Violent Memories

Violent Memories

Mayan War Widows in Guatemala

Judith N. Zur

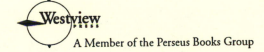
Westview PRESS
A Member of the Perseus Books Group

Copyright © 1998 by Westview Press, A Member of the Perseus Books Group

Published in 1998 in the United States of America by Westview Press, 5500 Central Avenue,
Boulder, Colorado 80301-2877, and in the United Kingdom by Westview Press, 12 Hid's
Copse Road, Cumnor Hill, Oxford OX2 9JJ

A CIP catalog record for this book is available from the Library of Congress.
ISBN 0-8133-2799-7 (hc) —ISBN 0-8133-3897-2 (pb)

The paper used in this publication meets the requirements of the American National Standard for Permanence of Paper for Printed Library Materials Z39.48-1984.

PERSEUS
POD
ON DEMAND   10   9   8   7   6   5   4   3   2   1

For Shimshon Zur,
Myrna Mack Chang,
and the Widows

Contents

Acknowledgements

I owe my deepest gratitude to the widows, their families, and to the family with whom I lived in Guatemala. They taught me much more than I have revealed in this book, for which I thank them. Unfortunately, they and many other people who gave me their time and hospitality cannot be named because insecurity and violence persist at the local level despite improvements in the political situation at the macro level. My thanks go to the many K'iche's, Guatemalan Indians from other ethnic groups, *ladinos*, and foreign religious who appear here either unnamed or under pseudonyms. The only people I can thank by name are two anthropologists: the indigenous priest Ventura Lux, who gave me many hours of his time explaining aspects of K'iche' life, and Myrna Mack, a *ladina* who, with her inimitable grace and generosity, provided me with both intellectual and moral support throughout the time I was in Guatemala and became a personal friend. Both are now dead: Father Lux was killed in a road 'accident' in 1993; Myrna Mack was assassinated in 1991.

I would like to thank the many Indians, *ladinos,* and non-Guatemalans working in non-governmental organizations (NGOs) in Guatemala, especially the NGO which made my research possible and helped me throughout. Again, most of them cannot be named without identifying where I worked.

I am also indebted to many other people whom I met in Guatemala for their kindness and generosity. In Antigua, Guatemala, I would like to thank the staff and visiting scholars of the *Centro de Investigaciones Regionales de Mesoamérica* (CIRMA) for providing a space in which I could work and allowing me access to their library during brief interludes from life in El Quiché; Amelia García, for generously welcoming me into her family and giving me another perspective on widows; Paola Ferraria and Ana Blume for their enjoyable and generous hospitality; Carol Smith for her encouragement; and George Lovell. Ana Blume, Lynne Jones, David Stoll, and Paul Yamauchi are remembered for carrying out fieldwork simultaneously with me and exchanging points of view. Paul subsequently provided me with generous help during the time I wrote my thesis. I would like to thank Agop Kayayan, then director of UNICEF Guatemala, for his support and friendship.

This book is based on my Ph.D. dissertation, submitted to the University of London in 1993. My research was financed by the Economic and Social Research Council, the Central Research Fund of the University of London, the Radcliffe-Brown Memorial Fund/Sutasoma Trust of the Institute of Anthropology, and the Malinowski Memorial Fund of the London School of Economics, University of London.

I am grateful to Mike Sallnow, Joanna Overing, and Alfred Gell for their supervision of my research. Mike Sallnow was a great source of inspiration and encouragement and his premature death was a blow. Alfred Gell's early death last year is also a great loss to everyone who had the good fortune to share his company. I would also like to thank Maurice Bloch and Peter Loizos for their careful reading of a couple of thesis chapters. I am also grateful to José Alejos of *Centro de Estudios Mayas*, UNAM (University of Mexico),for his comments on various chapters (and help in other ways). The work profited from instructive comments made by Stephen Hugh-Jones and Murray Last and participants at seminars at the London School of Economics, University College London, the School of Oriental Studies, and Cambridge University.

I am also indebted to all my friends who gave me succour and encouragement. I thank them all. I would like to give particular thanks to Julie Dockrell, who helped me so generously on various levels during the doctoral work; Julia Gonnella and Sam Landell-Mills, who helped to keep my spirits up; and Alex Radzyner for his generous friendship. Francisca Cooper gave me unwavering help and tremendous support during the writing of the thesis; without her assistance the editing of the manuscript into a book would not have been possible. Rachel Sieder has also given me valuable criticism on various parts of the text and generously copy edited the final draft.

I would also like to thank Susan and Michael Zur-Szpiro for their unerring interest and help when I was in Guatemala, Laura and Lawrence Sternberg, Norma Zur and Rachel Zur for their distinct forms of sharing this project, and most of all my husband Sergio Navarrete for his ineffable support and my daughter Sofia who was born during the preparation of this book and made it an especially joyous period.

I am grateful for Tim Girven's assistance with the index.

At Westwiew Press I would like to thank editor Karl Yambert and assistant editor Jennifer Chen for their kind patience and help.

I dedicate this book to the widows, my late father, and to my friend Myrna Mack.

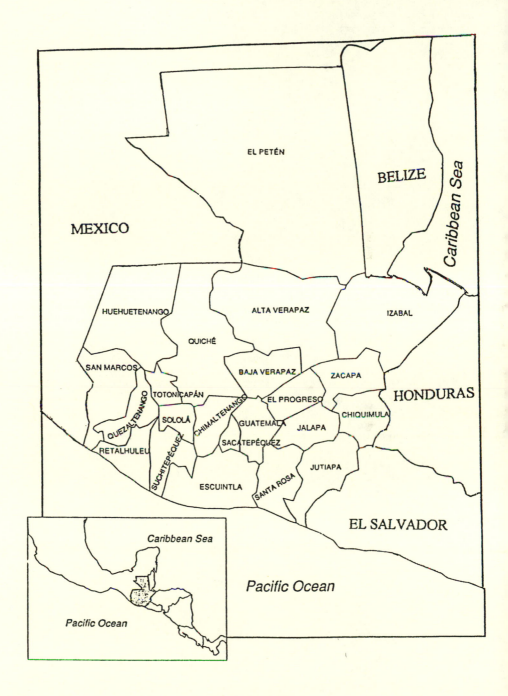

Guatemala

1

Introduction

I went to newly democratic Guatemala in 1988 to conduct research into how Mayan widows and orphans experienced their losses during The Violence *(la violencia)*[1] (1978-1985), only to discover that it was still going on — with a vengeance. I arrived just as the political situation was worsening, teetering on the verge of a return to 'that time'.

La violencia is the popular name for the former military dictatorship's overwhelming counterinsurgency campaign against Guatemala's rural, and mostly Indian, citizens. Through an unfortunate linkage of 'subversiveness' with 'otherness', the Spanish-speaking state linked the guerrillas with the traditional 'other': the wild and dangerous Indian with his 'natural' (magical) powers. This process resulted in a campaign to eradicate Indian culture and, in some places, Indians themselves.

The counterinsurgency campaign had ostensibly ended in 1985, when the military dictatorship called an election. Its reasons for doing so had more to do with Guatemala's international profile than conditions at home: the country had become an international pariah and the military dictatorship's reputation for corruption and cruelty had affected its ability to attract the foreign aid required to deal with the country's economic crisis. After seven years of internal war, the economy was in a shambles and private sector confidence at an all time low. U.S. advisers, concerned to support a right-wing, authoritarian regime to counterbalance 'communist' Nicaragua, persuaded the Guatemalan military government that democracy posed no threat to its power; it was merely a means of restoring Guatemala's international credentials and limiting internal social protest, thereby creating the necessary conditions to reactivate the economy.

U.S. advisers also showed Guatemala's military regime how to 'adjust' its counterinsurgency strategy (Jonas 1991:158) to democracy. All political

---

1. Spanish words (and a few Latin words) appear in *italics*; K'iche' words are underlined.

parties taking part in the election were approved by the military regime, which played an active part in the election process; the U.S. provided funds and the Reagan administration acted almost as the Guatemalan military's public relations firm. The net result was a civilian counterinsurgency state. The army, while taking credit for returning Guatemala to democracy, considered civilian rule as the third stage in its counterinsurgency campaign.[1]

In other words, the 1985 elections were a confidence trick on both the Guatemalan people and the international community.[2] However, the democratic aspirations of most Guatemalans led them to elect a man who had campaigned (presumably with the army's consent) on a promise to confront the military's entrenched and continued opposition to reform: Vinicio Cerezo Arévalo. Installed as president in January 1986, Cerezo said he anticipated wresting power from the army by degrees: 30 percent in the first six months, 50 percent after the first year, and 70 percent by his fifth and final year in office. This vastly over-optimistic aim does not seem to have been part of the agreed script.[3] The army responded in its customary manner and the death rate rose alarmingly.

Nevertheless, popular demand that those responsible for assassinations, disappearances, and rural massacres past and present should be prosecuted continued to grow. President Cerezo's response was that this would be political suicide. In 1986, he upheld the military's self-declared amnesty, granting immunity to those who had committed 'excesses' in the service of the state. He could hardly do anything else: apart from the material power of the army, there was the analytical problem of deciding where responsibility lay, something which Guatemala only began to address in the mid-1990s. In the interim, Cerezo (and subsequent presidents) offered a few sops to the public: Cerezo disbanded the hated Department of Technical Investigations (DIT), the police intelligence force modelled upon and subordinate to military intelligence (G2). This was the third time the unit had been 'disbanded' and renamed since 1966: although most DIT personnel were offered transfers to the uniformed police (only one was charged — with assault — in connection with atrocities committed by this force), the reorganization of its structure and methodology has only been superficial (America's Watch 1986); its activities continue as before. Equally meaningless was Cerezo's renaming, in 1988, of the civil patrol system to emphasize its 'voluntary' nature as set out in the 1985 Constitution (i.e., four years after it was forcibly imposed in rural areas). Yet the army's tendency to consider patrol refusers as members of the National Revolutionary Union of Guatemala (URNG)[4] persisted into the 1990s (El Grafico, 10 August 1992), that is, well after the instigation of talks between the URNG and the civilian government.

The installation of a civilian president had loosened the army's hold on the Guatemalan people, creating sufficient space for the formation of indigenous human rights organizations such as CERJ[5] and CONAVIGUA,[6] both of which originated in the department of El Quiché and were formally established in 1988 (GAM,[7] a *ladino*-led human rights organization, had been established in 1984). These groups promote the rights of patrol and conscription resisters, war-widows, and the relatives of the disappeared respectively; they also denounce human rights violations of any form. As their international profile increased, so had state-sponsored repression — even after the start of peace negotiations in the early 1990s. These days it is the membership of these groups which is being targeted rather than high profile leaders, a few of whom were elected to Guatemala's Congress of Deputies in 1995. An increasing number of indigenous women, especially widows who are members of human rights groups or even widows' groups run by neutral non-governmental organizations (NGOs), have been targeted by military and paramilitary forces. For example, María Mejía, the president of the CONAVIGUA group in Parraxtut, Sacapulas, was shot dead in her home by the local military commissioner in May 1990. A few months later, on 11 September, the British-trained, Guatemalan anthropologist Myrna Mack Chang, who had become a good friend during the course of our respective research in El Quiché, was murdered outside her office. Myrna's 'crime' was to denounce the appalling living conditions of internal refugees; she had compiled reports on the matter for AVANCSO,[8] of which she was a founder member. One interpretation of her death is that she was made an example of, to deter other educated *ladinos* from investigating 'matters'; another I heard is that certain interest groups were afraid that she would publish the sensitive information she had collected. Protests by the Catholic Church, the human rights movement, and especially by Myrna's sister, Helen Mack (who founded the Myrna Mack Foundation), eventually led to the assassination being traced to high-ranking army officers, including General Edgar Augusto Godoy Gaitán, the army's Chief of Staff at the time of the murder. In the interim, Noel de Jesús Beteta, a former army sergeant, was convicted of stabbing Myrna. The trial was especially noteworthy because, for the first time, responsibility for a political crime was placed on the Guatemalan state. Although Beteta's conviction is a 'victory' for those who want justice for their murdered kin, it is a hollow one: the deaths continue. For example, on 5 January 1996, Lucia Tiu Tum, a prominent local CONAVIGUA activist and her second husband, a member of CERJ, were assassinated.

Other targets of military opprobrium are foreign human rights organizations — the office of Peace Brigades International (PBI) in Guatemala City was bombed in August 1989 — and individual foreigners working for them. However discreet an outsider's behaviour, most foreigners who stay in an area, especially the remote Indian highlands, for any length of time are suspected of being human rights workers or guerrillas (which is the same thing so far as the military and local paramilitaries are concerned). Only U.S. Protestant missionaries are exempt.

Impeded by waves of military-inspired violence and attempted coups, Guatemala lurched erratically towards democracy. The impetus for change gathered momentum in 1993, with the appointment of the former Human Rights Ombudsman, Ramiro de León Carpio (1993-1995), as President. A series of accords were signed[9] but only one was effective immediately. This was the Comprehensive Human Rights Accord signed on 29 March 1994, which allowed for the presence of MINUGUA to investigate human rights abuses in Guatemala.[10] These developments gave hope to Guatemala's population and paved the way for the 1995 elections when they eventually got an opportunity to vote for parties and candidates which had not been vetted by the military.

The army's continuing power is evidenced by its opposition to the announcement, on 24 June 1996, that the civil patrol system was to be dismantled as part of the peace process. Although publicly agreeing that the patrols were no longer a military necessity, the army was still creating new patrols in areas where former military commissioners (the post was abolished in 1995) had been their main means of local control. Landowners and army-backed local power holders also called for the patrols to continue "because of the virtual public security vacuum in the countryside" (Popkin 1996:3), i.e., Indian areas. Some even demanded the creation of new patrols to combat 'crime'. By this time, the army (which has acquired large business interests) had been involved in the development industry for many years, offering improvement projects to 'loyal' communities, bribing 'less loyal' communities, and so on. Former President de León Carpio resolved the problem by suggesting that the patrol system be transformed into Peace and Development Committees (CPD), an idea which appealed to the army. In early 1996, the army claimed that more than 127,000 Guatemalans (about one third of continuing patrollers) had been organized into these groups (Popkin 1996:3). Such claims not only indicate the army's intention to maintain the patrol structure but contradict years of denial of military involvement in this supposedly 'voluntary' scheme. Today, it is the civilian authorities who profess ignorance of such structures (Popkin 1996:35-36). Resistance to 'peace' patrols involves opponents to the system in linguistic tangles and makes them easy targets of ridicule.

Throughout the 1980s and into the 1990s, violence changed in intensity but not kind. The Peace Accords may have abolished institutions but they cannot eradicate entrenched attitudes. GAM (1997) claims that 'impunity'[11] is government policy, citing as evidence the Law of Reconciliation (known as the Amnesty Law) which came into effect in January 1997 and pardons the army for its crimes during *la violencia*. However, this law is different from the twelve amnesties declared between 1982 and 1988 which protected both the perpetrators and the intellectual authors of the human rights abuses which not only comprised *la violencia* but followed in its wake. The Amnesty Law established a legal mechanism which gives relatives of the war dead and other survivors the opportunity to apply for a hearing to investigate individual violations. It is up to the applicants to prove that the violation is directly connected to the armed conflict. Although extremely few people are brave enough or sufficiently knowledgeable of legal procedures to make use of their new rights (which accounts for GAM's cynicism), Myrna Mack's family grasped this opportunity to accuse the men whom they had identified as ordering her assassination. They successfully argued that as Myrna had been neither a revolutionary activist nor a combatant, her killing was a criminal act and, therefore, the Amnesty Law had no jurisdiction in this case and, therefore, they were entitled to name names. However, it is not expected that the accused (who include General Godoy) will be convicted, let alone sentenced, for the crime.

Despite twelve years of civilian rule, unpredictable violence and impunity persist. In 1996, GAM (1997) alone registered 69 political killings, seven massacres, the murder of 58 children, and 109 disappearances, an 11 percent increase on 1995. Five days after the publication of GAM's annual report on 23 January 1997, Jorge Gonzalez, the founder of FADS,[12] was shot and wounded. There is considerable evidence to support the claim that the military continues to systematically hide and deny the crimes it commits not only to the families of victims and the citizens of Guatemala, but to the international community. It remains to be seen if there will be any military backlash to President Alvaro Arzú Irigoyen's efforts to retire officers opposed to his reforms.

Yet despite dramatic improvements at the macro political level, life has changed little for Guatemala's indigenous population. People's fears are not unreasonable: the conditions which gave rise to rural insurgency persist and the mechanisms of terror created to suppress it have been renamed rather than dismantled and in many places, not even that: according to recent army figures, nearly 400,000 men are still participating in the civil defense patrols (Popkin 1996:1). Many communities have found that abolishing the post of military commissioner or patrol chief has not abolished the post-holder's power: after fifteen years of impunity, no alternative authority structures remain. To many Indians, "the truth is that the violence always continues".

The Search for 'Emol'[13]

I originally planned to work in the north of the department of El Quiché which had been badly hit by *la violencia*; several ethnographies had been written about the area shortly before its eruption, which would have provided a base for comparison.

I met film producer Brian Moser at the offices of a human rights group and traveled with him to the Ixil Triangle[14] in northern El Quiché. At the time, the area was the army's showpiece for its pacification efforts.

When we arrived in remote and beautiful Chajul in the heart of the Cuchumatanes mountains, I immediately decided to do my research there. As we drove through the area, we were greeted by the first of many violent scenes I was to witness during my fieldwork: four women were being carried across the road on stretchers. Their bodies were covered with blankets; only their blood-spattered, bare feet were visible, sticking out from their traditional skirts. I was shocked by villagers' lack of reaction: no-one said who the women were, who had thrown grenades into their *adobe* bungalows, or where they were being taken. Later, I realized that the women were probably members of a local widows' group, their attackers men known to them.

An army intelligence unit arrived and started taking names. We left rapidly.

I then considered working in association with the Spanish medical team *Médicos del Mundo* in the Ixcán Jungle further north in El Quiché but fighting was heavy in the area: the army was trying to sever supply routes from the Mexican border to the Guerrilla Army of the Poor (EGP).

I headed south.

Southern El Quiché was tense[15] throughout the time of my fieldwork. I sought support (and cover) for my research from the Bishop of El Quiché but, despite the nuns' wish for my help with war-traumatized children — I am a clinical psychologist and family therapist — my request was rejected. The diocese had been re-opened for less than four years and the Bishop was probably loth to compromise both my safety and his own.

I eventually found a niche in an NGO which worked with war-widows. 'Carlos'[16] introduced me to the villages he had been working with for five years but when tensions increased, eliciting memories of his two brothers who had been killed by soldiers (who had been looking for him), he had a nervous breakdown from which he has yet to recover. The village where he had obtained permission for me to work refused to accept me without him.

Eventually, another NGO worker introduced me to Emol. It took several months and considerable help from the NGO and my interpreter and guide, *doña* Flora, to allay the fears and suspicions of those with whom I was in regular contact, including the village authorities — the patrol chiefs *(jefes)* and military commissioners — who were anxious about what people might tell me out of their earshot. Her bravery in undertaking this task on my behalf was impressive.

Doña Flora introduced me to Emol's widows' group, her family, and friends, 'selling' me as someone who could be trusted. Despite her efforts, many people retained their doubts about me which they concealed behind a screen of politeness. These doubts surfaced anonymously in the occasional rumours about me which seemed to spread through the village like wildfire: for example, I was a stranger who was not an Indian, a *ladina* or even a Guatemalan but a *gringa* who ate stews made of Indian children (a behaviour traditionally attributed to evil spirits, sorcerers, and Spaniards during the Conquest period). I suspect that most of these malicious rumours originated from the village's chief of patrols, Mario, who was suspicious of me from the outset. The first time I entered the village unaccompanied, he ignored my army-issued permit to be in Emol (he is illiterate) and, brandishing a loaded gun at me, accused me in his execrable Spanish of collaborating with some guerrillas who had just stolen guns from the police in a nearby township *(municipio)*. When Mario or his supporters called me 'blondie' *(canche)*, they used the term as the army do, as an allusion to the foreigners they claim lead the guerrillas; to most people who jokingly applied the nickname to me, the word is simply an affectionate way of referring to fair-skinned foreigners.

Equally dangerous was some men's speculation that I was an army spy or that I worked for the CIA; only men who had been involved in the popular movement had any idea of covert U.S. involvement in Guatemala's internal affairs.[17] In a village where I had planned to carry out comparative work (for reasons unclear to me, it appeared to have been little affected by direct violence), I was suspected of being an American missionary intent on converting villagers, who were all Catholic, to evangelical protestantism.[18]

I did not live in Emol for fear of bringing the widows more trouble with the authorities. Finding an indigenous family in the nearby town who were prepared to accept me as a paying guest was not easy. I was told, "Before *[la violencia]*, families in the town were pleasant and friendly and they would invite people to stay in their houses but now, after all the mistreatment and violence they suffered, they no longer accommodate anyone." I was eventually introduced to Emoltecos who had fled to the town following the abduction of one of their sons in 1984; they accepted me because another son had worked with the NGO with which I was affiliated. Both my worries about the family's well-being and theirs about mine grew in the last stages of my fieldwork (mid-1990) when the political climate deteriorated further. The family changed the locks on the door and told me to use them; they told me to be home before dark to avoid being accused of 'organizing' (being involved in subversive activities); only foreign friends were allowed to visit the house. Their anxiety stemmed from the reappearance of guerrillas in southern El Quiché; they knew the army would be close behind.

The protection I received as a foreigner cannot be overemphasized but even so, I had to tread with extreme caution. I had little preparation for the many harrowing incidents I encountered and had to learn on my feet. I was confronted with considerable intimidation throughout my fieldwork, particularly at the end. Luck, good advice, and a certain amount of skill meant that I encountered no serious problems. Perhaps denial rather than rational preparation saw me through such incidents.

There were other dangers outside Emol. Although I presented myself as a neutral social scientist, I had to take care that the army did not think that I was a subversive owing to my close association with Indians in general and war-widows in particular. In order to circumvent trouble, I visited the army base every three months (army units and their officers changed every quarter), explaining that I was studying K'iche' culture. With time, I included the effect of *la violencia* among the list of topics I was interested in.

The Widows

Widows' own accounts of their experiences of extreme violence and terror during *la violencia* — which they have been forced to 'forget' — form the basis of this book. This intense internal war created an unprecedented number of widows in rural Guatemala, a fact which the nation largely wants to 'forget' as the civilian government strides towards a new era built on the sandy foundations of a rewritten past.

The women whose voices appear here are all of Mayan descent and, until the advent of *la violencia*, had been relatively separated from the non-Mayan world. Socialized to be the 'conservers of tradition', most indigenous women's lives were restricted to hearth and home. The political, economic, and religious innovations since the 1950s had made little impact on the way most indigenous highland women perceived their lives; they had no conception of the battle for control of change. To them, the sudden, ferocious intrusion of *la violencia* which destroyed lives and livelihoods, a way of life and ways of interpreting that life, descended out of the blue.

The women's voices represent the broader realities of many unarmed civilians who survive political violence not only in Guatemala but in other areas of the world. Their experiences of repetitive violence are representative of the experiences of a large segment of Guatemala's female, Indian population. For almost every man killed or kidnapped, a dependent woman — wife, sister, mother or daughter — was left without male protection, a crucial concept in K'iche' social relations. Men protect women not only from physical dangers — other men, the outside *ladino* world — but from supernatural perils. Being without a man is an anomalous and therefore dangerous situation for an adult K'iche' woman; being labelled the 'wife of a guerrilla' adds another, terrifying layer of danger. Their putative association with the guerrilla means that their reports of atrocities they have suffered are discredited; whether or not they managed to 'forget' as ordered by the military and its local level collaborators, widows were definitely silenced and most remain so. The most insidious form of silence is the implicit prohibition of concrete markers of their status — funerals, graves, mourning ribbons, etc. Advertizing kinship with an alleged subversive can be fatal.

While I had intended to study the average person "that constitutes the heartbeat of society" (de Certeau 1980:3), the widows presented here are not representative of all women, nor of all widows. These very different but exceptionally courageous women, all members of Emol's widows' group, have recently been exposed to and have assimilated knowledge of the national political scene. Emol has several widows' groups but I worked only with those of the main village (Emol Central) and one of its outlying hamlets (Kotoh). The five principals are *doña* Eugenia (who has the title of Director of the village's widows' groups), *doña* Candelaria (Speaker for all Emol's groups), *doña* Consuelo (President, Kotoh group), *doña* Flora (my interpreter and the President of the Emol Central group), *doña* Josefina (Vice President, Emol Central). *Doña* Eugenia, *doña* Candelaria, and *doña* Consuelo (who are related by marriage) live in Kotoh, formerly the most progressive of Emol's hamlets; they are the widows of respected community activists. *Doña* Flora and *doña* Josefina live in Emol Central, the most conservative (and, today, predominantly Protestant) part of the village and Kotoh's traditional rival; their husbands, neither of whom had been prominent in the village or the movement, went to Kotoh to 'organize'. *Doña* Eugenia and *doña* Flora also lost their only sons; *doña* Josefina lost her grandmother; all of them lost other relatives. Despite their current activism, their life-stories are ordinary; there is little difference in the personal histories of the older women who are the groups' leaders and its younger members. The greatest difference between women over and under forty years of age is that the younger women have known nothing other than constant, rapid change (and resistance to change); although they were socialized into the Mayan traditionalist (*costumbrista* or 'pure' Catholic) world view of their mothers, they have not experienced the stability older women claim for life 'before'.

Doña Eugenia

Doña Eugenia was born to a respected *costumbrista* family in Emol Central. She neither knows nor cares how old she is; her identity papers *(cedula)* give her year of birth as 1920 but this is some clerk's estimate as her birth was not registered. Today, people have become used to the idea of registering births but even so, many are still not registered for one reason or another.

Her father, who was descended from one of Emol's founding families, was an outspoken man who played an important role in village affairs. *Doña* Eugenia describes him, with pride and affection, as "a bit of a rebel", who had explained *ladino* exploitation of poor Indian *(naturales)* to her as a child. He also drank. The combination drove the family to the coast:"Our whole family went, including my mother. We had to go because my father was very poor," she said; "he was a heavy drinker, we never had money for anything, even maize. We did not have enough land and had to buy our maize and this is why we went to the coast." *Doña* Eugenia earned her keep from a very young age:

> From the age of eight I was already working hard at home and then, later [from the age of ten] on the coast, where the work is much heavier. There, under the blazing sun and the sudden downpours, I cut coffee, worked in the cotton fields — I did all the work there is to do on the coast...

Doña Eugenia never went to school; there were no schools in Emol when she was a child, nor on the plantations *(fincas)*. There are still none on the *fincas*, where child labour continues as it always has despite fifty-year old laws compelling parents to send their children to school (they can be fined for non-compliance). *Doña* Eugenia remains illiterate although she has picked up a smattering of Spanish and understands much more.

Whilst the family lived on the *fincas*, two of *doña* Eugenia's siblings died of malaria and malnutrition; both are endemic on the coastal plains and remain a common cause of child mortality. After eleven years, her brother, by then a young man, insisted the family return to Emol. It was there that she met her first husband; they 'united'[19] when *doña* Eugenia was twenty years old. He came to live with her in her parents' home. She bore him two sons, leaving them with her mother while she and her husband returned to the *finca*; her father's land was insufficient to support them all. Her children died of measles, still a common cause of child mortality. *Doña* Eugenia blamed herself for their deaths (for leaving them) and not her mother who, she said, had not realized they were ill because she was so busy herself. After her children's death, her husband abandoned her for another woman. *Doña* Eugenia returned to Kotoh. She did not expect her father to support her, as is the custom when marriages end (chapter three), because he had warned her against the man in the first instance.

Life improved when she met Antonio, a landless pedlar and travelling musician. He had also been married before but told her that his former wife's child was not his; *doña* Eugenia believed him. She told me that he must have been speaking the truth because it was some time before she had Gilberto; she wanted more children but he was the only child of the marriage.

Antonio and Eugenia left her family home and began living in a house in the centre of Kotoh, where she still lives. Although they now had a small plot of land (acquired from a relative, which allows *doña* Eugenia to say her land has been in her family for generations), they continued working as seasonal labour migrants on the *fincas* because they needed the money to buy supplemental maize. They acquired more land over the years and eventually became comparatively well off in local terms. They sent Gilberto to school in another village. One of the first things he did for Kotoh as an adult was organize the building of the hamlet's school.

Doña Eugenia's husband Antonio was widely known locally because he was frequently invited by neighbouring townships *(municipios)* to play his shawm *(chirimia)* at village *fiestas*. His pioneering role in introducing the 'new' catholicism brought by Sacred Heart missionaries to Emol in the 1950s was more controversial, bringing him both friends and foes. *Doña* Eugenia converted, but retains her *costumbrista* sympathies.

Antonio and Gilberto became two of the most active and respected leaders in the village. Gilberto worked for an NGO which trained him as a health worker; he was President of Kotoh's Improvement Committee *(Comité de Pro-Mejoramiento)*; he was instrumental in building the road leading to Kotoh and many other projects. He worked hard and his achievements were impressive; he was much admired. Yet I heard rumours that Gilberto had been involved in tit-for-tat killings of army supporters; his mother denied all knowledge of this and denounced the tales as a vicious calumny. The story could be an expression of people's fear (and jealousy) of those who get ahead, which is expressed in terms of an old belief that advancement can only achieved at the price of human heads. On the other hand, the use of this myth could be an allegorical account of real killings.

When *la violencia* reached the area, Gilberto went into hiding; his father refused to flee, saying he had done nothing wrong. Shortly afterwards, the army occupied the village and began forming the civil patrols. At 75 years of age, *don* Antonio was far too old to join; he was also too respected and well known to ignore. He was abducted in full view of the community; such was his reputation as a mediator of disputes that, even though it is very unusual for an indigenous person *(indígena)* to travel in a car, no-one thought too much of it when he was taken away in an official car on Christmas Day 1981. Everyone thought he would return but he was never seen again. Gilberto returned to Kotoh soon afterwards but was killed in the village massacre on St. Valentine's Day 1982 (chapter five).

Like most widows in her situation, *doña* Eugenia has no satisfactory explanation for the deaths of her husband and son; she does not know why they were selected for death. She cannot reconcile their work for the community with 'subversion', a word she first heard when the army occupied the village and accused her of being a 'subversive' herself.

Following the deaths of Antonio and Gilberto, *doña* Eugenia invited her daughter-in-law Vicenta and her five children to stay on in the family compound with her. The women had always got on well but, following Gilberto's death, Vicenta descended into alcoholism. *Doña* Eugenia denies Vicenta an effective role in the household, so she has little incentive to sober up. It is now many years since her mother-in-law lost patience with her. *Doña* Eugenia also invited another widow and her two children to sleep in her overcrowded house because the woman was too afraid to stay in her own home after her husband was killed.

Despite all her losses to *la violencia* (other kin were also killed), *doña* Eugenia has not lost her faith. She remains a 'new' Catholic but invites *costumbrista* diviners (aj q'ij) into to her home to perform traditional rituals. I was surprised one day to see that the aj q'ij she had invited into her house was a man who had been involved in the massacre; he is reputed to have decapitated victims. In 1992, it was discovered that attempts had been made to decapitate only one victim: Gilberto.

Doña Candelaria

Doña Candelaria was born in Emol Central in the mid-1940s and is an exuberant mother of ten who is openly expressive with her grandchildren, frequently hugging and kissing them.

Her husband, Gilberto's cousin, was the President of Kotoh's Catholic

Action group; he played an important role in the hamlet's self-help projects. The success of these projects exacerbated tensions between Kotoh and its traditional rivals, Emol Central. One day, a group of men from Emol Central, including *doña* Candelaria's brother, took her husband and eight year old son Esteban to another part of the village where they shot him in front of the boy. She believes that her brother, a Protestant convert and, from 1982 to 1992, President of Emol Central's Improvement Committee, actually instigated her husband's assassination; Emol Central's resentment at Kotoh's progressiveness is said to be the cause. Talking about this reduced her to floods of tears. I had the impression that there was an unusual amount of affection between *doña* Candelaria and her husband; at least, communication about affection between spouses was unusual.

Doña Candelaria is a lapsed Catholic who has given up most religious rituals since her husband's death. She worked as a midwife to earn an income after her husband died, but gave this up when the political situation deteriorated. She claims that her sons did not want her to visit other people's houses, especially at night. Their request (which coincided with her decision to become active in the village's newly formed CONAVIGUA group) was couched in traditional terms, masking or normalizing their concerns that she might be accused of 'organizing'. Such an accusation is highly probable, as *doña* Candelaria had been a speaker *(vocal)* for the NGO-supported widows' group since its inception. She is one of the few Emolteco women who went on CONAVIGUA courses and demonstrations; she had even accompanied *doña* Manuela to a CERJ meeting. All of these activities are viewed as subversive by the army and civil patrol *jefes*, and remain so under Guatemala's fragile democracy. Rather than admit to her interest in the human rights movement, *doña* Candelaria cloaks her involvement in terms of financial help for her children's education — she is one of the few widows who is concerned that all their children, including daughters, should go to school.

Her sons' prohibition on her work as a midwife left *doña* Candelaria and her four youngest children almost entirely dependent on whatever her three eldest boys chose to give to the household; in 1988, they worked as street traders in the capital and one or other of them visited her about once a month. She continues to work as a healer but, in deference to her sons, restricts her clientele to children; she was frequently called out to help in the measles epidemic which killed 124 Emolteco children in 1990.

Doña Consuelo

Doña Consuelo was born around 1950 in a village adjacent to Emol's furthest flung hamlet — a good two hour trek across major ravines. Even today, the only way to get there by car is by going to the nearby town and then out again. The village is very different from Emol: there is less pressure for land and pockets of potters' clay have encouraged economic diversification into the earthenware which is found all over the area. *Doña* Consuelo's family have been potters for generations. These two factors result not only in a (slightly) higher standard of living but also different attitudes. *Doña* Consuelo was particularly fortunate as a child: her father did not drink away the profits of the women's work but confined his drinking to ceremonial occasions.

Like her daughters (one of whom won the village beauty contest three years in succession), *doña* Consuelo had been a striking young woman. She received many offers of marriage but chose a rather serious, devout young man from Kotoh who visited her village with his father, a godfather *(compadre)* to one of her uncles. *Doña* Consuelo's good looks and pleasant manner caught his eye in church and they were soon married. She was sixteen when he brought her to Kotoh and, although it was a love match and she was happy with her husband, she missed her family who seemed such a long way away. She began to feel comfortable in Kotoh as the size of her family grew and she developed friendships with the women of her husband's family, especially *doña* Eugenia and *doña* Candelaria.

Doña Consuelo's husband owned little land and the couple had to supplement their income by working on the *fincas*. This probably accounts for the gap between her eldest surviving child, twenty-two year old Manuela, and her other six children, whose ages (when I met them in 1988) ranged from sixteen to seven; it was not something she spoke about. The improvement in her children's survivorship probably coincides with her decision to contribute to the household income by exploiting her pottery skills.

Doña Consuelo supported her husband's community work and agreed with his decision to send all their children to school, including girls. He recognized the advantages of a Spanish-language education in terms of job opportunities; he was also concerned that Manuela would have no brothers to protect and provide for her (it was many years before a son was born). Ultimately, only Manuela received an uninterrupted education (to sixth grade, making her Emol's best-educated woman) because the family fled to Guatemala City during *la violencia*, where her father was abducted. *Doña* Consuelo did her best to send her younger children to school but their labour was often needed at home to make the clay ovens an NGO was encouraging highland women to use as a wood-saving device.

Doña Consuelo is a kindly woman who has a positive attitude to life; she inspires trust in others. These qualities led to her election as the president of Kotoh's widows' group, even though she is the youngest of its officers. When the group was taken over by CONAVIGUA at the end of the decade, she was again the widows' choice for president of the group.

Doña Flora

Doña Flora was born in another village, lower down the mountains, in the late 1930s. She describes her life as difficult from the start. Her father brewed bootleg liquor (kuxa) and spent most of his time drunk; he had little concern for his family's welfare. He frequently beat his wife because his meals weren't ready on time. *Doña* Flora's mother worked as a midwife to support the family, which included several children; *doña* Flora also contributed to the household from an early age, working in the village shop. There was an unusually high proportion of *ladino* families in *doña* Flora's natal village and she learnt to speak Spanish through her work and also from her mother, who had picked up some knowledge of the language from her *ladina* clients. Her ability to speak Spanish gives her more confidence than the average K'iche' woman. She did not go to school and her knowledge of the written word is limited.

Doña Flora's mother was cruel to her, taunting her that she would never marry because she was ugly, although I think she is an attractive woman, tall and elegant. *Doña* Flora's mother refused to allow her to marry the man she fell in love with because he had been married before; she married an older man who had been living with his landless parents in the town. He was clearly successful as he was able to buy land in Emol from a distant relative. Resentments triggered by this purchase may have contributed to his selection for death.

Soon after their marriage, *doña* Flora's husband began to brew <u>kuxa</u> for his own consumption and, when drunk, he beat her. The beatings intensified with the realization that they could not have children. He beat her until she collapsed on the floor and then he kicked her, calling her a whore. *Doña* Flora is an incredibly accepting person who frequently reminded me, when speaking about her hardships, "We have to bear it *(tenemos que aguantar)*"; she considers herself lucky as her husband allowed her to leave the house and to go about relatively freely.

After a few years of marriage, *doña* Flora consulted a doctor who told her that her husband was sterile; he advised her to find another man who could give her a child. Being a deeply religious person, she would not countenance the idea and, instead, adopted a baby boy (Juan) who she grew to love for what she described as his "hard working, honourable, and respectful" nature. Village women did not deride her for not bearing her own child; they saw her as a good woman who commanded respect.

Doña Flora and her husband sent Juan to school where, at the age of fifteen, he met and fell in love with Bartola, a fellow pupil. *Doña* Flora had not wanted Juan to marry so young but gave her consent when he threatened to 'steal' (elope with) his bride. Bartola's parents also gave their consent and the young couple began their married life in his parents' household (chapter three). Two years later, Juan was captured by the army and forced to do two years' military service. *Doña* Flora often made the fourteen hour bus journey to visit him in another province. She told me that she and Juan sat together and cried during her visits; he was opposed to killing alongside regular soldiers. If his views became known when he returned to Emol, this could explain why (insofar as a reason is necessary) he, too, was selected for death.

Unusually, it was *doña* Flora who had encouraged her husband and son to join the popular movement. Her curiosity aroused by talk of inequality and how the rich were living off the poor (which reminded her of priests' sermons about injustice), she thought that it must be something good. Besides, she herself had noted the truth in what was being said. She decided to go along and convinced her husband and son to join her. She told me there had been a good feeling of togetherness in the group; they were trained to be strong and to walk long distances but, she insisted, no firearms training.

Then *la violencia* began, with the killing of a village official. *Doña* Flora's husband was the first man to be kidnapped; he was taken naked from his bed and never seen again. She had persuaded Juan to leave but he soon returned; according to *doña* Flora, he said that he could not live without his father and wanted to join him (to die). In fact, he returned because Bartola's baby was due. Juan never saw his daughter Florinda because he was kidnapped almost immediately he returned to Emol. *Doña* Flora's brother persuaded her not to search for Juan, so she let the matter drop.

At first, *doña* Flora told me that Juan was away working. Some time later, she told me that she suspected that Juan had been killed; many months passed before she finally admitted that she knew where he was buried. She was too afraid to visit the site; she was also too frightened to report his murder or his grave — yet she condemned other women who knew where their menfolk were buried for not being 'good Christians' and reporting the site. She made many comments about other people's moral behaviour although she was even more critical of herself; she often refers with embarrassment to her phase of drunkenness after her menfolk were killed. *Doña* Flora's behaviour is fairly typical; inverting the usual K'iche' behavioural codes which insist on oblique criticism in order to obviate conflict, widows use other women's faults to castigate themselves.

Doña Flora turned to alcohol when her son was abducted. She told me, "I did not feel anything for a year." She sold her animals and some of her land at a very low price and, taking her eldest grandson, Eustaqio, with her, returned to her mother's house in another village. She remained there for a year before going to live in a nearby town with her brother. Her two younger grandchildren, Apolinario and new born Florinda, remained with Bartola, who returned to her parents' home in Emol Central. Two years later, *doña* Flora returned; Bartola and the younger children rejoined her and they live together to this day.

Doña Flora is a very religious Catholic who converted to charismatic catholicism after *la violencia*, primarily because the army permitted this sect to operate in Emol whilst the Catholic diocese was closed (1981-1984). Despite being the sect's co-ordinator, *doña* Flora retains her progressive sympathies. This is an unusual position (especially in Emol Central) as most charismatics value the separation the sect affords from all things radical.

Doña Flora has an air of serenity and benevolence about her. When I met her, she had many friends. She is better dressed than most Emolteco women as the nuns in a nearby convent sometimes give her clothes and her brother, a cobbler, occasionally provides her with the unclaimed shoes of the dead. She is also more of a free-thinker than the other women in the group. She is the woman to whom some of the village authorities appeal when they want the co-operation of other village women; for example, when the Christian Democrats wanted to secure the widows' votes, they asked *doña* Flora to tell the women to meet in a certain place so they could be taken to town by bus to vote for them.

Doña Josefina

Doña Josefina was born in the mid-1940s. When she was quite young, her father left for another woman (he still lives in Emol with his second family, but *doña* Josefina is estranged from him); her mother remarried, leaving *doña* Josefina and her brother with their maternal grandparents in Emol Central. Her labour was important to the household; her grandparents didn't send her to school. She is illiterate but has learnt a smattering of Spanish; after *la violencia,* she attended the adult literacy *(extrascolar)* class taught by *doña* Manuela but is still unable to sign her name.

When *doña* Josefina was twelve years old, her grandparents took her to live on the coast. She weeded coffee and cut cotton; she prepared food for labourers. Her grandparents didn't want her to marry young but, one year later, *doña* Josefina eloped. Her husband died three years later and, as a sixteen year old widow, *doña* Josefina returned to her grandparents' home. At seventeen she married a landless woodcutter and roofer who came to live in her grandparents' house, where she lives to this day (her brother married a woman with land in another village and went to live with her). *Doña* Josefina said that she and her husband generally 'lived well'; he only became abusive when he was drunk, which was only on ritual occasions. She gave birth to six children — the first two died before the age of eighteen months and a third, a daughter, died of malaria at the age of ten. She has another daughter and two sons who were only babies when their father was killed.

Doña Josefina's grandmother was kidnapped from the village square in 1982 together with everyone else at the market that day, plunging her grandfather into alcoholism; he is now senile. Three months later, in October, *doña* Josefina's husband was abducted; she has no idea why but believes that someone had informed on him. Referring to his political activities, she told me, "He did not tell me what he did." He had just returned home after completing his 24 hour patrol duty when 'they' (who are never clearly specified) came to take him and he was never seen again. She made no attempt to find out what happened to him. Some time later, 'they' told her where they had killed and buried him. After he was abducted, no one wanted to talk about it. She began to drink. Her little girl had to look after her baby brothers, her mother, and her great-grandfather. Despite frequent visits to a̱i q'ij for help to combat her alcoholism, it was three years before *doña* Josefina got her drinking under control.

For a long time, *doña* Josefina felt she could not cope without her husband and spent her small income on visits to 'spirit callers' (aj mes) asking them to contact her husband on every little thing. After a while, the aj mes refused her requests, saying he would only communicate with her husband on important matters. He said:

> Why do you want to suffer, to make memories and to make yourself sad? Your wish to speak to him all the time is an illness. You only come here to make yourself sad by hearing his voice. Your present worries should stop you from remembering this sadness...at least you should be feeling it less by now.

The aj mes also told her that another reason for her problems was that she was not following her destiny: he had interpreted one of her dreams to mean that she was destined to become an aj q'ij herself. He warned her that if she persisted in denying her destiny, she would have more dreams and become fatally ill — the usual fate of someone whose profession (or in this case, lack of profession) is at odds with their destiny. *Doña* Josefina accepted his interpretation but as she did not want to work as an aj q'ij, she rejected his advice. She began to suffer madness *(trastornos mentales)*. She went to another aj q'ij who performed a ceremony to enable her to talk to the spirits; she told them she would rather die than become an aj q'ij, even though she had worked, in an unofficial capacity, as a curer before *la violencia*. Her grandfather persuaded her to accept her destiny even though her training at 75 Quetzales (over US$15) a session was a big expense for them. She learnt to be a curer, midwife, and diviner; her madness disappeared. Becoming an aj q'ij gave *doña* Josefina a leadership position in the village, albeit restricted to *costumbristas*. She enjoys being able to help others and doesn't mind the dangers of having to stay out at all hours. Although she did not mention the minimal financial rewards of her work, clients' payments mean that unlike most widows, she does not have to do agricultural labour in order to survive, even on her own corn fields *(milpa)*. Diego, the boy she adopted during *la violencia* — the son of a war-widow who asked *doña* Josefina to look after him when she remarried — does this for her. He works in Guatemala City, visiting every so often to make a contribution to the household (not as much as she had hoped); he visits more frequently when work needs to be done on the *milpa*. He married while I was in Emol, leaving his bride with *doña* Josefina.[20] His visits became more regular.

At first, *doña* Josefina was reserved with me, but she became the most affectionate and humorous of all the widows I knew. She said that she had wondered if I had come to harm her; later she wondered if I came from a place similar to hers. She began to worry about my safety; she had dreams about me which she interpreted as warnings and passed on to me; interpreting dreams is one of an aj q'ij's roles. In one of her dreams, I was being pursued by horned animals, which the K'iche' generally interpret as a symbol of death; *doña* Josefina saw them as representing the patrols and their intentions towards me.

Doña Josefina is an emotional woman who suffers a great deal from *la violencia*; she does not understand why it happened. She says that the believers *(creyentes)* told her that it was written in the Bible, but she is unsure herself as she is illiterate. She expresses considerable guilt, sometimes castigating herself for not recognizing her destiny earlier; if she had, perhaps the ancestors would not have taken her kin (chapter eight). She suffers from innumerable physical ailments, including a terrible skin rash. She anaesthetizes herself with alcohol and is often found in a drunken stupor on her dirt floor. Her work contributes to her alcohol problem as clients often give local rum (*aguardiente*; kuxa) as part of their offerings.

The Anthropology of War:
Theoretical and Ethical Issues

Despite recent interest in the anthropology of war[21] there has been little documentation of how conflict is lived by the people caught in its midst or of how they themselves represent it.[22] Violence is often treated as a socio-culturally fragmented phenomenon which occurs 'outside' the arena of every day life.[23] Yet in most of the small wars currently being waged around the world violence has, more often than not, developed from long-existing animosities and rivalries ignited by some locally significant event or change. Yet theoretical attention to social conflict was new in the 1960s (Le Vine 1961) and remains relatively unexplored today. Instead, anthropology continues to focus on the 'objective' economic or political conditions which lead to revolt or war. Whilst analysis of 'structural' violence — which should include violence in a metaphorical sense such as the denial of civil, social and human rights or, in Weber's terms, "life chances"[24] (which have been systematically denied to the descendants of the Maya since the Conquest) — is clearly important, it does not tell the whole story: it misses the reasons people give about why a particular event sparks off violence, why this one becomes 'the straw that breaks the camel's back', what it means in terms of local values and beliefs, why some people interpret them one way, some another. It misses how an event between, say, two people, victim and perpetrator, suddenly belongs to everyone, escalates, and spins out of control, with the initial players as much caught up in subsequent events as anyone else.

Although violence can often be traced back to social, economic or political change, anthropological studies of communities undergoing change tend to emphasize the maintenance of community through rituals and other repetitive, relatively unchanging social actions.[25] Whatever is fuelling that change is often ignored — for example, Nash (1967) barely mentions the factory requiring a year-round workforce established in the midst of an indigenous Guatemalan community accustomed to seasonal subsistence agriculture and household autonomy. This type of innovation undercuts local beliefs which are literally grounded in the land, creating feelings of psychological displacement as people become increasingly divorced from the lived understanding of the reasons for their customs. People fight (literally and figuratively) not only for economic or political reasons but to protect and preserve their world view. They fight for the right to be who they are, for their "lived system of meanings and values" even though these are not necessarily in their own immediate economic interests (Williams 1977:110).

Internal war shatters social solidarity and compels people to make alignments and realignments based on economic, political, religious or family groupings or simply (and more commonly) the need to survive. It is this lived experience of community fragmentation and the redefinition of some of its elements whilst living in the midst of persistent conflict which interests me — the subjective perceptions of actors, how they respond to the various practices involved in physical and psychological violence, how they are affected by them. I wanted to know about variations in the way in which atrocity and war are conceptualized and managed, how violence is culturally articulated, how the horrors of conflict (and anxiety about them) are expressed in cultural performances or disguised in representations of the self at the local level; if everyday conversations or their repressive silencing provided arenas in which power struggles and aggression are given cultural voice. I wanted to explore the less tangible ideational manifestations of violence which indicate that violence continues long after the atrocities cease. I was interested in finding out how people survived and which cultural practices became meaningful in opposition to authorities who deny history on both a local and national level. However, "[d]ependence on a single kind of source or even on limited kinds of sources is bound to lead to a partial history" (Staves, in Hill 1993:38) and this book goes some way towards completing the picture.

The underlying assumption behind these questions is that many aspects of human cognition are founded on universals, that is, all human beings have the same psychodynamic blueprint and logically, these dynamics follow predictable patterns *vis-à-vis* certain external stimuli (such as extreme violence). This assumption is necessary in order to constitute the subject matter. That said, even if the physical forms of violence are similar across cultures, the same experience will be comprehended differently by people of different cultures for a variety of reasons, not least being that descriptions of the self are always culture-bound.[26] Culturally specific definitions of 'humanness' influence both perpetrators and survivors in situations such as Guatemala where much of the violence against indigenous people is committed by fellow Indians puppeteered by the *ladino*-run military. Thus, while biological death is a universal, the way a victim's body is disposed of or displayed bearing post-mortem mutilations provides the intended audience with a message only they can 'read'. For example, in the highlands, bodies are often dumped with objects stuffed into their mouths, which is believed to literally pin the victim's spirit to the spot, adding levels of supernatural danger to the denial of 'humanness' indicated by the corpse's nakedness (chapter eight). Response to similar events also differs, as they are expressed according to specific cultural idioms.

The answers to my questions were limited by a number of factors, not least being that most people known to have been 'organized' (members of the popular movements) are now dead, disappeared, in hiding, or have changed their allegiances. Another difficulty was that villagers thought my place was with the women; that I spent time with widows was understandable in local terms as I had not brought a partner with me. Trying to speak to everyone would have led to suspicions of betrayal which would have endangered my life and the lives of others too; a recent history of murders resulting from intra-community betrayals motivated by personal gain caused widespread mistrust and a readiness to jump to negative conclusions. In circumstances where "no neutrals are allowed" (Nash 1976:150), it is impossible to take a socially or politically neutral stance; it simply is not safe to do so. The virtues of distance which ethnographers claim to acquire for the sake of objective knowledge of other cultures obviously cannot be celebrated in this type of context. Indeed, it was an asset not to be so (Rosaldo 1984). That said, the problem facing all field researchers attempting to study violence and war close at hand — that of finding a position from which to speak and write against repression (Taussig 1987) — confronted me with a vengeance. It was a case of finding a safe distance where "it will not turn on you...and yet not putting it so far away in a clinical reality that we end up substituting one form of terror for another" (Taussig 1990:3). I empathize with Latin Americans working on the sequelae of terror who claim that the nature of the materials they deal with is so unnerving that no distancing from the material can ever be truly achieved (Jara and Vidal 1986; Balderston et al. 1987). I also understand the reluctance of some Latin Americans writing about terror to scrutinize the material beyond its testimonial value,[27] leaving testimonies to speak for themselves. Some offer their testimony in the hope that anthropologists, psychologists, sociologists, political scientists, and others will use the materials to help make sense of what has happened (Buda 1988).

Another practical problem is memory itself (chapter seven). Memory is more than the narrative of one's life experiences; it is a collaborative act and product between the narrator, the audience, the relationship between the two, and the spatial-temporal context (I am not concerned here with individual memories external to the social setting). Researcher and informants are not merely spectators and audience: "we are engaged. We are participants" (Grele et al. 1985:254). In the process of eliciting a personal experience, narrative that "has been unconscious, habitual, without meaning in a historical sense" is rendered significant when "we ask about it and thereby give it historical meaning" (Grele et al. 1985:253). I have attempted to be aware of the interaction between the narrating woman now and the remembered woman before, between present and past, and the impossibility of fully recovering that woman's world as it actually emerged.

My research elicited painful memories and I was concerned about the effects on the widows. My 'good intentions' — to give voice as best I could "to those who have been silenced" (Scheper-Hughes 1992:28) — did little to allay my concerns that the widows might resent my intrusions into their grief but it seems that many women found that "anthropology [insofar as they understood my explanations of what anthropology is] is not a hostile gaze but rather an opportunity to tell part of their life history" (Scheper-Hughes 1992:28). The life history approach I adopted has potential mental health consequences: the researcher's task, like a surgeon's knife, holds "the potential for both cure and disaster, for both illumination and confusion" (Ortiz 1985:101). Positive psychological consequences include the validation of the narrator's experience, conveying "the unambiguous message that the selectee is interested and that his/her life has value and meaning to someone else", which has a "cathartic effect". The narrativization and communication of one's life experiences to someone else provides "a grounding in reality" which has the potential for "increased family understanding and communication". Negative responses include a reluctance to delve into memories which are still painful and, for others, "fear reactions" concerning the revelation of certain details which could endanger the lives of family and friends. A rarer response is a "special sort of insight experience into subconscious processes" (Ortiz 1985:107-113, 198-9).

The pervasive gaze of a violent, oppressive state caused additional problems (Marcus 1992:104). The increasing instability of the late 1980s created a situation which was dangerous for the people under study. This raises serious ethical questions to which I have no answers. Although it is important to give testimony to individuals' experience of violence, especially when their voices have been silenced, it is not worth jeopardizing further lives. Because of my continuing concern, I have disguised the identity of the NGO to which I was affiliated, the village of 'Emol', the local town, and, of course, of the women whose voices appear in this book. The threat of further punishment remains.

My experiences in Guatemala have led me to question anthropology's prevailing concern with order at an abstract level of structure, where everything can ultimately be seen as self-regulating. This approach has led to a curious sanitizing of war and social and economic forms of violence (e.g., racism, poverty, and avoidable diseases); these practices and the horrors they entail need to be recognized and properly labelled within anthropological discourse. The sanitized language of abstraction denies the experiential reality of order, let alone that of disorder, the mechanism of which has no theory to explain it. Even less attention has been given to how unarmed victims of aggression express their social reality, even though 85 percent of all war-related deaths now occur among civilian populations (Renner 1989:133). This book goes some small way to remedying that situation as it addresses the question of how a community copes with fear in every day life when traditional forms of solidarity and the usual restraint mechanisms of social life collapse. I have related the women's testimonies as closely as possible to the way they were related to me, insofar as this is achievable when translating one language (K'iche') to another (English), sometimes via a third (Spanish). K'iche' women have no cultural means of producing themselves for they can neither write their own documents nor publicly construct their own versions of history; this book represents my attempt to write their voices back into history and to deconstruct their apparent eccentricity in the hope that their voices are more likely to be heard.

Organizational Structure of the Book

The book is loosely divided into three sections — life before, during, and after *la violencia*.

This chapter has, among other things, introduced the main characters in the book. Chapter two, 'The Setting', and chapter three, 'Gender Relations Before La Violencia', discuss the environment in which the women were socialized and the social, economic, and religious changes within that environment over the past forty years. Chapter three exposes the gap between an ideal of complementarity and balance between the sexes and a reality of female vulnerability and dependence.

The following two chapters chart the course of *la violencia*. Chapter four, 'La Violencia', describes the first phase of the military state's counter-insurgency campaign (1978-1982), when death and destruction were the work of external agents — usually the army but also the guerrilla. Chapter five, 'Village Patrols and Their Violence', describes phase two (1982-1985): the deliberate involvement of whole communities in the terrorization, destruction, and reorganization of those communities.

Chapter six, 'Women's Lives as Widows', describes the consequences of widowhood; women restructured their lives in the midst of unprecedented chaos and carnage. Chapter seven, 'Popular Memories of La Violencia', discusses the difficulties of accessing memories of chaos in a situation which denies their truth. Chapters eight, nine, and ten discuss the various cultural exegeses available to the widows and how they use them in their attempts to create meaning, continuity, and a new sense of 'self', both individually and as a group, out of their experiences..

The book concludes by describing the exhumation of the clandestine graves of Emol's massacre victims in 1992 and the subsequent implosion of the widows' group. The chapter describes the widows' lives in the present and looks at the varied, but typical, outcomes of their attempts to reorganize their lives.

Notes

1. cf. Jonas (1991:157): the 1985 election "was part of the war and it did not involve a real transfer of power from military to civilians. Once the army had completed the genocidal phase of the military campaign, and once the institutions of the counterinsurgency state were legalized in the 1985 constitution, elections and civilian government could proceed without requiring a fundamental change".

2. cf. Barraclough (1984), cited in Pearce (1986:302): "It is difficult to imagine how effective peasant and worker participation [in a more conventional democratic process] could be achieved in El Salvador and Guatemala without major social and political transformations in the whole society taking place first. In societies such as these, elections are often meaningless exercises".

3. The only other civilian president in the past forty years, Julio César Montenegro, elected in 1966, was only permitted to remain in office after literally signing a pact with the army (Jonas 199:60).

4. The *Unión Revolucionaria Nacional Guatemalteca* (URNG) was formed in 1982 as a result of the union of the Guerrilla Army of the Poor (*Ejército Guerrillero de los Pobres*; EGP); the Revolutionary Organization of People in Arms (*Organización Revolucionaria del Pueblo en Armas*; ORPA), the Rebel Armed Forces *(Fuerzas Armadas Rebeldes*; FAR) and the Guatemalan Workers' (Communist) Party (PGT). It is both the revolutionary movement's military high command and its diplomatic wing. The (civilian) government entered talks with the URNG in 1991. In February 1996, President Alvaro Arzú Irigoyen (1996-) "took the unprecedented step of meeting directly with URNG leaders" (Popkin 1996:1, fn 1).

5. Council of Ethnic Communities 'We Are All Equal' *(Consejo de Comunidades Etnicas* Runujel Junam). CERJ was founded by a *ladino*, Amílcar Méndez, a former elementary school teacher who had worked in southern El Quiché; it is based in the departmental capital, Santa Cruz. CERJ's aim in July 1988 was to use Guatemala's Constitution to protect peasants' basic human rights. The army has been known to tell villagers that the Constitution is a guerrilla document (America's Watch 1990). CERJ was formally recognized in December 1988 and its mostly Mayan membership grew rapidly; the organization was quickly harassed by threats in letters and telephone calls, verbal warnings of army reprisals, road 'accidents', the rape of a member of Amílcar Méndez' family, and televised denunciations of Méndez himself as a 'communist' and a 'guerrilla' at government-sponsored news conferences (America's Watch 1990). Several people have paid for their membership in CERJ with their lives.

CERJ is best known for organizing resistance to forced recruitment into the civil defence patrols and conscription into the army. It also carries legal claims to the civilian government which, despite the declaration of a new Constitution, usually ignores them.

6. The National Widows' Co-ordination of Guatemala *(Coordinación Nacional de las Viudas Guatemaltecas)* grew from the meeting of two widows' leaders, one from El Quiché and the other from Chimaltenango. Each had worked to unite groups of widows in order to look, in both local and national contexts, at their eco-

nomic and personal needs and the threats against their lives. With the support of an indigenous K'iche' Catholic priest and human rights organizations, they decided, in 1986, to form an organization for indigenous widows distinct from the *ladino*-run GAM. Most women date the formation of the organization from a mass for widows held in May 1987 which was broadcast over the radio, reaching thousands of women isolated in their communities by their experiences.

7. The Mutual Support Group *(Grupo de Apoyo Mutuo)* was established for relatives of the disappeared by a *ladina*, Nineth Montenegro de García. GAM seeks information and action on disappeared *ladinos* and Indians; supports Indian survivors' efforts to pressure the civil authorities to exhume their kin's remains from the clandestine graves which litter the countryside; and protests abuses by civil patrol chiefs and other paramilitaries. Most of GAM's members are indigenous.

Some GAM members have formed a separate organization: Families of the Detained and Disappeared of Guatemala *(Familares de Detenidos y Desaparecidos de Guatemala*; FAMDEGUA).

8. The Association for the Promotion of the Social Sciences in Guatemala *(La Asociación para el Avance de las Ciencias Sociales en Guatemala)* is an independent organization which sponsors and publishes sociological research.

9. Accords signed during de León Carpio's presidency include the "Agreement for the Resettlement of Populations Displaced by the Armed Confrontation, signed June 17, 1994; The Agreement on the Establishment of the Commission to Clarify Past Human Rights Violations and Acts of Violence that have Caused the Guatemalan Population to Suffer, June 23, 1994; and the Agreement on the Identity and Rights of Indigenous Peoples, signed March 31, 1995" (Popkin 1996:1, fn.1). These accords were implemented following the signing of the definitive peace agreement on 29 December 1996.

10. MINUGUA, the United Nations' Mission for the Verification of Human Rights in Guatemala, was established on 21 November 1994; its brief is to investigate current abuses and to verify the implementation of the Peace Accords.

11. As a psychological phenomenon, impunity cannot be separated from repression. Its purpose is to put into action ideological and psychological mechanisms to make permanent extreme fear and repression and the threat of further violence, thus maintaining the dominant regime. cf. Zur (1994).

12. Family and Friends Against Kidnaping and Crime *(Familiares y Amigos Contra la Delinquencia y el Secuestro)*. Founded 1996.

13. The names of this village and its surrounding hamlets are all pseudonyms.

14. The three points of this triangle are Chajul, Nebaj, and San Juan Cotzal.

15. Ironically, the town of Nebaj in northern El Quiché was "almost *tranquilo* [calm]" during this period, despite occupation by the Guatemalan army and regular problems caused by two columns of the Guerrilla Army of the Poor. No-one openly defied the army, despite the active presence of the guerrillas (Stoll 1993).

16. This name, and the names of the people of 'Emol', are pseudonyms.

17. The United States has shaped fundamental events in Guatemala through the Central Intelligence Agency (CIA). U.S. intervention began with the backing of the coup in 1954 which overthrew the reformist government of Jacobo Arbenz (1951-1954) (Jonas 1991).

18. North American contributions finance most missionary work in Latin America, including Guatemala (Stoll 1990:10).

19. 'Uniting' is the local term for marriage according to traditional customs; the resulting 'unions' were rarely registered with church or state.

20. Bringing his bride to *doña* Josefina's house is Diego's way of staking a claim to a share of her land. See chapter six.

21. For peasant war and/or rebellion, see, for example, Wolf (1969); Freidrich (1970); Alavi (1973). For the state or evolution of war, see, for example, Lesser (1968); Webster (1975); Otterbein and Otterbein (1985). Edited volumes on the anthropology of war include Fried et al. (1968); Nettleship et al. (1975); Bohannon (1980); Ferguson (1984); Haas (1990).

22. "The bulk of ethnographies that do consider warfare have tended to offer structural-functionalist analyses of inter-tribal feuding" (Wilson 1995:206). For instance, see Coser (1956) and Gluckman (1963) for examples of institutionalized conflict 'functioning' to maintain the social political order. Since the pioneering anthropological work of Wolf (1969) and Popkin (1979), much attention has been focused on 'structural' variables which influence conflict. Approaches in recent years have still not diverged much from that of sociologists (Scott 1976) or political scientists (Skocpol 1979). Exceptions include Das (1990) and Werbner (1991).

23. Research on the Guatemalan internal war which has not diverged much from this model includes Carmack (1988), Manz (1988), and Smith (1990a). To be fair, conditions of war (1979-1986) made fieldwork untenable and few ethnographies were produced during this time apart from the edited biography of Rigoberta Menchú (Burgos-Debray and Menchú 1984). Fieldwork became more tenable in some areas after 1986 (see, for example, Annis 1987). Analyses which deviated from the above-mentioned paradigm began to be produced in the late 1980s and include Smith (1988), Stoll (1990, 1993), Warren (1993), and Wilson (1995).

24. See Dahrendorf (1979:62) for an explication of Weber's concept of 'life chances'.

25. The focus on changes in material culture, artifacts, and human behaviour means that situations of political violence (which have occurred in many places where anthropologists have carried out fieldwork) are excluded from the study.

26. cf. Levett (1989:22): "expressions of emotion, self and subjectivity are culturally shaped and are embedded in linguistic repertoires". cf. Zur (1996).

27. See, for example, the critical literary essays in Balderston et al. (1987) and Jara and Vidal (1986).

2

The Setting

The province of El Quiché[1] is in Guatemala's remote western high-lands. These beautiful, verdant mountains are slashed by innumerable ravines *(barrancos)*, some of which drop over a thousand feet from plateaux up to 9,000 feet above sea level. For all their lush greenery, arable land and grazing are in short supply in the mountains, giving added emphasis to the K'iche's' traditional attachment to the land.[2] It is one of Guatemala's poorest provinces and also one of the least populated.

People live in dispersed hamlets *(aldeas)* collectively known by the name of the largest settlement or village *(cantón)* which houses the local administrative and economic centre. Emol is typical. It consists of a village (Emol Central) with some three hundred families plus five scattered hamlets — Kotoh, Raxa, Malah, Chi Te, and Pachaq, which are up to an hour's walk away from each other — with an average of eighty families each: approximately 3,000 people in all (prior to *la violencia*).[3] Equally typical is that most Emoltecos are descended from the original settlers of the village and are at least distantly related; most live on family-owned land. That Emol's five hamlets are interspersed with hamlets belonging to other villages probably reflects a historical resistance to the merging of disparate ethnic groups aggregated by the Spanish for administrative purposes *(parcialidades)* following the devastation of the conquest (Smith 1990b:28, n.10).[4] Centuries of intermarriage between adjacent hamlets belonging to different villages has not diminished local animosities.

Villages are grouped into townships *(municipios)* which have pre-his-panic roots (Lovell and Sweezy 1990), largely because *municipio* boundaries are predominantly shaped by the terrain. The differences in *municipio* topography result in variations in settlement patterns, house styles, methods of cultivation, and minor economic options which supplement the ubiquitous Indian occupation of subsistence corn farming.

Differences in pre-hispanic heritage and historical experience (Smith

1990b) are clearly discernable in the cultural diversity between Indians of different *municipios*, whom Emoltecos refer to as 'natural (indigenous) people' *(gente natural)*, 'poor people' *(gente pobre)* or 'the humble' *(humildes)*.[5] Other indicators of diverse histories are variations in traditional, *municipio* weaving patterns, traditional customs *(costumbre)*, and the proliferation of languages and dialects. The continued existence of twenty Mayan languages and dozens of *municipio* variants[6] also indicates the historic isolation of highland townships not only from the wider, Spanish-speaking state but also from each other (Smith 1990b).[7] Diversity is also discernable at village level — for example, Emol Central is quite different from, say, Kotoh: it is more conservative (not just in political terms), has a higher conversion rate (to evangelism), and a larger proportion of its inhabitants align themselves with the army.

Both Indians and *ladinos* identify themselves in terms of their natal *municipios* (Watanabe 1992; cf. Wilson 1995). The *municipio* is the smallest administrative unit of the nation-state. The organizational structure, established in 1954, consists of an elected mayor *(alcade)*[8] who appoints a deputy mayor, a secretary and an assistant, a treasurer and two treasury assistants, a chief of police, and a judge; office holders are nearly always *ladino*. Each village has an elected ancillary mayor, whose authority is confirmed by the *municipio* mayor; in highland villages, auxiliary mayors are Indian. Village mayors deal with petty offences and drunkenness. Crimes of violence (including rape), land disputes and rustling are dealt with by the town *alcade*, who may establish a commission to investigate the allegations. Emol has a mayoral office among its administrative buildings but, as in most villages since *la violencia*, it was virtually defunct for many years (1981-1992). Power had moved elsewhere.

Emol is located in southern El Quiché where the permanent population (excluding army personnel based in the area) is 93·5 percent indigenous. The high proportion of Maya reflects the inability of the Spanish *conquistadores* (and, until recently, their *ladino* successors) to penetrate the mountains; some Indian settlements are still only accessible on foot. The remaining 6·5 percent of highland residents are *ladinos*, who tend to be landowners, employers, or representatives of the state). Highland Indians have come to identify *ladinos* with both the state and class oppression (Smith 1990b:89).

One reason for this view stems from the demands of Guatemala's *ladino*-controlled, export-led economy which cross-cuts the neat patchwork of departments and *municipios*, drawing highland Maya to work in the plantations *(fincas)* on the southern coast. These fertile plains are only used for the export crops which contribute to Guatemala's position as the wealthiest nation in Central America.[9] In 1989-1990, agricultural produce accounted for 50 percent of total export earnings and cultivation employed 53 percent of the labour force (Economic Intelligence Unit, Country Profile 1989). This is seasonal work and most *finca* workers can be included among the 60 percent of Guatemalans who are unemployed or underemployed. With daily wages set for over a decade at Q.3·25 (75¢ US) despite 100 percent inflation,[10] migrant workers earn roughly Q.250 a season and generally return home with eighty Quetzales (about US$20, or the price of a young pig) for three months' work.

Advances in agro-technology since the 1960s led to the expansion of agro-export production and, in the 1970s, to new expropriations of land previously only cultivable by Indians. The landed oligarchy which supported the military regime (1954-1985) and is suspected of involvement in the various right-wing coup attempts of the late 1980s, was not loth to order the army to dispossess Indians of their lands. By the mid-1980s, fewer than two percent of Guatemala's landowners owned 65 percent of farm land (Barry 1989:68); more than 80 percent of Guatemala's arable land is owned by *ladinos*.

In Emol, 20 percent of families are landless, twice the average for southern El Quiché. The implications of being unable to produce corn, whether through landlessness or widowhood, go beyond the economic aspect for most Indians because "Without a territorial claim in a community of one's ancestors and the means to secure part of one's food supply, a Guatemalan Indian has great difficulty in retaining his or her identity as an Indian" (Smith 1990b:20). The importance of corn production is such that people cling to their land even though by 1979, 87 percent of family holdings were too small to meet household subsistence needs (Barry 1989:60).[11] Indian agriculture has collapsed dramatically following the initial tripling of yields resulting from Catholic missionaries' introduction of chemical fertilizer in the 1960s. For a few years, people were able to set aside some of their corn fields for commercial crops; even corn became a marketable commodity. But, as an old man explained to me, repeated applications of fertilizer "made the land tired". Today, only two percent of Emol families grow commercial crops and even these are minimal. The remainder (78 percent) need all their land to plant corn and beans; few families can produce subsistence crops sufficient for more than six months of the year. Emol's health worker estimates that 70 percent of the village's children under six years of age are malnourished, a higher proportion than a generation ago but probably 'normal' for children born before the 1960s. For example, *doña* Josefina (who was born in the 1940s) described a recurrent childhood illness, the symptoms of which can only be attributed to severe malnutrition, a connection she did not make herself. Many older many women told me that even in the reduced circumstances of the aftermath of *la violencia*, the food situation is better today than it was before the introduction of fertilizer. Yet the situation is likely to worsen, as family owned land is divided into ever-smaller plots every generation.

The combination of malnutrition and endemic disease (tuberculosis in the highlands, malaria in the coastal plains) exacts a high toll on indigenous children. Every year, 42,000 Guatemalan children die of preventable diseases. In 1984, a USAID study revealed that infant mortality was 160 per 1,000 in the highlands; in 1986, Agop Kayayan, then head of Unicef for Latin America, stated that "Guatemala has one of the poorest health records in Central America. Five children every hour die from diseases such as diphtheria, whooping cough, tetanus, measles, or polio" (cited in Painter 1987:4, fn.6).

With a doctor:patient ratio of 1:85,000 in the highlands and no doctors in the villages, an appallingly large number of people die following simple accidents or broken limbs. Indian life expectancy, at 47·5 years, is seventeen years shorter than *ladinos'* (Barry 1989). Health is another issue over which progressives and conservatives clashed: the former's commitment of a high proportion of local improvement projects to the provision of health clinics and potable water was resisted by traditionalists who believe that all illness stems from dissonant relationships between the spirits of the living, the dead, and the ancestors (chapter eight). Protestant converts side with traditionalists on this issue: they do not believe in doing anything to improve life on earth as everything is 'in the hands of God'.

Education and Language

Despite the state's avowed interest in transforming Mayan Indians into a Spanish-speaking, rural working class, the vast majority of Guatemala's indigenous citizens remain physically and socially marginalized from the benefits of participation in the world of the nation state.

There are many reasons for this, not least being the Indians' desire to retain their land and their way of life. Indians resist the state's programme of 'social integration' which they perceive as attacking their language and culture (Handy 1984:260). They are ambivalent about the Spanish teaching programme *(castellanización)* which prepares Indian children for standard primary school. The programme was established in the 1940s but it was another decade before schools began to be built. In the 1960s, bilingual teaching assistants were introduced. Known as *promotores*, they are unpaid community volunteers trained by either government or non-government agencies as their local intermediaries; in other words, the education of indigenous children depended (and largely still depends) on the willingness of their communities to educate them in an alien language and culture. State commitment to indigenous children's education has been very half-hearted and so the *castellanización* programme has been rather unsuccessful; today, only 50 percent of Indians are literate (Barry 1989:85) and, in most cases, only to a limited degree. Literacy in Mayan languages is even less common despite the efforts of North American Bible Translators from the Summer Institute of Linguistics: subsidized by USAID, this evangelical mission hoped to teach the Maya to read the Bible in their own languages (Stoll 1993:15).

Catholic missionaries were more successful in introducing Spanish to

Mayan communities than the state. Viewing the numerous Mayan languages and dialects as a hindrance to progress, they mounted a two-pronged assault on monolingualism. Beginning with bilingual Indian men in the mid-1950s, they organized Spanish-language catechist classes through which Mayans were introduced not only to orthodox catholicism but to a new understanding of their social, economic, and political position within the Guatemalan state. Spanish became the vehicle for new ideas, providing a new political language for the K'iche' who say they have 'ideas' *(ideas)* in Spanish and 'thoughts' in K'iche'. For the radicalized, *ideas* relate to new concepts and political matters inexpressible in K'iche'; people who have such *ideas* are said to have 'awoken' *(despertado)*. For their opponents, *ideas* refer to (the guerrillas') malevolent intentions. The K'iche' word for 'thoughts' refers to traditional affairs or mundane concepts.

The missionaries also encouraged the establishment of schools and adult education classes. Realizing that knowledge of Spanish was important in terms of acquiring a political voice, they aimed to create a new, bilingual, indigenous leadership core; it was this aspect of catechist-inspired education programmes which so inflamed the military state. Many of these schools were destroyed during *la violencia* because their very existence 'proved' that the village was 'organized' (subversive). For example, Kotoh's school, built by local catechists at the instigation of *doña* Eugenia's son Gilberto, was severely vandalized and children were educated in an abandoned house for several years; the *ladino* school teacher was one of the first people to be killed during *la violencia*. Kotoh's school has now been repaired but many villages still have no school at all.

The idea that knowledge of Spanish is useful, if not essential, in the struggle to protect their Mayan identity and culture, has taken root (cf. Burgos-Debray and Menchú 1984). The paradox of the politics of cultural preservation is that an activist such as Rigoberta Menchú has to know Spanish in order to be effective, even though this can lead to accusations of fraternizing with, or even becoming, the enemy, i.e., a *ladina* (Sommer 1991:35). Even more paradoxical is that the sense of identity of some indigenous communities in El Quiché was often enhanced when they adopted the Spanish language (Falla 1980:559). These profound changes represent a new stage in Indians' response to national society: a higher degree of articulation with the *ladino* world is part of their redefinition and recovery of identity as Mayans (Falla 1980; Lovell 1988). People who learn and use Spanish in order to protect their cultural identity are generally more secure in their personal identities than fellow Indians who merely want *ladino* power (chapter five). For the former, increased contact with the *ladino* is not a sign of *ladinization* in a simplistic sense. Such people tend to be more innovative and adaptable than the average K'iche' villager, most of whom consider Spanish the language of power: the power of the state, the army, the employer *(patrón)* — in short, of the oppressor. This is so engrained that some men attempt to appropriate the power of the language they had learnt outside the community by sprinkling their conversation with Spanish words and phrases in order to impress or dominate fellow villagers.

Knowledge of Spanish is also important in finding employment beyond cash-poor Indian communities. It is traditionally men who deal with the 'outside world' and consequently Spanish language and literacy rates are higher among men. Bilingualism is most common among young men, whose Spanish vocabulary is shaped by where they learnt it — army service, the catechist movement, or street trading in Guatemala City where they pose as Spanish-speaking *ladinos*; home again, they resume their K'iche'-speaking, peasant existence. To older men, having to know some Spanish is merely a fact of life which does not affect their perceptions of themselves as Indians; younger men, who are more proficient in Spanish, find the language spoken helps to compartmentalize their lives as, for example, they can attribute the awful things they were forced to do during army service to their 'Spanish'-speaking persona. Thus, depending on what is being spoken about and by whom, one can be 'human' in one language and not the other and vice versa (chapter five).

K'iche' women tend to consider Spanish the language of men; from childhood, they are 'protected' from contact with *ladino* people, culture, and language. Fathers, who have the final word on whether or not their children should attend school, often seem more concerned about the effect of a *ladino* education on their daughters; they are aware of the conflict between the girls' future role as 'conservers of tradition' and an education system which disparages local culture and encourages children to leave it and the land behind. Some parents deny their daughters an education for pragmatic reasons: although education is free, they consider the incidental expenses of pens, books, etc., a waste of their meagre cash resources as there are no job opportunities for girls which require Spanish. Consequently, girls are much less likely to go to school than boys, regardless of a mother's wish that her daughters should not be monolingual and marginal like herself. Women have few opportunities to learn Spanish through employment — unless they work for *ladinos* as children (as maids or shop workers, for example) or migrate regularly to the plantations *(fincas)* where Indians and poor *ladinos* work side by side. All contact with the *patrón* should be and generally is negotiated by men (fathers, husbands, sons) and most women are happy with this arrangement. Cultural restraints and domestic responsibilities meant that women also had less opportunity to learn Spanish through the catechist movement or adult education classes. These attitudes perpetuate low Spanish language and literacy rates among women: over 60 percent of Indian women are monolingual and only 15 percent are literate (CIT-GUA Studies 1987-1989). In Emol, the figures are 80 percent and 5 percent respectively. Few women speak Spanish although many understand a considerable amount.

As mothers, women are ambivalent about the merits of education; they see its theoretical advantages but they also know that most rural, educated Indians were killed during *la violencia*. K'iche' parents' concern about *ladino* schooling are borne out by an army officer I met in the Ixil Triangle: he told me that the army will only feel safe when it has taken over the Ministry of Education because "Guatemala's children are the subversives of tomorrow." In the mid-1980s, only 60 percent of seven to fourteen year olds were registered for school; only 10 percent finished sixth grade (Barry 1989). A family's need of a child's labour also discourages school attendance.

Some people retain their faith in education: for example, one widow, whose murdered son had been involved in establishing Emol's adult literacy classes, threatened her grandson that if he didn't go to school, he would be unable to get a job and would be taken into the army which killed his father. For other widows, the education of daughters has become more important since *la violencia*: the high number of male deaths means that women can no longer rely on men's presence to provide for and protect them.

Another factor in the complex education and language issue is that the powerful landowning class has a vested interest in maintaining the *status quo*: a bilingual, literate working class is unlikely to be as malleable as the separate, monolingual peasant groups who currently work on the plantations.

Ethnic Diversity and Class

About half of Guatemala's population is estimated to be Indian (Smith 1986, Barry 1989) — nearly five million people in 1990, of whom 550,000 were K'iche' (Government of Guatemala 1991),[12] the largest of the Indian sub-groups. The majority of the remainder of the population is of mixed descent *(mestizo)* which is generally interpreted as being of Spanish and Indian ancestry. In Guatemala, *mestizos* are known as *ladinos*, a word first applied by sixteenth century Spaniards to acculturated or Spanish-speaking Indians (Tax 1941:21; Sherman 1979:187); apart from Chiapas, Mexico, and El Salvador (Pearce 1986:45), both of which share borders with Guatemala, this usage has disappeared in Central America where the word *mestizo* is the norm. In Guatemala, where *ladinos* and Indians often share the same class position,[13] the upper classes prefer to call themselves Creoles, whites, or Europeans (Smith 1990b) in order to differentiate themselves from poor non-Indians (i.e., *ladinos*); yet Guatemala's elite is mostly *mestizo* rather than white. Few Europeans migrated to Guatemala (Morner, in Smith 1990b:3), which implies that most people who classify themselves as *ladinos* are of mixed Mayan descent and have little of the Spanish ancestry they claim for themselves.[14] This is rarely if ever mentioned (Smith 1990b): "What has distinguished Indians and non-Indians over time has not been biological heritage, but a changing system of social classification, based on ideologies of race, class, language, and culture, which ideologies have taken on different meanings over time" (Smith 1990b:3; cf. Wilson 1995).

In highland communities, class division commonly translates as ethnic and cultural division. The army, whose rank and file is predominantly extracted from the Indian peasantry, is employed to protect the interests of the *ladino* middle and upper classes, a role which later devolved to the civil patrols (chapter five), whose members are also predominantly Indian. In Uspantán, El Quiché, middle class merchants petitioned for the formation of the patrols when the town was occupied by guerrillas. A patroller recalled: "Since the guerrillas said they had come in favour of the poor, the *ladinos* knew that it would not be to their advantage to have them in our town since this could mean economic ruin for them" (America's Watch 1986:36). But, unlike their Indian neighbours, they were not obliged to join themselves; nor were they accused of subversion if they fled at the first hint of trouble.

Ethnic diversity elaborated within *municipio* distinctiveness generates a complex language for distinguishing the 'other'. The inhabitants of one *municipio* draw hierarchical distinctions between themselves and people from other townships; mutual antipathy flourishes as a result. Relationships with the outside on religious, cultural, and social grounds are permeated with mistrust. Indians meekly refer to themselves as 'little natural people' *(naturalcitos)* but barely hesitate to describe Indians from other ethnic groups or sub-groups (which are usually coterminous with *municipios*) as less civilized and less worthy, 'not too bright' or 'idiots'. These feelings are a behavioural habit, based on disparaging attitudes to different, 'incorrect' ways of doing things. Wealthier *municipios*, villages or hamlets are the subject of considerable envy *(envidia)* (Schultze-Jena 1954) and are the object of much criticism; this results in a decrease in solidarity or community (which is one of the definitions of *envidia* (chapter nine)). In a situation of 'limited good', one person's gain is another's loss as "there is no way directly within peasant power to increase available quantities" (Foster and Rubenstein 1965:296); the K'iche' express this in terms of a 'good' person being someone who is satisfied with his lot and lacks ambition. Jealously preserved ethnic, *municipio*, and village distinctions fragment indigenous Guatemalans, leaving them cruelly exposed to the attacks of the military state. The army capitalized on these traditional hostilities, actively setting one village, or even hamlets within a village (as in Emol, for example), against each other.

By far the deepest cleavage is between Indians and *ladinos*; even a ladinized (culturally assimilated)[15] Indian is not judged to be untrustworthy in the same way as a *ladino* outsider. Indians who adopt *ladino* ways are referred to as 'those who have advanced themselves' *(se superó)*, a remark which is redolent with ambiguity and conveys *envidia* rather than admiration. Indians say that both Spanish-speaking Indians and *ladinos* are 'civilized' because they are 'educated'; again, this attribution is ambivalent and often sarcastic.[16] Such people are disparaged by other Indians and contrasted with 'pure indigenes' *(puros indigenas)* (which in this context means an ideal type rather than genetic purity), but only in private, never to a person's face; unless inebriated, the K'iche' operate unwaveringly within strict cultural bounds of politeness. Indians who wear western clothes *(vestidos)* are said to be 'pure *ladinos*' *(puros* <u>moos</u>)[17] — this does not refer to the second-hand western clothes of most Indian men, which they tend to wear in traditional style. Women who wear *ladino vestidos* (usually only those who have moved away from the village) may even be deemed prostitutes. As 'conservers of tradition', women are much more likely than men to wear their *municipio* clothes *(traje)* and the change from traditional dress is somehow more shocking.

The division between Indians and *ladinos* is most apparent in the *municipio* town where the small *ladino* population is concentrated. It is here that Indians and *ladinos* have the most contact. Spanish-speaking *mestizos* wearing European style clothing dominate Indians socially and economically (Tax 1937:432); they abuse Indians physically and verbally, calling them 'dirty' and 'stupid', often refusing to pay in full for their market purchases. *Ladino* racism is endemic.

For their part, Indians stereotype *ladinos* pejoratively as selfish, untrustworthy, dangerous and 'without shame' *(sin vergüenza)*. Indians' negative evaluation of *ladinos* can be seen in the socialization of their children, who are given many explicit and implicit messages which aim to prevent them becoming ladinized. Indians perceive *ladinos*, with their appropriated Spanish ancestry, as the contemporary inheritors of the centuries-old hatred and fear of the *conquistadores* (cf. Burgos-Debray and Menchú 1984). Given that the *ladino* state and the landed oligarchy periodically utilize violence to enforce their interests, these emotions persist to the present, constraining Indian behaviour (Smith 1990b). Renewed *ladino* expropriations of Indian land and the 'regional-national restructuring' (capitalist expansion) of the 1960s and 1970s benefitted the upper *(ladino)* social strata and the army (which began to transform itself into a lucrative business) but, despite providing short term improvements for the rural population (higher wages, better yields), ultimately impoverished virtually the entire Indian population. This exacerbated Indian perceptions of *ladinos* as 'enemy' forces.

In reality, there is little interaction between Indians and *ladinos* on a day to day, person to person basis. Most of the ideas each has of the other are founded on prejudice and culturally elaborated mytho-history. *Ladinos* confuse social race with physical race to exclude Indians from the human community; they classify Indians as naturally inferior and non-human (that *ladinos* are generally taller and bigger than Indians indicates a healthier diet and less adverse living conditions, not different genes). These attitudes enabled the *ladino* military machine, like the *conquistadores* before them, to commit violence on Indian populations on a scale reaching genocidal proportions (Falla 1994; Jonas 1991).[18]

Ladinos see Indians as remote, wild and dangerous, like the mountains in which they live, as uncivilized, savage creatures with astonishing, enigmatic, and magical powers. These entrenched views of the Indian, which date from the conquest, lead not only to the ill-treatment meted out to indigenous people but also to *ladino* paranoia about the harm the uncontrolled Indian could do to them. Like the *conquistadores*, the Guatemalan army seems to subscribe to the paranoic's aphorism of attack before being attacked and uses the same mirror of terror which reflects the white man's worst fear in inverted form. *Ladinos*, and especially the *ladino* military, have projected into the stereotype of the Indian most, if not all, of those undesirable motives and characteristics they know best: their own (cf. Bettelheim 1986).

The mutual distrust and fear which characterizes relations between *ladinos* and Indians fed into *la violencia*. The great majority of people tortured, disappeared, or killed during this period were not white, middle class, or European in culture as, for example, in Chile or Argentina. Most were Indian who are 'other' in *ladino* cultural terms. As 'exemplars of chaos', Indians are the disorderly 'other' against which even Indian civil patrol chiefs *(jefes)* and military commissioners define themselves as civilized, rational, orderly, and *ladino*.

The complex nature of ethnic relations is illustrated by the army's attitudes towards its rank and file. Before conscription was abolished in the mid-1990s as part of the peace process, up to 8,000 (mostly rural) young men were inducted into the army every year, often forcibly; as a result, 20 percent of all rural (mostly Indian) young men between the ages of eighteen and twenty-four were part of the military machine which terrorized their communities. Although my enquiries at the end of the 1980s revealed that most young men were against performing their military service, the army has had little difficulty in gaining recruits since the end of conscription. It is not simply that being a soldier brings status, skills training, and perquisites but rather because army service is such an integral part of male adolescence that many Indian teenagers continue to present themselves for induction. Thus the proportion of young Indian men in the army has remained more or less constant; equally unchanged are army attitudes towards them.

At induction, a significant proportion of Indian men are monolingual and most are illiterate in Spanish: they are indoctrinated with army propaganda as they learn the limited vocabulary of the military. Individual soldiers responded differently to this indoctrination: some became brutal patrollers, *jefes* or military commissioners (chapter five); others could not hide their repugnance at being expected to kill other Indians; for example, when *doña* Flora visited her son in camp, he wept for the horror of it all. Faced with the overwhelming power of the army, most recruits merely comply and hope to survive. Indian soldiers become invisible because they are sent to areas of Guatemala where they do not speak the local dialect: they are forced to speak Spanish which identifies them as *ladinos* in the eyes of the communities they are sent to subdue. Their uniforms, new imported weapons,[19] and Spanish-speaking officers are all emblems of the *ladino* state. Former conscripts spend an indefinite period in the army reserves in their home villages, where they are obliged to exercise every Sunday, in uniform but unarmed. They are again Indians like any other; army service and compliance with local paramilitaries is not enough to protect them from being disappeared or killed (which is what happened to *doña* Flora's son, among others).

Indians are politically used by both sides. The lower ranks of both the national army and the guerrilla are predominantly Indian (the remainder are poor *ladinos* with the same class position), whilst the highest echelons are always *ladino*. However, by the early 1990s, the lower ranks of the guerrilla had disappeared into the social landscape from whence they came.

The Development of Religious Differences

Traditionally, the Indians of the western highlands followed 'custom' *(costumbre)*, a word which is applied to rituals and other behaviours associated with Mayan tradition rather than the Catholic church or the nation. *Costumbre* can be described as a synthesis of ancient Mayan beliefs and sixteenth century Spanish folk catholicism; it has also been described as Mayan religion in Catholic garb. Although there is validity in both descriptions, Mayans refer to themselves as being 'of the custom', *costumbrista*, or 'pure' Catholics (as opposed to the 'new' catholicism introduced in the 1950s and the charismatic catholicism of the 1980s).

There has been a Protestant presence in northern El Quiché since the 1920s but another fifty years passed before the K'iche' began to convert in significant numbers. By then the *costumbrista* system of civil-religious offices, steadily undermined since the arrival of 'new' catholicism, was in disarray.

By the late 1980s, Emol was 60 percent Protestant, 25 percent 'new' or charismatic Catholic, and 10 percent 'pure' Catholic *(costumbrista)*; the remaining 5 percent were 'without religion'. The high proportion of Protestants indicates Emol's recent history: nationally, Protestants only account for 17 percent of the population, despite a seven-fold increase in converts between 1960 and 1985 (Stoll 1990: Appendix 2).

Costumbre

The colonial *cargo* system,[20] which revolves round the worship of Catholic saints, provides the moral basis for the traditional gerontocratic authority structure. Authority is vested in elders *(principales)*, men who rise through the ranks of the saints' brotherhoods *(cofradia)*;[21] communities are ruled through rotating civil and religious offices designed to promote the common good and ensure the survival of the community *qua* community (Farriss 1984:265). Holding office entails heavy expenditure, obviating the accumulation of capital; as such, the *cargo* system has been described as a powerful leveling institution, keeping families equivalent from generation to generation (e.g., Wagley 1949; Nash 1957; Carmack 1983:230). In fact, the system actually legitimizes the position of wealthier Indians who solicit contributions to saints festivals from the community rather than pay all the expenses themselves (Piel 1989). In other words, despite vigourously promoted 'norms' of economic equality within the community, Indians lived with the experience of differential wealth and power. Nevertheless, the saints festivals did function as a means of intra- and inter-community cohesion and co-operation as people joined in the processions and the feasting, each village and hamlet parading its patron saint icon. The custom disappeared during *la violencia* (cf. Wilson 1995:247) but has since made a small comeback.

Several factors contributed to the decline of the *costumbrista* authority structure. The military coup of 1954 saw the introduction of mayoral elections and political parties, which had a minimal effect on highland communities. The coup also ended peasants' hopes for land reform, which had serious long term consequences. In the short term, the coup led to the unprecedented commercial growth of the 1960s because it created "a 'safer' investment climate [for] national and international elites [who] promoted the development and diversification of Guatemala's economy" (Arias 1990: 231). Guatemala 'diversified' by increasing the cultivation of existing export crops (such as coffee) which can be grown at higher altitudes.

The renewed emphasis on the export-led plantation economy with its voracious appetite for land and cheap, seasonal labour drew increasing numbers of Indians from their communities for months at a time. This had a detrimental effect on village life (Smith 1977; Brintnall 1979) in that it loosened community bonds. The coffee boom (1960-1974) increased demand for labour at a time when Indians had least need of it because of the recent introduction of fertilizer. Higher wages (which were still extremely low in real terms) had to be paid to entice workers down from the mountains. Many Indians invested their hard-earned pay in local ventures such as petty trading and land improvement (Lovell 1988) rather than in their community's spiritual welfare (e.g., sponsoring *fiestas*, endowing the *cofradia* with new regalia), a rebuff to *cofradia principales* which was encouraged by Catholic missionaries and catechists (cf. Arias 1990). During this period, some returning labour migrants 'leapfrogged' over their richer neighbours who had been able to afford to stay at home. In an environment where even good luck is unlucky, this created significant tensions.

Principales' economic control of their communities was further undermined when Indians involved in the commercial sector began to consolidate their economic power by buying and selling outside *cofradia*-controlled, local markets (cf. Arias 1990). That catechists were getting better crop yields — not everyone could be persuaded to use the new fertilizer straight away — cannot have improved the *principales'* reputation. By the time the government's Village Improvement Scheme was relaunched in the 1960s, many younger men had gained positions of authority outside the traditional schema by converting to 'new' catholicism and participating in missionary-led organizations. In the late 1960s, tensions were high between *costumbristas* and supporters of Catholic Action *(Acción Católica)* and clashes were frequent (Warren 1978; Brintnall 1979; Cabarrús 1979; Falla 1980; Wilson 1995). In very divided communities, each group had its own separate mass on Sundays, used the Catholic church on alternate days (Colby and van den Berghe 1977:146), and marked saints' days and other village events with processions on consecutive days.

During *la violencia, costumbristas* were attacked by the military and local vigilantes because of their perceived alignment with 'new' Catholics. This is ironic, considering the tensions which then existed between them, but the military state saw both as expressions of insistent Indian 'otherness'. At the beginning of *la violencia,* one of the few things they had in common was their opposition to the growing number of Protestants; later, both groups had a greater tendency to resist the patrols. In Emol, following the return of Catholic religious to El Quiché in 1984, solidarity has increased as the new local priest was popular with both groups.

Particularly subject to lethal attack were *costumbrista* diviners *(zajorines*/aj q'ij); it was believed that they were using their powers to protect the guerrillas. Despite their religious authority, aj q'ij were easy targets because they lacked collective organization. Some aj q'ij took refuge in conversion to protestantism; people said these diviners were seduced by the possibility of payment for preaching in evangelical churches.[22]

A villager told me *costumbristas* were killed simply because "the evangelicals hated them". In Emol, the targeting of traditionalists was explained in terms of local enmities: one *jefe* was a former *costumbrista* sorcerer *(brujo)* who had been involved in witchcraft battles with other villagers; killing aj q'ij, who offered rituals of protection, rendered his opponents more vulnerable to his illicit spiritual and temporal powers. Eventually, he decided bullets were more efficacious in settling the battle 'once and for all'.

The *cofradía's* power base collapsed completely during *la violencia* and the saints brotherhoods now exist in very depleted form. In Emol the *cofradía* are being revived, though increased poverty since *la violencia* discourages many families from participating in the *cargo* system. One *mayordomo* houses two saints because a replacement could not be found when one hamlet's last *mayordomo* died;[23] its saint's statue is paired with that of another hamlet and they are taken out together for *fiesta* parades. Overall, there are not enough members to rotate the offices: the same officeholders *(mayordomos/cofrades)* house the saints and perform duties as though members of an exclusive club. Die-hard *mayordomos* persist with their rituals such as the small saints processions, to the derision of both Protestant and Catholic evangelicals, who ridicule *costumbrista* rituals such as the dances *(zarabandas)* and the alcohol consumption at such events.

Costumbre has lost its *raison d'être*. Intra-communal cohesion has collapsed because of fragmentation into different groups. Inter-village celebrations, where they still exist, are now banded by interest group: in Emol, *costumbristas* and some 'new' Catholics from other communities still visit on the annual festival of a village's patron saint; patrols across communities were led to celebrate the anniversary of their foundation. Yet despite rapid social change and religious conversion, most Mayans people's understanding of the world they live in is still informed by the *costumbrista* norms they absorbed as children from their mothers, who are responsible for their primary socialization.

'New' Catholicism and Catholic Action

The European and American priests sent to Latin America as part of a papal crusade to bring believers closer to orthodox catholicism proved to be the major catalyst of change in highland Guatemala. The missionary-priests arrived around the time of the 1954 military coup, which had had the support of Guatemala's clerical establishment (which also supported the counter-insurgency campaign of 1966-1968, their professed apolitical nature notwithstanding). The missionaries were shocked by the social injustices they witnessed and deliberately tried to engineer change from the bottom up. Identifying *costumbre* as the main impediment not only to conventional catholicism but to social improvement, they personally directed the task of breaking the *costumbrista* civil-religious hierarchy. Catechists were encouraged to throw villagers' personal idols (*icons*; saints statues from domestic altars) and aj q'ij's divining beans (*piloys*; tz'te') into the ravines.[24]

The priests established catechism classes and trained lay catechists *(catequistas)* whose ideology has been said to espouse "ladinization as a means of achieving social and economic equivalence of Indians and *ladinos*" (Warren 1978:94; cf. Falla 1980:545). Rather than making *ladinos* out of catechists, the catechist movement created an intermediate position "between the rest of the indigenous people and the *ladinos*" (Colby and van den Berghe 1977:115),[25] splitting Indian peasants into traditional and modernist (catechist) factions.

The first local catechists, initially all male, already spoke Spanish (catechist services were in Spanish); they were responsible for taking 'new' catholicism to their communities. For example, *doña* Eugenia's husband Antonio, whose job as a pedlar required him to speak Spanish, trained with catechists in Malah hamlet; he then worked as a catechist himself in Kotoh and, as a result of his efforts, many of the hamlet's residents converted. Through catechism classes, villagers learnt about the 'new' catholicism and discussed community problems (Barry 1989:98). Study groups addressed topics such as peasant rights; the country's constitution was also studied in order to contrast what was written with reality (Arias 1990: 241). Catholic Action *(Acción Católica)*, a supra-communal pastoral movement started by

Spanish priests, developed as a result. This Catholic renewal movement, fused with traditional paganism (Dunkerley 1988:474), became known as liberation theology but is known to peasants as 'the Word of God'.

The catechist movement promulgated through male rural leaders challenged the established norm of spiritual resignation.[26] With its focus on developmentalism, reform and self-help measures, Catholic Action served as the point of departure for the missionaries' search for a replacement for the ancient, sacred bonds familiar to the *cofradia* (Arias 1990). The peasant co-operatives and community improvement projects, established with Catholic Action help and funding, created novel organizational structures which challenged and undermined the authority of *costumbrista principales*: younger men gained authority outside the *cargo* system. However, the missionaries' idealism was exposed by their failure to organize the distribution of the benefits of co-operative farming: they failed to realize that the obverse of emerging 'proto-capitalist' agriculture is "proletarianization and land hunger" (Hill 1993:29); in other words, their success in introducing new forms of agriculture contributed to the high percentage of landless Indians locally.

Of the men who grasped the advantages offered to them by the missionaries, some used their new authority to raise themselves through the civil-religious hierarchy, becoming *principales* out of turn; others used their position to gain control of Indian land and labour for their own benefit. For such young men, being able to avoid dissipating their meagre capital on the heavy expenses of being a *mayordomo*, including financing the *fiestas* the missionaries so disapproved of, was one of Catholic Action's main attractions. By the mid-1960s, many proto-capitalists had left the social activism of Catholic Action behind. As part of the emerging, Indian, commercial sector, they were anxious to support groups opposed to more radical forms of social change, such as land reform, and therefore aligned themselves with the right-wing Christian Democrat Party (established 1955). Although many of the 'co-operatives' they developed were no more than a form of sharecropping, these petty entrepreneurs established rapport with Catholic Action (Falla 1980:427) on a different axis: the movement against traditional beliefs. Proto-capitalists willingly challenged *costumbrista* control of religious rites and codes. In many areas, the major struggle at village level in the mid-1960s was between *costumbristas* and the commercial sector (Arias 1990:51).

Catechists, also known as progressives *(progresistas)*, posed a very real threat to traditionalists as missionaries demanded the "complete or partial abandonment of the whole *[costumbrista]* world view, which also included agricultural methods" (Carmack 1979:384). Tensions were high between priests, Catholic Action, and *costumbristas* before *la violencia* (Warren 1978; Brintnall 1979; Falla 1980). In the villages, activists' influence and authority was resented by traditionalists as they had not met the requirements of the civil-religious hierarchy. These sentiments allowed government and local elites to assassinate local leaders of Catholic Action-inspired self-help organizations with impunity.

Local struggles took place against a backdrop of revolution. The predominantly *ladino* uprising of 1966-1968 did not directly affect highland communities but its indirect consequences were immense. Catholic Action and the Peasants' League it had established in 1965 began to be labelled 'communist' (Arias 1990) and stigmatized, as were self-help community projects. The government's response was to centralize improvement projects through the creation of a national committee which directed local, official Improvement Committees *(Comités de Pro-Mejoramiento)* towards government and non-governmental fund holders. The state hoped to control both donors and recipients but in many villages, these committees were run by the very people whom the military state had begun to label pejoratively.

By the mid-1970s, highland villages were divided into three groups: *costumbristas*; the commercial sector, now clearly delineated as the Indian bourgeoisie, who leaned to the right and the far right; and the radicalized, predominantly Catholic, Indian peasant *(campesino)* who leaned to the left (and sought convergence with poor *ladinos*) and recognized neither of the previous groups as their natural leaders (Arias 1990).[27]

Social instability worsened following two national events: rapid inflation in 1973 (the oil embargo created a monetary crisis, overwhelming the Central American Common Market) and the massive earthquake of 1976. Catholic priests and foreign aid workers witnessed the army reselling international aid for personal profit while the intended recipients starved to death. These events propelled the transformation of the literacy work undertaken by catechists: "The young leaders talked in general about the need to 'organize'. But practically speaking, none of the 'organizers' had any meaningful experience that would allow them to decide what type of organization they sought or needed" (Arias 1990:244). 'Organizing' required a high degree of secrecy because repression had already begun in El Quiché; an open organization would have been immediately destroyed.

The Committee for Peasant Unity (*Comité deUnidad Campesina*; CUC) grew out of the catechist movement; its origins are in Catholic Action's socratic-style consciousness raising *(concientización)* efforts.[28] Formally established in 1978, CUC became a national, Indian-led, broad-based workers' union with little leadership structure; it sought no recognition from the state. CUC agitates for higher wages and advances a positive programme for economic and social justice. The exploitation of Indian labour on the plantations made the *fincas* good recruiting grounds; for example, migrant workers from the Emol hamlet of Malah discovered the CUC on the coast and brought its ideas back with them. CUC's agenda only came to include organizing the masses for insurrection after heavy army onslaughts; highland members of CUC/Catholic Action were involved in establishing links with the Guerrilla Army of the Poor (EGP). Emoltecos insist that very few members of Catholic Action and perhaps a few more from CUC actually joined the revolution;[29] former sympathizers say that only those known to be (or suspected of being) armed are 'really' guerrillas and, one way or another, there are none left in the village.

The military state, dismissing socio-economic conditions and particularly the land crisis as a cause for rebellion, considered Catholic social teaching and its focus on co-operative action as the cause of highland insurgency. Repression of catechists and Catholic clergy escalated in the late 1970s (Diocesis del Quiché 1994). This led to increased militancy among the popular organizations which had subsumed the Catholic Peasants' League. Army action also drove villagers to become more militant; one villager told me, "The killing made people organize more." Indians began to organize in earnest for their economic rights and to protest against repression. Religious conversion had been a precursor to their political 'conversion', i.e., joining the revolutionary process (Brintnall 1979; Falla 1980; Le Bot 1983).

Local activists became disillusioned with the results of development schemes, feeling that they had made no impact on traditional constraints to progress — "the most profound being respect for authorities" (Guatemalan Church in Exile 1990).[30] Yet they were being attacked by the state for their efforts. They gave up trying to effect change through economic means and turned to revolution: "Development did not lead to an insurrection in Guatemala but violent repression of development engendered support for an insurgency" (Wilson 1995:209). Revolt erupts not when conditions are at their worst but when hopes of improvement have been frustrated (Storr 1989).

After several priests were killed and their bishop threatened because of their development of a 'counter-ideology' and creation of grassroots popular organizations (Frank and Wheaton 1984:44-45), the bishop of El Quiché closed the diocese in the summer of 1980 and was forced into exile (Diocesis del Quiché 1994). The priests' absence made it difficult for Catholics to hold any programme together.

When *la violencia* reached Emol, 60 percent of villagers were 'new' Catholics and 40 percent were 'pure' Catholics although the ratio varied in different hamlets. Kotoh's inhabitants were almost entirely 'new' Catholics, which led to heavy army onslaughts. Malah, the first part of Emol to join both the catechist movement and the CUC, was even worse hit; both hamlets were abandoned for several months. Some survivors promptly converted to fundamentalist protestantism; others went into hiding (many people in other hamlets did likewise). As people returned to Kotoh, an evangelist from Emol Central 'entered' them into a charismatic Catholic sect known as Catholic Renewal *(Renovación Católica* or *la Renovación)*[31] which the Catholic Church describes as a pentecostalist version of catholicism (Diocesis del Quiché 1994). The sect is so similar to Protestant evangelism that members have been called "crypto-Protestants" (Stoll 1993:104). Like Protestant evangelicals, charismatic Catholics address each other as 'brother' and 'sister', invoke the Holy Spirit, speak in tongues, heal by faith, and prophesy (Stoll 1993:104). The sect stresses its separation from both 'new' and 'pure' Catholics, claiming to be abstinent from "impure acts" (Stoll 1993:264); it rejects both the *cofradias'* saint worship and the political activism of liberation theology, defining itself in opposition to the guerrilla (Stoll 1993:105). Many Emoltecos include charismatic Catholics with Protestant evangelicals when describing current allegiances and some charismatics even refer to themselves as evangelicals.

La violencia divided 'new' Catholics. Some , such as *doña* Eugenia, the Director of Emol's widows' group, are tolerant of *costumbre* and even retain some of its practices; she remains loyal to the principles of Catholic Action. Most, however, prefer to distance themselves from radical catholicism. Former 'new' Catholics, many of whom were at least sympathetic to the popular movement, hope that their new self-definition as charismatic Catholics will be perceived as politically neutral, especially by locals: they know that 'pure' Catholics suspect them of involvement in the disappearance and death of *costumbristas* who had refused 'to go over to their side' which, as former catechists, the charismatics have now betrayed themselves. Although betrayals stemming from pre-*violencia* disputes did occur, most victims were merely Indians in the wrong place at the wrong time — being any kind of Catholic was a secondary consideration. Nevertheless, Catholics in general continue to feel that they have to tread with extreme care.[32]

Protestantism

Despite its long presence in Guatemala, conversion to *evangélico*, meaning any non-Catholic religion (Stoll 1990:4), was insignificant until the 1976 earthquake which ruined the adobe houses in Indian towns and villages, killing thousands. While soldiers looted aid, Protestant evangelicals distributed food and corrugated iron roofs direct to survivors. A wave of conversions followed, almost in spite of the army, even in Emol which was not badly affected (although it was already incurring the consequences of being labelled 'Catholic').[33]

As the political situation deteriorated, more and more people, including entire families and sometimes whole communities, began attending evangelical services to protect themselves from being accused of sympathizing with the radical elements of the Catholic Church (Barry 1989:103); the number of converts multiplied rapidly in the early 1980s (at the height of *la violencia)* when evangelical leaders (unlike their Catholic counterparts) supported the military regime. In the highlands, the army's counterinsurgency campaign was the most important incentive for conversion. Only the most courageous held steadfast to their religion and the ideals of the popular movement.

During *la violencia*, which reached its peak during the presidency of the born-again Christian general Efraín Ríos Montt, most Protestant 'soul winners' were vowing not only to "win Guatemala to Christ" but also to save it from revolution (Stoll 1990). Many survivors of the repression were pushed into this politically conformist fundamentalism and, in parts of the western highlands, *evangélico* became the dominant religion (Stoll 1988). K'iche' testimonies suggest that pragmatic self-preservation motivated most conversions: for example, a few women admitted they had converted because they had been promised their husbands would be returned to them if they did so. The men did not reappear.

People occasionally admit that the language of neutralism used by Protestant and Catholic evangelicals was a means of escaping confrontation with either side:

> Catechists and traditionalists could also adopt the language of neutrality, but evangelicals seemed to use it with most skill. In contrast to Catholic Action's language of commitment to the community, conversionist religion offered a convenient rhetoric of escape (Stoll 1993:179).

It has been said that conversion during and immediately after *la violencia* was necessary rather than escapist (Cook 1985) because *evangélico* provided safety and a means of dealing with disaster by separating converts from the past; there is also the millenarian idea that salvation is at hand. In practice, surrendering to 'divine power' allied people to the army. The struggle for survival led villagers to criticize each other for converting for reasons of self-interest *(interés)* or handouts *(ayudas)* rather than conviction *(convicción)*.[34]

Evangelical sects flourished (with generous support from the United States) amidst the survivors of crushed radical movements, who are said to have 'changed their minds' *(cambiaron sus cabezas)* in order to survive; they are viewed as opportunists who would do anything for a small payment and are described as having 'two hearts' (ka'ib' k'u'x). This pejorative comment reflects the belief that if people cannot be true to themselves, then they are capable of betraying others and have probably done so. Protestant converts are especially mistrusted by 'new' Catholics and *costumbristas* who have remained loyal to their faiths and political beliefs. Protestants, in turn, fear that both 'new' and 'pure' Catholics will take revenge. A well-worn phrase indicating general mistrust resulting from all the conversions and reconversions is 'every head is another world' *(cada cabeza es otro mundo)*.

The conversion rate fell as *la violencia* calmed. The reasons for conversion changed; they have, perhaps, become more genuine. Some widows, who abandoned religious rituals a decade ago when they lost their menfolk, have become receptive to evangelical proselytizers; they are converting with the realization that their disappeared husbands will never return and perform *costumbre*, which means they feel they have been left with nothing. Evangelical sects are popular with women because they listen to their grievances and

have notable success in changing Indian men's attitudes towards sexual li-
cence and alcoholism (at least temporarily; some men find it too difficult to
give up drinking); it also offers counselling to women whose grief led to
alcohol abuse. According to the head of the Evangelical Alliance, the Catholic Church is merely keeping alive "idolatry, fetishism, alcoholism and
machoism — all that it defends is 'tradition'" (Larmer 1989:72). One widow
told me that she felt comfortable among the evangelicals because the Protestant emphasis on predestination corresponds with the Indian stance of resignation to fate.

Although *evangélico* is the fastest growing religion in Guatemala, it is
the most fragmented. Former catechists who joined the Protestant movement in the search for a safe haven while maintaining supra-communal links
were frustrated by the rapid proliferation of sects (some sects in a nearby
town comprise only one family). The interminable division is both representative of and contributory to increased village factionalism; it also reflects the
endless searching which ensues when people seek explanations for tremendous adversity, both chronic (hunger and alcoholism) and acute *(la violencia)*. The end result is increased fragmentation and dissention among people
who already suspect others' motives for conversion.

People with No Religion

A few villagers now live without religion *(sin religión)*. Some had converted to protestantism for pragmatic reasons but abandoned the religion
when *la violencia* eased without reverting to their former faith; others who
had converted in search of answers also abandoned protestantism, despairing
of support in any religion (chapter eight). Some people who never vacillated
in their religious alignments lost faith in their priests or traditional practition-
ers; such people had the most difficulty in finding satisfactory explanations
for their losses.

A few *costumbristas* describe themselves as being *'sin religión'*. For
such people, *costumbre* cannot be separated from lived understandings of the
universe; they view catholicism and protestantism as 'religion'. Others use
the phrase to obscure their religious affiliation

Religious Identification

Religious identifications spilled over into political loyalties and different support and information networks, further atomizing family and village
life. For example, when Santa's alcoholic father broke his skull in an accident, the family knew he would have wanted treatment from an aj q'ij, but
he was too ill to decide. Santa and her sister, both liberal 'new' Catholics,
thought an aj q'ij's treatment would be helpful; their *costumbrista* brother
also wanted their father to have traditional treatment. Their Protestant, maternal half-brother suggested taking him to a *ladino* doctor. Santa's mother,
a devout convert to 'new' catholicism, wanted to take her husband to the

priest (ordinarily he would not set foot in the church) but her sons' conflicting advice rendered her incapable of reaching a decision. Her indecision was exacerbated by her fear of potential malicious gossip about how her husband met his injuries. Surprisingly, Santa's father survived.

In other families, different religious/political loyalties were much more damaging. For example, *doña* Candelaria is a lapsed 'new' Catholic; her Protestant brother not only worked closely with the village's patrol *jefes* and military commissioner but had instigated the murder of her husband (chapter one). Although this man is distrusted by the widows, he is invited to family life-cycle celebrations; he is ridiculed for drinking fruit juice instead of sharing the local rum (kuxa) with the rest of the family.

The most ambiguous identification is found among Emol's charismatics. Despite the sect's stated opposition to 'the Word of God' (liberation theology), some members, such as *doña* Flora, the sect's co-ordinator and President of Emol Central's widows' group, claim to belong to Catholic Action. Other members of *la Renovación's* congregation are active in national human rights' groups. *Doña* Flora told me, "There are evangelicals [charismatics] who are organized." She added, "The evangelicals [charismatics] say that the organizations are in the Bible and that we have to organize." This confusion is not limited to Emol: in areas which converted to *la Renovación* prior to *la violencia*, people professing no interest in the things of this world had suddenly joined the Peasants' League.

Any one person can be simultaneously involved in more than one religion. As pressure eases, some pragmatic converts stop attending services; others remain nominal Protestants and attend services now and then. People who turn or return to alcohol (which is not uncommon; cf. Hinshaw 1975) give up attending services to avoid embarrassing condemnation of their drunkenness. Some Protestants (and many Catholics) consult aj q'ij; they do so surreptitiously for fear of the disapproval of more avid converts.

Some people consciously identify with one of the newer religions and conscientiously follow its particular beliefs and practices. However, in the same way that 'new' catholicism is syncretized with traditionalism, *evangélico* is syncretized with both 'new' catholicism and *costumbre*. The fluidity of current religious alignments renders precise distinctions impossible; they are mixed up to different degrees. Not only do some people's statements reflect a lack of firm identification with any one religion but 'new' Catholics, charismatics, and Protestants all tend to revert to former religious practices at times of crisis. One effect of this is that a decade after the end of *la violencia*, a person's claimed religious affiliation at any one time does not necessarily imply political alignment, not that Emoltecos seem ever to have had strong ideological beliefs; their political sympathies are not based on, say, Marxist communism, but on pragmatic considerations.

Repression splits the corporate community (Wolf 1967).[35] Villagers blame decreased village solidarity on an increase in *envidia* since *la vio-*

lencia (chapter eight). The mistrust and discord which prevents Emoltecos from interacting with many of their fellow villagers, including members of their own families, causes them to realign themselves in new ways. These new alignments bring material benefits to particular groups. For example, prior to *la violencia*, the Improvement Committee favoured hamlets where 'new' catholicism had most support; afterwards, the position was reversed for several years and Protestant hamlets received the meagre benefits of the Improvement Committee's efforts. The allocation of basic utilities such as latrines causes further argument and division between and within hamlets.

Conclusion

Prior to *la violencia*, the K'iche' experienced over two decades of spectacular change: new authority structures (some imposed by outside institutions), new economics, and new religions. Re-establishing and re-asserting reality after the eruption of chaos that was *la violencia* was thus extremely difficult. The distortion of affective bonds and the destruction of communities through terror and deprivation (chapters four and five) seriously undermined epistemological systems which normally provide the raw material for repairing depleted frameworks of knowledge and meaning. The changes which preceded *la violencia* meant that people did not have anything approaching a stable cultural bedrock to return to. The basic institutions that ground life, the structures that substantiate knowledge, had already been badly shaken.

Notes

1. Guatemala is divided into twenty-two provinces or departments, each with an administrative centre (in El Quiché this is Santa Cruz) through which state-appointed bureaucrats, invariably *ladinos*, direct local politics.

2. For labour in the *latifundia/minifundia* system in Guatemala, see Figueroa Ibarra (1980).

3. Malah and Raxa are the most dispersed Emol hamlets; in 1982, they were divided into Mala I and II and Raxa I and II to make patrolling easier (chapter five).

4. See Sapper (1985) on the mixing of ethnic groups during the Spanish invasion.

5. When applied to Indians by *ladinos*, *'humildes'* has connotations of 'people of no consequence'.

6. There are also wide variations in the way common words are pronounced, spelt, and, of course, transliterated into other languages.

7. Of Guatemala's 325 *municipios*, 150 are Indian and located in the Western Highlands (Smith 1986). There are twenty *municipios* in El Quiché, all of which are slightly different in their customs and dialects.

8. Between 1982 and 1985, mayors were appointed by the military state.

9. Other natural resources include petroleum and nickel.

10. Wages, including 'maintenance benefits', average US$1.10 a day (Schmid, in Handy 1984:207). Low wages and appalling conditions contributed to the massive strike on the *fincas* in the early 1980s.

11. In the 1930s it was estimated that an 'average' family needed between fifteen and twenty *cuerdas* of land to meet their subsistence needs. There are sixteen *cuerdas* to a *manzana*, which is about 1.75 acres (Stadelman 1940:130). Even without taking the poor quality of highland soil into account, two acres seems too little to support the average family. Only about a dozen Emol families have more than ten *manzanas* and not all of that is agricultural land.

12. This is the population for 1990, taken from *Estimación de Población Urbana y Rural por Departmento y Municipio 1990-91*; see also *Nacional de Estatística* [National Statistics], Government of Guatemala, February 1991.

13. "With the advent of the coffee economy [1960-1974], the class positions of Indians and *ladinos* began to diverge" (Smith 1990b:86).

14. The genetic inheritance from African slaves brought to Guatemala in the early colonial period is largely forgotten and indeed hardly visible in the highlands.

15. Brintnall (1979) discusses the process of becoming *ladino*; Colby and van den Berghe (1969) discuss Indians who adopt *ladino* traits, 'pass' as *ladinos* and abandon their Indian identity.

16. A widow said of Emol's most hated *jefe*, who had reclassified himself as a *ladino*, "Some say he is very civilized. But although he speaks Spanish [badly], he doesn't know what he's saying... They *[jefes]* are all brutes." In other circumstances, being 'educated' is a reference to good manners and is expressed with admiration.

17. Xñorá for women, from *señora*. Mo's or moos for men; sometimes a general category without gender. The expression r'mo's is also used to refer to the army "because the commanders of the army are *ladinos*".

18. On 11 December 1946, the General Assembly of the United Nations defined genocide as "a denial of the right of existence of entire human groups" (Resolution 96-I) (Kuper 1981:23). The 1948 U.N. Convention on Genocide defines the crime of genocide as "acts committed with intent to destroy, in whole or in part, a national, ethnical, racial or religious group, as such [by] (a) Killing members of the group; (b) Causing serious bodily or mental harm to members of the group; (c) deliberately inflicting on the group conditions of life calculated to bring about its physical destruction in whole or in part; ..." (quoted in Kuper 1981:19).

19. Both Israel and the United States supply arms to the Guatemalan government — the U.S. as part of aid packages to both military and civilian regimes.

20. Patan, patinah: literally, burdens; also means duties/destiny/tribute/service, as in the 'burden' of holding office in the saints' brotherhoods, which is a person's duty, a tribute to the ancestors and a service to the community. The *cargo* system was a Spanish institution adapted by the Maya to their own ends (Farriss 1984). See Wagley (1941), Bunzel (1952), and Reina (1966) for descriptions of the traditional *cargo* system.

21. *Cofradia* (brotherhood) and *cofrade* (brotherhood member) are Spanish loan words used by the K'iche'.

22. Like Mayan converts in Mexico (Aulie 1979), Protestant pastors in Emol seem mainly interested in increasing their incomes.

23. In other areas, such as San Pedro Jocopilas in southern El Quiché, the *co-fradia's* position is more stable than the catechists' because of the former's ability to "mediate a situation of subordination" (Rojas Lima 1988:214).

24. It is ironic "that the indigenous population [was] converted to catholicism largely at the hands of Spanish priests, no longer the companion of the *conquista-dores* but proponents of popular liturgy" (Dunkerley 1988:474).

25. cf. Smith (1988:209): The "Indian 'rebel'...assimilated just enough of Western ways to effectively resist Western incorporation".

26. cf. Bruneau (1979:225): Christian-base communities are the "seed bed for popular initiative under authoritarian regimes".

27. The argument could equally be described in economic terms: *costum-bristas* idealized economic autonomy; emerging capitalists wanted to keep their money for themselves; the 'organized' wanted to invest in community infra-structure.

28. See Diocesis del Quiché (1994) for an explanation of the spirit of the CUC.

29. According to Arias (1990), the Catholic Church did join the guerrilla movement in the late 1970s. This was at local level; at national level the hierarchy of the Catholic Church has always been conservative.

30. The Guatemalan Church in Exile is a revolutionary support group estab-lished by some Sacred Heart priests after they were forced to leave El Quiché; it serves refugees and publicizes atrocities.

31. The sect arrived in the area in 1976 but the Catholic priest 'kept it at bay'.

32. This preoccupation is justifiable. In El Quiché, two prominent lay consult-ants to the diocese were murdered in 1990-1991: a Guatemalan anthropologist and an agronomist working for the Catholic agency Caritas. The killings were in retali-ation for the bishop's concern for the Communities of Popular Resistance.

33. The apparent contradiction between being accused of being 'Catholic' in a Catholic country is resolved by the belief that Indian catholicism bears no relation to the catholicism practiced by *ladinos*.

34. cf. Stoll (1993:273): "Ixils' pragmatic attitude towards religion [is] con-firmed by the frequent complaint that wayward members joined a Church for *interés* rather than *convicción*".

35. Communities can be closed with respect to some practices (e.g., marriage) but not in relation to economic or political ones "as long as the political changes did not threaten the unity of Indians *vis-à-vis* the state" (Smith 1990b:20).

3

Gender Relations Among the K'iche'
Before 'La Violencia'

When attempting to understand their own lives in the present, widows refer to the time before *la violencia* when social roles in general and gender roles in particular were more clearly defined. Older women also refer to village life before the arrival of Catholic missionaries some forty years ago: Mayan traditionalism, known as 'pure' catholicism or simply as 'custom' *(costumbre)*, is the base point from which most changes are measured.

Traditionally, gender roles are guided by the concept of complementarity: husband and wife are likened to the sun and the moon. Neither can exist without the other and each has its own sphere of activity although one (the man; the sun) has more power and a greater range of influence than the other. Women's roles were a recognized integral part of the schema though they had limited power within it. The changes of the past forty years have resulted in the peripheralization of Indian women within their communities, and especially of the widows of the war dead: for them, life has changed beyond comprehension.

Religion and Politics

'Pure' Catholics and the Traditional System

Community religion and secular politics have always been male dominated and, since the Spanish established the civil-religious structure after the Conquest, they have also been inextricably intertwined.

Women played an important part in the civil-religious hierarchy through their participation in the saints brotherhoods *(cofradías)*: each *cofradía* had (and, where they still exist, still has) an equal number of male and female office holders *(mayordomos)*. In Emol, unlike some areas of Guatemala,[1] female *cofrades* can stand in their own right; women do not have to be *mayordomos'* wives. However, both male and female *cofrades* do have to be married. There similarities between men and women end: there are no female elders *(principales)*. Even though some post-menopausal women command respect and their opinions sometimes incorporated into decisions affecting the village, their position is unofficial; that these women are referred to as elders relates to codes of respect, not the civil-religious hierarchy. Women are given secondary importance by men, who make most of the decisions whether acting as *principales* or husbands. The slow disintegration of the *cofradia* following the introduction of 'new' catholicism in the 1950s resulted in a reduction of women's influence in the community as they lost their only legitimate contact with people outside their families.

The *costumbrista* hierarchy of diviners (aj q'ij) is also male dominated; there were few female aj q'ij in Emol prior to *la violencia* and, in some areas, none at all. An aj q'ij is literally a 'worker of the sun' or 'day-keeper';[2] according to *"Popul Vuh"*, the sixteenth century anthology of Mayan custom, myths, and history, 'day-keepers' are the husband and wife Xpiyacoc and Xmucane (Tedlock 1985:35). In some areas aj q'ij are referred to as 'mother-father' (chucuqaaw) (Bunzel 1952:79). The obligatory references to the importance of the married couple notwithstanding, the highest position — that of a spirit caller (aj mes)[3] who is believed to be able to summon the spirits of the dead — is limited to men. Unaccompanied access to sacred sites beyond the township *(municipio)* is also restricted to men.

There is also a division of labour among aj q'ij within the community. Although both male and female aj q'ij divine and treat the causes of illness and misery and are concerned with matters of protection, male aj q'ij are more concerned with the well-being of the community as a whole (they will help individuals when asked).[4] Female aj q'ij are more concerned with the individual and often act as midwives and as children's healers.[5]

The number of female aj q'ij has increased in recent years because so many male diviners were killed during *la violencia*. Some people feel uncomfortable with this development, accusing women of practicing as aj q'ij when it is not their destiny (patanih)[6] to do so (the Mayan concept of destiny encompasses ideas of obligation, calling, and the fulfillment of one's proper role in life; one's destiny can only be divined by a high ranking aj q'ij). The use of traditional concepts to accuse women of inappropriate behaviour masks people's discomfort about the danger posed to the community by the number of lone women (widows). Members of the newer religions — evangelical Protestants and charismatic Catholics — refer to aj q'ij as "either gender deceivers *(charlatanes)*".

The New Religions

'New' catholicism and evangelicalism have undermined women's influence within religious spheres as Catholic priests and Protestant pastors are always men. The only role available to lay women in 'new' catholicism is that of catechist, from which most Indian women were initially excluded because of their monolingualism; later, as language classes were established, some women learnt Spanish through becoming catechists.

From the outset, then, most catechists have been men. Although the presence of women was generally accepted by Indian men, the idea that there should be equal numbers of both sexes (as in the *cofradía*) was never considered because participation in catechism involves mingling with people from other communities, a male role (communication with political networks was handled exclusively by men). The inclusion of women was not, at least initially, considered by the (predominantly Spanish) missionaries even though, as part of the consciousness-raising process, indigenous men were led to address the issue of gender (in)equality. Both priests and Indian men learnt from the process. One result was that some men began to allow their wives to leave the village on their own when on catechist business. Women's success as catechists or political activists depended, as always, on the willingness of other members of the community — especially male villagers and family members — to let them hold positions of (limited) authority. A few exceptional women became influential in religious and political spheres following involvement in the catechist movement and some became involved with the Committee of Peasant Unity (CUC); since *la violencia*, these women have been ostracized and marginalized in their communities.

There is no official leadership role for women in Guatemala's evangelical sects, despite the varied roles played by women in many of the American churches which fund them. Many women who followed their menfolk's lead in pragmatic conversion during *la violencia* liked what they found: evangelicals insist on high standards of male behaviour. Evangelicals have, to some extent, assumed the moral authority once exercised by *principales* and *aj q'ij* over the private sphere. Many villagers, especially women, find this reassuring and the network which reproduces 'cells' of protestantism is now found among women. In 1993, I saw women from a radical Protestant sect in Quezaltenango make regular visits to Emol, where they preached to local women.

Yet evangelicals are aligned with the state and the patrols (chapter five), the most *macho* and violent institutions in Guatemala. Women's position has deteriorated rapidly since the patrols' usurpation of power, irrespective of their religious, political, or other affiliations: the patrol system is a completely male organization which aims to control every aspect of village life. Women have no voice of their own at all in their villages.[7]

The apparent contradiction is resolved at local level by the pentecostalist dictum that everyone is equal before God (cf. Stoll 1990:319). Protestant pastors encourage their congregations to contrast *evangélico* with the historical, deep-rooted, male authoritarianism of *ladino* catholicism which has greatly affected the status of all Guatemalan women. This potentially radical message is attractive to indigenous women who, in some areas, now account for as much as 80 percent of recent converts to the various Protestant sects (Navarrete 1997); today it is indigenous women, rather than men, who make the first move to conversion.[8] An added bonus is that many evangelical sects encourage talking in tongues and trance states, during which women can say what they please in safety: responsibility for their utterances rests with God. They are familiar with the idea of being 'invaded' by supernatural beings (chapter ten); what is new is that this is now viewed as beneficial.

Marriage and Remarriage

K'iche' Marriage Traditions

Marriage is virtually mandatory. Unmarried men are not economically and socially respected; women still unmarried by their mid-twenties are usually suspected of being witches. Although arranged marriages and the pressure to marry both diminished after people converted to 'new' catholicism, unmarried adults are still considered anomalous.

Marriage is one of the most potent symbols in K'iche' culture. It is said to be 'natural', a statement some people support by reference to mythology in which gods appear in divine pairs, in male and female couples (Tedlock 1982:72). Dualism is viewed as an essential feature of both the living Maya and their sacred universe; being without a spouse is considered contrary to nature and an obstacle to the achievement of the ideal of complementarity and 'balance'.

The pervasiveness of the concept of dualism is evidenced by people's choice of marriage partners as, despite a stated norm of *municipio* endogamy, many people marry within traditionally paired hamlets or villages. This custom has survived the change — from complementarity to rivalry — in the relationship between these settlements. The practice can have harrowing consequences for women who move to their husband's home on marriage: when inter-hamlet antagonism intensifies, men become suspicious of their wives' loyalties.

The creation of the marital unit used to be a highly formalized process extending over twelve months during which the groom provided labour for his future father-in-law[9] — unless the girl eloped (a common way of avoiding an arranged marriage). Such girls are said to have been stolen *(robado)*; the term also applies to hasty marriages following a short engagement (or none at all), little ritual, and a token marriage payment of fruit, bread, chocolate, and cash rather than the traditional groom service (cf. Bossen 1988). These gifts are an acknowledgement of the bride's family, a sign of respect which indicates the groom's family's acceptance of his choice.

Traditional marriage customs fell out of use due to religious conversion and economic hardship. Prior to *la violencia*, only a small proportion of villagers, mostly *costumbristas* and, to a lesser extent, 'new' Catholics, were still conducting the full range of marriage rituals. Arranged marriages have disappeared since *la violencia*; men no longer perform agricultural labour for their future fathers-in-law. Nowadays, in some areas of El Quiché, a desirable bridegroom is not so much someone who is 'honourable' (a virgin like his intended bride) but a man who has performed his military service, a fact which partly explains why young men continue to join up now that conscription has been abolished. Yet many K'iche' boys marry well before the age of eighteen, the age at which they used to be conscripted, as marriage remains the passport to adulthood.

Residence After Marriage

A bride's transfer from her natal family to her husband's household marks a dramatic change in her life. The move is accompanied by powerful sanctions which force girls to tolerate their treatment as 'strangers' in their husband's home — girls whose marriages do not conform to the norm of *municipio* endogamy are particularly badly treated in this regard.

For at least the first year of marriage, the newly-weds live with his parents and any other siblings still at home in their one-room, adobe house. During this period, the young wife is under the authority of her mother-in-law; she has to prove her worth to her husband's family by working hard, learning the ways of their household, and 'respecting' (conforming to) family customs which include speaking their dialect and wearing their particular design of clothes (I heard of one marriage which collapsed because the wife refused to change her smock top (huipil), woven to her family pattern for one woven to her husband's family design). Complaints are likely to engender conflict, particularly with her mother-in-law.

It is during this period that the wife grows into her new identity: she is addressed as 'wife' (ixokil) by her husband's relatives of his generation, as 'daughter' (u mial; ral) by his parents' generation, and as 'mother' (nan; chuu) by the junior generation. Although she takes on her husband's patrilineal name and retains her own, her personal name virtually disappears with her previous identity. Her relationship with her natal family often suffers during this time: her husband's family may forbid her to visit her parents' home if they suspect that she might gossip about them with her family.

A wife's position improves when, usually in the second year of marriage, the young couple create their own household. The husband asks his father for his land inheritance and, once this is given, the family continues to work the land co-operatively as father and sons help each other on each other's land on a reciprocal basis.[10] The couple build a one-room adobe house close to his parents' home, or merely added to it. A wife's contact with her natal family, who have minor but continuing responsibilities towards her and her children, become less restricted. Nowadays, religious and political alignments can take precedence over family ties, leaving wives more vulnerable to abuse within the marital home.

Traditional marriage practices have also been affected by changes in men's labour migration: Guatemala City is now the preferred destination, especially for younger men. Working in the city allows men to evade their obligations to form separate households and to take full responsibility for their wives and children, whom they leave under their parents' supervision. This arrangement leaves men free to assume a second identity in the city and a second wife to go with it.

A woman may be reluctant to leave her natal home if she envisages a life alone with her husband's parents. In such circumstances, a husband is invited to live at her parents' house. If the groom has little or no land or money, his family is normally very willing to take advantage of this option. Fifty years ago, *doña* Eugenia's landless husband came to live in her natal household; over thirty years ago, *doña* Josefina's husband came to live with her on land belonging to her grandfather, now a senile alcoholic. Although one in five Emolteco peasants are landless, uxorilocality is still considered the exception rather than the rule.

The Relationship Between Spouses

Marriage is idealized both as an institution and as a way of life, yet it is within this culturally crucial relationship that the largest gap between ideal and reality occurs.

At the time of union, couples are formally advised that they should not separate until death. Should troubles arise, then parents usually do everything in their power to discourage a separation; keeping the marital unit together, despite problems, is highly valued. Seen in this light, the loss of husbands and children to *la violencia* is not only a personal tragedy but also a visible social failure.

Villagers say marriages are generally stable and monogamous and that separation is rare. Individual life histories repeatedly contradict this. One widow, born about 1940, told me that her father "had many women when he went travelling" in pursuance of his trade; he had a son with another woman whom he brought to the marital home for his wife to raise. She did not know who her half-brother's mother was and nor did she know whether to believe her father who said she had died; she may have married and needed somewhere to leave the boy. Her husband's family was even more irregular: her father-in-law had had "many women in all parts [of the village]", several of them simultaneously; her husband had six siblings by different mothers in different hamlets. I heard many similar stories, mostly from older women; younger women seem to have absorbed the 'new' Catholic doctrine regarding divorce, welcoming the emphasis on life-long unions which, in this instance, reinforces the traditional ideal.

Emotional reserve within the marital relationship is an ideal which makes it very difficult for the dependent wife to comment on her husband's infidelities, his drinking or any other failing he may have. Parents (and, for *costumbristas,* aj q'ij) offer guidance on how to attain this rarely achieved ideal. Over the years of marriage, the couple work towards 'balance' within the family unit; 'balance' relates to the couple's behaviour towards each other, the wider family network, and especially to the division of labour. A man who fails to tend his fields properly or to contribute enough money for weekly household expenses *(gastos)* is admonished by his parents and family elders; a woman who does not complete her wifely duties within the household may be similarly cautioned or accused of laziness and unceremoniously returned to her parents' home. *Doña* Angela's first marriage dissolved when she became ill; when she became too unwell to walk, her husband's parents tied her to a chair and carried her back to her parents' house, where they left her 'once and for all'.

Mutual respect and a meticulous regard for individual property rights are another marital ideal, although considerable tension existed in the conjugal unit well before *la violencia.* Many Indian males are socialized into masculine violence through exposure to male violence within the family: masculinity and violence are linked through the role played by the family in the construction of male identity, in which violence is accorded a socially sanctioned space.[11] The corollary is that women were well-versed in local-level violence before *la violencia:* as children, they were likely to have been abused by angry grandparents; to have witnessed their fathers beating their mothers; to have been raped by their own fathers. The incidence and severity of domestic violence increased in the aftermath of *la violencia.*[12]

Outside the home, women witnessed drunken brawls in the street; if they attended school, which became more common after the 1950s, then they were likely to have received corporal punishment from racist *ladino* teachers (nowadays, this is less common). Women were also all too conversant with violence in the form of *ladino* racism and exploitation, especially on the *fincas.* *Doña* Eugenia told me:

> The owners of the *fincas* didn't treat us well and we had little to eat; [as a child], I was always getting diarrhoea from drinking dirty water from the river. They only gave us beans and one gets pretty bored eating the same thing all the time. We also worked long hours and they always had us work longer and longer hours without increasing our wages. And then if one did not work well, they would not pay us for the work we did. Let's say we picked two *quintales* (200 pounds) in a day but the owner thought we didn't work hard enough, then he would discount some of the work and only pay a proportion of the full wage. It was better at home than on the coast.

Doña Eugenia also remembers getting up at three in the morning to help her mother make *tortillas* for the labourers; she remembers living with dozens of other families under makeshift shelters. She was describing her experiences as a teenager and young wife in the 1930s and 1940s, but younger women's descriptions indicate little improvement in conditions over the decades. Today, only the destitute, which includes war-widows, take young children to the *fincas* as chronic malnutrition and endemic malaria still result in very high child mortality rates.

Surrounded by physical violence both within the community and in the *ladino* world beyond, girls know that they are likely to get more of the same when they marry. K'iche' men tend to be very possessive; they often suspect their wives of having illicit affairs, although it is usually they who are duplicitous. It is said that some men's jealousy led them to kill their wives during *la violencia*, when murder was committed with impunity (a contemporary black joke was that divorce was no longer necessary). One young man told me his drunken father killed his mother; his maternal uncles then killed his father in retaliation, leaving four young children to fend for themselves. Domestic violence has always been extremely common, contradicting the marital ideals which all K'iche' claim to espouse, and has increased in severity and frequency since the onset of *la violencia*.

If the erring husband continues to meet his commitments to the domestic corn economy, then his activities in the city are not seen (at least by men) as affecting the household back home. But, as men move away from the subsistence sector, "The transition to high individual cash income upsets the balance of mutual needs. The higher earning husband begins to feel that his spouse is rather expendable and that he could easily replace her. He tries to provoke her to leave" (Bossen 1978:154).

The consequences of separation are such that "women tenaciously remain" (Bossen 1978:154). Economic dependence forces women to tolerate polygamy, abuse and poverty; one of women's most common sayings is, "I must bear it". Wives can leave abusive men (Bunzel 1952:131), but cultural pressures, their own religious beliefs, and, latterly, the dearth of marriageable men, oblige them to stay.

Separation, Divorce, and 'Natural' Widowhood

Under the traditional schema, a divorced or widowed woman returned to her parents' home and began afresh. She was expected to leave her children, especially her sons, with her husband's family; women agreed to this in order to protect their children's inheritance rights and also because second husbands are generally loth to support non-biological offspring. Daughters and unclaimed sons were usually placed within their mother's extended family. Occasionally, these landless boys were lucky enough to inherit land from their foster-parents or other relatives; most grew up to be landless.

The widowed or divorced woman was supported by her father and brothers until she remarried. The widow was expected to deny her grief and the divorcee to hide her feelings about being abandoned for another woman (the most common reason for marriage dissolution); both were to seek a new partner as soon as possible[13] and look forward to their future families. It was as if the woman's first husband (and their children) never existed. A previous union is usually kept secret (even by men), a difficult feat in a face-to-face community. Reasons for this are largely expressed in terms of jealousy of prior relationships. Another reason for secrecy is that widowed and divorced women, even before conversion to 'new' catholicism, were considered less attractive marriage partners[14] as virginity at marriage is valued by both partners.

Widows and divorcees were divided by what happened to marital property. A divorcee usually had to give up the property accumulated during the marriage, even the crops she helped to cultivate and the animals she bred; separation was a personal failure. Widowhood was a community matter which traditionally entailed the involvement of village elders who directed the disposal of any land, property, and children. This was often a complex affair if, for example, families only had daughters (in which case, girls sometimes got a share; this is more common nowadays) or no surviving children at all. In such instances, land was distributed among other relatives. Occasionally the children from a long dissolved marriage or an illicit relationship claim some of their father's meagre assets. Elders also had to consider what type of land it was and where it was: marriage across hamlet and village boundaries meant that family-owned land could be spread throughout the area; one of the elders' roles was to ensure that no one acquired a disproportionate amount of local land. All this was 'men's business' and supposedly no concern of the widow, who was to remarry and move to another man's land. Yet most widows are reluctant to leave their husband's home and land; once a separate household has been established, a husband's allocation of his family's land belongs to his household alone and his widow generally takes it over. Being able to hold on to this land provides the children of the marriage with greater security. One a woman has established her right to inherit land, she alone has control of it.

Widowhood was rare until *la violencia*: indigenous women's life expectancy is lower than men's and women expect to die before their husbands. Separation and divorce, on the other hand, were surprisingly common although both acquired more of a stigma after most Emoltecos converted to 'new' catholicism and began marrying in church. These weddings had secular consequences: marriages recorded in church registers are legally binding. Many villagers were slow to absorb the significance of state administrative records which, apart from the identity papers *(cedulas)* people are obliged to carry, seemed irrelevant to them. Mayan attitudes to marriage dissolution result in people carrying papers saying they were married to one person when they consider themselves married to another. This situation became more common after *la violencia*, when people could not prove their spouses were dead. The names of the war-dead remain on their partners' *cedula* because the death and its cause are denied by the authorities. The process of declaring a person legally dead is beyond most Guatemalans' comprehension and definitely beyond most Indian pockets.

Locally, people know who is dead and the community generally accepts second unions as valid under customary law; they are often blessed by the village priest. The unscrupulous took advantage of the situation, using national law to declare second marriages invalid or bigamous and the children of the union illegitimate, thereby legally validating culturally invalid appropriations of land within the community. Once village elders were killed or neutralized and replaced by patrols chiefs, this type of theft became unstoppable. The idea seems to have originated with the army, who bribed patrollers with the possibility of taking over 'subversives'' land.

The Sexual Division of Labour

Subsistence Agriculture

Subsistence production takes place at the level of the household. This is envisaged as a group of patrilineally related men together with their wives and unmarried daughters; the husband is the head of the household. In practice, a household can consist of the conjugal pair, their elderly and probably widowed parents (whose voices must be heard), adult offspring, spouses, and children or, since *la violencia*, virtually any combination of relatives.

Economic autonomy for the household is the ideal[15] and production is guided by ideals of complementarity but not equality between the sexes. Within the household, the traditional division of labour by gender ranges from pragmatic flexibility (men and women can usually do each other's tasks) to nearly absolute (tasks which define a man and a woman). Corn production defines a man; transforming it into edible products defines a woman. Maize is **the** valued food; the word for food (wa) means 'transformed maize products'. If a meal does not contain wa from one's one home, then one has not eaten. The female role of transforming corn (and other domestic produce) into food is seen as integral to the whole subsistence process. Women have the monopoly in food preparation, including the lengthy and laborious process of turning dry, hardened corn kernels into soft *tortilla* dough. Grinding corn is such an important part of women's identity that when electric corn grinders were introduced, many women preferred to continue spending five or six hours a day grinding corn with a heavy stone grinding pin and slab because "it tastes better that way". Just as women do not normally participate in maize production, men do not normally help in maize dough preparation.

Men are responsible for maize crop fertility; there is an association between maleness and corn production. Apart from weeding and gleaning, women only work on the corn fields if a man cannot find anyone else to help; this is done as inconspicuously as possible for fear of ridicule. When asked if they ever help to plant, women reply, "That's what we have men for", "No, the women here make the *tortillas*", and, "No, the women here are weavers". Their embarrassment stems from a "overt association between the planting activity and the human sexual act" (Wilson 1995:111): seed corn is associated with semen and the earth is considered female during planting. The sight of women planting corn is interpreted as evidence of a serious aberration within a family. As I passed two women planting corn, my male companion asked me if I could see anything strange. I thought he was referring to the fact that planting is the definitive male task. He told me the older woman's husband was also having sexual relations with their daughter, the second woman planting in the field. This state of affairs was clearly visible to him; he asked me if I too could see it too. To him, this aberration in the treatment of the land betrayed the breaking of other taboos in the family; it also 'confirmed' rumours he had heard about the family.

Men plant one type of beans, *frijol de milpa* (kinaq' rech abix), with the corn. About six weeks later (when the corn has germinated and the earth's gender is masculine again), women plant the *frijol de surco* (kinaq' rech poq'op), using dibble sticks, in the furrows between the corn. Women's planting of beans is a recent practice; fifty years ago, they did "nothing whatever" in the fields: to do so was considered to be "against the whole theory of marriage and household economy, and the relations of men and women for women to have any part in the providing of food" (Bunzel 1952:53). Today, women are exclusively in charge of the production of secondary crops which grow between the rows of corn and in their vegetable gardens. They are also responsible for gathering herbs and wild plants for dietary and medicinal purposes from the surrounding countryside. They are always accompanied by female friends and children on these expeditions; they never go alone.

Women are also responsible for domestic livestock — a cow, a few sheep, a pig, some turkeys, chickens or rabbits — which they buy from the profits of sales of animal products or other female-gendered work. Grazing and fodder *(zacate)* are women's responsibility: they take their animals to pasture, always accompanied by a child or two or a friend who also brings her animals (and children); they collect and prepare corn greens and cob kernels for their livestock. The animals are not raised for household consumption; even eggs and milk products are sold to pay for more basic necessities. Animals are slaughtered at fiesta time or for some life transition ritual (such as funerals) when their meat is shared by everyone attending. Domestic livestock, especially cattle, also represent the family's savings and are sold at times of need.

Gender roles are clearly separate though interdependent. Husband and wife have distinct areas of responsibility. Senior men specialize in the long term management of the family's generally very meagre capital assets (excluding livestock) and senior women supervise the day-to-day administration of the household (in the 'best' households, men and women make decisions about everything together). Men do not interfere with their wives' decisions when they act in their capacities as wives. In general, men are not coercive over women who act in accordance with their prescribed gender roles; there, women have independence.

Community Self-sufficiency

The ideal of household autonomy used to be sustained by a network of kin and godparents or fictive kin *(compadres)* which provided a moral economy of mutual support based on deferred reciprocity. Help was only solicited outside the household for specific tasks: for example, men assisted their *compadres* with house-building and, in special circumstances, corn planting; women helped each other after childbirth or when large amounts of food had to be prepared for life crisis rituals such as funerals. The erosion of this ostensibly cash-free economy began before *la violencia*: diminishing community solidarity resulting from the growth of individualism and competition within villages involved a certain withdrawal from each other's personal problems. As the *compadrazgo* system unravelled, there was a corresponding move towards cash payment for work done for others, emphasizing the fact that help for others had never been a pure gift. Woodcutters, for example, now sell their timber to house-builders and coffin makers who work for cash rather than as part of a family network building each other's houses and burying each other's dead.

Romanticized memories of highland autonomy in 'time before' — it is not always clear if people mean before *la violencia*, the arrival of 'new' catholicism, or the Conquest — mask Indians' need of a cash income in the present. Men need money to meet their traditional obligations to the household economy: seed corn, fertilizer (the most expensive item), and supplemental corn when home-grown supplies are exhausted. Changes in the local economy have increased husbands' need for cash; for example, for the last twenty years, house-building materials and labour have had to be paid for. In Emol, where women stopped weaving a couple of generations ago, men have assumed the responsibility for buying the family's new clothes for the village *fiesta*. Men are also responsible for obtaining, and paying for, health treatment beyond their wives' herbal treatments; even though Kotoh has a health clinic, people still have to travel to the departmental capital to buy most medicines in the pharmacies there.

The village market also contributed to perceptions of self-sufficiency: home produced goods were exchanged for other local goods (only one or two people traded in items imported from other regions). Even though cash was involved, local marketing rarely increased household income: the market was a mode of simple commodity exchange mediated by money — for example, a woman needing say, soap and some sugar, went to the market with a milk product, sold it, and bought the required goods. This began to change as Catholic Action encouraged their supporters to by-pass the village market, which was controlled by *costumbrista principales*; one consequence was that people had to make more frequent trips to the bi-weekly market in the nearby town, where transactions are solely in cash. This is in the *ladino* world and hence dealing with it is a man's responsibility. A 'good' husband takes one of his sons with him to the market to purchase items not produced by the household and pays with money he earns outside the subsistence sphere; he gives his wife *gastos* for necessities purchased in the village during the week (Emol has four or five shops, each selling a similar and very limited range of goods). In reality, women have always gone to market together, whether or not their husbands are at home in the village. Men often can't be bothered to go when they have no corn to sell (or no need to buy any); women often prefer to go with their friends because household produce and corn are sold in a different parts of the market.

The emphasis on protecting women from contact with the *ladino* world masks, or at least helps to undervalue, women's contributions to household income. Women's autonomy in their specific areas of household responsibility includes the ability to exploit their traditional skills for cash. As a rule, they produce both a greater variety and a greater quantity of saleable goods than men: they grow garden produce, prepare animal products, raise livestock, and make handicrafts for sale. The money women earn is their own and, like their husbands, women use their income to subsidize their traditional responsibilities within the household. Prior to *la violencia*, women sold most of their goods in the village market, only occasionally accompanying their husbands to the town market; the closure of Emol's market following the mass disappearance of everyone in the market square one winter Sunday in mid-1982 forced women to go to town more often which, in the midst of *la violencia*, many women found frightening. It was particularly hard for the newly widowed who were unsure whether anyone was prepared to accompany them: leaving the house without an adult member of her husband's family exposes a woman to malicious gossip *(chismes)*. Gossip is a common, veiled form of aggression used by both men and women; in a face-to-face society such as Emol where reputation still has some currency, *chismes* provide a relatively safe means of social sanction or bullying — even war-widows who assume the responsibilities of a household head need to be wary of malicious tongues. Thus women's ability to earn an income is dependent on another person's agreement to escort, chaperone or protect them. Their children have been drafted into the role.

Labour Migration

Villagers say that only husbands and teenage sons leave the village to work in the outside, *ladino* world. This is another generally unrealized ideal, although conformity to it has increased since the 1960s. Many village men have taken advantage of the new highways built during that decade, opting to work in the national capital, provincial cities, and even the borders with Mexico and El Salvador. Younger men, usually those with most initiative, prefer petty commodity trade — selling cheap modern knick-knacks *(fantasía)* from street stalls — in urban areas to the heavy work on the plantations. Older village men accuse them of 'not wanting to get their hands dirty' and express concern about the city's negative influence on their young men; they consider young city workers morally degenerate. It is certainly true that young men are exposed to *ladino* values in the city and ladinization is most likely to occur among them.

Work in urban areas is not seasonal and the young men stay away for long periods, usually visiting the village one week in four. Two of *doña* Candelaria's married sons, one a policeman and the other a soldier by the end of the 1980s, own Kotoh's shop: they return more frequently to ensure that their wives keep everything in order.[16] Some men prefer the traditional pattern of coastal work, returning home every few months; others return home only to work the land or for special occasions (a life cycle ritual, a *fiesta*); some hire a seasonal worker *(mozo)* or a day labourer *(jornalero)* to care for their fields. I was told "every man comes home to plant" and most do; in other areas, even guerrillas are said to do so (Stoll 1993). Men who spend nearly all their time in the city send money home with a friend or a child. Wives rarely have any idea how much their husbands earn or what they get up to in the city.

Children

Women's scant knowledge of the outside world reinforces their position as 'conservers of tradition'; they tend to be monolingual and wear traditional clothing *(traje)* indicating *municipio* identity. These factors ensure that the care and primary socialization of K'iche' children is centred on distinctly non-*ladino* concepts of family, household, and community. Their frequently absent fathers may speak reasonable Spanish, wear western clothes, travel with varying degrees of confidence to *ladino* market towns, but this has little bearing on the lives of women and children in the village.

Fathers are responsible for their children's moral education and for teaching their sons specifically male tasks, a difficult role for men whose presence in the village is, at best, erratic. Nevertheless, it is still fathers who have the final word on whether or not a child should attend school (chapter two) and also when a child should begin contributing to the household — usually around the age of six or seven. At this age, boys should start learning the mysteries and practicalities of corn production but, even before *la violencia*, many fathers were not there to teach them.

Girls help their mothers with household chores such as sweeping the house and washing. When they are a little older, girls help with gardening, collecting medicinal herbs and fodder for the family's livestock, grinding corn, and making *tortillas*. Both boys and girls look after younger children, herd the family animals and collect firewood. Pragmatism encourages a certain amount of cross-sex training, particularly if a family has children of only one sex, but major dividing lines for the central subsistence tasks are rarely breached.

Conclusion

The ideal of complementary on the cosmological level translates into male subordination of women in every day life. *Ladino machismo*, epitomized by the military man who is violent to women and distant from children, is absorbed by K'iche' men as they work in the city, do their military service and/or patrol duty, and even through membership of guerrilla organizations and some popular movements. The result is increasingly *macho* attitudes towards women, undercutting the cultural ideal that a woman be supported and protected throughout life by a succession of men — father, brothers, husband, sons (and in the case of divorce or widowhood, husband and brothers again, followed by second husband and subsequent sons) — who provide agricultural labour, *gastos*, and ritual protection by performing *costumbre*. The risks and problems attendant on increased dependence on wage labour — men's prolonged absences, the possibility that they may take up with another woman, the separation from the land, exposure to *ladino* ways — strain the cultural ideal of complementarity and place extra burdens on marital relations and on women themselves. The rapid changes preceding and during *la violencia* skewed relations between men and women further. Yet women's responsibilities remain centred on the household and they remain confined to the home; conditions are such that their role as conservers of tradition can hardly be avoided.

Notes

1. For example, among the Q'eqchi' (Wilson 1995:164).

2. One of an aj q'ij's roles is to count the 260 days of the Mayan short calender (Wright 1991). They use red coral beads for this purpose.

3. Literally, a 'worker of the table'. From the Spanish word for table, *'mesa'*, which refers to the small wooden altars these diviners use in their rituals.

4. Few surviving aj q'ij will perform rituals of protection against *la violencia* type dangers.

5. Not all midwives and curers are aj q'ij. Among the widows I knew, *doña* Ana was a midwife (aj kunib); *doña* Candelaria was an aj kunib and healer (of children's complaints), as was *doña* Josefina who was also an aj q'ij.

6. See chapter two, fn 20.

7. Paradoxically, the very silencing of women, and especially war-widows, has pushed the few women brave enough to demand to be heard into national human rights groups and hence into the national political arena. For example, Rosalina Tuyuc, an indigenous war-widow, became the leader of CONAVIGUA; she was elected to Guatemala's Congress of Deputies in 1995.

8. In the rest of Latin America, it is usually men who take the first step to conversion. In some male-headed households in the Guatemalan highlands, "Some men too become willing accomplices in conversion: they too wish to escape the destructive influences of *machismo*" (Stoll 1993:318-9).

9. See Bunzel (1952) and Burgos-Debray and Menchú (1984) on K'iche' marriage rituals.

10. Fathers divide their land between their sons or other heirs in return for their keep in their old age.

11. This is then given expression within the wider society in many forms (McKendrick and Hoffman 1990) and vice versa. Men who were small children during Ubico's dictatorship (1930-44) were socialized according to military values absorbed by their fathers.

12. See Manz (1988:78) for other reasons why civil patrols cause increases in marital violence.

13. A Maya-Mam group in Chimaltenango, a department south of El Quiché, were encouraged to re-marry immediately following the twenty day ritual mourning period (Wagley 1949:46).

14. cf. Bunzel (1952:131) on the undesirability of female divorcees.

15. Collective farming, where land was held and cultivated by people not of the same kin group, has long since died out as a tradition in Emol but still exists in Q'eqchi' areas such as Cobán (Wilson 1995).

16. *Doña* Eugenia's grandson Saturnino told me that corruption in the army and the police force enabled his cousins to obtain the shop. By 1995 they had drunk all the profits away and the shop had closed, leaving Kotoh without one.

4

'La Violencia'

The period of rural terror popularly known as The Violence (*la violencia*, 1978-1985) has been described as a full-scale civil war (Dunkerley 1988). It was triggered by the expansion of agro-export estates following the massive foreign investment of the 1960s; this exacerbated existing social tensions by severely disrupting Indian subsistence agriculture.

From the military dictatorship's perspective, *la violencia* was a confrontation between military and guerrilla forces, a battle against Marxist communism, against an armed and dangerous delinquent within. Constant government rhetoric proclaimed the army's purpose to be defense of the country *(la patria)* against alien enemy forces and ideas, not unarmed civilians. Though guerrillas were the initial target of the counterinsurgency campaign, the boundaries of this category expanded to include ever-increasing numbers of (predominantly Indian) people within the victim class; the army soon turned its attention to innocent but 'potentially dangerous' civilians. As President Ríos Montt (1982-1983) explained, "the problem of war is not just a question of who is shooting. For each one who is shooting there are ten working behind him" (Amnesty International 1987:96).

The military onslaught reflected state paranoia and hostility towards an ideologically selected scapegoat: the Indian. This became increasingly explicit as *la violencia* progressed. By 1982, the category of 'enemy of the state' included anyone the army deemed capable of subversion; Indians no longer needed to be suspected of subversion to be attacked. The genocidal nature of state violence against the indigenous population (Falla 1984; Jonas 1991)[1] was not a new phenomenon, merely its most brutal expression to date. No-one felt safe; the deaths of innocent victims, including women and children, became almost routine. Francisco Bianchi, President Ríos Montt's press secretary, explained the government's (syllogistic) reasoning:

The guerrillas won over many Indian collaborators. Therefore the Indians were subversives. And how do you fight subversion? Clearly you had to kill

Indians because they were collaborating with subversion. And then it would be said that you were killing innocent people. But they are not innocent, they had sold out to subversion (Amnesty International 1987:96).

Military paranoia about Indian subversiveness persists: in 1990, an army officer told me, "Before, we thought we could defeat the guerrillas but when you kill a hundred, another five hundred appear."

The Course of 'La Violencia'

The counterinsurgency apparatus was established to quash the *ladino* uprising in eastern Guatemala of 1966-1968. The structural changes which gave rise to this rebellion intensified over the next ten years (Reyes 1986; Smith 1990b), profoundly affecting Indians' self-conception (Arias 1990) and providing the basis for the Indian uprising in the late 1970s (Jonas 1991).

The guerrillas began to regroup in the early 1970s: "as their only escape from being trapped between the pincers of economic strangulation and political suffocation", many peasants, trade unionists, religious workers, students, and intellectuals turned to armed opposition (Painter 1987:xiii). In response, right-wing terrorist groups (death squads) murdered some 15,000 people in the five years prior to *la violencia*; they became autonomous units, taking full initiative in seeking out victims. Clandestine detention camps and cemeteries were established, as were installations to house and torture the kidnapped. As one man told me, the 'tradition of death' had begun.

By 1975 the landed oligarchy, which depends on compliant Indian labour, felt seriously threatened by Indian farming co-operatives and peasant *(campesino)* groups. The military government also felt that Indigenous 'new' catholicism posed a serious threat to the state and began selectively suppressing (i.e., disappearing and killing) local catechist leaders. The dictatorship had support in some surprising quarters: many 'pure' Catholics *(costumbristas)* also felt threatened by 'new' Catholics. For example, in November 1975 the commander of the military base in the capital of El Quiché, Santa Cruz, received a request from a local community "to come and finish off the village's guerrillas" who were "pure Cubans fighting against us with co-operatives and other idiocies" (Guerriaran n.d., in Arias 1990).

A year later, in 1976, the military government began violently repressing members of popular organizations, directors of village self-help improvement schemes (even members of the government scheme came under suspicion), and members of local co-operatives. Victims were almost entirely indigenous 'new' Catholics whom the state labelled 'communists' and 'subversives'. The massive earthquake of the same year, which left 25,000 Guatemalans dead and 1·25 million homeless (Jonas 1991:95), failed to deflect the government from its purpose: between 1976 and 1978, 168 co-operative leaders are known to have been killed in El Quiché alone (Handy 1984:244). The guerrillas responded by taking selective action against known army sympathizers.

Following General Lucas García's accession to the presidency in early 1978, the military dictatorship decided to prevent revolutionary forces from prevailing in Guatemala, no matter what the cost. The president re-activated the counterinsurgency apparatus almost immediately, unleashing a campaign of terror "which has been rarely paralleled for its savagery (and lack of publicity) in the history of Latin America" (Painter 1987:xiv).

By May, army massacres had galvanized peasants to revolutionary militancy (Burgos-Debray and Menchú 1984), leading the Committee of Peasant Unity (CUC) — which had just absorbed the Peasants' League established by Catholic Action — to make an open declaration of war. This effectively dissolved CUC as most of its militants joined the guerrilla organizations (Arias 1990) and it was several years before CUC resumed its own identity. In terms of bringing Indians into the armed struggle, the most important event was the massacre of 700 Q'eqchi' in Panzós, Alta Verapaz: they were slaughtered as they peacefully protested eviction from their lands.

Recognizing Indian catechist and peasant groups as the main source of guerrilla support (other supporters included urban intellectuals and poor *ladino* peasants), the government classified these groups as subversive. Catholic clergy and catechists were targeted because of their influence and leadership roles within communities. Survivors of army attacks tell of catechists being garrotted, hanged from trees, chopped to pieces with machetes or locked in churches and burnt to death.

By 1979 the military had begun to terrorize Indians as a generality, threatening them with death should they talk about 'injustices' (land expropriation, exploitation, and, later, military atrocities). 1979 was also the year the first Emolteco was killed by the army: I was told, "They falsely claimed he was one of the captains in charge of the guerrilla and they burnt him alive to make an example of him."

By 1980, the insurgents presented a serious threat to the state. By this time, Bishop Gerardi of El Quiché had received death threats because of his sympathies for the Communities of Resistance in the north of the department; several of his priests had been assassinated. The Bishop fled, ordering all religious to leave the diocese (Simon 1987:77).[2] The abandoned churches and church houses were taken over by the army (Carmack 1988:62). The military probably thought it would be difficult for the K'iche' to keep their supra-communal organizations going without the support of their priests, but the loose structures the priests had established were strong enough to withstand their absence. The guerrillas fought on.

Starting in the predominantly Indian provinces of El Quiché and Alta and Baja Verapaz in 1981, the military retaliated with a scorched earth policy, bombing and burning villages. The army torched houses and crops;

stole or killed livestock; maimed and raped women; kidnapped villagers singly or *en masse* and killed men, women, and children for reasons survivors cannot fathom. Also destroyed were Catholic churches, health clinics, schools, and co-operatives: the existence of developed local institutions was sufficient reason to fall foul of what one missionary described to me as "the army's 'preventative' measures". The state visualized non-governmental organizations (NGOs) — especially Catholic-backed NGOs — as an armed force acting with guerrilla organizations in an attempt to disturb the *status quo*. The repression wiped out local NGO-trained volunteers *(promotores)* who worked as teachers and health workers. As a result, many foreign NGOs curtailed their programmes or withdrew from Guatemala in the early 1980s (Davis and Hodson 1982).

The guerrilla responded with major attacks, beginning in mid-1981 and continuing into 1982. At one point it seemed they would gain control of the highlands. In Santa Cruz del Quiché, the town guerrilla unit blew up the tower of the governor's administration building; other guerrilla units blew up roads leading in and out of the town, sometimes trenching them to stop traffic flow and painting *"Viva EGP"* on the highways. At the end of 1981, a guerrilla force (said to be 5,000 strong, though this is unlikely) attacked the town's military base; in early 1982, guerrillas blew up its electrical transmission tower, leaving it in darkness for four hours. The army increased its presence and regained control of Santa Cruz and the roads around it.

The Violence in Emol

Emoltecos mark the beginning of *la violencia* in a local, personalized way, often attributing the initial incident to an 'unknown' person *(desconocido)*; for example, *doña* Flora told me it began with the kidnapping of her own husband from his bed but another Emolteco woman said:

> It all began in 1980 when two *judiciales*[3] murdered two men and then looted houses. Then five people were taken from their houses at night, one night after another. From that time onwards, the villagers were terrified. People moved from their houses if they were on the road-side or further inland [from the village centre]. When the army came, everyone fled into the ravines...

A few people said *la violencia* began when some villagers were killed by the guerrillas, non-locals who carried out their 'task' and left; people who mentioned these events indicated that they had occurred prior to the violent military action of the late 1970s. For the majority of Emoltecos, the beginning of *la violencia* is marked by army atrocities.

Emol's troubles really began when the army embarked on a major campaign against the remote highland villages of El Quiché in the second half of 1981, in the hungry months before the staple corn crop is ready for harvest (in the mountains, this is usually October/November). The timing was probably deliberate: it is, after all, difficult to deeply terrorize a well fed and housed community (Bettelheim 1986:297). Alternatively, perhaps it was just that the corn, which grows to eight feet, was burnt to prevent people hiding in it. Be that as it may, the creation of conditions of extreme insecurity (arbitrary death and destruction) and increased deprivation (hunger and homelessness) was certainly deliberate, forming part of the 'softening up' process which involved repeated assaults over a period of months. This was not because they met with any resistance (armed opposition was rare and ineffectual); rather, it was the initial stage of an overall plan to terrorize villagers through destroying individual autonomy and destabilizing their communities.

Emol was selected for particularly severe attack on the basis of its local notoriety as a 'Catholic' village[4] and the progressive politics of two of its hamlets. These factors were sufficient to give rise to Emol's reputation as a 'guerrilla' village (which still persists) even though there is little if any evidence that the EGP was active there. The village suffered several military bombardments which killed hundreds of people and caused extensive damage to property (houses, crops, and livestock). Kotoh, which was especially noted for its successful development projects, was so severely attacked that it was abandoned for several months. A woman describes the atmosphere:

> When the people in the village saw the soldiers coming from afar, they began to scream with fear because we thought that the soldiers were coming to kill us... As they got closer, all you could hear was people sobbing...it was like nothing I had ever heard before. There were moments when they were weeping like it was the end [of the world]...

Although a permanent watch was kept for soldiers and the church bell tolled if any were spotted, the army sometimes managed to descend without warning. Encircling a village was the most common counterinsurgency technique; soldiers closed in, lobbing grenades and bombs as villagers fled in panic. Villagers fled to the ravines where they remained for days, sometimes months, at a time. Highland residents describe a time when their families slept hidden in mountain thickets, under trees or in the forest, living on wild plants. Some widows spoke of having only *tortillas* and salt to eat and only water to drink, a succinct way of expressing the idea that despite the hardship, life was in some ways lived as it should be — they were still able to perform the defining task of womanhood, turning corn products into food (wa); factions and feuds were temporarily forgotten as everyone found themselves in the same boat, attacked by the same enemy. This seemingly romanticized view is a metaphorical statement of their continuing humanity, a refutation of any possible inference that they had lived 'like wild animals in the mountains' (as the army say the guerrilla do).

Women describe this period as a time of unmitigated terror. Avoiding the dangerous phrase *'la violencia'*, the use of which the army and its supporters take as evidence of subversion, the women refer to it as 'that painful time' (uq'ijool k'ax k'oliil), 'that desperate time' (uq'ijool paxi b'al k'ux). They say blood ran in torrents. It was a time of intense fear and panic as people ran from soldiers, when they did not think but were like mindless zombies with their eyes to the ground, trying to survive. Some women admit that at such times they were so frightened that they 'no longer felt human'; they say it was as if they were in a dream, just wandering around, having lost their sense of time and place. People can no longer remember how often they fled to the ravines or how long they spent there; without the normal time-fixing events of the religious calendar and the agricultural cycle, time became a meaningless concept. When they returned to their homes, people's only source of food was the maize they had in storage (if it had not been destroyed or looted); they ate no beans and little maize. Some widows ground corn cobs, usually fed to animals (now mostly dead or stolen), to make flour. Water supplies were often contaminated by human bodies and animal carcasses. It was a time of scarcity, hunger, and disease.

The army finally occupied Emol at the end of 1981. The murder and mayhem continued. Pervasive surveillance and monitoring *(control)* became the norm. I was told that brother fought brother, sons fought their fathers, killings occurred between spouses and fear *(miedo)* caused pregnant women to miscarry.[5] The end of the world, as foretold in the Bible, had arrived.

Pacification and Psychological Warfare

In 1980, the military designed strategies to pacify areas of greatest guerrilla activity and support, implementing them from 1981. Although 1981-1982 saw the largest number of guerrillas bearing arms and mounting successful attacks on the military and its installations, it was also the period they were routed as a fighting force: the army cut off the guerrilla's support base.

Firstly, the military redeployed its forces. The army had been concentrated in four urban bases; by 1988, it had major bases in each of Guatemala's twenty-two departments and garrisons in most towns with over 10,000 inhabitants. Military squadrons remain permanent fixtures in highland townships *(municipios)*. Next, the military began to reorganize civil society on military lines (Smith 1990a; 1990b). As part of their overall plan to assert the dominance of the national identity (Barry 1989:112), penetration roads were built to provide military access to isolated villages; evangelical proselytizing, with its emphasis on the individual, was encouraged. Obligatory civil patrols, which undermined all community power structures, were an essential feature of the plan to obliterate actual and potential resistance.

Strategic re-education camps were created for people flushed out from the mountains. In the Ixil triangle in northern El Quiché, 'model villages' and other concentrated resettlement villages were established between 1983 and 1985 in order to regiment the population and separate them from guer-rillas. The idea is borrowed from the Conquest period:

> Model villages are designed to serve similar purposes as colonial *congrega-ciones* — to function as the institutional means by which one culture seeks to reshape the ways and conventions of another, to operate as authoritarian mechanisms of resettlement, indoctrination, and control (Lovell 1988:47).

By 1990, Guatemala had twenty-four model villages, containing some 70,000 people from different ethnic and language groups — all mixed up like 'scrambled eggs' *(huevos revueltos)*, as their inhabitants say. Guate-mala's State Department refers to such places as 'half-way houses' and 'rural settlements' but most people call them 'concentration camps' (Simon 1987).

Psychological warfare played an important part in the pacification pro-cess. The army created networks of trained psychological warfare operatives and other informers, who were paid by results;[6] the responsibilities of mili-tary commissioners *(comisionados militares)* were reorganized and extend-ed to other, often clandestine, work for the army.[7] Spying and informing be-came endemic and fear of both even more so: people conflated the army's and the *jefes'* temporal powers with the supernatural powers of sorcerers *(brujos)*, who are believed to make themselves invisible in order to spy on others for nefarious purposes (cf. Madsen 1967:630). *Brujos* have a unique place in the K'iche' construction of good and evil: 'ordinary' people who 'succumb' to antisocial behaviours are seen as being invaded by malicious spirits (chapter ten) but the *brujo* is viewed as actually courting and manipu-lating the negative forces of the K'iche' social universe. Hence consistently antisocial individuals are thought to be *brujos*; for example, long before *la violencia*, Emol's *de facto* chief of patrols, Mario, was widely believed to be *brujo*, an attribution he enjoys as it increases villagers' fear of him (chapter five).

Witchcraft *(brujería)* thrives on the chronic factionalism and covert feuding which exists in indigenous communities which have few effective means of dispute resolution. Retaliation through direct violence is rare unless the injured party is drunk, in which case the individual is not considered responsible for the attack as actions committed under the influence of alco-hol are considered in the same light as spirit invasion. Nowadays, people are often drunk. Killing is traditionally regarded as an illegitimate response to disputes and is deplored. Justice, which in K'iche' eyes, is inseparable from retribution, is said to be in the hands of God; as former CUC activist ex-plained, "If one does the right thing on the land and you die unjustly, then God settles the matter." The living should not take the law into their own hands, but they do. They are accustomed to the idea of taking illicit revenge within the community, albeit obliquely, through *brujería*. This had appalling consequences when the circumstances of *la violencia* encouraged the reification of previously hidden aggression towards local enemies.

Disinformation was another important tool. For instance, the army claims to have captured the CUC leader and radio announcer Toj Medrano in 1981, forcing him to broadcast anti-revolutionary messages to the so-called guerrillas — "the struggle is useless" — not only over the radio but through a megaphone as he was flown over the villages of Chichicastenango and Santa Cruz in a helicopter; to make the story more credible, the army even admitted giving Medrano 'repressive treatment' (torturing him) to re-orient him to act as their informant. But the man who told me this story said Medrano escaped and "continued to work as a liberator of the people, as one of the original four surviving members of the founding members of the CUC". Neither version reflects what happened to Medrano: he was found dead in May 1980, the day after he was kidnapped, with his hands tied and skull crushed (Carmack 1988). But what is important here is how Medrano has become part of villagers' myth making, providing the grains of hope essential for resilience — hardly the army's intention when killing him.

Myths of violence — the relation of grotesque incidents of violence and unconfirmed rumours — were also instrumental in 'softening' individuals and communities (cf. Scarry 1985). In Emol, rumours centred on activities in the abandoned church, which the army requisitioned when they occupied the village; its reputation as a torture chamber was confirmed after its departure by the blood on the walls (soldiers not only tortured prisoners to extract information about the 'organized' but freely admitted that torture was used as a means of punishment). The truth or otherwise of rumours is irrelevant (the origins of some are the military's psych-ops): their importance lies in the cultural elaboration of terror (Taussig 1984:469). Starting rumours — about whose name was on a death list, for example — is a very effective means of heightening levels of fear in a community which is accustomed to such oblique messages of disapproval and considers them dangerous. *La violencia* exacerbated people's fears and created the terrifying impression of a proliferation of internal enemies, "like thousands of eyes posted everywhere" (Foucault 1979:214), which strung out "the nervous system, one way towards hysteria, the other way numbing and apparent acceptance" (Taussig 1990:3).

One of the most insidious manifestations of psychological terror was the military regime's manipulation of language. The military and their henchmen *(esbirros)* add connotations of their own to ordinary Spanish vocabulary, creating a euphemistic language for public discourse which keeps certain social facts out of sight, masking and sanitizing the many nasty truths of domination. This is designed to obscure the use of coercion and increases the sense of intimidation.

Formerly ordinary words such as 'disappeared'[8] are themselves 'kidnapped' for use in the state's euphemistic discourse; for the rural population, the word then comes to represent collective terror, producing a chilling effect even in intimate discussions between people 'from the same side who understand' (ju maaj wach). The word is then 'blacklisted' by the military and its use becomes dangerous; even mentioning new terms such as *'desaparacido'* can lead to the speaker's death. People search for other words which they can use to mean the same thing without incurring military and paramilitary wrath and the whole process begins again. In the late 1980s, local use of 'kidnapped' *(secuestrado)* had become almost as dangerous as using the word it replaced *(desaparecido)* so Emoltecos had moved on to using more ambiguous phrases such as 'taken from' *(llevado)* or 'taken out' *(sacado)* when talking about this taboo subject. The term *'la violencia'* has a similar history.[9]

Meanings, like the acts to which they refer, thus live a clandestine existence. While apparently describing certain events, words such as *desaparecido* simultaneously mask the real meaning of what actually occurred. Many expressions are employed by people to nullify impact by expressing what they say only by using a construct which intimates that it is not saying it. This forms part of the "discourse of denial which recognizes and reproduces the initial denial, instead of denying it in order to discover what it denies" (Bourdieu 1991:153). The use of words like 'disappeared' stimulated a form of pre-rational thinking: just as a child or husband 'disappeared' one day, so they could reappear another (chapter eight): but they never do. The word simultaneously carries both irrational hope and connotations of death and torture.

Having the power to stigmatize persons and activities which question official realities is another aspect of the manipulation of language (*vide* the extension of the category 'enemy of the state'). The military encourages and accentuates recourse to gross simplification and generalization, persuading people to put themselves and those like them into broad categories over and above the individual. The resort to stereotypes diverted attention from the political claims of people the army have labelled as subversive; by denying status to rebels (or ordinary people perceived to represent them), the authorities assimilated their acts to a category that minimizes their political challenge to the state. Although ultimately unsuccessful — ten years after the end of *la violencia*, several former 'subversives' had been elected to Guatemala's Congress of Deputies (parliament) — the message behind the military's assault on language was loud and clear: people should not discuss what happened. Both the military's euphemisms and the neologisms people create for their own use are idioms for representing the epoch of the unspeakable (chapter seven). Even death became euphemized: through the deletion of human agency in the classification of the cause of verified deaths, accepted by survivors who feared further casualties, the deaths were garbed in a false cloak of normality.

At the same time as the specifics of *la violencia* are denied through censorship and the manipulation of language, the bodies of the dead display literal and metaphoric wounds. In making innocent Indians repeat the fate of the few guerrilla sympathizers, the process of mimesis and metonym are used to link the killing of guerrilla sympathizers to the killing of innocent Guatemalans. Opposition to (supposed) communist ideology is expressed through brutal attacks on the bodies of the Indian. These actions are a "kind of grisly polemic directed at the onlookers and the wider national audience" (Sallnow 1989); each death is the death of the guerrilla in microcosm.

Whilst adopting these new tactics, the army continued its policy of arbitrary and unpredictable violence, destruction and terror. The security forces and their henchmen *(esbirros)*, who serve under military authority, continued likewise. Although Guatemala's military dictatorship, like other repressive regimes, maintained its authority by keeping its repressive style and techniques secret and private (Martín-Baro 1990), it made no secret of its desire to terrorize the population.

Like most stigmatized groups, Mayan Indians are accustomed to being blamed for the country's ills; they have little knowledge of their rights under the constitution or the law because their experience over the centuries has told them that they have no way of enforcing them. Indians evade the issue by avoiding contact with *ladinos* as much as possible; they live as self-contained an existence as they can at the fringes of *ladino* society. *La violencia* brought *ladino* realities into village life, with the result that all Indians found themselves labelled as actual or potential subversives[10] and criminals, regardless of their individual beliefs and actions. In such conditions, concepts of innocence and guilt lose their meaning and become irrelevant.[11] Identifying guilt or innocence through traditionally legitimate or legal means is supplanted by terror; social and legal structures collapse, leaving everyone feeling insecure. The techniques and language for defining, controlling, and neutralizing suspected terrorists are applied to arbitrary victims (Indian civilians) selected by the state for the purposes of political theatre and the periodic advancement of hegemony.

La Violencia Peaks

La violencia crested between 1981 and 1983, when the army and its local *esbirros*, especially the 'voluntary' civil patrols (chapter five), were active in eradicating previous authority structures in order to impose their own. During this period, 440 Indian villages were razed to the ground (Painter 1987:xiv); an estimated one million people — roughly 12 percent of the population at the time — fled their homes (Manz 1988:7), at least temporarily; hundreds of thousands became internal refugees; tens of thousands were concentrated into new villages controlled by the army (Jonas 1991: 183). An estimated 90,000 people were killed (excluding Guatemala City); thousands more were disappeared. At least 80,000 women were widowed during General García's dictatorship (1978-1982) (Comité pro Justicia y

Paz de Guatemala 1985), up to 200,000 children lost at least one parent (Government of Guatemala, National Institute of Statistics, 1991) and an estimated 100,000 lost both (Jonas 1991:183-4). Countless women were raped: the army encouraged soldiers to gang rape women: the multiple rape dehumanized the women in the men's eyes, making it easier for the soldiers to kill them (Stoll 1990:203-4).

Three provinces accounted for 25,000 adult deaths (Carmack 1988:7); the highest number of deaths was in the province of El Quiché (GVIS 1992), which experienced considerable guerrilla activity and hence bore the brunt of military attack. A map[12] published by the Guatemalan Church in Exile shows fifty-four known massacres in El Quiché in 1982 alone. Information on population loss in El Quiché is fragmentary. A population shortfall of 48 percent has been estimated for one of the hardest hit areas, the Ixil triangle in the north of the department (Stoll 1993:5). Emoltecos told me that over one thousand people, a third of the village's population, were killed or disappeared in less than twelve months over 1981-1982. In other southern *municipios* such as Chiché and Chichicastenango, population loss also reaches 33 percent if permanent migrants are included (Smith 1990a:20). Approximately 15,000 of Chichicastenango township's 60,000 inhabitants were killed or abducted; each of its villages has an average of eighty widows and 150 orphans (America's Watch 1986). The departmental capital, Santa Cruz, and adjacent communities lost at least 10 percent of their Indian population, excluding refugees (Carmack 1988:57).

These are survivors' and witnesses' estimates: hard data on population loss does not exist in any meaningful sense and records which do exist are often kept under lock and key. Registers for 1981 and 1982 in Santa Cruz, for example, list only 4,077 deaths, of which 2,020 are attributed to 'unnatural' causes. These figures are too low (Carmack 1988:56); they exclude the thousands of disappeared people whose bodies were dumped by government killers in clandestine cemeteries. There are thousands of these cemeteries, big and small, in the country's interior (La Crónica, 20 September 1991); by 1990, according to GAM, 108 had been identified in El Quiché, Huehuetenango, and San Marcos alone.

Survivors contribute to the undercount: they were too afraid to report 'unnatural' deaths because the army considered anyone killed by either military or paramilitary forces a 'subversive' and relatives feared being similarly labelled. Many people deny that relatives have been killed or disappeared, which amounts to the same thing as no-one has ever reappeared (although the disappeared are more likely to have been tortured before being killed (Amnesty International 1987:8); instead, people claim their dead or disappeared kin are working away from home.[13] Having a political death or 'disappeared one' *(desaparecido)* in the family is like admitting to a contagious disease.

Privately, away from the dread hand of the state, informants report that the army killed people in most of the villages of Chichicastenango and Santa Cruz. People arriving at a village after a massacre sometimes found no one alive in sight; in one instance, villagers came under fire as they transported forty bodies to the mortuary. In this period, the number of deaths attributed to any one army unit during their three month tour of duty in any one place ranged from one to one hundred.

A member of the voluntary fire brigade *(bomberos voluntarios)*, established to recover the corpses strewn across the countryside,[14] told me:

> The numbers of bodies began with one or two, steadily increasing to fifteen. Eventually massacres of a hundred at a time were taking place in the villages. These included women, children, and babies.

The formation of *bomberos voluntarios* bears witness to the extent of this undocumented carnage — 200,000 unarmed civilians had been killed or disappeared by government security forces and semi-official death squads by 1991 (Jonas 1991:2). The *bomberos* were usually townsmen (including some altruistic *ladinos*) who decided they could not tolerate the large numbers of dead bodies being left to rot. In Chichicastenango town, which had a population of 35,000, government firemen estimate that they collected over 1,300 bodies over 1981 and 1982. As the bodies were neither identified nor claimed, these victims of the violence were not entered into official records.

Characteristics of 'La Violencia'

Visible and Invisible Violence

Invisible webs of causation were characteristic of *la violencia*. The military state's construction of the suspected subversive was shaped by its own atrocities; political assassination was presented as a 'natural' consequence of subversives' violence and disorder. Being arrested became sufficient cause to consider that person a guerrilla; having confirmed this association to their own satisfaction, the counterinsurgency forces felt they had legitimate cause to subject the victim to a series of processes of annihilation — including interrogation under torture and covert assassination.

La violencia was relentless and unavoidable. It comprised two types of violence: the visible and the invisible. Overt violence consisted of burning and bombing villages, a tactic called 'operation cinders' within the army; it was also referred to as a 'clean up' of a group the army portrayed as less than human: the guerrilla.[15] Visible violence also included public executions and massacres which addressed no one but were an end in themselves: they were intended to completely efface the identities of individuals and Mayan populations.

Invisible violence was (and still is) covertly performed by clandestine organizations belonging to the army, the security forces, and the police. Army intelligence officers are believed to be responsible for many killings and disappearances. Most feared are civilians attached to this branch of the army, who are believed to be former soldiers with a propensity for murder. Both the military and the government disclaim any involvement in their atrocities and blame the guerrillas. Victims simply disappear, leaving a silent space. Sometimes villagers are themselves unsure which side did the killing during the worst period of *la violencia* and, in cases of unwitnessed abduction or assassination, evidence of culpability is occasionally flimsy; at other times, their uncertainty reflects a reluctance to attribute blame for fear of physical or spiritual retaliation.

Invisible and visible forms of violence aim for completeness and silence on the one hand and brutal suppression on the other. This is revealed with ruthless clarity in atrocities comprising both types of violence such as the dumping of mutilated bodies in public places following unwitnessed abductions and secret murders.

Anonymity is another controlling mechanism: both assassins and assassinated were anonymous. Most bodies are unidentifiable. Many had been transported from elsewhere, stripped naked[16] and disfigured. Death is more disturbing when recovered bodies show signs of torture, as approximately 50 percent of recovered corpses do (Adamson 1992); these include fire and acid burns, flayed skin, mutilated genitals, amputations, and stake insertions. Sense organs are a common target of both symbolic and literal assault: ears and tongues sliced off, eyes gouged or burnt out. This is a potent meta message: all sense is attacked, leaving the population without 'sense', without the means to perceive, reason, criticize, or, most crucially, name the guilty.

Local killers exploit traditional beliefs to add further layers of terror. Defacing and mutilating corpses transforms victims into condemned spirits *(condenados)* who cannot complete the transition to the other world. Especially dangerous are corpses with objects stuffed into their mouths, blocking the spirit's exit. Stripped naked, victims are rendered invisible to the ancestors, who cannot recognize the dead as their own (chapter eight).

Bodies placed openly in towns and villages evoke terror among the local population; so do less immediately obvious disposal sites such as deep gullies, rivers or clandestine graves. Liminal places such as crossroads, river banks, and roadsides became regular dumping grounds: "It was horrifying," said *doña* Flora; "they just lay rotting on the ground...or in rivers..." Two villagers describe the scene:

> The bodies were dumped at the crossroads which lead to several villages... they were not from here...we did not know where they came from, nor do we know when they were dumped. Many of them would appear just like that, usually in the morning. They were like the trees that the army had cut down

and lined up along the road.[17] They were in such a state, all mutilated, with their tongues and genitalia missing, sometimes in the nude. Many were not from here; we could see that when they still had bits of clothes on.

It was terrible...there were dead all around. Since we could not bury them,[18] the dogs ate them. They carried bits of them round in their mouths...the dogs were fat in those days... Everyone saw the dead in this state... The dogs were so used to seeing the dead that one day one went for the arm of a man who was stone cold drunk and it almost dislocated his arm before he was roused.

Mass abductions which leave no witnesses are another form of invisible violence. A widow told me:

One market day in Chichicastenango, a black-hooded man *(encapuchado)* pointed out the 'bad people' (guerrillas) from Emol to the plain-clothed army man accompanying him. The selected victims were then thrown into trucks and driven away. When the trucks were full, they were slung into jail until the next day. All the people identified in this way were never seen again. On the next market day in Emol the army rolled up with several trucks. Everyone attending the market and living in the houses surrounding the square was thrown into the vehicles and driven away. Over a hundred people vanished.

Victims were men, women, and children, the very young to the very old, *costumbrista*, Catholic, and Protestant. It was an event which made no sense. That was the point. It caused a major disruption of life and time and became a marker for both. But the event itself has no meaning. Survivors fear their disappeared kin have been dumped on other people's doorsteps.

The Suppression of Religious Practice
The suppression of 'pure' and 'new' catholicism was designed to stifle all community organizations not integrated into (or aligned with) the army. Even Indian army recruits were debriefed in the first days of training; they were told most vehemently, "God does not exist, only the army".

Mayan Indians are not accustomed to separating religion from local politics; community leaders' legitimacy was grounded in the religious structure, be it 'new' Catholic or *costumbrista*. Both religions were suppressed. *costumbrista* confraternities *(cofradia)*, already under threat prior to *la violencia*, collapsed in most villages (including Emol), only re-appearing after *la violencia* in a reduced form with no political influence. In areas where the *cofradia* continued to exist with any force, they usually formed a symbiotic relationship with the army. Sometimes political parties also vie for *cofradia* support, offering money for their 'co-operation' (votes).

Costumbrista diviners (aj q'ij) are also severely restricted in their ability to practice in their communities. It is still dangerous to visit the sacred sites where many ceremonies are performed at night: aj q'ij run the risk of being accused of subversion or being shot as a guerrilla. The army continued its repression of independent minded aj q'ij whilst simultaneously attempting to harness Mayan religious symbolism to legitimate its position of power through the co-option of other aj q'ij "to Indian militia divisions and even to bases in Guatemala City" (Carmack 1990:121). The army's attempts to 'retraditionalize' *costumbre* were largely unsuccessful as the *ladino* authors of the scheme failed to understand aj q'ij's relationship with the sacred landscape (chapter eight).

Many people converted to protestantism as a survival strategy. Evangelicals are believed to be given new identity cards by the army, specifying their religion; people wanted this extra protection. Despite high conversion rates, villages such as Emol remain criminalized for having had a high proportion of catechists.

The Guerrilla

Supporters and Sympathizers

Guerrilla strongholds were in the rural areas. People in the highlands organized spontaneously along either class or ethnic lines in the hope of improving their lives. They had no ideological programme (Arias 1990); the guerrilla leadership's professed Marxism-Leninism had little if any relevance to most Indians who joined the 'organization'.[19] Some people say this lack of resonance led to the failure of the movement; new Mayan movements criticize past resistance movements for preaching foreign ideologies (cf. Le Bot 1995).

Rebellion developed within village religious structures. The catechist movement was the only supra-communal organization among the K'iche' (other than the localized saints brotherhoods); catechist courses were one of the few venues in which K'iche' and other Maya from different villages could formally gather to discuss important issues. Highland catechists helped to establish the *campesino* leagues and then the CUC which subsumed it; when the latter declared war on the state in May 1978, most K'iche' activists followed the CUC's leadership in joining the Guerrilla Army of the Poor (EGP). The Organization of People in Arms (ORPA), which also emerged in the 1970s, worked in other parts of Guatemala. High profile killings, such as the assassination of Andrés Avelina Zapeta y Zapeta, the Indian mayor of Santa Cruz in 1981, pushed many Indians, already radicalized by their participation in catechism and other popular movements, into joining the guerrillas (Carmack 1988:54).

In January 1982, the EGP joined with ORPA, FAR, and the Guatemalan Workers' Party (PGT) to form the National Revolutionary Union of Guatemala (URNG) which functions as the diplomatic and military command of the revolutionary movement (chapter one). While Marxism-Leninism is the dominant ideology within the URNG, there are also strong liberation theology and social-democratic tendencies.

Some families were divided over the issue of incorporation into the successive movements; not everyone followed their local leaders through the chain of revolutionary groupings, which partly explains the confusion about who was involved in what. In local terms, being a guerrilla implies taking up arms: "The people do not believe what the army say as 'they' [the army] accuse them of being guerrillas", an 'awoken' woman told me angrily; "CUC was here and they are not guerrillas, for they do not carry guns."

Even more people 'began to work' (to fight back) after the Spanish Embassy massacre in January 1980[20] in which a local man died. This incident radicalized many people who had not yet made the transition from the CUC to the EGP. They worked either directly or indirectly by, for example, providing guerrillas with food, clothes and, occasionally, shelter: it has been estimated that between "250,000 and 500,000 highland people participated in the war in one form or another" (Arias 1990:255). Although support in southern El Quiché was never as great as in the north among the Communities of Population in Resistance (CPR), most hamlets in the mountainous areas of Santa Cruz and Chichicastenango *municipios* harboured guerrillas (Carmack 1988):

> Paramilitary organizations, forms of self-defence, were organized to provide food and clothing for the permanent guerrilla units whose members were mostly Indians with relatives in various villages. Indians also began to collaborate in large military operations (Smith 1990b:255).

An exile claimed that more than one thousand Indians from Santa Cruz *municipio* alone joined the guerrillas:

> These and many others recruited from surrounding communities were organized, trained, and armed by the Guerrilla Army of the Poor (EGP), the organization that for ten years had been operating in the northern part of the department of El Quiché (Carmack 1988:56).

At its peak, the guerrillas had seven fronts (including two in southern El Quiché), totalling between six and eight thousand armed men. The guerrillas had strong support in some areas, and relatively well-organized supply lines; in other areas, the infrastructure was less established and arms scarce (only a few antique rifles), so few supporters actually became active aggressors. Generally, villages under guerrilla control laid traps — staked pits — along their boundaries; people were instructed in the placement of sentries and the planning of escape routes into the canyons and forests.

The scale of military repression made guerrillas desperate for recruits. They visited Indian villages to elicit their support (Carmack 1988); coercive strategies were sometimes used but conscription was unknown. An old man from Chichicastenango told a U.S. reporter that guerrillas arrived in the village centres, called the population together, and stated their case; no problems arose, he said, if people listened quietly: "...but if you object to something then they will come to your house at night and kill you. His daughter ...spoke out and was killed by the guerrillas" (Carmack 1988:59). The two facts may or may not be linked; the girl is dead and this is the only reason her father can find to explain such a pointless death.

Five years after the official end of *la violencia*, it was difficult to assess support for the rebel forces and I was unable to gather much information regarding guerrilla action in and around Emol; discussion of the subject causes obvious discomfort and fear. I was given to understand that most village militants were dead. Later, in another village, I was told that communities never allow people who join the guerrilla to return home. It is both safer and easier to attribute *la violencia* to a force which no longer has any hold over them. Thus, on the rare occasions that people do admit to knowing any guerrillas, they are all said to have left the area or to have sold out to the army.

People are afraid, with good reason, to admit that anyone in their family or village became an armed guerrilla. Part of the difficulty is that the army had created the impression of potential, if not actual, total support for the guerrillas and had apparently convinced itself, by its indiscriminate reprisals, that all Indians are subversives. Indian villagers give the impression that they are themselves unsure how widespread support for the guerrillas had been, though their evasiveness could well be an example of traditional survival techniques (chapter seven).

Some people admit they had been 'organized', a general expression which, when used by men, indicates that they had belonged to a popular organization, trade union or guerrilla group. Fear prevents survivors from specifying which; it is extremely rare for anyone to admit to belonging to anything more radical than the unarmed CUC; most villagers were unaware of the CUC's 1978 declaration of war and those who did know let their memories slide over it. Others flatly deny that they had belonged to the guerrilla or that the guerrilla ever came to the village. Some Emoltecos insist that the most villagers did was supply food and shelter to the guerrillas; some (including patrollers) claim that they were coerced into doing so. Another villager said there had been about a dozen active sympathizers in each hamlet who had carried out propaganda and training; they had been involved in attacks in other areas but not in their own village because the advantages of local knowledge were offset by the danger of being recognized. Some people said guerrillas from other *municipios* carried out military actions in the area and then left; others said that local guerrillas carried out actions (such as blowing up bridges) in nearby towns. Others said guerrillas 'from outside' brought good guns which they left with locals; others said local guerrillas were never armed with more than the antique hunting rifles used to shoot birds. Guerrillas from one village were also said to come to the aid of people from another who were being attacked by the army (cf. Carmack 1988:59).

Some villages, including Emol, were politically polarized before *la violencia*. At this time, differences in political alignments reflected different distributions of religions. A woman recalled, "There were two groups here, those who wanted to learn [about equality etc.] and those who didn't because they were afraid." Villagers from Emol Central accused people from Kotoh of being 'progressive' (which they had been and proud of it until the army came and destroyed everything they had built for themselves); they were envious of what Kotoh residents had accomplished, but refused to 'work' themselves. *Doña* Rosaria told me:

> They organized themselves in this hamlet [Malah] and then another hamlet [Kotoh] got involved. And then the hamlets became each other's brothers *(hermanos)*. In other words, when *la violencia* came the guerrillas had already formed groups and so had the army. It was not the guerrillas themselves who came though. They sent their representatives who 'organized' people from the community. So, you see, the community became divided in two. There were some who accepted the side of the guerrilla and others who didn't. Among those who didn't were the 'ears' *(orejas)* who spied for the army.

Many Emolteco women had not known what a guerrilla was until the army accused them of being one and even then, most of them failed to understand the concept — beyond realizing that the label was (and remains) dangerous. Their monolingualism, together with the gender barrier which separates male and female activities, prevents all but the most determined women from participating in the popular movements. Women are less susceptible to outside influences, whether the new cosmology of catechists, guerrilla ideology or, later, military propaganda: all these discourses were (at least initially) presented in Spanish and directed at men. Extremely few local women became involved in the popular movement. Some women were persuaded by friends and relatives to go to the meetings without knowing what exactly they were about; one attraction was the promises of material benefits, especially land and higher wages. It was unusual for a woman to persuade her menfolk to join the 'organization' as *doña* Flora had done.

Women give the impression that, until the early 1980s, involvement in popular movements was a male prerogative. Women who joined were usually young, single catechists who became politicized through the teachings they received. Older women were politicized and pushed into participating in 'the struggle' as a result of their experiences. As one widow told me, "If your husband died, you have to organize more, you have to 'work' more because of the blood and love."

Current Views of the Guerrilla

Many subversive crimes, if actually committed at all, were wrong only when viewed from the perspective of the state's overweening interest in social control. While government authorities and their newspapers generally succeeded in stigmatizing subversives as evil through and through, members of local communities often supported their activities. Local residents often perceived village 'subversives' to have been a less than threatening presence in the village; they had even felt protected by them.

People's perception and opinion of these forces varied over time and, perhaps, in different contexts, when talking to different people, and so on. In general, people who had previously perceived the guerrillas positively now tend to see them more negatively.

Despite the processes of condensation and association typical of memory, most people clearly distinguish between the early and later guerrilla periods (with a corresponding changing view of the old and new army). What was initially seen as offering a millenarian future is retrospectively viewed by some as 'deception'; even people who had been involved at the time, said the guerrilla only came to 'ruin them'. People more susceptible to army propaganda likened guerrillas to coyotes,[21] deceiving villagers.

Some people felt let down by the EGP because it had not fulfilled its promises of a 'new law', a new social order to end exploitation and ethnic discrimination. Indeed, according to some, the guerrillas ran off with their guns when the villagers were bombarded by the army. People who are more politically aware attribute failure more accurately to the overpowering army onslaught followed by the militarization of the countryside. Such opinions are more common among men.

Many people spoke about the guerrilla in general terms because certain ordeals remained outside personal family discourse. People elect to remain silent about a family member who is or was a guerrilla. Only once did someone (not from Emol) admit to me that a member of his family was a guerrilla. Usually the perception of heroism *vis-à-vis* guerrillas was blocked by the discourse of the family at home. It was not that families felt anger and frustration because they had fought without achieving the promised millenarian dream but, rather, that they did not want to admit that they had been involved in the first instance.

Doña Lydia expressed many widows' romanticized image of the left-wing forces, referred to in general terms as 'the organized', when she remarked:

> They had many good ideas and they spoke of equality. They spoke really well and raised people's consciousness, making us aware of how we worked for the benefit of the rich and not ourselves... But then they disappeared like the spirits do.

Voicing such an opinion is unusual: most people will not admit to having any positive opinions about the guerrilla. It is more common to hear analogous stories told via dreams; for example, one woman dreamt of soldiers coming into her house and everyone abandoning her, leaving her to face them. She explained to the soldiers that her visitors were 'teachers' — that is, organized men who teach less learned villagers about equality, etc. — who had "not been doing anything wrong". Despite her protestations, her dream that they ran away expresses her ambivalence towards the organized.

Gradations of 'Guerrillaness'

Villagers' concepts of the guerrilla are no more an absolute than the military's, although each measured 'guerrillaness' along different axes. For villagers, one could be more, or less, of a guerrilla and therefore more, or less, dangerous. The familiar discourse of 'otherness' is used to distinguish gradations of guerrillaness: being different, standing out in any way, is contrary to K'iche' values of community conformity. Already differentiated by their actions and beliefs, the 'otherness' of those who left during *la violencia* was confirmed by their flight. Anyone who fled the village, even for a short time (other than during the mass evacuations during army bombardment), was suspected of being a guerrilla by villagers who returned to their homes as soon as the shooting stopped. People who did not go far or remained outside the village for only a short period say that those who went further afield or stayed away longer are guerrillas. The further people went and the longer they stayed away, the more of a guerrilla they are perceived to be:

> One man from Emol left during the worst part of *la violencia*. He went to work on the coast. He did not return for two years. During this time his family, his wife, and children did not know if he was dead or alive. He came back after amnesty was called but was not among those who were killed [by the patrol chiefs]. Now, because he left, people say that he is a guerrilla...

On returning to the village, such people said the **real** guerrillas were still in the mountains.

This ranking was motivated by people's hopes of saving their own skins by 'passing the buck', an idea encouraged by the army who extracted information from people, sometimes under torture, leading them to believe that they could save their own lives if they supplied the right answers. Some qualification is needed here: families who became separated when some members were forced down from the mountains never refer to relatives who remain behind as 'guerrillas'. I heard of only one exception: an abandoned wife whose husband had taken another woman in the mountains.

Knowing or suspecting that one's name was on a hit list, or having close kin who had been killed or kidnapped, also indicated 'otherness'. Men in this situation fled; very few took their families with them. Most sought safety in the relative anonymity of urban or coastal areas; some crossed the border into Mexico. The choice often depended on the presence of family or like-minded friends with whom they could seek refuge. People working on the coast, receiving word of the situation at home, just did not return. At least 100,000 terrorized *campesinos* remained in the plantation zone after 1982 because they were afraid of being perceived as having fled and thus rebel supporters (Dunkerley 1988:496). Displaced persons were considered subversive by the army because they came from areas which it deemed subversive; they were hunted down by military intelligence units, kidnapped, and killed by plain-clothed army personnel or gunned down by death squads. Several women told me that their menfolk had been pointed out to these clandestine forces by fellow villagers, their faces hidden behind black balaclavas. A woman told me, "Our men went to the Guatemala City and became *judiciales* so that they could kill..."

People who left were generally the most resourceful, both in terms of material wealth and connections. Their ability to survive outside the village reconfirmed their 'otherness' and gave rise to suspicion: survival 'outside' was seen not only as a denial of K'iche' values and but also of identity, which is conventionally tied to one's place. Villagers have a point here: the displaced person and the refugee have to construct a self which can survive and an identity which can withstand the abandonment of the land. Life 'outside' exposes refugees to 'otherness' and so returnees are seen as frightening even if they are not associated with being guerrillas: however, they invariably are. Returnees who believed that their innocence would ensure the ancestors' protection were soon asking whether the ancestors had, in turn, abandoned them.[22]

Conclusion

La violencia descended with shocking suddenness on a people completely unprepared for the idea that the *ladino* nation state, which has abused, exploited, and segregated them for centuries, should bother with them at all.

The K'iche' traditionally present a passive, closed face to outsiders. They are accustomed to being subordinated to *ladinos*, a way of being that has been internalized; they are not geared to political action. They perceive themselves as victims of violence, not its perpetrators, an ideological perception reinforced by their experiences of colonial domination and exploitation.[23] Some men, particularly the formally 'organized', are aware of the similarities between the government's counterinsurgency campaign and the Spanish conquest of the K'iche', an event which has never lost its contemporary relevance: indeed, "it is disconcerting to think how much the twentieth century resembles the sixteenth, for the parallels between cycles of conquest hundreds of years apart are striking" (Lovell 1988:47; cf. Manz 1988).[24] The role of victim is familiar to them and, during *la violencia* and its immediate aftermath, they were re-victimized. They have no more institutions with which to counter external violence than they had five hundred years ago: they are unarmed, have no military organization, no cult of violence. Indeed K'iche' cultural norms proscribe violence (at least in public) as a means of settling arguments; the emphasis is on conflict avoidance, an important behavioural strategy in a society — and nation — with few mechanisms of dispute resolution.

To maintain this façade, K'iche's conventionally attribute all calamities to some personified, outside agency which can be human (anyone from a fellow villager to the *ladino* army) or supernatural (God, ancestors or the spirits); neither source of misfortune is seen to be under the control of the living. Straddling the two categories are *brujos*, living fellow villagers who attempt to influence the negative elements of the spirit world. Witchcraft *(brujeria)* is considered illicit — it's not just that the K'iche' believe one cannot act on the world, but that one should not — and unjust: it can kill the innocent.

Fear of *brujeria* is very real and expresses the insecurity and doubt which accompanies rapid change (cf. Marwick 1965:247-8). There are less innocent ramifications: the concept provides a ready-made blueprint for the execution of antisocial, illicit desires (see Heusmann and Eron 1984). Resort to *brujeria* or *brujeria*-style activities becomes even more attractive when the few legitimate means of dispute resolution — elders, customary law (Sieder 1996) and the national judicial system[25] — are destroyed or become non-functional in times of war. People learnt to obtain redress and exact retribution by denouncing their enemies to the army as 'subversives' instead of visiting the local *brujo*.

What horrified and terrified villagers was the ease with which some people switched from one mode of attack to another when, in 1982, the creation of the patrol system provided a cover for overt violence, shattering community solidarity probably for ever. Even families were riven apart by suspicion: a few men told me that they no longer trusted their wives because of the number of women who denounced their husbands as guerrillas. This male myth is based on the contemporary consequences of traditions of marriage between rival hamlets: I found several instances of a woman's brothers being involved in the murder of her husband.

Notes

1. See chapter two, note 18.

2. One Guatemalan priest remained cloistered in the Bishop's headquarters in Santa Cruz. When I met him, he hardly left his parish for fear of his life.

3. In Guatemala, *'judiciales'* refers to any section of the security forces which carries out disappearances and killings — which includes the police, who are involved in assassinations and torture as well as the disappearances they are supposed to investigate. The national police force is officially under the jurisdiction of the

Interior Ministry although it was subordinate to the army during the dictatorship; police links with the military persist to the present.

4. See chapter two, note 35.

5. See Wilson (1995:113) on the treatment of pregnant women and the association between production and reproduction.

6. "It is widely believed that the army has established broad networks of informers in most communities. Some people suggested that the soldiers dress up like guerrillas, trying to engage people in conversation to see if they criticize the army. Prior to the counterinsurgency campaigns of the early 1980s, local military commissioners and their assistants primarily carried out and coordinated army intelligence. Now the military directly coordinates a more elaborate informer network, probably through the G-2 (military intelligence). The common perception is that those who act as spies are trying to clear their own names or are paid for the information they pass on" (Manz 1988:70).

7. The post of military commissioner was created in the 1930s. Commissioners are village men who have completed their military service; they act as the army's (unpaid) civil agents and serve under military discipline for a fixed term. The town-based head of the commissioners is often a *ladino*; commissioners in smaller towns are often self-appointed (America's Watch 1986). In Emol, commissioners are elected and invariably Indian.

Commissioners are responsible for public order, army recruitment and training military reserves (former conscripts). The requirements of the post changed in the late 1970s to include spying, informing, and other tasks for the army; a few years later, commissioners often helped to organize the patrols (Smith 1990b:272). Commissioners who worked for the good of their community were replaced. Men who wanted to refuse the appointment (two years' army service does not necessarily imply army sympathies) were afraid to do so for fear of being labelled 'subversive'.

Guatemala's 33,000 military commissioners were demobilized as of 15 September (Independence Day) 1995. However, many commissioners "remain armed and continue to exercise authority within their communities" (Popkin 1996:3).

8. The term *desaparecido* (literally 'disappeared', referring to governmental kidnapping) acquired its grammatical versatility as a verb and participle ('to be disappeared'; 'he was disappeared') in Guatemala almost a decade before it was exported to Chile and Argentina (Simon 1987:14).

9. Several synonyms for *la violencia* are commonly used, including 'the repression' *(la represión)*. More oblique references include: that time *(aquel tiempo;* uq'ijool); the epoch *(la época)*; the thing *(la cosa)*; the situation which happened *(la situación que pasó)* or just *'la situación'*; the pain *(el dolor)*, that painful time (k'ax k'oliil); that sad time (uq'ijool b'iis); the despair *(la desesperación)*, that desperate time (uq'ijool paxi b'al k'u'x). These apparent synonyms carry different meanings and are employed to different effects.

10. Political groups are excluded from the U.N. Convention on Genocide (Kuper 1981: chapter 2). But, as one representative pointed out, "since it was established that genocide always implied the participation or complicity of Governments, that crime [i.e., genocide] would never be suppressed: the Government which was responsible would always be able to allege that the extermination of any group had been dictated by political considerations, such as the necessity for quelling an insurrection or maintaining public order" (Kuper 1981:28-29).

11. Conditions of legality imply there must be a way of being innocent (Walter 1969:342) yet innocence is impossible if there is no means of avoiding spurious accusations.

12. Entitled 'Massacres committed by the army 1981-1985' *(Masacres cometidas por el ejército 1981-1985)*.

13. The victims' killers and their accomplices also claim that the men are still alive, living with the guerrillas in the mountains.

14. It is illegal for civilians to move bodies before obtaining permission from local legal authorities who, ordinarily, inspect the corpse and make preliminary criminal investigations; the police remove the bodies (a function they resumed after 1985).

15. cf. Suárez-Orozco (1992:239): in Argentina, "the perverse medical-hygienic and surgical imagery which accompanied the operation...point to the paranoid ethos that engulfed the 'dirty war'...indeed, a *dirty* war was required to 'cleanse' the country of ideological contamination" (italics in original).

16. Corpses were stripped to prevent identification by the living and the dead (chapter eight). Only women wear traditional clothing which identifies their *municipio*; most corpses are male.

17. The military felled numerous trees when building access roads in the wooded highlands; the trunks were then regularly spaced to buttress the cuttings.

18. Villagers were not allowed to do so; this was the *bomberos voluntarios'* job. People were generally too terrified by the condition of the corpses to touch them. Fear of being labelled 'subversive' prevented them claiming kin for burial (there is no tradition of burying non-kin).

19. Most people's concepts of 'communism' derive from what they were told by the army, which represents this ideology as a catch-all category containing anything and everything the military state considered negative (chapter ten). If communism did not exist, the military would have had to invent it and it can be said that it has.

20. Rebuffed by the U.S. Embassy, a delegation of protesters (including K'iche' from Santa Cruz *municipio*) tried to peacefully occupy the Spanish Embassy. When state security police fire-bombed the building, 23 Indians died.

21. The coyote is the Mesoamerican trickster figure; one of his attributes is cowardice.

22. Even though the U.S. (the source of most of Guatemala's aid and the destination of most of its exports) is less concerned about the communist threat since the end of the Cold War, Guatemala's democratic government views refugees repatriated from Mexico in the 1990s as guerrillas and communists. Communities of returnees are among the most politicized of Indian communities, having acquired an awareness of their rights during their sojourn in Mexico. They are perceived as a threat to the state and stigmatized as guerrillas and communists.

23. cf. Hawkins 1984: "Indo-*ladino* ideologies [can be seen] as part of a single system of inverse images of domination and subordination".

24. The Spanish *conquistadores*, after accepting the K'iche's' offer of peace, seized the kingdom's rulers and assassinated them. They burned the capital and then terrorized the surrounding rural peoples who, by then, had taken up arms. Spanish victory was achieved through superior weaponry (horses and firearms) and ruthlessness. Indians were massacred or enslaved. In many ways the army's recent actions

in El Quiché (for example, public executions of community leaders, the scorched earth policy, terrorization, etc.) symbolically duplicate the Conquest.

Historical sources (Remesal 1932, Juarros 1981, Ximénez 1929, Las Casas 1909, Estrada Monroy 1979) indicate that the military massacres of the 1980s were worse than those committed by the *conquistadores*.

25. According to the Lawyers' Committee for Human Rights, "The actual practice of the Guatemalan judicial system...often bears little resemblance to the procedures mandated by law, especially when the circumstances of the crime suggest involvement by the Guatemalan army or security forces" (LCHR 1990:5). In the indigenous highlands, the army is the ultimate judicial authority (Jay 1993:57). Although recourse to *habeas corpus* has been incorporated into the Guatemalan Constitution since 1945, it has little, if any, impact.

5

Village Patrols and Their Violence

The patrol system has left tragic scars on the Guatemalan highland communities, where poverty, fear, petty feuding and the replacement of traditional legal systems by arbitrary military force have made the patrol system a dangerous conduit for vigilante justice and abuse of power. The cultural landscape of rural Guatemala has been more profoundly altered in the past six years than the past century (America's Watch 1986).

La violencia can be divided into two phases. In the first, violence was committed by outsiders (the army and the guerrilla); in the second, from 1981, violence was also committed by insiders (village men incorporated into the patrol system). In both, violence was perpetrated predominantly against Indians by Indians under *ladino* (state) control; in the latter phase, this was denied and deliberately obscured. A veritable smokescreen obscured the third phase of the military's counterinsurgency campaign from 1985 (chapter one) and although the violence continued and even worsened during the early years of 'civilian' rule, this phase is not popularly included in *la violencia*.

The Army and the Patrols

The civil patrol system (*Patrullas de Autodefensa Civil*; PAC) developed from the army's desire to reorganize the countryside in its own image. There was more to this than the military's perception of the necessity of pacifying rural areas, namely, its overweening interest in social control. This extended to a desire, if not a felt need, to control interpersonal relationships, something which had eluded them as far as the Indian population was concerned.

The army already had a presence in highland communities in the person of the local military commissioner, a post established in the 1930s.[1] The army was "part of village culture, having long since insinuated itself into levels of local meaning" (Wilson 1995:21). As rural unrest intensified in the mid-1970s, commissioners' responsibilities were increased to meet the army's revised perceptions of its needs. But military commissioners in highland villages were invariably indigenous and elected bi-annually by fellow Indians, making the system suspect from the army's point of view. Army paranoia was exacerbated by information received from commissioners and the new networks of informers,[2] much of which seemed mysterious and 'other' and hence dangerous and subversive. There is little if any understanding of Mayan culture within the *ladino* officer class.[3]

The army realized that a different kind of local, indigenous intermediary was required to fill the communications gap arising from the political and cultural disparities between the *ladino* state and the Indian, one that could be controlled without the subject's conscious knowledge.[4] The army decided to look for potential collaborators, men whose personal identity could be exploited in order to penetrate Indian communities and their value systems. They wanted the type of man who could be relied upon to lose control of the inhibitions which restrict the expression of the "unintegrated, asocial tendencies [which] are always present in man[kind]"; indeed, the army relied on the "open, unrestrained expression" of these tendencies (Bettelheim 1986:16). The army benefitted from the differences in their intermediaries' backgrounds — army supporters, guerrillas, catechists, *cofradia*, etc. — as the variety masked the common denominator between them. Significant secondary benefits included the co-option of political adversaries: neutralizing opponents and gaining access to (or at least terrifying) other members of the popular movements far outweighed the disadvantages of close supervision. Yet selecting existing community leaders to lend "legitimacy and a semblance of continuity to the army's new local structures" (Wilson 1995:240) often backfired as villagers frequently recategorized the army's intermediaries as spies or '*ladinos*', i.e., as outsiders.

Having decided what kind of man would most suit their purposes, the army then designed the circumstances which would bring him to local power and keep him there: the civil patrol system. Designed to be a coercive means of military control of an enemy as elusive and intangible as the spirits, the patrol system was carefully calculated to involve everyone in the terrorization of their own communities, initially as perpetrator or victim and ultimately as both (cf. Jay 1993). The intention was to ensure submission through locally produced terror, a tactic which has been sustained over the years since the end of both *la violencia* and the military dictatorship.

Trials were launched in southern El Quiché in late 1981. Emol was a late addition to the experiment but the script had already been finalized and has not been revised since.[5] The delay in its inclusion was due to its reputation: there were arguments within the military about the possibility of arming guerrillas. (I was told that this had actually happened elsewhere but army intelligence officers had disarmed the 'guerrillas' when this was discovered.) The solution was not to arm Emol's two most progressive hamlets, Kotoh and Malah. Years later, Kotoh residents claimed they had refused the army's guns.

Initial trials were so successful that the new President, General Ríos Montt (1982-1983) expanded the system to virtually every highland township *(municipio)*; by this time, all Indian villages were considered subversive although some were considered more so than others. Civil defense patrols were promoted with a fanfare of publicity in the government controlled media. A promotional booklet, published by the government in 1982, describes patrollers as "having organized themselves with minimal hierarchy ...to repel terrorist attacks" but a secret army document circulated in the same year disproves these claims (America's Watch 1986:19). The hierarchy was anything but minimal:[6] patrols were fully supervised and controlled through a military-style hierarchy by each army command (McClintock 1985).

The barrage of disinformation masked the scheme's coercive nature. Government rhetoric insistently described the patrols as a 'spontaneous expression of patriotism', an opportunity for the 'ordinary citizen' to police and eradicate 'subversive elements'. Its 'spontaneous' nature can be gauged by the fact that the government even wrote the Civil Patrol Code of Conduct — in Spanish: one wonders who its intended readers were. (Item ten reads "I will respect community customs and traditions as well as the civil and military authorities" (America's Watch 1986:100), an implausible combination.) Throughout its remaining years in power, the military regime persisted in its claims that the system was independent of official structures. The official line was that the patrol system's 'spontaneous' and 'unofficial' nature precluded the necessity of giving it legal status; the dictatorship considered the 'war' situation sufficient authority for their creation. In reality, the lack of formal decree or law defining civil patrols' roles and responsibilities was to its advantage and "[t]he civil patrol system became the cornerstone of military control over Indian communities, in-so-far as it organized (and continues to organize) Indian communities into paramilitary forces under direct military command" (Smith 1990b:272).

The military state also offered inducements: amnesty was offered to rural 'subversives' in early 1982 on condition that they returned to their villages and joined the patrols. Further 'hands off' support was given to the scheme by extending the 'beans and bullets' programme[7] to communities with successful patrols; villagers saw few of the former and plenty of the latter. They were unimpressed with the government's offer: they heard the threat behind the words. Nevertheless, many returned.

During General Ríos Montt's short presidency, numbers rose rapidly from 25,000 to 700,000 men and continued to rise under his successor, General Oscar Humberto Mejía Victores (1983-1986), who extended the scheme throughout rural Guatemala. When a civilian president was elected in 1985, an estimated one million men were serving in the patrols nationwide (America's Watch 1986); in other words, 10 percent of Guatemala's total population (McClintock 1985) was under direct military supervision. The department with the most extensive patrol network (with an estimated 86,000 members) was El Quiché which, like other areas with extensive systems, has a high concentration of Indian villages.

The elections weakened the military's hold on the national psyche and prompted the resignation or flight of many patrol *jefes* involved in the atrocities which accompanied the establishment of the system. Installed in January 1986, the civilian president, Vinicio Cerezo Arévalo, confirmed the army's self-declared amnesty; he knew prosecuting the guilty would be political suicide. Perhaps unconvinced by previous government 'amnesties', fleeing highland *jefes* generally stayed in hiding for two or three years. Although returning *jefes* feared vengeance from their victims' relatives (and posted guards on their homes to protect themselves), many resumed their now doubly illicit authority behind the scenes, working through their successors. They "still have their little ways," said Saturnino, whose father and several other male relatives had been killed by the *jefes*; "they do not respect the community." Even stripping *jefes* of their rifles (as happened in Emol in 1992) has had little impact on their power.

The army met Cerezo's attempts to fulfill his campaign promise to confront its opposition to reform with fierce, if underhand, resistance. International human rights organizations documented systematic human rights violations and a serious deterioration of the political situation. There were more assassinations and abductions in 1987 than in 1985 (Infopress Centroamérica [IC], 21 January 1988). The trend accelerated in 1988 and 1989, when the army attempted to reassert its authority in earnest, both nationally and locally: the army is suspected of being behind the right wing coup attempts of the late 1980s and the resumed activities of local death squads (Amnesty International 1989; America's Watch 1988, 1989).

In 1988, as the country became increasingly unstable, Cerezo renamed the patrol system to emphasize its voluntary nature[8] — a hollow compromise between his campaign promise to guarantee villagers the right to vote on whether or not to keep the patrols and the army's successful resistance to the idea. Within a year, 7,000 men (less than one percent of all patrollers) were resisting patrol duty, despite retribution — a new round of assassination, kidnapping, intimidation, etc. (Jonas 1991:185). A few communities disbanded the system although it was (and in some areas, still is) dangerous for patrollers and especially *jefes* to be seen to be attempting to circumvent the military's intentions; those who do so show great courage. Emol retained all its patrols until 1992; two hamlets still have them.

The emptiness of the gesture was exposed the following year, by which time violence had escalated sharply, prompting fears of a return to *la violencia*: the civilian government allowed the military to re-equip communities which had retained their patrols.[9] For some patrols, the number of working weapons doubled overnight (Emol and three of its five hamlets received their new rifles in early 1990).[10] The distribution of modern, effective weapons at a time when the political situation was becoming increasingly volatile terrified so-called subversive communities who had been issued very few rifles, or none at all, when the patrols were first established. The iniquitous labelling of settlements as 'loyal' or 'subversive' thus persists to the present. In the early 1990s, differences between communities have been further emphasized by the tendency to allocate government and army sponsored development schemes to places which retain their patrols.

By 1996, mounting pressure to disband the patrols was met with the usual military resistance. The solution was the customary tactic of re-organizing and renaming the offending institution: patrols are now called 'Committees for Peace and Development' (chapter one) — the 'beans and bullets' programme in new guise. It has been said that the new title is intended to pull the wool over the eyes of the international community, which does not realize that the army has yet to relinquish control over the patrol system. Knowing the army's definition of 'peace', villagers greeted the news with incredulity. Few expect the planned 'dismantling' of the patrols, announced on 24 June 1996, to have much effect on local power relations.[11] This has had the unfortunate effect of reducing faith in the Peace Accords, of which dismantling the patrols was an integral part.

Despite over a decade of civilian rule, the patrol system remains the military's main local-level political weapon. Even where it has been disbanded, lapsed patrollers are left with the disturbing knowledge that not only could they be forced to reinstate the patrols but they could also be forced to commit further atrocities. Many indigenous men learnt more about what they are capable of, or can be forced to do, than they ever wanted to find out.

Instituting the Patrols

Trials of the patrol system began at the height of *la violencia*, at a time when a few thousand poorly armed guerrillas seemed about to gain control of the western highlands. The mountains swarmed with government troops who, unable pin down the elusive guerrilla, turned their attention to unarmed villages. The resulting extreme insecurity, deprivation of basic necessities such as food and safe shelter, not to mention the threat of loss of life itself, prepared the ground for the institution of the patrols. Conditions deteriorated to such an extent that Indians were easily victimized.

Within this chaos, the military selected villages for inclusion in the experiment; softened by repeated assaults (chapter four), they were then occupied. This effectively separated and isolated the community from its neighbours, denying residents a reference point from which to judge normality and giving the army a free hand to manipulate reality. This was merely the first step in a series of separations and forced choices[12] designed to destroy any remaining feelings of 'communitas' (Turner 1969) and undermine personal autonomy.[13] Each separation isolated villagers further until people hardly dared to trust anyone but themselves.

Once the community had been subdued and its inhabitants had returned from their hiding places in the ravines, the local army commander and his delegates from the psychological warfare branch began combing the village for suitable intermediaries. Thinking soldiers were only looking for the 'guerrillas' who had given the village its bad name, dazed and terrified villagers identified the usual suspects — catechists, health workers, teaching assistants, members of the Peasants' League or Catholic Action, non-Protestant community leaders, personal enemies, and their relatives. Suspects' kin were included because, until *la violencia* shattered family solidarity, people were identified by their household or extended family rather than as individuals with their own allegiances. The fear generated by having a dead or disappeared relative among one's kin is driven by the residuals of this traditional way of identifying and placing others. It was a time of multiple betrayals and these betrayals have scarred the community more than the deaths themselves.

Villagers' reactions to the horror visited on their communities helped the army to identify suitable candidates for the new role of civil patrol chief *(jefe)*. The choice of mediator was pivotal to the scheme's success; they were to become the village's new authorities but, at least during initial trials, neither they nor their fellow villagers were aware of this. In some places, the army sought recommendations from influential community members known to support the army (cf. Stoll 1993:183); in others, military commissioners sympathetic to the army selected *jefes*. Perhaps their recommendations would have been different if they had understood what the men's roles were to be. In areas of particular unrest, the army chose all levels of *jefes*. At start-up, villages had between four and ten *jefes*; the number depended on alleged subversiveness more than population size. Emol had nine.

Having selected their intermediaries and despatched them to a nearby army base for three month's training, the occupying force turned their attention to remaining villagers. An army *oficial*[14] informed them that they could save themselves from further death and destruction by volunteering to form civil defense patrols to protect themselves from the guerrillas and other subversives supposedly lurking in every corner of the village. Faced with a detachment of heavily armed soldiers who had already tortured and killed in the village and looked as if they would not hesitate to kill again, most men rapidly complied. Unless they managed to escape in time, resisters were shot or, if they were lucky, merely slung into jail. Emol's tiny jails were full of patrol resisters while common criminals walked free.[15]

Villagers had no option but to comply with the army's demands if they wanted to stay alive. Both negative incentive (literal survival) and forced

choice worked against passivity and stimulated villagers' active co-operation. Villagers 'chose'[16] to form patrols rather than trust their fate to the
army. They had no alternative as any lack of co-operation was met with
force; the futility of resistance led people to submit to coercion, thus creating
a new form of authority (Barnard 1968). At the time, villagers had no idea
what they were being coerced into and with hindsight, many people regret
'deciding' to comply. Years later, Emoltecos likened army attacks to unpredictable, destructive tornados: one lives in dread of them but there are
periods of respite in between. There was to be no respite from the patrol
system, especially for widows with no male protection.

Formed into units *(pelotón)* of between fifteen and thirty men, patrollers
were told to choose a leader from among themselves. This was the only part
of the charade which was voluntary: all village men between the ages of fifteen and fifty-five were obliged to join. Even the developmentally delayed
and the physically handicapped were inducted into the patrols; only the most
incapacitated are excused.[17] Fear of falling foul of the army and, later, of
local *jefes*, was so high that old men and ten year old boys joined the patrols,
sometimes with disastrous results; whilst I was in El Quiché, one boy acci-
dentally shot and killed another. Sometimes the under-age sons and elderly
fathers of known activists who had fled the community were forcibly inducted into the patrols as hostages; this happened *doña* Eugenia's fourteen
year old grandson Martín when his father, Gilberto, went into hiding.

Continuing with the theme of separation and isolation, patrollers were
ordered to build a patrol base *(destacamento)* in the village centre and
mobile outposts *(garitas)* which could be moved from place to place as required. Barriers were erected on the roads connecting village hamlets and on
the isolated tracks to the mountains; initially staffed by armed soldiers, these
checkpoints isolated villagers both from each other and from the outside
world, giving the army and its local cohorts control of the dissemination of
information and disinformation and so maintaining high levels of terror.
Strangers, which could even mean villagers walking between hamlets or
even married daughters resident in neighbouring villages visiting their parents, were interrogated about their destination, the purpose of their visit, and
length of stay. Genuine strangers were a rarity.

The patrols also enforce an unofficial curfew: anyone out after dark —
night falls quickly around six o'clock — is suspected of 'organizing'. Most
catechism meetings, literacy classes, and political gatherings had taken place
when the day's work finished at nightfall but such activities had usually been
suspended by the time the army entered a village. The blanket ban on night
movement primarily affected the weak and vulnerable: women in need of
midwives, the sick in need of healers, the dying in want of the rituals only
a traditional diviner (aj q'ij) can perform. Surviving aj q'ij were particularly
hard hit by the curfew which prevented them performing night time rituals
at secluded locations in the nearby hills.

I was told that one former Kotoh *jefe*, whose patrollers were unarmed, ordered his men to kill everyone walking down the hamlet access road at night by hitting them over the head. This hand-to-hand killing was a 'punishment' of both the victims and the perpetrators, for whom murdering people they knew well was not only a torment but has long term consequences in this world and the next (chapter eight). Their *jefe* had no such qualms about shooting anyone who survived his subordinates' assault. I was told, "The ones they didn't kill were obviously their friends *(compañeros)*." A former Kotoh patroller told me of the murder of a local family who tried to flee when the patrols were first established:

> [Patrollers from Emol Central]...hid near the road and kidnapped everyone walking along it...one woman tried to plead with the patrollers not to take them away [kidnap and kill them] and she even offered them her body... Why did she do this? To save her life but they only violated her and then killed her. And she was pregnant. First they killed the others [by shooting them], then they raped her and then they killed her when she was only trying to save her life.

I heard many similar stories and such atrocities were still taking place in neighbouring villages when I was in the area several years later; by then, victims were usually patrol resisters and members of human rights organizations such as CERJ, GAM, and CONAVIGUA. I found it difficult to associate the patrollers I saw outside Emol Central's patrol base with any action, let alone atrocities: sitting with their rifles slung over their shoulders, they stared vacuously into space, only their fingers busy plaiting straw fronds *(trenzas)*. Most murders occur at night; patrollers are rarely bold enough to do their kidnapping and killing in daylight.

Corralling villagers inside the new boundaries was more important than keeping others out, though few people dared to visit a community so clearly labelled 'subversive'. In at least the first year of the system's operation, hardly anyone dared to leave to follow the customary practice of labour migration in order to earn the household's meagre cash income. Later, as people learnt to accommodate the system, labour migration resumed though absent patrollers not only had to obtain the permission of the new village authorities but supply a substitute in their stead. Some men sent their young sons or elderly fathers; some paid other men to do their shifts for them.

Psychological isolation is added to physical isolation. (The use of the present tense is intentional: the mechanisms of terror invoked by the patrols has persisted beyond their supposed dissolution fifteen years later; in 1996, a third of all men eligible for duty were still patrolling). Patrollers work twenty-four hour shifts every four to ten days (the shorter the rota, the more subversive the army deemed the community to be). Separating men from their families and customary social networks encourages identification[18] with their *pelotón*, the patrol system, and the army; together with sleep deprivation, this reduces men's resistance to orders contrary to cultural and personal values as they operate in more normal times, making them more amenable to army propaganda and indoctrination (cf. Sapir and Croker 1977).

Patrollers' day to day duties — becoming the army's eyes and ears, placing the whole community under surveillance *(control)*, reporting (betraying) what they see and hear to their *jefes* — not only reinforces men's separation from conventional social relationships but undermines those relationships. Normal social interaction came to a grinding halt as people realized that where they went, who they talked to, etc., is constantly monitored by the patrols. Constant *control* also affected the subsistence sphere: men found it difficult to work land they owned in other hamlets; women found themselves challenged when they went to the surrounding hills to pasture their animals or to forage for fodder, firewood, and herbs. But even more pernicious is patrollers' unwitting role in the destruction of family life: the scheme forces them into a situation where they cannot avoid being the link between the public and private spheres, mediating between the army and their own households. Patrollers provide the army with a spy and an enforcer in every home and hence control over it (female headed households are an obvious exception, at least until their sons are old enough to patrol).

More important from the army's point of view was the survival of the patrol system following the soldiers' departure. Villagers had expected the army to leave when the *jefes* returned and that life would return to some semblance of normality. They were wrong. No one seems to know what the *jefes'* three months' training entailed, but separating them from their cultural inhibitions concerning the expression of violence clearly played an important part. People say that on return from training, the *jefes* were 'fierce' *(bravos)*, an attribute contrary to Mayan cultural and behavioural norms of respect.

The *jefes* were escorted to their villages by soldiers who publicly installed them in office and then remained on hand for six months to provide what can euphemistically be called 'on the job' training to ensure that they were sufficiently brutal. It was during this probationary period that the worst local violence occurred. Army-instigated, high profile atrocities compromised *jefes vis-à-vis* the rest of 'their' communities and obliged them to remain loyal to the army — *jefes* cannot resign without engendering life-threatening suspicions about their loyalty. *Jefes* unable to hide their repugnance for their duties were disappeared and replaced.

Eventually the soldiers left, leaving patrol *jefes* in charge. Emoltecos say that one thousand villagers, a third of the village's population, had been killed or kidnapped between the initial army attacks in late 1981 and its departure in mid-1982; this level of population loss is not unusual in the highlands. In Emol and elsewhere, the deaths continued as the *jefes* re-affirmed their army-given power. They were assisted (or, in some instances, monitored and supervised) by military commissioners and Presidents of local Improvement Committees sympathetic to the army. There are no hard and fast rules about who is in charge: power at the local level depends more on the individual history and personality of the particular villager as his position (this is evidenced by the fact that the power of many commissioners and *jefes* was unaffected by the abolition of their posts in 1995 and 1996 respectively). Although the *jefes* normally takes the lead, sometimes the military commissioner is the most brutal. In the vast majority of cases, both use their authority and access to the army to abuse the local population. Idiosyncratic factors such as whether the *jefe* has done his military service — most have no previous connection with the army — play a part in the anomalous power relations between *jefe* and commissioner. In Emol, the patrol hierarchy was obscured and one man had assumed the role of *jefe* of the village's patrols; he worked together with the military commissioner (who was subordinate to him at the time of my fieldwork) and the President of the village Improvement Committee;[19] they became Emol's 'new authorities'.

The army expects *jefes* to keep each other and their communities (including patrollers) in line but rarely concerns itself with the ways that personal domination takes place at the local level. To the military, the patrols whether in their original form or their new guise, are simply a means to an end — bringing Indians under national, military control. In the process, many elders who survived the initial army onslaught were killed by their successors, the *jefes*. Among other things, elders are the repositories of history and ritual; connections with the past and certain kinds of access to the ancestors died with them. Traditionalist diviners (aj q'ij) were another frequent target; although the army had not recognized their importance, local *jefes* were aware of aj q'ij's religious authority and the respect accorded to them by villagers. They knew that villagers would be demoralized by not being able to perform life crisis rituals or obtain rituals of protection. Six male aj q'ij were killed in Emol; the remainder joined the patrols with the rest of the men. Also targeted were other surviving community leaders such as health workers, teaching assistants, and local Catholic Action leaders.

Villagers were deliberately left with nowhere to turn for protection on any level. Supra-communal links created through the catechist movement and popular organizations had been destroyed not only by the formation of the patrols but by the army's fomentation of the traditional suspicion of and hostility towards neighbouring communities. This was fostered through the issue of weapons: 'loyal' communities (such as Emol Central) were given enough rifles — outdated army surplus — to arm the duty patrol; particularly 'subversive' communities were given none at all. In Kotoh, only the *jefes* were armed, enabling them to terrorize and massacre fellow villagers. In other places, villagers were forced to buy guns from the army, each family or patrol unit seriously impoverishing itself by contributing to the purchase. The inadequacy of the arms provided (in quality and numbers) means that many men patrol armed with machetes, sticks or hand-carved replica guns, leaving their communities vulnerable to attack from better armed neighbouring villages.[20] The army ensured that animosity remains high between villages by using patrollers as shock troops in raids against such unarmed 'guerrilla' villages. Separation from the outside world, initiated by army occupation, is maintained through the patrols who continue the army strategy of exacerbating local factionalism within and between villages. Many patrollers are too busy saving their own skins and settling old scores to realize that the army has succeeded in its desire to shatter any feelings of Mayan solidarity almost beyond redemption.

Less familiar sources of support also disappeared during *la violencia*. Even the rural administration, established by the military dictatorship in 1954, was suspended between 1981 and 1985. Elected mayors were deposed (or, like the Indian mayor of Santa Cruz del Quiché, assassinated) and replaced by army appointees. Power, formerly based on age and prestige and enforced through social sanction, is now based on violence and memories of violence.

The military state had set out to deprive rural Indians of their autonomy and, through the institution of the patrols, largely succeeded. The chronic fear, hunger, and exhaustion of the start up period — the duty rota interfered with men's ability to farm their own land, much of which needed remedial work following army bombardment — deprived men of their autonomy. The humiliation of not being able to protect and provide for their families — the traditional practice of providing economic and labour support for widowed kin was abandoned as men were forced to concentrate on their immediate interests[21] — led to anger and resentment, which some men took out on their wives (cf. Manz 1988:78). These factors contributed to a loss of identity as a male, Indian agriculturalist associated with locality.[22]

Having set in motion the conditions to create patrollers' feelings of alienation, the army and its local cohorts proceeded to manipulate them, promoting the patrols, with their emphasis on violence, as a new space for the reassertion of male dominance. The military dictatorship also offered its (voluntary and forcibly enrolled) followers a new, tenuous identity through identification with the Guatemalan state and an equally suspect self-respect through its ideology of the superior, military/*ladino* race. Such satisfactions are said to be necessary for the state to gain complete external control of the individual without bringing about his immediate and utter disintegration. Identification also provides a sense of connection and support (Staub 1989): the patroller's alliance with the *jefes*, like the *jefes'* alliance with army *oficiales*, shatters his solidarity with his own social group and reinforces his active co-operation with the military (Walter 1969:286-7). For some persecuted, weak, and vulnerable villagers, attachment to the powerful army fulfills a frustrated need to belong and provides feelings of control (Staub 1989). These identifications are as flimsy as the obligatory uniforms patrollers wear on duty: a straw hat, painted green or camouflage, and a tee-shirt stamped with the local patrol emblem, their company number and the name of their community.

Joining the Patrols

Patrollers' Motivation

The startling rapidity with which highland Indians were absorbed into the patrols was primarily activated by fear. People's fear of arbitrary victimage was exacerbated by the army's psychological games. First, villagers had to be taught what a 'subversive' was. Many people told me that they had not heard the word before the army accused them of being one. In Emol, villagers of all political and religious affiliations were shaken by the assignment of the 'subversive' label, from which they wished to escape; membership of popular movements rapidly lost whatever positive identity it had had. Located in the war zone between rebel and national armies, their position was precarious: the army labelled anyone suspected, for even the flimsiest of reasons, of collaborating with the guerrillas as 'subversive' and the guerrillas deemed anyone not co-operating with them 'army collaborators'.

Next, villagers had to be convinced of the seriousness of the guerrilla threat. They were warned of the peril of the continued presence of 'subversives' such as men who opposed the establishment of patrols or refused to participate in the system. Particularly recalcitrant men were killed or disappeared. Even men who complied but without the requisite amount of enthusiasm — by not keeping strict hours, for example — were tortured or killed by the rest of the group who feared collective punishment from higher up the system. Lesser punishments included stints in jail or public humiliation through being forced to undertake nonsensical tasks such as carrying rocks from one place to another and back again. This type of punishment is particularly galling as one of the strongest K'iche' values is to work hard and not waste time doing things 'just for the sake of it' *(por gusto)*.

Indians' general ignorance of their rights in the world beyond their immediate areas contributed to their co-operation with the system. Most men joined under the mistaken impression that they were legally required to do so, although the legality or otherwise of the system is irrelevant when one is faced with the overwhelming brute force of the army. Most men continued to patrol even when it became general knowledge within indigenous communities that participation really is voluntary under the constitution. This says more about continuing levels of fear than it does about support for the army; it also points to the irrelevance of the Constitution to Indian life — despite the many 'good things' written in it, the legal system still does not operate for them.

Cultural values, especially the high value placed on conformity, play an important part in men's compliance. The importance of conformity is inculcated from early childhood; deviation from the idealized village mean is considered threatening and can provoke jealousy and anger which is usually expressed in hidden aggression (cf. Foster 1979:137). Overt ideological differentiation in indigenous communities began following the introduction of 'new' catholicism (chapter two) and this, according to many villagers, ultimately led to the army's devastating onslaught. Severely battered by the softening up process, villagers sought any means to protect themselves, one of which was conforming to the army's demands.

The negative aspects of the extreme emphasis on conformity in the K'iche' socialization process became glaringly apparent during *la violencia*. Its potential to result in outward conformity and inner alienation — a combination which has been identified with the potentially assaultive, over-controlled person (Zimbardo 1969) — was realized as fear of others' failure to comply intensified pressure within the community. Culturally induced denial and repression of and unresponsiveness to hostility, even in the face of extreme provocation, suddenly snaps; extremely aggressive behaviour results — in this instance, dramatic demonstrations that they had never been on the 'enemy's' side. This analysis applies not only to particularly brutal patrollers and *jefes* but to K'iche' society as a whole.

The importance of conformity to community norms can be gauged by the fate of men who responded to the amnesty which was part of the promotional package accompanying the introduction of the patrol system. Returnees discovered to their cost that their flight had confirmed their non-conformism, their 'otherness', and, ultimately, their 'subversiveness'. So labelled, returnees were not only 'enemies of the state' but 'enemies' of the community; most were massacred by fellow villagers afraid of being criminalized and hence attacked on account of tolerating the presence of such dangerous 'guerrillas' in their midst. The incredible intra-communal violence within K'iche' communities in the early 1980s can be partially understood in terms of the creation of this 'enemy' in fulfillment of the military's ideology. The killing of K'iche's by K'iche's is the reification of an ideology on the bodies of its victims. The result was the creation of a pervasive sense of terror which became part of the everydayness of life.

Obedience to authority is another major K'iche' cultural value which is so entrenched that many people prefer the terror of the new authority structure to the chaos of none at all (the abhorrence for disorder is evidenced by the fact the same word (ch'u' jiaj anón) is applied to *la violencia*). As a former patroller explained, this was exploited by the army:[23]

> The army came to threaten the *jefes* of the civil patrols. They told us to pluck out the rotten apple from the community so that it would not contaminate the rest. They told us that if we didn't, it would indicate to them that we were also guerrillas. So the patrols did it to avoid being killed themselves. But the fact is that many of the victims had no connections with the guerrillas.

Showing respect for authority is another important value which has been inculcated since the Spanish invasion, if not before. This too can work against Indians' own interests in a terror situation: a culturally induced respect for authority can join with governmental propaganda and repression in creating uniform views about events (Staub 1989:65). People who grow up in an authoritarian culture can have difficulty in assuming responsibility for their own lives (Fromm 1965); consequently, men acquiesced not only from fear but also from well-worn codes of respect. Some men's (and many *jefes'*) deep need to identify with strong authority results in behaviour which exhibits a curious amalgam of the cult of obedience and complete lack of control: the destruction of world views (as happened in *la violencia*) freed them from traditional restraints whilst simultaneously offering untrammelled authority, if within parameters defined by the army.

But there are different types of respect just as there are, or were, different types of authority. Within rural communities, respect is traditionally given to one's elders in general and to men who have risen through the gerontocratic hierarchy in particular. *Jefes* try to utilize this imbued respect by appealing to the K'iche' value of behaving as a respectful Indian by serving the community (through carrying out patrol duty); they present themselves as being dedicated to the community, perhaps even believing it (it will be even easier to present this façade if one is a *jefe* of a Peace and Development Committee). But the *jefes'* alignment with the army brings them within the ambit of the 'respect' given to *ladinos*, towards whom most Indians present a silent, deferential face (cf. Hobsbawn 1973:13). *Jefes* recognize this mask. While some enjoy this oblique confirmation of their *ladino* status and power, others are reminded that their power is not legitimately grounded in the community but rests solely on external support and, formerly, the power of the gun. The respect *jefes* receive, even from their own patrollers, is based on fear, not esteem.

Jefes' Motivation

At the outset, *jefes* had no idea what the job entailed although they knew it would bring some reward: for those who feared death, it promised life; for those who sought power, it brought status.

Personal safety was a common motive: the post offered the victimized Indian hope of defence against further attack. Former guerrillas or guerrilla sympathizers who feared for their lives welcomed the role, at least initially. They saw it as a means of regaining social acceptance: in theory, the terrified ex-guerrilla could surrender to the army, express true repentance by providing the names of fellow members of the same popular organization and becoming a *jefe*; in practice, it is almost impossible to shake off the guerrilla label. Ultimately, local factionalism determines whether 'guerrillas' survive or not.

For former guerrillas and known supporters, becoming a *jefe* was a safer option in terms of long term survival than being a patroller. A few did volunteer, although forced choice ensured that men who had not done so did not reject selection: the line between volunteering and being selected is not as distinct as might, *prima facie*, appear. Some former guerrillas had personal reasons for their willingness to betray their former colleagues such as dissatisfaction with the level of power allotted to them by the guerrilla. As one Chichicastenango *jefe* told 'his' community, "I used to be the guerrilla's mother, now I'm the army's" (America's Watch 1986:35). In other instances, the successful power of the army in defeating the insurgents had such appeal for insecure guerrillas that it became internalized as their standards and values (as interpreted by individual K'iche'). In a village near Emol, two former guerrillas who became *jefes* terrorized the local population (and probably still do): one denounced villagers as subversives and asked the army for permission to bring them in to the army base (from which no suspected subversive ever reappears); the other had become a serial rapist and boasted about how many people he had killed since becoming *jefe*. Many *jefes* who originally resented the army's control over them were unable to resist the tremendous appeal of the military's power (Staub 1989).

For many *jefes* the main attraction of the post is the prospect of exerting power over fellow villagers. These are men whose hunger for power excedes their ability to achieve it either through traditional means or the new opportunities offered by NGOs or the popular movements. Men who had previously sought power through illicit means such as sorcery welcome the new means of regaining control over clients who had converted to protestantism; some also welcome the change from earning an income to being able to expropriate labour, goods, and services from villagers.

Power is sought by and granted to the frustrated, to men who crave authority and are willing to venerate hierarchic authority in order to obtain it: the immediate power of a rifle and the ability to evoke fear in fellow villagers is a more than satisfactory compensation for all the years of disrespect. Even *jefes* who are aware that the job is fundamentally despicable cling to the advantages of the appointment because it confers the most authority within the new social structure.

Power is also sought by many of the oppressed who unconsciously strive to identify with their oppressors. For *jefes*, 'identification with the oppressor'[24] is bound by, or oscillates with, an identification with the oppressed; although token *ladinos*, *jefes* are still Indians, some of whom had been literally beaten into shape before being allowed to assume their posts. When performing their role as *jefes*, they identify with the army and its objectives — they are the saviours and protectors who kill for the public good. In their own eyes (and those of the army), their behaviour is seen as moral and righteous, a common belief among mass killers (Staub 1989). Army indoctrination causes *jefes* (and through them, patrollers) to identify with their aggressors and commit themselves to the cause they fought for. Villagers' identification with the aggressor makes them, like their oppressors, genuinely fear the guerrilla; indeed, as described by the army, the guerrilla is a frightening prospect (see Figures 1 and 2). The military state's description of the subversive is based on customary *ladino* definitions and cultural devaluation of the Indian, not that Indians recognize themselves in the resultant caricature. The basic *ladino* stereotype of the Indian as unworthy and inferior is then expressed in terms of anti-communist ideology, which the military use to define groups challenging the *status quo*.[25] The army cynically translates this as meaning anything and everything antithetical to the way of life they have done their best to undermine. The military deliberately maintains high levels of fear by, for example, incessantly producing and reproducing the fear of being infiltrated and overrun by 'bandits' or 'devils' (i.e., subversives, communists or guerrillas), constantly alluding to the perils inherent in their return. Taking their cue from the army, *jefes* see 'guerrillaness' as spreading like a disease.

Other men welcomed the role as a means of reclassifying themselves as *ladino*, appropriating the *ladino's* power *vis-à-vis* Indians for themselves. This self-identification encourages *jefes* to abuse and exploit fellow villagers as they themselves had been exploited by *ladinos*, including faux *ladinos* such as soldiers, in the past. Like everyone else in their communities, *jefes* have had many opportunities to observe *ladino* behaviour towards Indians; what is different about *jefes* is their readiness to seize the opportunity offered by their new post to imitate soldiers' intense aggression against their relatives and neighbours.

The assumption of a *ladino* identity gives access to a different view of humanity which categorizes Indians as a sub-human species. By casting his lot with the army, the *jefe* can see himself as 'more' human than his fellow villagers; over time, as he becomes increasingly separated from 'his' community, a *jefe* comes to see himself simply as 'human'. This has ramifications with regard to a *jefe's* treatment of the patrollers under his command. Unlike the undifferentiated mass of villagers, the position of patrollers is ambiguous. They are simultaneously part of the *jefe's* team and 'other': his claim to be a *'ladino'* rests on their obedience to his command, yet they are his relatives. Such artificially constructed dichotomies resulted in the *jefe's* unpredictable behaviour towards the people of 'his' community: frantic switching from camaraderie and affection to violent abuse and punishment was typical of *jefes* installed when the patrols were established. *Jefes* became the terror of their communities because, like the fascist or torturer, they can turn their identity into violence and pain at random (Taussig 1987:3-72). The power of the role led to greater devaluation and cruelty towards the 'other' (Zimbardo et al. 1974). A widow explained that part of the problem was that

...not all of them were used to authority. They had never held such a position and they did not know how to handle it. They believed they had many 'tasks' to carry out. They steal, they rape women, they mug people. And what's more they don't care who they rob or rape...be they elders, women or children, they don't care. They are killers.

That the patrol *jefe* is always on duty is probably more significant. Unlike his men, who patrol a maximum of one day in four, the *jefes* can be called out at any time; his gun is always to hand. Thus even when he returns home to his role as an Indian agriculturalist and household head, he is still, at some level, always the *jefe*. The oscillation between his role as an adjunct to the *ladino* military and the 'off-stage' world of the Indian (where he may have to answer for his behaviour in the former) tends to collapse as the *jefe* becomes increasingly distant from his community through the performance of his role. In the process, men experience confusion, self doubt, and, perhaps, self hatred; this is evidenced, for example, by surreptitious visits to aj q'ij to confess their sins and seek rituals of protection. One aj q'ij told me he has *jefes*, patrollers, and soldiers among his clients.

Not all *jefes* take the opportunity to wallow in their antisocial desires. A few *jefes* help their villagers by, for example, securing the release of non-compliant patrollers from jail, turning a blind eye, giving a helping hand or failing to report people out of friendship, goodness of heart, or calculated self-interest (cf. Carmack 1988; Stoll 1993). One *jefe*, a former member of the local Peasants League, helps village women whose husbands had been disappeared. Others who want to help find their wishes frustrated: for example, *jefes* who did not want to kill fellow villagers acceded to village-level decisions that a few people should be killed to prevent the destruction of the whole community (cf. Carmack 1988:63). But it cannot be assumed that all *jefes* (or military commissioners) who help their communities are former radicals, although most of them are: *jefes*' different roles in life affected their perception of the post but not necessarily their execution of it.[26]

Many men merely comply with the dangerous authorities rather than take on their agendas as their own; they merely want to "make it through the night" (America's Watch 1986:47); however, it is very difficult to stay alive and unchanged inwardly, for efforts to avoid change endanger lives (Bettelheim 1986:127). Survival in terror situations depends on a certain flexibility; the question for reluctant patrollers is how much they internalize the roles whilst wearing the mask (cf. Scott 1985). *Jefes* who are neither pro-military nor ambitious are presented with tremendous dilemmas and little reward; yet their compliance, however reluctant, reinforces their position as accessories to and accomplices in military atrocity. Co-opted catechists and health workers are more likely to be in this category.

Emol's *jefes* exhibit a mixture of all these motives in various combinations. They also come from a variety of backgrounds: Emol Central's *jefes* are former *costumbristas* who converted to protestantism: one is a former aj q'ij and another is a former sorcerer (*brujo*; aj itz). Remaining *costum-*

bristas, now mostly found in other hamlets, see these men's assumption of the role as a double betrayal. One of Kotoh's *jefes* is a known former guerrilla, a circumstance which causes great fear amongst the formerly 'organized'. Several *jefes* are related to one another, allowing a couple of families to run large parts of the village as their own personal fiefdom, creating a network of power which survives the eclipse of the patrol system.

Mario: Emol's Most Feared Jefe

Mario is the *de facto* head of the village's patrol system and the only one of Emol's original *jefes* to remain in power following the 1985 elections. Mario demonstrated his power and fearlessness (or perhaps merely his psychopathic tendencies) by staying put when his colleagues fled. He lives in the most conservative of the village's hamlets, Emol Central, which he controls with the aid of two former *jefes* who are his brothers-in-law. Another brother-in-law is a former Kotoh *jefe*.

When I met him in 1988, Mario was about fifty years old. He is noticeably different from Emol's other *jefes*, whether installed in 1982 or 1985. Especially distinctive is his demeanour and way of strutting round the village in his scruffy clothes — the second hand cast-offs worn by most Indian men are in notably better condition — and, sometimes, an old pair of army boots. He does not wear the uniform; everyone knows who he is.

Mario is taller and more brawny than the average Indian, and people describe him as even larger (cf. Watson 1971); his size leads to scurrilous jokes about his parentage (*ladinos* are generally larger than Indians). Some women suggest that, like soldiers, he eats more meat than the ordinary Indian. This is a macabre pun. Mario, now a Protestant, is a former *costumbrista* and sorcerer *(brujo)*; at night, *brujos* turn themselves into spirit animals which 'eat' (kill) people;[27] as a *jefe*, Mario has certainly 'eaten' many villagers, often at night. To speaker and listener, this association brings to mind other aspects of witchcraft (*brujería*; itzel) such as *brujos'* power to cause demons to enter others (patrollers, for example) who then abduct people and rape women. Beliefs in spirit invasion help to account for the noticeable lack of antipathy towards off-duty patrollers: blame for local atrocities is almost always placed on the *jefes*, especially Mario. The army may see him as their mediator but to many Emoltecos, Mario is the mediator of the devil. Women describe him as someone 'whose wisdom is evil' (itz'el u no'j). Mario's reputation as a *brujo* predates his appointment as *jefe* and probably reflects villagers' assessment of his anti-social nature. In some areas, *jefes'* power comes from villagers' implicit permission for them to take over *brujos'* malevolent powers.

The venom and fear Mario inspires in widows and the venom which he himself exercises against his fellow Indians are also unique. Women notice how similar Mario is to the military in both his behaviour and attitudes towards 'humble Indians' *(humildes)*; they suggest he has added the military

agenda which he learnt as *jefe* to his own which has always been different
from that of the ordinary Indian. But Mario is impervious to the hatred he
engenders in widows who claim he is still a sorcerer and that he had had
pretensions to authority when he was only a *brujo*. The following conversation is representative of women's malicious gossip concerning him, and
expresses their antipathy towards him and the women associated with him:

Doña Flora:
> You know they say that this old man *(viejo)* who is in charge of justice
> [Mario] went [had sexual relations] with the wife of another. He was doing
> lots of things with her...they say that there are three women with this wrinkled
> old man *(viejo arrugado)*.[28]

Doña Eugenia:
> Jesus! Jesus!

Doña Flora:
> And the woman [Mario's wife] has a female worker who lives with her.

Doña Eugenia:
> Ahh [she says with admiration].

Doña Flora:
> And the girl now has a baby.

Doña Eugenia:
> She already has a child?

Doña Flora:
> Yes, they say that the woman's [Mario's wife's] daughters-in-law taunt her,
> asking her who the father of the child is, but the wife denies it [that the child
> is Mario's] because it is convenient for her. And her boss (*patrona* [Mario's
> wife]) tells them not to bother the girl asking them, "Why are you inter-
> rogating her? She is my helper, she's the one who feeds my cows and sheep,
> you've no reason to ask her questions." She tells them, "I'm here to attend to
> her basic necessities", and she does all she can to block her servant from
> answering herself... I expect that the two of them are in cahoots.

Doña Flora leaves the implications hanging in the air. There are at least
two: that Mario's wife allows him to commit adultery with the girl or that
she is Mario's second 'wife' — generally only rich, *ladino* townsmen have
the power and money to do this and few are bold enough to keep both
women in the same house.

Villagers have no idea how Mario achieved his position and speculation
is rife. The most common interpretation is that Mario plotted to obtain the
position, using his powers as a *brujo* to obtain it; the implication is that

Mario lusts for power, a totally inappropriate desire in conventional K'iche' society. A few people suggest that Mario's somewhat disreputable air made him attractive to the army who recognized his capacities as a competent puppet. *Doña* Josefina's suggestion that "Mario had contempt for the poor and that is why he allied himself with the army" indicates recognition of the problem of class as opposed to race. On another occasion, *doña* Josefina hinted at political motives: "Mario killed them because he had a bit of money and because of this he didn't want to accept the other type of poor. This is what he did not want." The 'other type of poor' are not just literally paupers but members of various scapegoated groups — widows, Catholics, *costumbristas*, the landless, etc. Surviving relatives of victims of *la violencia* are among the poorest of the community and Mario apparently has no compunction about victimizing them further as difference violates K'iche' norms of balance and conformity. Thus Mario can justify (at least to himself) his continuing persecution of Kotoh, the hamlet which has both gained and lost the most over the past two decades.

Within a very limited sphere delineated by the army, Mario presents a façade of exerting his own will. His autonomy is largely based on self-deception, as *jefes* conceal "from themselves and others the social bases upon which their power...depends" (Bourdieu 1991:27). Mario came to share the army's twisted megalomaniacal illusions to such an extent that he sees himself as part of the military rather than dependent on them. His vision of himself is distorted by the fact that he and other *jefes* like him have accrued power over and above that of the civilian and supernatural authorities: an impotent judicial system coupled with a collapsed traditional authority structure created a power vacuum which men like Mario are happy to occupy.

Mario's illusions about his position have never been challenged and, although his behaviour is brutal and sadistic, he is smart enough not to go too far, i.e., not to commit an atrocity of such appallingness that it would unite the various village factions against him. Some *jefes* do cross this invisible line, prompting villagers to call in the army to rescue them from their *jefe*. Paradoxically, posing as the community's saviours restricts the army's atrocities rather than the *jefes'*. Although the army has been known to kill or disappear psychopathic *jefes*, what usually happens is that a big play is made of reprimanding the *jefe* in public while the real discussion between *oficial* and *jefe* takes place behind closed doors. So far as villagers are concerned, such incidents illustrate that the *jefe* is as subordinate to the army as they are. Some *jefes* are not so amenable to this message because of the strength of their identification with the army.

Mario readily identifies with army *oficiales* who, in the late 1980s, occasionally visited the village to speak about the need to continue with the patrols (not being in a position to speak with him, I was unable to ascertain if his identification with the powerful is deliberate, knowing or unconscious). I watched him imitate people whose power he desires — *ladinos* in general and the *ladino* army in particular. His identification with and imitation of soldiers is apt, as most soldiers' *ladino* status is, like his own, restricted to the job.[29] Most soldiers Mario meets are Indians from other ethnic groups and it is this element of difference which he relates to: the soldiers are no more like 'his' villagers than he believes himself to be.

Mario zealously endeavours to copy the behaviors and learn the cultural codes of *ladinos* and soldiers, not realizing that they do not necessarily overlap. He emulates their beliefs (he attends the evangelical church which has been associated with the military state since Ríos Montt's presidency), public ceremonies, gestures, and expressions; rituals of group identification and the use of a special language are common among perpetrators of terror (Gibson and Haritos-Fatouros 1986). Taking his cue from the army, Mario alleges that "human rights activists are killers"; in May 1989, he ordered a villager to kill five CERJ members on these grounds. The order was not carried out, although similar orders issued in nearby villages were and Emoltecos who belong to, or sympathize with, human rights organizations know this. At the time, the military-dominated civilian government was campaigning against CERJ and other human rights organizations with significant indigenous memberships. Mario had seen the videos of army organized national press conferences at which people described as 'guerrilla defectors' accused CERJ of links with the armed opposition. Army *oficiales* who promote the video in areas where CERJ is active warn villagers they will be killed unless they denounce CERJ organizers (America's Watch 1990). Mario shares the army's concern about CERJ which (among other things) helps parents, and especially widows, who want to keep their teenage sons out of the patrols.

As a consequence of his efforts to be a militarized *ladino*, Mario sees himself as his community's lord and saviour and, as such, appears to have no qualms about the atrocities he commits; he is even conceited about the fact that he takes army orders further than they were intended to go. He holds steadfast to the army's view that he is ridding the community of 'subversives' and 'bandits'; he is saving the nation *(la patria)* from the evils of a godless, alien, Marxist infiltration.[30]

Mario relishes his role; he loves authority and exercises it with devastating effect. His authority is facilitated by his brutal durability and smooth adeptness with *oficiales* who doubtless encourage him on his path and profit from his flair for sustaining power through terror. Like other frustrated men who appointed themselves *jefe*, Mario tasted power and became intoxicated by it. He suffers from the well-known syndrome of prolonged and unchallenged power and its symptoms are visible in him: dogmatic arrogance, clinging to the levers of command, regarding himself as above the law. Mario seems oblivious to the inevitable mockery of the military, who are indifferent to his fate; he lacks the sophistication to realize that the military architects of the patrol system intended it (and the atrocities its members were encouraged to commit) to be 'deniable'.

Kotoh's Public Massacre

The injury that a crime inflicts upon the social body is the disorder that it introduces into it, the scandal that it gives rise to, the example that it gives, the incitement to repeat if it is not punished, and the possibility of becoming widespread that it bears within it (Foucault 1979).

The event which gave Mario his power was the village massacre, which the army forced him to organize and carry out in broad daylight. Unlike many newly installed *jefes* faced with this part of the army's standard script, Mario was apparently not loth to comply. Told to make an example of the village's 'subversives', he chose his victims from Kotoh, Emol Central's traditional rivals and, with the kind of sadistic flourish which he later became proud of, forced unarmed Kotoh patrollers to round up and kill them. There are many reasons why this event is so shocking, including one which the army was unaware of when calculating this collective spectacle of torture: the idea that victims, perpetrators, and witnesses are not only participants in an event but united by it in this world and the next (chapter eight). The massacre was an identity fixing event: it simultaneously created a closed community of experience whilst inducting both everyone present into it.[31]

It was some time in 1982 when the village massacres began. I actually witnessed the one that occurred in Kotoh. A friend *(compañero)* and I happened to visit that day. In fact, I remember now that it was the St. Valentine's Day *(Dia del Cariño)*. As we approached the village it could have been any other day. It was early and everything was shrouded in the freezing mist so we were unable to see much as we entered from the road. Then, as we drew closer, I heard shouting. I remarked to my *compañero*, "The patrollers must be doing their exercises early today." But, then, as we drew nearer still, I realized that the patrollers were doing no ordinary exercise. No, it was not ordinary at all ...for they were clubbing men...to death. I remember that there were about twelve men and two boys and they were lying on blankets, some were under them. They were groaning and bloodied.

[Were they guerrillas?]

...No, I do not think they were guerrillas for they carried no guns... They were local men.

[Who was doing it?]

The *jefes* were...well, at least they were giving the orders to the patrollers who were the ones who were actually doing it. One *jefe* noticed us advancing and he quickly put us in the school with the children who were already locked in. Some had hoisted themselves up to peer out of the windows. In horror they watched the fate of their relatives. Their mothers and grandmothers stood out-side...staring, paralyzed, in silence... When the men were virtually dead they locked the women in the church so they would not follow them when they dragged the bodies down a canyon to two big holes which the men had un-knowingly prepared earlier, for their own burial. Apparently there, before their graves, another man, not a *jefe* or patroller but a village *brujo* took it upon himself to perform the final blow... (Local witness, not from Kotoh).

The massacre was a most arresting rite of legitimation. This "festival of punishment" (Foucault 1979:8) engaged the villagers as "audience-guarantor in a system that transforms spectacular atrocity into political power" (Grazi-ano 1993:64), simultaneously transforming more or less equivalent villagers into victims and perpetrators (patrollers were one or the other depending on whether they were on duty or not). Massacres reinforced the *jefe's* violent authority, consecrating the arbitrary boundary between him and other vil-lagers; it was an act of communication which simultaneously signified to the *jefe* how he should conduct himself towards the 'enemy' and other scape-goated villagers whilst signifying to the latter how he could act towards them. It also had the effect of discouraging the *jefe* from deserting his role: if he crossed to the other side, he too could become the object of violence rather than its agent.

Massacres are also a most effective way of mortifying the Indian, an extreme means of degrading an already devalued population through de-humanizing them. Sheltering behind their new, *ladino* definition of human-ity, *jefes* utilized their local knowledge to devalue victims in terms of their own culture: "They were tied up and thrown on the ground, like animals for slaughter," said one outraged witness. Being treated like an animal is one of the worst insults one can pay the K'iche'.

Massacres conducted under army coercion affected the perpetrators, beginning a process which *jefes* continued in an apparently auto-suggestive fashion, convincing them that they had the ability to make further displays of power; even self-selected perpetrators "evolve along a continuum of de-struction" (Staub 1989:18). The violence they were forced to commit seems to have anaesthetized their emotions and diminished their sensitivity to the suffering of others. Massacres transformed the representation which the *jefe* had of himself and the behaviour he felt obliged to adopt in order to conform to that representation. Given his previous (and, to some extent, current) membership of the group being devalued, the *jefe* has to devalue them with a vengeance in order to protect his own newly formed identity (Staub 1989).

The massacre atomized the links among the objects of this act (vil-lagers) which had the effect of increasing mistrust and, hence, terror. The place of the atomized, subsumed subject (the villager) is determined by a central authority (the *jefe* who, in turn, is under military authority) (Foucault 1979). Atomization arose partly because of the betrayal involved when one neighbour killed another while others stood by, paralyzed and unable to pro-

tect or aid victims. Survivors feel guilt and shame because their awareness
that interference would have led to their own deaths prevented them from
doing anything. A man from another village describes the situation:

> One villager stood, waiting to be killed by the army, having been erroneously
> accused of being a guerrilla. He turned to other villagers who he thought could
> have saved his skin by telling the army that he was innocent. As he tried to
> catch the eyes of others they averted their gaze. Finally, he caught the atten-
> tion of one man who looked at him reacting as though the devil himself had
> peered at him and he said, softly, knowing what it was he wanted, "I am
> afraid" and with that he walked away (Montejo 1987).

Like other elements in a whole series of official rituals, the massacre
quelled villagers' remaining will. There was no choice other than to comply
with this rite. Both those selected for death and those forced to watch were
unarmed victims, socialized to be passive in the presence of authority and
especially *ladinos*. Faced with overwhelming brute force, they were denied
the possibility of defending themselves against the intense anxiety which
results from seeing the intentions of harm-doers. As the continuum of annihilation progresses, there is a parallel progression of psychological change
in the victims, who give up hope and move along a continuum of victimiza-
tion. Families and other villagers (most of whom are at least distantly related) became passive or more active participants in these atrocities; the affective bonds between parent and child, husband and wife were severed with
the resultant reorganization of the family unit: "suddenly an entire culture
based on familial love, devotion, the capacity for mutual sacrifice, collapses"
(Timmerman 1981:148).

Army-ordered massacres committed by newly formed patrols were presented as the ultimate punishment of so-called transgressors. In reality, massacres are less intended to 'punish' than to force villagers to do as the state
wishes: villagers will refrain from involving themselves with the guerrillas,
patrollers will co-operate with the patrol system and the *jefe* will carry out
massacres — willingly. In this sense the process of massacre and abduction
illuminates, in the form of a new political ritual, the essential relationship between a totalitarian state and its chosen scapegoat. *Ladino* power in relation
to the K'iche' has always given them the ability to exercise power over the
Indian. The *ladino* tendency to devalue Indians as 'other' and inferior is a
long-standing precondition to harm them. This is a prevailing human tendency, as is the process of scapegoating (Staub 1989:48-49).

Undermining the Social Fabric

Assaults on the Family
Prior to *la violencia*, the home was a place of refuge where the family

congregated at the end of the day's work for the main meal of the day, conversation, relaxation, and sacred rituals. People return to their own homes: there is no tradition of inter-household visiting, especially after dark; even day time visitors are regarded with suspicion and rarely allowed beyond the patio. Night, traditionally feared because of supernatural dangers, has become a time of increased insecurity because of the many violent acts committed under cover of darkness; even today, everyone stays at home to avoid accusations of being involved in seditious activity ('organizing'); night-time classes have not resumed.

The home was women's main, everyday sanctuary until *la violencia*, when they were raped within it and their relatives disappeared from it, activities which were continued by *jefes* and zealous patrollers (and in some places, still continue despite the 'disbanding' of the system). In Emol at the height of *la violencia*, soldiers killed women within the adobe sweat baths *(temascales)* which are an important part of every traditional household: it is where children are born, where sacred rituals are performed, and where the ancestors are said to reside (cf. Bloch 1995). A naked, pregnant woman was abducted from her *temascal* during an army round up and never seen again. Such atrocities led widows to abandon their homes, which were then looted and razed to the ground. These days, houses burnt down usually belong to members of human rights and widows' groups.

The army's and the *jefes'* looting of abandoned houses and their continued forays into inhabited homes while women are present has particular significance to the K'iche' who expect others to honour the privacy of their homes. Such intrusions are an "assault on a woman's sense of self and [a] manipulation of her traditional role as wife and mother. The protection and refuge of the home is shattered, and the control and coherence she maintained in the intimate sphere of the home is destroyed as well" (Bunster 1986 :304).

The *jefes* flaunted their new found authority by entering any house at any time. They take who they want (a man to kill; a woman to rape) and what they want (food, property) — as one woman told me, village men abandoned their previous roles to become *jefes* "and now they are *jefes* of the thieves." Widows are the primary targets of their abuse: the abolition of the patrols has made little , if any, difference to the relationship between victim and perpetrator. Intruding into their houses and extracting goods, labour, and services from them, the *jefes* ensure that widows (and their children) know they can fulfill any violent or other whim with impunity. The *jefes'* creation of a plethora of social experiences of indignity (control, submission, humiliation, forced deference, labour and sexual exploitation,[32] and punishment) form the foundations of women's fear, anger, and resentment; each episode increases their sense of impotence and frustration.

Widows are subjected to chronic, severe intimidation.[33] Threats of rape, abduction, and massacre are issued almost as a matter of routine. Women

know these were not idle threats as they and their kin have already been subjected to such experiences by both soldier and *jefe* (cf. Manz 1988:92).
Widows who join human rights organizations or neutral NGOs are threatened with having bombs dropped on their gatherings and with being disappeared on the way to meetings; *jefes* warn that they might be forced to take them
to the military base or kill them 'once and for all' *(de una vez)*. Emol's *jefes*
intimate that further violent acts are likely to occur, reminding widows of
past incidents of violence against them. Allusions are made to particularly
repugnant incidents such as the fate of a group of widows from a nearby
village who were left to drown after being beaten senseless and then shoved
into a cesspit. Parrotting the army, *jefes* claim that guerrillas are connected
to widows' organizations and are attempting to recruit new members from
them; they organize demonstrations against CONAVIGUA and other human
rights organizations, forcing patrollers and other villagers to take part.

More effective are the *jefes'* threats against the widows' children. Their
monothematic message of silence — "don't talk to anyone or your children
will be killed" — permeates the community. Widows often told me that fears
for their children's safety constrain their behaviour. But war-widows are not
the only people targetted through their children: the army hands out leaflets
to all school children in an attempt to organize them into informing on their
families. Children whose fathers or other male relatives are known to be in
hiding (or, later, refusing to patrol) are questioned about their whereabouts,
the implication (and threat) being that they have joined the guerrillas. Soldiers warn children against becoming 'subversives' too. One way of discouraging this is forcibly inducting schoolboys into the patrols, a tactic
which has the support of the army, which distrusts Indian education. One
young man who lives in town told me he cannot return to his village because
he is afraid of the "hatred in the peoples' eyes" which, he claims, is fuelled
by the fact that he had left to study and had not carried out the patrol.

Encouraging children to inform on their parents robs family life of its
intimacy.[34] The knowledge that they can cause a parent's death is intended
to destroy the respect children have for their parents. Few children have denounced a parent but the threat looms large. When denunciations do occur,
their terrible consequences are widely publicized and are enough to sow distrust. Fear of denunciation from within damages the family as a source of
inner security. Especially destructive is people's fear of the consequences of
what they might inadvertently say or do in front of other family members.
This fear grips parents and elders, weakening their security within the home;
it dries up the main source of the self respect which feeds their sense of
worth and inner autonomy.

Fear, more than the fact of betrayal by children, spouses or siblings,
makes it impossible to lower one's defenses even within one's four walls.
Family relations are now driven by continuous caution; people live with the
strain of being constantly on guard, if not openly distrustful of family mem-

bers; the 'enemy' could be residing under the same roof or within one's extended family. Needless to say, the extended family is said to have disintegrated as a result of *la violencia*. The family became a weakening experience at a time when people most needed its security. Trust, the greatest value in intimate relations, is one of the biggest casualties of *la violencia.*

The splintering of the community down to the level of the individual (one of the army's declared aims) means that villagers can no longer discern a single frontier; many, perhaps innumerable, confused frontiers stretch between them. The solidarity formed in the early stages of *la violencia*, already fragmented through suspicion of betrayals among villagers before the formation of the patrols, disintegrated. The hoped-for allies were no longer there. Insecurity was deliberately created through the destruction of private life. No-one feels confident about who is friend or foe. People continue to search and hope for security, self-respect, and respect from others — that is, the experiences which breed autonomy and, after bare necessities, are the most important in terms of survival as a human being — in situations which no longer offer them. The patrols destroyed people's assumptions that everyone inside the community and especially within the family is benign and everyone outside is dangerous (cf. Wolf 1967). Instilled from childhood, these expectations are a prime motivating force in community life; they do not change over night. So people continue to seek security in their homes and communities and the relationships within them even though they know, at some level, that it no longer exists: "at this point we can see the psychological appeal of tyranny" (Bettelheim 1986:293).

Psychological violence, which includes the dissemination of rumours or myths of terror, severs connections between people, controls their ways of being together and relating to each other, and attempts to destroy the possibility of free dialogue and thought. This is crucial to the cultural elaboration of terror (Taussig 1984:460). Terror ultimately destroys the network of stable expectations which lie "at the core of any set of organized relationships" (Moore 1954:175-6), feeding into highland communities' tendency to be isolated, atomized, and divided by suspicion and mutually destructive rivalry. Such communities prop up systems of terror more effectively than those without chronic hostility (Walter 1969). Hostility within Emol has always been chronic; *la violencia* brought it inside the family.

The home became the space over which both sides fought for the attention of those within it. Some people say guerrillas come to give talks *(platicas)* to villagers in their homes at night; in 1990, a man told me he had recently been asked if his house could be used by the guerrillas as a look out post. Others told me of disguised, anonymous men *(desconocidos)* — usually members of the right wing forces — who visit people at home, trick them into making 'subversive' statements, and then return to abduct them (cf. Manz 1988:70). These generally unverifiable stories help maintain high levels of terror.

The Climate of Fear

At the end of the 1980s and the beginning of the 1990s, villagers' spoken words attested to the general sensation of a 'climate of fear'; by mid decade, fear had lessened though it still exists. For different reasons and to different degrees, everyone in El Quiché is afraid. Widows fear the violence of *jefes* and some patrollers who in turn fear the power of the women's words and vengeance from the relatives of those they have killed; their response is to terrorize each other and the people of 'their' communities, including patrollers. All parties to this vicious circle of terror are Indians subject to government terror and manipulation. However, the scripts they are meant to follow as participants in *la violencia* are not the same.

Women's Fear. Women's constant fear that *la violencia* is about to return is fed by sporadic news of military or guerrilla violence committed in other areas of Guatemala; such news intensifies their fears. Yet despite the devastating destruction directly perpetrated by the army, Emolteco women feel that their worst enemies are the *jefes* and their informers. In other areas, such as Nebaj, local discourse emphasizes the external origin of violence, thus deflecting blame from local men who commit crimes under duress from outside forces (Stoll 1993:262). In southern El Quiché violence is often attributed to local, non-political causes (chapter nine).

Women's reports of being treated as subversives are based on reality: women have also been tortured and disappeared. Their anxiety is exacerbated by the fact that no soldier, policeman, member of the security forces *(judicial)* or local perpetrator of violence has been arrested, charged, convicted, and imprisoned for their crimes against Indians in the highlands. One of the consequences of this is that women live in a climate of terror stemming from the impunity of officially protected killers. Although men too live with the fear of death and disappearance, to which they are actually subject with far greater frequency than women, their experiences are different: men are not assaulted by continuous violence from the same directions, nor are they subjected to the same kinds of harassment (i.e., sexual exploitation, rape, the murder of children). Gender effects not only the kind of violence offered to a person but the way it resonates within the person. Thus grown sons, unless unusually close to their mothers, do not identify with the position of victim in the same way that adult daughters do (K'iche' children are encouraged to identify with adults of the same gender).

The mere presence of current and former *jefes*, particularly murderers such as Mario, is a continuing source of intimidation. Mario is seen by some to be the sole instigator of the massacres in Emol and the person behind the persecution and intimidation to which widows are continuously subject. Women's anxiety concerning the *jefes* they see daily is complex. They fear the *jefes* will kill them; they are also afraid that they might become like them by, for example, taking revenge, something which they sometimes express in their fantasies. The easiest way to quiet such anxiety is to believe that one is made of 'different stuff' and could never fall so low.

Whether married or widowed, women are excluded from contemporary power structures which render them mute, silent, non-existent. The new local authority structure precludes the performance of women's traditional, supportive roles. In that sense, they remain victims.

The Jefes' Fear. *Jefes'* fears changed over time. Their fears of vengeance have been succeeded by fears of justice being brought to bear by trial. Most of all, *jefes* fear the loss of position and power.

Fears of *brujería* vengeance attack led Emolteco *jefes* to massacre the village's *brujos* to prevent victims' relatives from seeking their services. It is difficult to imagine a clearer statement of the killers' beliefs in the efficacy of *brujería*. Other *jefes*, less concerned with threats from the living, were unable to rid themselves of the traditional idea that the ancestors will punish them on the day of reckoning; they also fear the malicious spirits of the people they killed. Such fears often survive *jefes'* conversion to Protestantism, leading them to seek rituals of protection from traditional diviners. Unlike most people whose conversion to protestantism during *la violencia* was motivated by the need for a safe haven from army persecution, some *jefes* were motivated by the need to seek refuge from the spirits which share the K'iche' social universe. For many *jefes*, conversion indicates not only an identification with the *ladino* army and its 'modern' ideas but also a conscious rejection and attack on Indianness.

Fears of supernatural attack were superseded by the equally intangible threat presented by women's words. Most *jefes* are frightened of widows because they are outside their control. Particularly threatening from the *jefes'* point of view are widows who are leaders such as aj q'ij, women who refuse to convert to protestantism, and members of indigenous women's groups such as CONAVIGUA or other human rights groups; women who petition for exhumations are even more dangerous from *jefes'* point of view. Such women have access to knowledge, information, and support which are completely closed to *jefes* who do everything they can to undermine the camaraderie of women whose husbands were killed or disappeared by the same side (the 'same mind'). A popular strategy is fomenting suspicion among women in order to discourage them from becoming a strong force. This tactic is quite successful in Emol, where women are deterred from joining widows' groups by suspicions that other women's surviving male kin may have betrayed theirs (which is known to be true in some cases), or because they believe other women obtain greater benefit from membership than they do and so on.

Motivating this persistent harassment of widows is *jefes'* fears of the women's memories. They fear that widows will expose their atrocities, turning public secrets into public facts. They are also afraid that widows will report them to the civilian authorities. *Jefes'* fears of legal justice arises more from the rhetoric of human rights agencies than from the government, which has granted them amnesty from prosecution. However, it seems that *jefes* have as much faith in government amnesties as their fellow villagers.

What *jefes* really fear is loss of power, a fear which has haunted many *jefes* since the 1985 elections, although Mario took this in his stride. The civilian government's confirmation in 1988 of the patrols' voluntary nature posed more of a threat as increasing numbers of formerly outwardly compliant patrollers began to resist the system. In Emol, the patrols continued until 1992, when armed patrols were disarmed and unarmed patrols disbanded. Even this did little to dent Mario's power; even without his army rifle, he is still an intimidating presence. The plans to re-educate patrollers and their *jefes* contained in the 1996 Peace Accords do not affect him, as the patrols he commanded imploded after their disarmament. Although protected by the decision to blame institutions rather then individuals for the atrocities of *la violencia*, he could, following the precedent created by the Myrna Mack case — her family had successfully argued that the protection provided for perpetrators under the Amnesty Law only applies when the victim had been involved in the conflict (chapter one) — be vulnerable to prosecution for his crimes. Such an eventuality is unlikely. Even if they have heard about the law, it is highly unlikely that Emoltecos would know how to use it against him and even less likely that they would bother to find out: they know that even if Mario's crimes were to be proved, he would not go to jail. Mario therefore continues to intimidate the relatives of the dead and witnesses to his atrocities with impunity. His continuing employment of spies and exploitation of his reputation as a *brujo* (about the only part of his Indian identity he seems to find useful) can be seen as evidence of his power mania or, perhaps, of his insecurity. Perhaps his knows that the ground is shifting under his feet.

Jefes fear the loss of their assumed *ladino* identity which is tied to their position and hence only valid within their communities; outside it, they are just Indians like any other. Demotion to the ranks of the 'other' among whom they have kidnapped, tortured, and killed, would expose *jefes* to both physical and supernatural danger.[35] The prospect of loss of position, power, and/or identity has led some former *jefes* commit suicide.

One thing does disconcert Mario and his ilk: they know that despite their fear, the widows laugh at them; they sense that the women's laughter is different from the socially sanctioned custom of laughing at misfortune. The women's laughter stems from the need to find relief from the mental strain of exercising self control; the slightest pretexts, a simple play on words, is enough to provoke an outburst of laughter. There is an increased propensity to grasp double meanings in the absence of the freedom of expression and such laughter acts both as a safety valves "for venting secret resentments" (Freud 1960) and a substitute for protest. One characteristic of this laughter is that it functions as a symbolic compensation for impotent political status; another is its ambivalence. Indeed, the excessive care needed to avoid getting into trouble with an authoritarian regime makes people more susceptible to laughter. Not understanding the phenomenon, *jefes* (and men generally) are bewildered and offended by the women's laughter, their 'lack of respect', and wonder what they will do next.

Patrollers' Fears. By the beginning of the 1990s, many patrollers were even more opposed to the system than ever, having had to suppress their opposition for so long and having seen that the rewards, if any, are so meagre. As one man explained, apart from a few people who had 'changed their minds' *(cambiaron su cabeza)*, "the majority of Catholic Action people do not want to participate in the patrols." Nevertheless, Emoltecos continued patrolling for several more years; they feared being victimized by the army, their *jefes* or even their fellow patrollers.

Ordinary patrollers also fear being blamed for the atrocities they were forced to commit. Some take refuge in the traditional idea of spirit invasion, which allows them to disclaim responsibility for their actions; others convert to protestantism in the hope that survivors' revenge sorcery will be unable to touch them once they had leave their traditional beliefs behind.

Many men are frightened by the ease with which they had stepped over cultural boundaries and are unable to reconcile themselves with what they had done. In order to kill one another, it is necessary (sadism aside) for villagers to believe that there is a separateness, a boundary, an inferiority of the victim in relation to the persecutor. Perpetrators need to believe that they do not share solidary relations nor common substance with their victims, and that they are not the same category of person. Many ordinary patrollers have never been able to make this mental leap, seeing no difference between themselves and the men they were ordered to kill; nor were they ever totally convinced by the army's attempts to persuade them that war was actually raging inside their communities. Nevertheless, patrollers have been the instrument of that war within their villages.

Conclusion

The patrol system has proved to be as destructive as it was designed to be yet its originators failed to realize that there are limits to what can be achieved through terror. K'iche' society has adapted to militarization as best it can; in their day-to-day choices, individuals take account of the army's demands and the resources it offers, assessing in turn what it is opportune to accept and what not. Certainly, this takes place within the margins allowed, but it leaves some room for manoeuvre.

Women's statements expose an environment full of arbitrations linking villagers and military authorities, permitting domination by the army and their local mediators, the *jefes*, to be simultaneously sanctioned and revised. This unofficial, secret arbitration has serious implications because as long as such acts remain publicly silent, it is responsible for maintaining the impunity of officially protected killers: "over a period of years, public silence can reshape memory, history and even the notions of right and wrong to the point that might makes right" (Stoll 1993:302). Whilst this does occur, there is a limit to this: although the army has penetrated the private sphere through the institution of the patrols, it never gained complete control over it; nor does the military seem to realize that, despite terror, censorship, etc., it cannot prevent the private sphere and private memories leaking into public consciousness.

Notes

1. See chapter four, notes 6 and 7.

2. See chapter four, note 6.

3. The guerrilla's *ladino* leadership was similarly ignorant of Mayan culture. See Le Bot (1995) for criticisms of guerrilla sociopolitical ideology.

4. This realization has been attributed to the discovery of the work of anthropologists and psychiatrists by the army's psychological warfare branch; a certain amount of understanding of Indian culture can be retrospectively detected from this time.

5. Although most of this chapter is based on events in Emol, events in other highland villages followed an identical pattern and sequence. Differences in the type of atrocities committed in different communities reflect differences in local history, distribution of religions, local factionalism, etc.

6. A typical structure was (1) military zone commander; (2) lieutenant of local army detachment; (3) head of the military commissioners; (4) military commissioner; (5) *jefe* of the civil patrol; (6) *jefe* of the civil patrol battalion; (7) *jefe* of the civil patrol platoon; (8) *jefe* of the civil patrol squadron; (9) rank-and-file civil patrol member (America's Watch 1986). This was the blueprint; I found that authority belongs to whoever has the power to take it.

7. This propaganda programme offered peasants a choice between death or flight (bullets) or military 'protection' including limited hand-outs (beans) in army-controlled areas.

8. The name was changed to 'Voluntary Committees for Civil Defense' (*Comités Voluntarios de Defensa Civil*, or CDVC).

9. These weapons were part of a U.S. aid package. The military regime's request for U.S. economic and military aid had the support of Washington's liberal Democrats. After the installation of Guatemala's civilian president in January 1986, U.S. congressional Democrats increased Reagan administration military aid from US$5 million to $9 million; they also approved the sale of 20,000 rifles in early 1989 (Jonas 1991:21, fn.2).

10. No training was given in the use of these new rifles: one newly appointed commissioner, running out of his house in response to the sounding of an alarm, shot himself in the foot.

11. "The announced plan calls for a first phase of *concientizacion* [consciousness raising], explaining why civil patrols are no longer necessary; a second phase of disarming the PACs; and a third phase in which patrollers would be presented with the option of remaining organized, presumably for other ends" (Popkin 1996: v). Many people believe the army has no 'other ends' in mind.

12. Forced choice occurs when people are forced to "choose between two evils, both of which would be rejected in an 'open' situation. As people move to avoid the more noxious alternative, the struggle mobilizes their energies and they actively co-operate with political authority to gain the positive increment of the lesser evil" (Walter 1969:286-7).

13. The concept of autonomy has to do with a person's ability to govern him [her]self and with a conscientious search for meaning despite the realization that, as far as we know, there is no purpose to one's life. It is a concept that does not imply a revolt against authority *qua* authority, but rather a quiet acting out of inner conviction, not out of convenience or resentment or because of external pressure or controls.

14. *Oficiales* are not only army officers but anyone who speaks on the army's behalf on an official basis, which is not always the same thing.

15. Defining a 'common criminal' in times when the powerful can rob, rape, and kill with impunity is problematic.

16. See Barth (1981): choice is not synonymous with freedom; people rarely make choices under circumstances of their own making. In normal circumstances, values and intentionality play an important role in shaping behaviour.

17. I only met one man excused from patrol duty on health grounds. He had always been of a rather fragile disposition and the torment he received from the *jefes* and other patrollers caused him to suffer a break from reality from which he never recovered. He remains bedridden and incontinent.

18. 'Identification' is a psychological process whereby the subject assimilates an aspect, property or attribute of the other and is transformed, wholly or partially, after the model the other provides. There has been a good deal of anthropological discussion of what 'identification' might be (e.g., Rigby 1969).

19. See America's Watch (1986) for other examples of Improvement Committee members being instrumental in imposing order.

20. cf. Carmack (1988:63): a foreign diplomat told him "Patrols from six small villages went to the town of Chijtinimit [Chichicastenango, El Quiché] in July and August of 1983 and confronted the local patrol with a list of villagers whom they suspected of being subversive. The visiting patrols threatened to attack the town if the local patrol did not execute the reputed leftists, so the patrol complied by killing 25 of their own men".

21. Provisioning the guerrilla — the ostensible reason for the erection of *garitas* — also became impossible. Some patrollers claim they had only done so under duress.

22. Identity in respect to one's physical location has been more important than any essence or being among the K'iche'.

23. cf. Milgram's (1974) research indicating that ordinary people can be provoked by someone of limited authority to dispense life-threatening electric shocks. People enter an 'agentic' mode in which they surrender individual accountability and no longer evaluate the morality of an action independently.

24. 'Identification with the aggressor' has been described within the psycho-analytic literature as a defence mechanism; this may be achieved by appropriating the aggression itself, by physical or moral emulation of the aggressor, or by adopting particular symbols of power by which the aggressor is designated. cf. Anna Freud (1937) who describes the variety, complexity, and compass of mechanisms of defence including repression, projection, and turning against the self.

25. See chapter four, note 10.

26. cf. Bettelheim (1986:16): "if different persons react differently, if the inhibitions of some stand up while those of others fail, if some even strengthen their defences against behaving asocially, it can all be ascribed to their different life histories or personality make-up".

27. This verb (to eat, i.e., kill) is the one most commonly used to express other notions such as exploitation and betrayal. Here the K'iche's' historical preoccupation with food and the accusation of what amounts to savagery and even cannibalism are joined together in a powerful, evocative metaphor.

28. Mario, *doña* Flora and *doña* Eugenia's daughter-in-law Vicenta (Mario's sister) are close contemporaries.

29. This is something which many returning Indian conscripts fail to realize, believing that their long held elite status has become their inalienable, 'natural' right (cf. Staub 1989:226).

30. In reversals of morality, leaders of mass killings often come to regard their actions as good, right, and desirable (Staub 1989).

31. Induction is an unavoidable rite of passage of defilement which strips inductees of many outward components of their identity, leaving them with very few resources with which to counter this massive socializing onslaught (Goffman 1961:18-30).

32. Widows sexually exploited by *jefes* were accused of being prostitutes by the *jefes*' wives (chapter six).

33. Intimidation is "a symbolic violence which is not aware of what it is (to the extent that it implies no act of intimidation) and which can only be exerted on a person predisposed...to feel it, whereas others will ignore it. It is already partly true to say that the cause of the timidity lies in the relation between the situation or the intimidating person (who may deny any intimidating intention) and the person intimidated, or rather between the social conditions of the production of each of them. And little by little, one has to take account thereby of the whole social structure" (Bourdieu 1991:51).

34. See Timmerman (1981:149) regarding the use of children in the reproduction of terror.

35. The lack of blood vengeance among the K'iche' is more apparent than real, for anger over a murder is as potent as any other cause for hatred and has repercussions for the future. On rare occasions, people intimated that *brujeria* was performed against the *jefes* although they were generally reluctant to admit to knowing anything about such malevolent practices lest they themselves be suspected of them.

6

Women's Lives as Widows (Malca'nib)[1]

The loss of a marriage partner creates a sharp break in the surviving spouse's social and personal identity which the K'iche' believe should be repaired as soon as possible in order for the widow(er) to resume his or her full adult status. For the K'iche' (whatever their current religious affiliation), this means remarriage. Being married is the most of important of "those attributes, capacities, and signs of 'proper' social persons which mark a moral career (and its jural entitlements) in a particular society" (Poole 1982:103); among the K'iche', widow(er)hood renders the surviving spouse less of a person. The impact is greater on women than men even in more normal times, because a woman is the less powerful of the two complementary elements comprising, in this instance, the conjugal pair/household. K'iche's are socialized to think of women as being supported and protected by the man on whose land they live, be it father, brother, husband or son. As a rule, land belongs to men and is inherited patrilineally (cf. Wagley 1949). In some areas, such as Emol, this principle is cross cut by the idea that land belongs to the household rather than the individual man or his patrilineage which means that in some circumstances a widow retains her rights to her deceased husband's fields. These conflicting notions provide considerable scope for friction between widows and their in-laws.

The end of a marriage through death, separation or divorce throws into relief the inequality between K'iche' men and women, husband and wife, which is largely masked by the ideology of complementarity within marriage. Prior to *la violencia*, being a malca'n was rare and so the community and a woman's family could afford to support her until remarriage. The unprecedented slaughter of Indian men during *la violencia* meant that widows could not be re-integrated into the K'iche' world in the traditional manner. This led villagers to take many different and novel approaches to their war-widows, as *don* Alberto explains:

Every village *(cantón)* had their own concept of widowhood and this affected
the way they treated them. Some tried to integrate them, others rejected them,
controlled them and harassed them. Their conception depended, in turn, on the
information they received, usually from the patrol chiefs *(jefes)*. Some de-
segregated them because they were afraid that they would be called the 'wife
of the guerrilla' and then this would spread to the whole village. They thought
it was better to incorporate them into the community so that there will be no
distinction between widow and non widow. Others decided to assimilate them
because they thought, "If we leave them aside, then they will take revenge on
the community." Some, while realizing this, still rejected them because they
could not bring themselves to do otherwise. They thought, "How do we support the widows if they are the ones who caused the trouble in the community
in the first place?" They decided that they must be punished for what they
imagined they had done, whether in fact they had or not.

In Emol, most female-headed households are socially isolated. Even
though most killings had no apparent political or ideological basis, villagers
tend to follow the army's lead in assuming or contriving a story that the dead
men must have been involved in some political activity. Lack of personal
contact among villagers allowed malicious rumours *(chismes)* to develop,
causing people to ostracize war-widows. They dwell in a twilight zone of in-
definition, which is neatly summed up in the derogatory appellation 'wives
of the guerrilla': they are not wives, but neither have they been able to take
on the traditional status of widowhood or move on to a new status which has
meaning within the traditional K'iche' world view; they form a new category of 'otherness'. Women whose husbands have been disappeared suffered
a double dose of liminality, not knowing whether they are wives or widows.

Obviously, the women were not socialized to become war-widows, nor
to deal with the hostile world into which they were cast; they had to be resocialized. They also had to look to new ways to survive. This chapter looks
at how they achieved this and how they, and others, assess the experience.

Residence Following Widowhood

The chaos of *la violencia* emphasized the fragility of widows' position
in K'iche' society. Fear of being associated with a deceased 'guerrilla' led
many women's families to abandon or reject them; similar feelings on the
part of widow's in-laws were exacerbated by greed for the dead man's land.

A war-widow's place of residence depended on economic factors such
as whether or not her husband had received his land inheritance (chapter
three) and if she could hold on to it: some families decided to redistribute
their land to the exclusion of the dead man's widow and often his children
as well. Personal factors such as a woman's relationship with her husband's
family, especially his mother, were very important in this regard. For many
widows, mothers-in-law were a source of harassment.

Widows were often evicted or terrorized into leaving. Tactics included sexual harassment; widows whose fathers-in-law were village *jefes* or military commissioners were particularly vulnerable. Threats to rob widows of their houses, land, and property were commonplace and led many women to flee; some widows fled when the threats were carried out. Other ruses employed by families included accusing a daughter-in-law of complicity in her husband's death or of involvement in subversive activity. Widows with no male kin to support them were particularly vulnerable to intimidatory tactics.

Widows with neither land nor family are forced to uproot themselves and their children to the town, the capital or the coast in search of a livelihood and shelter. In urban areas, women take a room, paying the rent from the small income they earn as laundresses, cleaners, and cooks in *ladino* or relatively affluent Indian households. In the capital, many widows and children move to the squatter settlements on the outskirts of the city[2] where there has been a "marked feminization of poverty as half the families in the huge El Mezquital shanty town, for example, are headed by women" (Jonas 1991: 183). If widows have somewhere to leave their children, they work as live-in maids (*ladinos* usually stipulate no children). Some desperate widows abandon their children, leaving them to fend for themselves, occasionally with disastrous results. Such women are the least fortunate of widows, alone and landless; people told me that many of them died of 'sadness' (bis; *tristeza*),[3] fear *(miedo)* or fright *(susto)*.[4]

On the plantations *(fincas)*, many women, weakened by their harsh experiences during *la violencia*, find they can no longer cope with the severe conditions (cf. Hoyt 1959; Dassaint 1962; Melville and Melville 1971; Schmid 1973); some, such as Natalia's mother, died from a combination of exhaustion and 'sadness'. She had taken her children to the coast after the abduction of her son and the disappearance of her husband from Emol's Sunday market; she did not have the option to return to her parents' home and nor could she maintain her family home in Emol. She died shortly after arriving on the *finca*, leaving four orphaned children. Natalia, the eldest, was only twelve years old at the time and had to take sole responsibility for her siblings. I was told many times about people who had died of 'sadness', though such comments also reflect speakers' own experiences of overwhelming distress and their own wish to die, which a few confessed to more directly.

Many widows are afraid to stay in households where other adult men (sons, father- or brothers-in-law) are also dead or missing, leaving two or more widows without any men. Such women leave if they can. *Doña* Flora had already lost her husband to *la violencia*; when her son was killed a few months later, she and her daughter-in-law, Bartola, went their separate ways. *Doña* Flora went first to her brother's house in town and then spent two years in her natal village with her mother; Bartola stayed with her parents in Emol. *Doña* Flora paid someone to look after her land in her absence; Bar-

tola's family also kept an eye on it (it was in their interests to do so, as the
land would eventually be inherited by their grandsons). Thus she was able
to return when amnesty was called. Other women retain their land rights by
cultivating it; they arrive with male helpers at corn planting, weeding, and
harvest times. Yet others work their land but do not stay in their homes at
night for fear of intimidation by the *jefes* and being bothered by the spirits
of kin who had met violent deaths. Such widows sleep at other widows'
houses.

Most women who abandoned their husband's land for any length of
time are unable to reclaim it; some tried. Women can seldom prove ownership; even if the land is registered in a husband's name with the civil administration, which was often not the case, wives are rarely in possession of the
deeds (as women cannot prove their husbands are dead, they have no legal
reason to have the deeds transferred to their name anyway). Monolingualism
and distrust of the *ladino* legal process further hamper women's attempts to
regain their land. I only met one widow trying to seek legal redress for the
theft of her land. *Doña* Christina had fled to her parents' home when her
husband was abducted; she and her mother fled to the town when her father
was also killed. Malicious gossip identifying her as a prostitute pushed her
into remarriage. She returned to her first husband's land with their children
and her second husband, who proved to be an alcoholic; she left him and returned to the town with her mother. When she next visited her first husband's home, she was stoned by her male cousins who, having heard a rumour that she had lost her senses, hoped to take over her land.

Women who fled with their husbands rarely resettled in their communities following their husband's death or disappearance. A series of atrocities brought Juanita back to Emol, however. Her mother called her home
when her father was killed; her husband remained in Guatemala City, only
visiting the village to plant his mother-in-law's corn as a good son-in-law
should (he was landless himself). He abandoned them when Juanita became
pregnant as a result of being gang-raped by fifteen soldiers, returning to his
work in Guatemala City. Two years later, marital relations resumed when he
came to live in the village during periods of unemployment; by then the patrols had been set up and attempts were made to force him to participate. He
refused and returned to the city, taking Juanita with him but leaving her son
(whom she called 'Army Child') with her mother. They visited the village
when her mother needed help with the land and it was on one of these occasions that he was killed by the patrols. Juanita, who was pregnant again, remained in the village with her mother. Another woman who returned was
doña Lydia, who had been left on her own with three small children in
Guatemala City after her husband was kidnapped from his street stall. At
first she took over his stall to earn money to feed the children but then, she
told me, her husband appeared in her dreams and told her to plant the corn
fields *(milpa)* as he used to do. These widows are fortunate in having land

to return to: other widows who attempted to return following the 1985 elections found that their homes had been looted, burnt out by the army or taken over by their husband's family, together with his land. I traced some of these widows in Guatemala City and found that theft by fellow villagers is a major source of resentment; fear of the power of the men who had stolen their land prevents them from attempting to resettle in their villages. Contact with the village is rarely severed entirely; most women pay short, secret visits to their extended family and close friends, remaining as hidden as possible from the rest of the village. Their hosts collude with the surreptitiousness of these visits because of the dangers in allowing 'subversives' to stay.

Some women refused to flee. They were convinced that no harm would befall them because they were innocent of any wrong-doing; others, like *doña* Luisa, simply say, "I did not want to go to Guatemala [City]...I did not like the idea of going to another place." As a further justification of her decision to stay in Emol, she mentions lack of money: "I did not have enough money to pay for the bus fare. And even if I could have got there, I couldn't have found food, having no money."

Other widows were determined not to desert their land at all costs; they are hardier and more resourceful than most and their circumstances were more favourable than those of women who left. They also tend to be older and more secure in their position in the household. *Doña* Eugenia, who was in her sixties when she lost both her husband and only son within weeks of each other, has a strong attachment to her land which she claims has been in her family for generations. She suspects that 'they' are trying to force her to leave in order to take over her land and her house, which is on a prime site near Kotoh centre. *Doña* Eugenia's resistance stems from her determined personality and also from the fact that she has nowhere to go.

Younger widows who were not displaced remained in their husband's house (if a separate one had been built) or their mother-in-law's, only leaving if they remarry or, in cases where the land was not owned, when they cannot pay the rent. Although help from in-laws is unusual, it is fairly common to find households consisting of mother- and daughter-in-law who are both widowed and share similar beliefs; for example, both *doña* Eugenia and *doña* Flora have their daughters-in-law and grandchildren living with them. In these instances, mutual assistance occurs mostly on a practical level: the grandmother looks after the children while their mother earns what money she can. The arrangement is more beneficial to the mother-in-law as a daughter-in-law, even with sons, remains under the older woman's authority; the death of a husband weakens the daughter-in-law's position and it is the older woman who becomes the household head.

Female Headed Households

Female headed households were uncommon before *la violencia*, when natural widows were rare though not as unusual as the women remember: deaths following quite mundane accidents are quite common. Nevertheless, female headed households, as defined by the K'iche', usually result from widowhood. The K'iche' do not recognize *de facto* female headed households arising from male migration, divorce or separation (which, since *la violencia*, elicits considerably less stigma than widowhood), female assertiveness or male delinquency, incompetence or drunkenness. Even if a man leaves his wife on his land for another woman (a very rare event), she is unlikely to become the household head unless there are no other adult men (defined locally as married and earning a good income) in the household.

Many women learnt to fend for themselves and their families before *la violencia*. The changes in men's work patterns (chapter three) and their prolonged absences during *la violencia* when they were forced into hiding (chapter four) meant that women in less poor households were left alone in the village for considerably longer periods than the familiar seasonal male labour migrations. Long separations were detrimental to both marriage and household: some men's second relationships in their place of refuge became permanent and they stayed with their new partners after *la violencia*, especially if their land in the village had only been rented (a couple of women admitted that they did not know whether their husbands were dead or living with someone else). Meanwhile, their wives not only had to cope with the consequent reduction in income and support but had to pretend that their husbands were away working and not in hiding. In such circumstances, the husband is still considered the head of the household.

The negative consequences of separation during *la violencia* prepared women for the transition to widowhood to some extent. Women assumed economic and other responsibilities under extremely difficult conditions; they learnt to take decisions in their husbands' absence; they had to leave the house with greater frequency and go further afield, which most women initially found distressing. Women's routines seldom stray beyond the village[5] — even if they had, say, travelled to the market when their husbands were away, the ideology remained that their place was in the home with the children and animals. Many wives' economic circumstances barely changed when their husbands' status changed from absent to dead, though the psychological repercussions were immense. *La violencia* brought the outside world to the village and many women found they had to deal with it completely on their own.

The experience women gained during these periods of separation sometimes led them to question their husbands' decisions. For example, although the tradition of virilocal residence predisposes women to defer to their husbands on such matters, some wives had considerable influence on decisions such as whether or not a husband or indeed the whole family should flee during *la violencia*. *Doña* Ana used economic arguments to persuade her husband to stay in Emol, thus tacitly accepting responsibility for his death:

> My husband was the one who usually gave the orders but this situation was a little different for I really did not want to leave the house. I was thinking of my animals because, you see, they are mine. If we left, then we would have to sell the cows. But if I had sold them, then I would have had no way to make money for myself. So I told him, "The cows are mine, I will not sell them and no one orders me around!"

Most men considered that the hostile, external world was not part of women's domain; hence *doña* Josefina's husband was unconvinced by her understanding of the situation, which she expressed through the common idiom of a dream:

> I had a dream about two weeks before they kidnapped my husband... In the dream he was abducted, so when I woke, I told him, "Leave man! Go to the *fincas*! Go wherever you can so that you will be spared. Then, once it is all over, come home."

In the late 1980s, between 10 and 25 percent of household heads in southern El Quiché were women;[6] in Emol, 25 percent of households contained widows but the number of families which have lost menfolk is, of course, higher. An estimated 80 percent of widows live without another adult (excluding grown sons) in the household. The balance live with both parents, both in-laws, their mother, their mother-in-law, another lone woman (a spinster or a widow) or a subsequent husband (in her home or his). Households containing widows generally fall into four types: single widows, 'nuclear' widows (with unmarried children), 'affinal' households (with their in-laws) or 'filial' households (with married children and perhaps others).

The Collapse of the Traditional Support System

During and after *la violencia*, the community support women had been socialized to expect on widowhood (chapter three) failed to materialize. Most widows can identify with *doña* Eugenia's statement that widows

> ...feel undermined because no one cares for us. They call us 'women without men'. In this way they deride us. They gossip about us when we are forced to work the *milpa* because our men are not here and we have no money to pay for a agricultural labourer *(mozo)*. There are so many splits in the community these days that we do not receive help from others. Before, everyone helped each other. We would join together, lend a hand to those who needed it... But not any more.

One reason for the scant support given to widows is the dearth of able bodied men. *La violencia* cut a swathe through some families, leaving surviving menfolk with such overwhelming responsibilities under the traditional system that most do not attempt to meet them. Another reason is men's time-consuming patrol duties and the reclamation of their own fields which had returned to scrub during *la violencia*. Some women feel that these were merely excuses offered by kin who do not share their husbands' political beliefs. The main reason for men's reluctance to help their widowed kin, fear of being associated with a 'wife of the guerrilla', confirmed this view for many widows. *La violencia* caused the network of male kin and fictive kin *(compadres)* which underpinned traditional community support to collapse as survivors formed themselves into ever-smaller interest groups.

Some men do help their sisters, despite religious and political differences which are a source of fear and friction within the family. For example, *doña* Candelaria distrusts her Protestant brother because of his role in the murder of her husband. She only asks him for help when she is desperate; as part of the village's new authority structure, he feels secure enough to assist her. *Doña* Candelaria accepts his help, but criticizes him for his attempts to convert her to protestantism.

Widows receive new kinds of limited help which fell outside traditional concepts of reciprocal assistance. For example, *doña* Candelaria's brother gives her cash; *doña* Flora's brother, a cobbler, gives her shoes. Neither man helps with his sister's *milpa*. War-widows have been forced to look to themselves and their children of both sexes (who were often referred to as 'children of the guerrilla') in order to survive. Sons help their widowed mothers with the *milpa* but even they expect reciprocation — the land they will eventually inherit.

The lack of community support compelled women to develop new support systems through their children and, later, other widows, which were more dispersed or merely different from the traditional pattern; they learnt the value of self-reliance.

Widows' Income Generation

Widows are disadvantaged by their low earning power and limited opportunities for generating the income they need in their new roles as household heads. Widows were particularly hard hit by inflation and static wages (and sometimes reduced wages) which resulted in a tripling of prices (in real terms) for basic goods during the 1980s. The widows' situation is exacerbated by their fear of leaving their homes; fear of losing their land is as much a factor as their fear of the unknown outside world. Widows who remain based in highland villages continue to work within familiar spheres. Subsistence farming continues to be the mainstay of the household economy.

Women miss their husband's nurturance, which largely centred on the provision of foodstuffs; they compared the family diet before, during, and after *la violencia*. Malnutrition existed before *la violencia*, worsened during it, and lessened afterwards though many families' diets are still extremely poor. Malnutrition is rife in war-widows' families.

Widows particularly miss their husbands' agricultural labour because the barriers to women's cultivation of corn are still enforced. Thus any males in the family — usually boys too young, or men too old, for patrol duty — are recruited to tend the *milpa*. For example, *doña* Flora's grandsons, both under ten in 1988, struggled with their father's and grandfather's heavy hoes when planting the family corn. *Doña* Josefina's grandfather, with whom she lives, cares for her *milpa* but, because of his age and chronic alcoholism, his work is slow; her adopted son Diego, the child of a friend whose second husband refused to accept him, provides less help with this work than she had hoped. Widows only cultivate their own corn as a last resort as this provokes humiliating jeers from passers by, who call, "What's the matter, haven't you got a man?"

Cultural constraints force widows to employ *mozos* to work their *milpa*, increasing their need for cash just as family income drops to almost zero. *Doña* Flora hires an old man to do most of the heavy work — an old man costs half as much to employ as a young, able bodied worker;[7] *doña* Josefina sometimes hires her fourteen year old half-brother. It is increasingly difficult to find men to do this work: young men have become accustomed to city work and are 'badly educated' *(malcriado)* so far as agricultural work is concerned and older men are usually busy with their own fields.

Meeting the expenses of corn production is a major problem. Even comparatively well-off widows such as *doña* Flora, who obtains a small income from renting out some of her land, cannot afford to hire a *mozo* to work all the land she wants to cultivate herself, so some of it lays fallow; nor can she afford to buy enough fertilizer to spread within the optimum period on the fields. As a result her corn yields are low, only lasting the family six months of the year. Other women sell a range of maize foods, such as *tortillas, tamales,* and cornmeal drinks (*atol,* **the** drink), prepared from their meagre corn supplies, in order to meet these costs. They also sell their garden produce, poultry, and eggs which cannot by any stretch of the imagination be called surplus to the household's requirements. In large baskets on their heads, women carry enormous loads of home-produced edibles to the bi-weekly town market. Always accompanied by a child, the women trek for hours to save the bus fare. In between sales, women invariably keep themselves busy in order not to waste time, embroidering belts and doing other handiwork which they sell to directly customers or to a middleman who has a stall in the market.

Widows work at traditional handicrafts on a year round basis. They earn a meagre income by making straw plaits *(trenzas)* which are sold to be made into straw hats.[8] They plait as they walk to fetch water, with a basket of corn on their heads, a baby on their backs; there is hardly a moment when their hands are idle. Their earnings are so minimal — about five *centavos* daily; less than a penny — that it is really not worth the effort, yet people are judged by how quickly they can *trenzar*. This reflects the need to maintain a sense of continuity in their identities in the face of monumental change.

Women weavers sell smock tops (huipiles) though they earn very little for this skilled work. Some women slowly work at a commissioned huipil in order to earn a few *centavos*; producing a huipil takes a married woman three months and a widow even longer. Many widows say they have little time for weaving now that they have to take on men's work. Others have been forced to give up weaving altogether which entails a loss of identity, a loss of continuity with the past (cf. Annis 1987; Elhers 1990).

Widows also sell their animals in the market to meet major expenses which would have been met from their husbands' earnings. They sell a pig, sheep or cow in order to buy medicine or, when times improved, new clothes for the village *fiesta*. Women are reluctant to do this because they have less livestock than before *la violencia*, when many animals were stolen, killed or simply died. Only sheer desperation (caused, for instance, by a husband leaving his widow with huge debts to pay) forces widows to sell land.[9] Widows have no access to credit and, desperate for cash, they are sometimes forced to sell land at ridiculously low prices, even after taking inflation into account.[10]

At the end of the market day, like their husbands before them, many widows squander their hard-earned money on alcohol. Women sometimes end up in a drunken stupor in the road (a very rare occurrence prior to *la violencia*), their children sitting protectively beside them, waiting patiently for their mothers to sober up — just as the women themselves had waited for their husbands. Going to market with a child rather than a husband is a very forceful reminder of the latter's absence; K'iche' culture, with its prohibitions on the expression of grief and its pragmatic acceptance of alcohol's role in loosening inhibitions, almost pushes the bereaved women to drink. Women's resort to alcohol can be seen as a temporary relief or as a negative aspect of the male responsibilities they have assumed.

Most widows also work as seasonal agricultural labourers. Some hire themselves out locally as female peasants *(mujeres campesinas)*, for which they earn the same as an elderly male *mozo*; over the year, they earn about Q.84 (US$20). More commonly, widows migrate to the coast, repeating their experiences as children and newly-weds when they had made *tortillas* for *finca* workers; like their parents before them, they come home with about Q.80 for three months' work. Working in the *fincas* is often the first way widows made a wage following a husband's death or disappearance, even though they knew they were likely to experience further losses by taking their children there (chapter three).

A less common way for widows to earn an income is through specialist activities such as midwifery or curing. The work is not lucrative as women empathize with other women's poverty and normally charge according to means. Some women began working in these professions out of necessity: for example, *doña* Ana began working as a midwife when her daughter went into labour in the mountains whilst the family was hiding from the army.

Doña Josefina had practiced (informally) as a diviner (aj q'ij) before *la vio-lencia* but had stopped because she was 'seriously affected' by what was going on; she said she was not in a position to help anyone for three years (because she drowned her sorrows in alcohol). After considerable persuasion from an aj q'ij and her grandfather, she agreed to accept her destiny and undergo training (chapter one) because so many aj q'ij had been killed during *la violencia* — six in Emol alone. The income she obtains from this work means she does not have to hire herself out as an agricultural labourer or go to the coast like other widows (she still *trenzars*, but this is more of a habit than an economic activity; it is what Indian women do when their hands are free and as such is part of her identity). Less tangible benefits include her leadership position among the village's 'pure' Catholics *(cos-tumbristas)*; she also enjoys serving others, despite the danger of being out at all hours. Rumours circulate that women become midwives, curers or aj q'ij to legitimate staying out late at night to 'organize' or cavort with men. The latter accusation was levelled at midwives and female aj q'ij before *la violencia*, when the threat implied by such rumours was relatively minor.

Widows also earn an income in new ways; for example, *doña* Consuelo makes clay stoves for sale; her daughter Manuela earns a few pennies teaching adult literacy classes.

Children

It is considered better to have children of either gender and of any age than none at all. Even though it means having more mouths to feed, children provide valuable companionship at a time when several losses were incurred:

> If only I had [more] children I would not miss my husband so much. And if I had several children, I would feel better. You see, when my only child goes to graze the animals, I have to stay alone in the house and this makes me feel very alone. *Doña* Chepa has children who take the animals [to pasture] and others to keep her company at the same time. She always has someone talking to her.

A widow's children are an important source of emotional support and women often become dependent on them. Widows receive little emotional support from their peers, but such behaviour is generally muted in K'iche' society; they receive even less practical support from fellow widows.

Bereaved mothers are more likely to provide each other with emotional support as a mother's loss seems to carry more weight than a wife's: for example, both *doña* Eugenia and *doña* Flora feel their grief for their dead sons is greater than that of the men's wives, a rather extreme internalization of the idea that one should only grieve for one's husband during the funeral period. The lack of support between mother and daughter-in-law also reflects the reserve demanded by elders. Less mentioned is the support widows do get from their own mothers and daughters; even though mothers and their married daughters frequently live in different hamlets or villages, relationships between them are often close. *Doña* Flora now has a good relationship with her mother, who lives in another village; she says she takes strength from her mother's ability to survive on her own as a (natural) widow. *Doña* Josefina, *doña* Consuelo, and many other widows have strong and affectionate relationships with their own daughters. Mother-daughter relationships carry little economic weight and are therefore not, at least officially, highly valued.

For younger or lone widows, the need to send children (especially daughters) away from home to earn an income is particularly harrowing. The marriage of daughters is also traumatic, especially if the mother is then left alone in the house; nevertheless, a mother might prevail upon her daughter to marry quickly for economic reasons, including the hope that a son-in-law might help with her *milpa* and wood supply.

Children's contributions to the household, already important in 'normal times', became increasingly significant. Similarly, children have always been a source of social (economic) security for their mothers and this too was emphasized following a father's death when their widowed mothers felt incapacitated by the experience of *la violencia*. *Doña* Ana commented, "Other women [with husbands] can lift one hundred pounds *(quintal)* but I need my children's help. Actually, I can lift a *quintal*, but then I can hardly walk... My children help me, they take the place of my husband."

Extremely limited female employment opportunities means that child labour, however scanty, is the main source of income in many female-headed households in El Quiché. Children were set to work immediately following their father's death.

Girls. Girls were generally kept at home. They began performing women's tasks, often working independently of their mothers at an earlier age than normal, while their mothers tried to fill the roles of their missing husbands. Five year old girls were sometimes left to look after younger siblings while their mother works away from the village;[11] even toddlers were abandoned on their own. To avoid this separation, some widows forced their daughters to stay up all night making things to sell in the market. When talking about this, women express guilt about the harsh way they were forced to treat their children to make them work harder.

Girls accompany their mothers to the *fincas*, where they help their mothers fill baskets with coffee or make *tortillas* for the workers; some girls are taken on as maids by the *finca* owner. Sending girls to work as maids in *ladino* households was rare in southern El Quiché prior to *la violencia*.[12] Parents are reluctant to send their daughters not only because they know that mistreatment is common — physical and sexual abuse by the men of the house is not unheard of — but because they were concerned that their daughters will pick up bad habits from their *ladino* employers. Parents are afraid that girls will forget their culture as they work among *ladinos* and wear *ladino* clothes and shoes from an early age; some maids are as young as eight, although older girls are preferred because they can work harder. Maids only return to their villages once a year, although luckier girls come home more often, bringing a small contribution to the household. Poverty-stricken families, whether or not they had lost members to *la violencia*, have little option but to send their daughters to work as maids. Sometimes girls want to go because they see it as an opportunity to learn Spanish (cf. Burgos-Debray and Menchú 1984). Among the Emolteco women I knew, only *doña* Candelaria sent a daughter to work as a maid; she suffered remorse over this and, of course, her daughter's departure caused further loss to the household.

Boys. Older boys become the family breadwinners. *Doña* Candelaria's two eldest boys, Pedro and Santos, were teenagers when their father was killed; Pedro was already working as a street trader in Guatemala City and Santos, who had planned to become a teacher, had to give up his studies and join him in order to support their mother and younger siblings. Her third son, Esteban, soon joined them.

Many widows with older sons find they have control over a greater proportion of their sons' wages than they had had of their husband's income. Some women proudly told me that their sons give them Q.100 or so from their month's wages, saying, "Here, you know what to buy." This is more than they had received from their husbands, who only gave them household spending money *(gastos)* after they had done the weekly marketing, something which widows had to take over. Other widows discovered that their sons are just as selfish as their husbands had been. Nevertheless, widowhood generally gives at least senior women economic control of the household.

Boys also act as their mothers' protectors. Mothers say that eldest sons who take on their father's work take on their father's position in the family and often imbue them with the characteristics of the person whose tasks they have taken over. *Doña* Flora jokingly claimed of her eight year old grandson, "Now Eustaquio is my husband, he plants my fields and he goes with me to the market." Sons sometimes take on their dead or missing father's authority and exercise it over their mothers. *Doña* Candelaria's son Santos (now a policeman) forbade her to continue practicing as a midwife, an occupation she had taken up after *la violencia* in order to earn an income. He objected to the gossip about his mother 'talking' (having sexual relations) with other men when she visited her clients' houses; he thought that she should be at home. His objections to his mother's work coincided with an increase in violent activity in early 1990, which made people more afraid to visit each other's houses because of its subversive connotations. Santos was afraid for his mother because she had begun to participate in CONAVIGUA activities, but found a culturally acceptable and altogether safer way to justify restricting her movements. Like a significant proportion of the police force (which is subordinate to the army), Santos had become a policeman simply to earn a living. At the time, he was not against the aims of CONAVIGUA *per se* but his mother's active involvement was not only dangerous for her but could have caused problems for him.[13]

In many families, elder sons had also been killed in *la violencia* so the boys who worked were very young. Boys were given the responsibility of men's work as agriculturalists before they are considered old enough to leave the home to earn a cash income. One eleven year old boy told me, "I have no father, I have to keep my mother and work the land so we can eat." *Doña* Eugenia's grandsons Saturnino and Martín, then in their early teens, had to leave school when their grandfather and father were killed and immediately set to work. Initially, their efforts were not very lucrative, especially as both boys were forced to join the patrols.

Other families sent boys as young as seven years of age to seek employment in urban areas or on the coast, preferably accompanying an adult male relative or friend. By the age of eight to ten (instead of the pre-*la violencia* norm of eleven to thirteen), many boys travelled together without adult accompaniment. On the coast, they harvest coffee and cotton; in the towns and cities, they shine shoes, sell ice cream or help on street stalls selling cassettes, cheap watches, and other paraphernalia.

Many widows forced to send their sons away to work were afraid that their boys will become undisciplined and turn to alcohol and stealing (which are considered *ladino* traits). Women see discipline and education (in terms of the transmission of cultural values) as a man's role; mothers do not have the same authority over their children (especially their sons) as fathers do; widows often bemoan the absence of someone to take this authoritative role. In fatherless and grand fatherless households, there is no one to tell children stories which carry moral import or that they should remember the ways of the ancestors; no one to tell boys that one only becomes a K'iche' man through performing the functions of one. Mothers felt this lack most keenly during and immediately after *la violencia* when K'iche' moral values were inverted by the new local power-holders and children grew up knowing that men can acquire power, status, and material goods by killing with impunity. This has implications for sons' treatment of mothers and husbands' treatment of wives, given that *machismo* has increased. Boys see the army and the village patrol *jefes* as the strong ones; they contrast this with their own female-headed and female-dominated households, in some of which agriculture has become women's work. For some boys, being male has changed from being Indian agriculturalists to being rich and powerful *ladinos*.

Many boys who lost their fathers at an early age lose the motivation to assist their mothers with their *milpa* by the time they reach adulthood. They had worked in the capital, associated with *ladinos*, and boasted that city folk took them for *ladinos*. Some boys disappear into the ranks of the capital's estimated 10,000 street children who come under attack from the security forces. The price some women pay for their families' survival is the de-culturation and sometimes even the loss of their children.

Yet despite mothers' anxieties about their boys, widows with no sons or only young sons and grandsons sometimes complain about their relative disadvantage. *Doña* Flora remarked, "I tell the woman that she should feel consoled by the fact that she has three sons... They take the place of her husband. But me, I am on the streets once and for all."

Attitudes to Remarriage

Marriage Opportunities

Despite the cultural and pragmatic reluctance to mention previous liaisons, the incidence of remarriage among Emolteco war-widows is clearly low. The main reason for this is the lack of marriageable men: nationally, war-widows outnumber widowers by four to one and the ratio is considerably sharper in areas of heavy army involvement. Consequently, men are able to normalize their social position by remarrying almost immediately. Most of these second marriages, even those performed by local priests who accept their parishioners' widowed status, are bigamous in the eyes of the state which persists in its claims that the unregistered dead are not only alive but living with the guerrillas. These second unions are socially valid to the K'iche', among whom the concept of registering a marriage with the civil authorities is relatively new.

The highest incidence of remarriage is among young, childless widows. Most widows had children: even seventeen year old widows are likely to have at least one child. In Emol, the youngest widow was only nineteen when her husband was killed; she had four children. However, it is more common for a woman with four living children to be in her mid to late twenties on widowhood.[14] Such women have less opportunity to remarry.

In Emol, land is an important issue in remarriage.[15] From a prospective groom's perspective, a young, childless widow living on her husband's land is a very desirable marriage partner. They are targeted by men desirous of increasing their landholding by living on the widow's land while continuing to cultivate their own. Such behaviour is viewed as particularly dishonorable and provokes malicious rumours *(chismes)* and envy *(envidia)* — it is not so much that a man has a lot of land but how he acquires it which is important. Many widows are prepared to face the *chismes* accompanying an in-marrying husband because they are desperate to remarry: they want male protection in a household which has lost all its adult menfolk. The need for protection increased owing to *jefes'* constant threats of sexual harassment which contribute to women's feelings of helplessness. Women ask rhetorically, "How can I defend myself?", referring not only to practical matters but also to the supernatural threats which fill a woman's world.[16]

Remarriage is the simplest and most conventional way for a natural or a war-widow to overcome the loss of a husband's income and labour, but the scrabble for land in Emol complicates matters considerably. Older widows who wish to remarry because they want help with their land are sometimes prevented from doing so by their adult sons, who are understandably suspicious that the prospective groom is more interested in their mother's land than the woman herself. They present their mothers with a choice: "You will have to choose between him and your home; if you marry, we will only allow you here for a visit, no more."

Land inheritance is also an important issue for women considering moving to a new husband's home. A woman may be prepared to forfeit her own rights to her husband's land in return for the safer status of a wife, but a widowed mother is generally reluctant to risk her children's. Even if a second husband accepts his wife's children, they have no rights to his land, although this does not necessarily stop them from trying to obtain a share. One woman told me of the fighting between the adult children of her first and second marriages: the children from her present marriage did not want her older sons to have a share of their father's land. Trouble often arises between the children of both partners' previous marriages.

Most men do not want the financial responsibility of a widow's children and mothers-in-law are usually unwilling to accept a new wife's children into the household (some men do not even want the responsibility of their own children from a second union: a widow who had 'united' with a man on a *finca* and was abandoned when she became pregnant, suspected he already had a wife at home). Many widows are forced to leave their children with their paternal grandparents, which protects their land inheritance; leaving them with their mother's extended family or friends generally leads to its loss, especially if they move to another hamlet or village. Children whose parents had lived on rented land are sometimes simply abandoned.

Many widows say they have not remarried "because of my children". *Doña* Candelaria assumed that she would have to leave both her house and her four dependent children if she were to remarry: "How can I remarry when all my things are here?" she said; "I have my children and I would not leave them alone here in the house." In fact it is unlikely that *doña* Candelaria will remarry; she has dependent children, little land, and is considered too old in a marriage market overburdened with women. Yet she is more fortunate than most widows as her older children now have steady jobs and support the household; for *doña* Candelaria, remarriage is not an economic necessity.

Other widows tolerate an unhappy second marriage because of their need for financial security:

The death of my first husband changed virtually everything. I was left feeling disconsolate, desperate, and lonely. I was even at the point of committing suicide. You see, he was everything to me. But a year passed and then I began to live with another man in another village. This union was not a great success. I never felt that he was equal to my first husband because he beat me frequently. I would leave him but then we would get back together again. I tell you he was not a good man. But in the end I decided that I would tolerate all his madness for I didn't know how I would manage without him.

Other widows remarry to obscure their past. They are anxious to hide the fact that their husbands are among the war dead; they want to avoid accusations of being a witch, a whore or a 'wife of the guerrilla'. One widow told me she felt coerced into remarriage to end the *chismes* which surrounded her. This did not end her problems: her second husband was an alcoholic who, knowing how dependent she was on him, began to abuse her; his parents exacerbated the acrimonious situation between them and ended up snatching her eldest son.[17] *Doña* Luisa's description of her second marriage illustrates the complexity of relations within the household:

> I left my second husband because he beat me and he gave me no money. This was in part due to my mother-in-law, in whose house we were living. She encouraged me to leave once when her son was away on the coast. She said that I should leave before he returned to beat me again. So I left and returned to my parents' home. But then he came to get me. I soon realized that my mother-in-law was not trying to protect me but in fact it was sometimes her fault that he hit me. Although she supported me at times, at other times she turned against me. She also undermined me by asking me why I had married her son knowing that other women had left him before. But I decided that I had better tolerate it for if I left him, I'd find it exceedingly difficult to live. Also our people (qa winaq) would think badly of me.

Remarriage does not necessarily indicate that a woman is resigned to the death of a disappeared husband. They are vulnerable to the same pressures as widows and remarry for the same pragmatic reasons. One woman, who hoped her husband was still alive, said: "My husband was kidnapped, I still don't know if he's dead; all I know is that he is not here. I couldn't manage the children, so I married a man who agreed to support us." Other women indicate that their uncertainty about their husband's fate prevents them from remarrying.

A few women with their own homes and land obtain financial security by becoming a man's concubine; as neither partner changes residence, the arrangement protects women and children, except from potentially dangerous rumours which may circulate about the liaison. Widows living in their mother-in-law's house have less opportunity to form such liaisons. Such widows have fewer opportunities all round: several widowed mothers-in-law prevent their daughters-in-law from remarrying by refusing to give their permission. A common reason for this is that many widowed mothers-in-law have dependent children of their own and cannot afford to raise their grand-children as well.[18] More frightening to older widows is the prospect of being left alone without another adult in the house.

The Rejection of Remarriage

Some women have clearly made a positive choice not to remarry though the distinction between deliberate rejection and external obstruction is not clear cut: widows' chances of remarriage depend on the opportunities they face, the support they and their children can expect, and their 'habitus' (cf. Bourdieu 1977).[19] Many women struggled on by themselves, finding a temp-orary *mozo* instead of a permanent husband to work their land; over time, widows began to view this necessity as a positive choice.

Some women who had had a negative experience of conjugal life de-cided not to repeat the experience. They see no advantage in having another husband who gets drunk, beats them, and fails to provide them with *gastos*. Younger women are prepared to 'tolerate' men and their sometimes violent ways within a marriage but older women have the opportunity to avoid this a second time round.

Older women with a positive experience of conjugal life also avoid re-marriage because they wish to preserve the image of their husbands; their determination not to remarry reflects their resolve to maintain psychological ties with him. This is typically expressed in terms of 'remembering'[20] a dead or disappeared husband: "How would I act if I saw another person who wasn't my husband when I still remember him so well? Listen, if another man came who wasn't my husband, I honestly think that I wouldn't be able to stand it."

A woman's perception of her late husband not only as a good man but as a valued authority in the community can influence her decision not to re-marry. Men who had been community leaders, (Catholic) presidents of local Improvement Committees, and health workers are viewed as 'honourable' by their widows, who tend to share their politics. These widows are inclined to see their husbands as martyrs; such idealization relates to their refusal to remarry. Remembering a perfect relationship with a dead or disappeared husband, coupled with incomplete mourning, hampers many women's ef-forts to rebuild their lives (Bowlby 1961:335).[21] Many if not most widows have been deprived of the opportunity to perform funerary rituals (chapter eight) and some have been denied confirmation of their spouse's fate. Many women, even the most resourceful members of the widows' group who have successfully held their families together, are unable to let go of the past.

A woman's religious beliefs and identifications also influence whether or not she remarries. Catholic women sometimes convey the image of being like Penelope, waiting. This is encouraged by Petronila, an unmarried female catechist who speaks to them 'in the name of the Virgin' (chapter seven). Some *costumbrista* widows told me that their husbands had told them (via a 'spirit caller'; aj mes) not to remarry but to 'act well' (be chaste), although this can be seen as a projection of their own. A few women simultaneously boast and lament their chaste ways; other widows claim that women who, like themselves, have not remarried are 'honourable', 'respectful', and 'imaginative'. They say they have no desire to marry again, sometimes intimaating a notion of destiny: "I became a widow and that is how I have to remain," said *doña* Candelaria. The same women often joke and gossip about other widows who have remarried. *Doña* Tomasa caused ribald laughter when she observed of another widow, "She remarried because she did not like being alone...who knows why...I suppose it's because the body doesn't like to be deprived of satisfaction."

Women who decline remarriage indicate that it would entail taking on an older, divorced man, a widower or someone who wants a second 'wife' (a bigamous relationship). They have lost trust in men, viewing them as lascivious and 'no good'; widows suspect almost any surviving male may have betrayed their husbands. I heard many conversations expressing women's fears of male intimidation and their own ambivalence towards remarriage. The following exchange is typical:

Doña Ana:
> A man came two times and almost entered in the animal pen *(corral)*. I was not in the house the second time he came so he spoke with my son, Santos, asking for me. This man's name was *don* Juan. I didn't know him personally but I know his wife had died the previous year. I said to my Santos that maybe he had come to ask after [propose to] me. What an unnerving thought! If he comes again I would not know how to respond.

Doña Flora:
> You must say to him, "Excuse me, I do not want to talk to you"...that's all.

Doña Ana:
> Yes, I suppose so, for apart from anything else he's already very old.

Doña Flora:
> And if you did [marry him], you'd only be left in his house for him to die with you. And what would you want that for?

Doña Ana:
> You know, on another occasion I attended mass with my children and we saw him there and he was with another woman [that's awful, interjected *doña* Flora]. Yes... It was a Wednesday when I saw the old man at mass and then he came to look for me again the following Friday. I thought that he was very ugly. So after that I asked my children to accompany me [when she left the house]. I also told them that should this man came to look for me when I was out, they should tell him not to come again. I insisted on this because, really, the man is very old and it appears he's after all the women. In fact, it seems

that he goes around chasing all the widows, at least that is what his daughter-in-law told me. They are pure filth *(son puros desaseados)*, these men.

Doña Flora:

They are all like that. *Don* Tomas did the same with *doña* Cecilia and not only with her but with all of them. But if this man has daughters-in-law who wash his clothes and cook for him, what does he want with a wife...perhaps he's a little crazy or something.

Doña Ana:

Yes, now I can't trust them [men] because, who knows, perhaps they ate the brains of the poor ones [killed their menfolk]... Did he come here as well?

This conversation is both an expression of envy in the light of their own lack of opportunity to remarry and a justification of their own refusal. Widows who say they do not wish to remarry occasionally admit that life is just not the same without a husband. Women who express this sentiment include widows whose financial worries have decreased because their sons or grandsons are now old enough to provide the household with a constant income. Ambivalence is typical of many widows who are still in a general state of disequilibrium: "But isn't it good that you were left with two young [grand] sons?" asked *doña* Flora. "It's some consolation," replied *doña* Eugenia, "but it still not the same, because one always needs a husband." *Doña* Flora conceded, "Yes, I suppose they are necessary." *Doña* Eugenia replied, "It's different when one is a couple." She began to cry.

But women's overt rejection of remarriage is, to some extent, a means of saving face in the light of scarce opportunities. Older widows with children have less opportunity, but they sometimes have less need to remarry; they also have more authority to refuse. This is often couched in terms of economic independence: if widows have the use of their husband's land (cf. Wagley 1949:46) and the means to maintain themselves, they can refuse to remarry, even if their sons are very young. *Doña* Ana thought that if a widow is financially secure, then there is no need to remarry: "You know they tell me that a man fell in love with *doña* Tomasa but she didn't want him because she has grown sons who maintain her and she therefore has nothing to worry about." These are *post-hoc* rationalizations, made when the women had successfully survived for many years on their own. Widowhood is not a steady social state at all, even for those women who have accepted the role as irreversible and fixed.

Relations with Others

Solidarity and Conflict Among Widows

Solidarity exists among widows whether their menfolk died from natural causes or were war dead, though there is a limit to the understanding and empathy between them. The experience of unnatural widowhood also differs: women whose kin were killed by the *jefes* and the army (by far the numerical majority) are called 'wives of the guerrilla' by army sympathizers whereas the widows of army sympathizers are not pejoratively labelled. Some women spontaneously differentiate widows whose husbands are believed to have been killed by the guerrilla. Members of the widows' group often identify other widows and survivors in terms of 'organizing': in private, when discussing other women, they say, "She was an organized person *(organizada)*" or "Her husband wasn't an *organizado*", and so on. *Doña* Flora is one of the few women who, impromptu, labels people as having been 'organized' or not; it is apparent that she trusts *organizados*. Knowing that being 'organized' covers everything from joining an adult literacy class to being a gun-toting guerrilla, I asked for more details of what this meant. I was invariably dismissed with the answer, "These were meetings which were held at night." Then the subject was changed.

Widows whose husbands and/or themselves are viewed to be on opposite sides keep an eye on each other and generally do not mix, other than to greet each other politely as a way of avoiding conflict. There are exceptions to this: *doña* Flora, for example, invited an old woman to live with her for a while when the latter's husband died: not only was this woman not an *organizado* but *doña* Flora believed her to be a q'ol q'ol, a person who, at night, can transform herself into an animal which goes about 'eating' (killing) children. She had recognized her house guest as a q'ol q'ol because of the barely perceptible white streak in her hair. I never understood why she did it, but she told me that she was trying to act on her Christian principles.

There is a further differentiation between widows and women whose menfolk were disappeared. Women whose relatives were abducted have a different experience from those who knew their men are dead. Like 'real' widows, they too are considered to be malca'nib, regardless of any personal hopes that their husbands might return.

Difficulties sometimes arise from the recognition that others experienced different degrees of loss. A widow whose children were also killed might ask rhetorically of another widow, "Why did her children live while mine died?" At times she holds the woman with children responsible for this, especially if she is on the 'other side'.

While some widows co-operate with one another, at least in some domains, others are competitive. Conflict and jealousies are common among communities of survivors (Lifton 1967; Das 1990). Conflict is chronic in Emol, and widows are not immune. Competition for scarce resources makes them each other's rivals; factions suddenly form if they suspect resources have been unfairly distributed. Most rumours of this nature originate with the village's *jefes*, who do their best to foment discord between widows. The tactic lead some widows to withdraw from the NGO-supported widows group. Other women lost faith in the benefits of membership when their un-realistic expectations of material help were not realized. Most widows who dropped out of the NGO widows' group did not rejoin when it was taken over by CONAVIGUA; others rejoined because they heard that the organi-zation was issuing free fertilizer to widows; a few more joined because they had a mission to exhume their kin and rid themselves and the community of the dangers of both the malicious spirits of the dead and the *jefes.*

Conflict also arises because widows cannot agree on how they should behave now that they have been compelled to leave their traditional roles behind. The argument rages both within the widows' group and between its members and other widows who, for various reasons, are too afraid to join it (the desire to reintegrate themselves into the community through remar-riage or the marriage of their children is strongest among these women). Widows adopt various ways of being which allow survival but each has dif-ferent capacities to be innovative. Socialized to be the 'conservers of tradi-tion', many widows feel uncomfortable with the changes they have had to make and are uncertain of the best way to proceed. *Costumbrista* women probably feel the least uncertainty because they consult aj q'ij who make mirror-like interpretations of dreams and signs to help people relocate them-selves, confirming their sense of orientation and identity, and even telling them, in the most practical terms, what to do.

All widows tend to observe and be highly critical of each other. Wid-ows cannot avoid the public attention their situation brings yet find them-selves criticized by others, including widows, for not abiding by the cultural norms of avoiding public attention. Their disapproval of one another reflects their own insecurity as they adopt new roles. It is also a projection of the conflict which many women experience because of the demands made of them and their own self-doubt and self-criticism. The women's narratives of the explanations they receive from the spirits regarding their aberrant behav-iour also reflects this. *Doña* Josefina communicated with the spirit of her husband (through an aj mes) to obtain an explanation for her alcoholism fol-lowing his death. The explanation indicates the aj mes' (and possibly her own) attempt to reconcile her behaviour:

> I went to ask him why I liked to drink so much. I was desperate about this. I said, "When you were living, I didn't have the urge to go in all the bars."

> [And what was his response?]

> He said, "The truth is, it is not your fault. They [sorcerers] did this in order to destroy you. Ordinarily you would have no reason to drink but since the people killed me and since you already had this [tendency],[22] you've suc-cumbed to it."

One of the most common and acceptable bases for widows' overt criticism of each other revolves around moral and religious differences. Widows attempt to correct one another when they perceive others to behave immorally. *Doña* Josefina related how another widow told her she was behaving incorrectly:

> One woman, Santa Yac, who came to visit me when I was ill[23] told me off, saying that I only got drunk for the sake of it. She said that she thought it was dreadful that I let my children go without food while I get drunk. She said I got drunk to make trouble.

Even widows who form supportive networks within the community according to affinity, natal family, religion or other group membership such as popular movements and widows' groups, resort to gossiping about one another sooner or later. For example, *doña* Josefina and *doña* Flora share similar politics but *doña* Josefina, who remains a *costumbrista*, feels criticized by *doña* Flora who has converted to *la Renovación*, the puritanical charismatic Catholic sect which criticizes alcohol consumption, playing or dancing to the traditional wooden xylophone *(marimba)*, and so on. As an aj q'ij, *doña* Josefina drinks as part of her duties and *doña* Flora criticizes her on these grounds and for 'talking to' (have illicit relations with) men. She once suggested that *doña* Josefina had even killed a child conceived in one of her illicit affairs by drowning it in a water hole.

Doña Flora, in turn, feels criticized by another widow: "I am desperate because this woman tells me that I'm ill [immoral] because I am never in my house. She says, 'Now two weeks have passed and you have only gone around frivolously while I am here doing all my chores.'" The bone of contention here is leadership within the widows' group, which some women consider incompatible with traditional female roles. Such criticisms indicate that widows do not wish to entirely relinquish a woman's traditional place despite being forced to assume responsibilities outside their usual domain.

Yet despite the suspicion, rivalry, and competitiveness, widows draw strength from their relations with one another:

> The consolation we have is that there are several of us widows and we advise each other. The others tell us, "Leave your concerns aside, for it is better that you should not be sad."

Widows' Autonomy

With their husbands dead or missing, women learnt to make important domestic decisions and take public action. They are sometimes unwilling to remarry, thus resuming a more dependent role. These women implicitly contest and challenge male constructions of the female role, usually only in private with female interlocutors.

Women realize that despite preaching about equality in their catechist classes, men do not change their behaviour but still expect the traditional divisions of labour to operate in their personal lives. Many of the tasks pertaining to family life which women have had to take over and reorganize had been hidden in normal times, as *doña* Candelaria explains:

> He was head of the house, he was the one who worked and earned money, he was everything. He cultivated the *milpa*, I never touched the hoe when he was here, nor the fertilizer, much less do the work itself. I only carried out the preparation of the food, looked after the children, and kept the house clean. This was my work but now everything is in my hands.

Widows who venture into traditionally male domains do not necessarily expect a new division of labour at home; in fact, many women seem to want to maintain the domestic division as it is. Such women frequently refer to the loss of someone with whom to make decisions. They complain, for example, "Now there is no one with whom to decide which colour corn to sow..." *Doña* Josefina often consults her husband's spirit on agricultural matters, thereby continuing to make decisions with his help several years after his death.[24] "The others have planted their corn," she said; "but my worry is that we've yet to do this. This is the most problematic consequence of not having a man in the house."

Yet despite their complaints and their heavier work load, widows do not want to relinquish their broadened repertoire of roles, including participation in economic and other public spheres. Becoming the breadwinner brings control of the family economy and also a new identity, making women more self-reliant and confident. *Doña* Teresa describes the process:

> We were sad for two long years. You see, when they were alive, our husbands looked after all our necessities. They got the fertilizer, they were responsible for the expenses of the house, etc. Without them we could find little consolation. The first year was the most difficult, then the next year we learnt new skills little by little. I taught myself how to work, how to buy things, and how to maintain the family. We learnt to be both father and mother to our children.

Many women derive an everyday feeling of accomplishment in their non-traditional roles and thereby experience a diminution of their depression. As *doña* Josefina said, "When our *milpa* grows then, little by little, our sadness disappears..." *Doña* Teresa also felt comforted when her corn grew:

> Only then did I find some consolation. Now we still think of our husbands but it is less painful than it was before. We have finally learnt how to live without them. Now and then we still get sad because of them...well, not because of them, as such, but because we have necessities which we can't fulfill given that we are widows.

Despite the burden of their double role of being women and men, mothers and fathers,[25] widows have become confident of their ability to move in heretofore relatively unknown, male, spheres.[26] Once they got used to it, many women began to enjoy their freedom, newly acquired knowledge, and sense of mastery. *Doña* Flora once told me:

> *Ladinos* treat us badly in the market place and on the buses. They say that we want loads of money but we, as widows, are beginning to know a little. Before, as wives, when we used to go to the town, we would not even think of ascending the steps of the town hall. Now we not only ascend the steps but we even talk to the mayor![27]

The widows' survivorship increased their self-esteem: "We've been alone for eight years," marvelled *doña* Flora. *Doña* Josefina agreed, "Yes, we've been alone for eight years and we're still alive." *Doña* Flora repeated proudly, "We're alive, and we're dressed, and we've done on it on our own."

Normal life cycle events, such as a child's marriage, makes widows realize that they have managed, despite the odds stacked against them. *Doña* Eugenia was particularly happy when her granddaughter married and the wedding took place in her house. This had been difficult to arrange because the groom's parents wanted to see her father's official documents. Gilberto's papers had been confiscated by the *jefes*, which means his death cannot be registered.[28] The marriage took place and the family achieved a degree of normalization and re-integration as a result.

It was not only the widows who realized they had not only coped but had achieved a degree of autonomy in terms of control of economically productive resources and their own activities; married women noticed it too. The wife of an alcoholic admitted, "We too would be better off alone. We would be able to work better. If only men did not exist...then we would be able to decide what to do without needing to follow their orders."

But the widows' autonomy was to cause a different set of problems.

Perceptions of Widows

Married Women

Married women fear that widows could jeopardize the stability of their marriages. "They suspect that we intend to steal their husbands," *doña* Josefina said; "they taunt us in public, saying, 'Why don't you stop scrounging and go to work yourselves.'" Wives blame widows for the continuing poverty of married women; they fret that widows' apparent economic autonomy results from illicit affairs with their husbands, whom they suspect of giving cash and gifts to their mistresses. This dignifies the men's relations with the widows; according to them, patrollers take what they want.

Widows told me that patrollers force themselves on widows and that "when the 'wives of the patrols' find out that a widow slept with their husbands, they take revenge on all the widows", singling out the victim for special abuse. "They accuse them of all sorts of things and collectively they ask the accused widow, 'Why do you sleep with our husbands?' So in daylight, no one knows which man it was." Everybody knows which man it was, but no one is prepared to identify him publicly.

Poverty is the driving force behind local attitudes towards polygamy. Scarce resources are a constant source of conflict between wives and widows. Married women are envious of the widows' supposed ability to obtain economic assistance from development agencies and the government but aid is minimal. Government aid was issued just once in Emol. Few women dared to collect it because they were afraid to display their status. Widows who did apply showed considerable restraint and dignity; there was little of the covetousness and greed married women accused them of. NGOs distributed food at the height of *la violencia*; later, they gave widows loans in the form of livestock which were to be repaid when the animal was sold. The scheme was not as successful as had been hoped because many of the animals died: some widows could not afford to feed them.[29] A more serious consequence of this gift of what the K'iche' consider to be a major capital asset was the reaction of other villagers, especially those who had lost kin but were not widows. They expressed their enviousness of the 'compensation' given to widows indirectly, through ridiculing them. NGOs realized they were exacerbating conflict within villages by distinguishing between wives and widows and that all women were poor.

Married women are perceived to be angry at, and jealous of, widows for the mere fact that they managed. "Women who still have their husbands are very angry with us," said *doña* Flora; "they act as though we have done something to harm them." The perception of other women's anger provokes indignation among widows. *Doña* Josefina:

> Before when I went out, say, to the market, my husband accompanied me and there were no problems. But now I go out and I encounter some women who appear to be angry with me. They insult and offend me. Perhaps they would have reason to treat me so badly if I were divorced or something. But I did not separate with my husband out of choice, did I?

Despite her indignation, *doña* Josefina takes pride in her ability to survive: "We succeeded, we have managed in the end. Because of this the women who are still married say, 'These women are pure shit. Who knows why they've acquired so much intelligence.'"

Some widows believe that wives' attitudes towards them "have been affected by the fact that their men have carried out so many assassinations". *Doña* Josefina's remark shows an instinctive understanding of the process by which cultural norms and morality have been contaminated by patrol duty, leading to new definitions of humanness which exclude 'subversives' and their surviving kin (chapter five). She can see no valid reason for wives' attitudes towards widows and suggests they have 'caught' these new understandings of humanness from their husbands.

Men's Attitudes

Widows' successful performance of male roles is confusing for men because of K'iche' society's traditional strict divisions of labour. Many men feel their masculinity and traditional male roles as sole providers and negotiators with the outside *ladino* world have been threatened by the widows: perceiving them as competitors for traditionally male-gendered activities, power, and resources leads to increased attempts to marginalize widows. What it is to be a 'strong' man changes in the context of war.

Widows' independence is threatening to *jefes* who fear the women's growing strength might lead them to find the courage to report their crimes (chapter five). *Jefes*, who no longer identify with their roles as Indian agriculturalists, have a vested interest in maintaining their violent, *macho* image.

Women's Self-perceptions

Widows have been forced to alter their image of themselves in the world although, in order to maintain a sense of continuity, thoughts about the self lag behind actual changes in behaviour and role position.[30] Widowhood presented a major change in self-perception: women no longer had the protection of their menfolk and now had to go into the male, outside world, alone.

Many women learnt Spanish after widowhood, through attending *doña* Manuela's language class, but they do not view themselves in any way as *ladinas* (chapter two). One woman expressed her satisfaction at mastering rudimentary Spanish by saying, "All our lives we had big ears...we were like donkeys, unable to speak." Just as it had for their late husbands, learning Spanish facilitates the widows' movement in the *ladino* world and provides them with access to certain types of knowledge. *Doña* Josefina explains:

> I have changed a little in all ways now. I feel that I have more knowledge about things. I feel that I have learnt how to speak [Spanish]. Now, with ease, I can enquire about different subjects. Whereas before I did not realize about things and neither was I able to think.

It is not that the women think speaking K'iche' is unimportant; rather, they have a sense of achievement about adding a new and useful dimension to their lives. Their attachment to their own language is demonstrated by their response to *doña* Candelaria's new daughter-in-law, a woman from the Ixcán area who defines herself as Indian but only spoke Spanish when she arrived in the village; behind her back, widows gossiped that she was 'really'

a *ladina*. The girl's readiness to learn K'iche' and wear local clothes helped
with her (admittedly slow) integration into the community.

Taking on men's roles added to the widows' multiple identities with
both positive and negative repercussions on psychological, social and economic levels; yet they do not perceive themselves as 'male' because of the
roles they have been obliged to assume[31] — despite their complaints that
they are both 'mothers and fathers' to their children. It is very important for
them to continue with their own work as grinders of corn and to wear their
traditional clothes which state that they are available for the men of their
own community and not 'ladino' soldiers or civil patrollers.

Although (among Chichicastecos), "one's occupation is one's distinguishing characteristic, as inseparable a part of one's personality as one's sex
[and] the fulfillment of life consists of the completion of what is expected of
one" (Bunzel 1952:34), I did not get the impression that women who assume
male tasks (apart from those which are taboo and cause mortification to perform) are degraded by carrying them out. If anything, women's self-esteem
increases through the performance of tasks which are accorded more value
in the male world.

At the same time, a widow's thoughts of herself as an attractive sexual
being diminish. In the early stage of fieldwork, I asked *doña* Ana, via my interpreter (*doña* Flora), how she thought that the rest of the community view
widows. *Doña* Flora answered me herself, saying, "I believe that we aren't
pretty any more now that we are no longer with our husbands... How can I
think about how I am when I do not even have time to look at myself?" She
then asked her friend a different question: "How do women seem now that
they were widows? Are they still pretty, does anyone [men] want them?"
Both women laughed. *Doña* Ana answered, "I think we are not very pretty
nor much good because we are unable to do it [have sex] any more." On another occasion I unwittingly provoked raucous laughter when I asked women
if they missed their husbands' company other than as providers; they thought
I was referring to sexual relations which, except when gossiping or drunk,
they only address obliquely.

Widows identify themselves as 'other' in contrast to their memories of
what they used to be as marriage/sex partners, which they see depicted in
traditional married women. They view themselves not only as both 'women
and men' (with attendant positive and negative effects) but as children:
"Now we have been left alone," asserted *doña* Eugenia, "we seem like
children." Her remark refers not only to their chastity, but to the traditional
criterion for adulthood: marriage. In this regard, the women's hard-won
autonomy is irrelevant; it is a statement of their perception of their damaged
personhood. By referring to themselves as 'child-like', women are saying
that not only have they lost their menfolk but have also lost the power to
think or speak about what happened to them (cf. chapter seven); they have
lost what little power they had to make themselves heard (Bourdieu 1977).

By not being allowed to conform to the cultural model of wife or widow, women are anomalous beings whom different categories of people in K'iche' society attempt to categorize. Persistent intimidation and the relentless accusations of 'subversiveness' and 'sinfulness' encourages low self-esteem and undermines women's sense of self. Some widows' behaviour indicates their acceptance of the negative identities ascribed to them; motivated by either conscious fear, an unconscious drive to act according to the role they have been assigned (thus eliciting further abuse), a culturally inculcated desire to please authority or a mixture of all three. Such women sometimes 'fell into' a position of dependency or prostitution with *jefes*. A woman may even be flattered by the attention of a powerful man (one widow intimated this about herself). A few widows, demoralized by a recent history of abuse which resonated with their own personal history of abuse, may have elicited further abuse. For example, telling the widow that she is 'the wife of a guerrilla' with the life threatening danger this implies, means that over time she may be resocialized to respond to the *jefes* as if she is truly guilty.

Some widows remarry in their attempt to reject the identities others try to impose on them. Some widows, perhaps strengthened by their solidarity with other women, take on new, positive identities, which in a few cases have even been mobilized to political ends such as participating in demonstrations as a member of CONAVIGUA or GAM for example.

Conclusion

The unprecedented slaughter of Indian men during *la violencia* not only deprived women of their complementary partners and other adult male kin but destroyed the system of economic and labour support which they had expected would support them in their hour of need. Women were forced to take on traditionally male roles to varying degrees and, despite the extra laborious work this entailed, gained a sense of esteem from this; they say that they feel more knowledgeable and more capable *(más capaces)* as a result.

Denying war-widows re-entry into 'normal' social life means they are no longer harnessed to male authority. This has had both positive and negative repercussions. Their new responsibilities bring them into contact with women in similar positions, allowing widows to create new networks of support which, unlike those of previous family constellations, are relatively free from social control (and especially male control).

With time and the help of available grown sons, many widows have acquired a degree of economic self-sufficiency, independence, and self-esteem. Some of the more resourceful widows enjoy greater autonomy than previously, but with this comes greater responsibility which not all widows want; given the chance, widows, especially younger ones, opt to marry again.

Neither younger nor older women mention the possibility of redefining gender relations as a way of dealing with male violence. Wife beating has always been seen as 'very manly' and worsened during *la violencia* as indigenous men became increasingly influenced by the patriarchal norms of the *ladino* military. Many men have ceased to regard women as essential complementary partners, reclassifying them as inferior and subordinate. For such men, all women become legitimate targets of abuse.

Widows who survive in the face of so much male antagonism and violence are actually rewriting the rules of gender relations whether they intend it or not. Younger widows see that it is possible to survive without a husband and a few have decided not to remarry; some of them are active in human rights organizations and it seems they believe marriage is incompatible with their political activities. Other politicized women are beginning to question gender roles more directly.

Notes

1. The term malca'nib (pl.), malca'n (sing.), is the K'iche' word for widowed, divorced, separated or abandoned women and single mothers; it is used to imply a permanent state although since *la violencia* the term has been used by the wives of the disappeared who do not necessarily think their husbands are dead. In Spanish, different terms are used for widows *(viuda)*, divorced *(divorciada)*, abandoned *(abandonada)*, and single women with or without children *(soltera)*.

2. Guatemala City's population doubled between 1976 and 1987; massive migration following the earthquake continued through *la violencia*, creating a broader axis of poverty. Half a million people live in squatter settlements on the outskirts of the city; 50 percent of shanty town dwellers live in extreme poverty and a further 25 percent live in poverty.

3. The K'iche' word bis is a much larger concept than the Spanish *'tristeza'* or the English 'sadness' as it encompasses ideas of loneliness and social isolation, which the K'iche' consider unnatural and hence dangerous and frightening.

4. *Susto* (xib') also has connotations of being terrorized by spirits, soul loss, and death.

5. Even when girls and women worked on the coast their (work related) contact with *ladino* overseers and *finca*-owners was practically non-existent because migrant labourers virtually take the village to the *finca*: families travel together and preferably work alongside others from their home communities. This did not, however, prevent the sexual abuse and rape of Indian women by *ladino* overseers.

6. Similar figures have been reported for villages in Chimaltenango, a department southeast of El Quiché (Green 1995).

7. Old men earn two Quetzales (plus meals) a daily.

8. In Emol, making *trenzas* was men's work when women were still weavers.

9. Since an Indian holds his land "beneath the hands of [the] ancestors and as a trust which [he] must pass on to [his] children, the sale of land is a great sin against the ancestors as well as against one's children" (Bunzel 1952:23). Nevertheless, it occurred.

10. In 1989, land three miles from town cost Q.3,500 per *cuerda* (0·9 acres), about US$1,000 per acre; land considered far from town was worth Q.500 per *cuerda*. In the early 1980s, i.e., at the height of *la violencia*, women sold their land

in remote areas for Q.100 (roughly US$25) or less per *cuerda*.

11. Children of this age sometimes have to look after younger siblings even if both parents are still alive. One woman told me she had been left to look after her younger sister while her mother accompanied her father, who was an aj q'ij. cf. Burgos-Debray and Menchú (1984:334).

12. This was more common among the Ixils or Uspantecos further north. cf. Burgos-Debray and Menchú (1984).

13. By 1993, Santos had internalized military values.

14. On average, women had four children on widowhood: approximately 45 percent of widows had four to six children and 55 percent had one to three children.

15. In contrast, marriages or 'unions' among the Ixils of northern El Quiché are uncomplicated by economic considerations and take place between people whose spouses are known to be dead or are just missing. Their villages have been razed to the ground in 1980-1981 and they have no possibility of recovering their lands; they live a nomadic existence in the mountains, facing repeated displacements to escape the army.

16. *Costumbrista* women also lost the protection solicited by their husbands in daily rituals carried out in the home at the home altar (chapter three).

17. Children, especially boys, are seen as an investment. For example, *doña* Eugenia's daughter-in-law legally adopted a friend's orphaned son; years later, his father's family tried to reclaim him. *Doña* Eugenia's rejection of their claim was expressed in terms of the money invested in the boy way of medicines, food, etc.

18. As many Emolteco girls marry before the age of sixteen, it is common for a woman to have grandchildren older than her own youngest children.

19. By 'habitus' Bourdieu (1977) means the propensity to select responses from a particular situation or field. Unlike the concept of 'rules', habitus has the great advantage of allowing its users to recognize the extent of individual freedom within certain limits set by the culture.

20. The same term is used in connection with the ancestors, although men who died less than twenty years ago have yet to become ancestors. Remembering the ancestors involves adhering to traditional customs and mores.

21. cf. Raphael (1983:44): "In the earliest phases of the bereavement one's review of the image and memories of the dead are often idealized, the deceased and the relationship remembered in perfection. Then, if mourning is progressing satisfactorily, more of the real memories, the positive and negative aspects representing ambivalence inevitable in human relations are recalled".

22. A reference to her nahual. See chapter nine.

23. *Doña* Josefina is referring to the years she spent drowning her sorrows in alcohol following her husband's death. The K'iche' word for 'ill' also means 'immoral', reinforcing the link between sin (mak) and ancestral punishment (illness).

24. Western psychologists reporting on people who say their dead loved ones appear in their dreams and are their companions whom they continue to consult, say they have "denial woven into their dreams" (Stewart and Hodgkinson 1988:13).

25. Only one type of being in the K'iche' natural and supernatural universe combines both elements of the complementary, male-female pair: the aj q'ij. Hence, being 'mother and father' to someone is not an unknown concept, even if it is one that is usually applied to sacred matters.

26. This had already begun with catechization (chapter two).

27. Only a select group of women, the leaders of the village's widows' group, have the courage to do this. Most Indians — and especially monolingual women — are deterred from this type of task by the pervasive climate of racism.

28. Gilberto had attempted to give his papers to his mother, *doña* Eugenia, when he was taken to her house by the patrols before being murdered in the village massacre. His mother reported: "At that point the patroller shouted, 'keep quiet!' (Xo!) [an expression used to animals] and pointed his gun at me, so I was unable to take his papers and who knows what became of them."

29. The idea of granting loans in the form of livestock seems eminently sensible until one remembers the subsistence farmer's perennial cry of "God rot a gift that eats".

30. cf. Bettelheim (1986:79): "when social change is rapid, there is not enough time to develop the new attitudes needed for dealing with an ever changing environment in terms of one's own personality. This makes the individual 'confused' and uncertain...weakens his integration and he grows less and less able to respond with autonomy to new change".

31. The only 'ordinary' context (i.e., unconnected with *la violencia*) in which I heard a woman say she was a man — in fact, 'very male' *(muy hombre/macho)* — was when she described herself as very angry, almost to the point of violence. The most common expression of being 'very male' is wife beating; anger is a 'male' emotion.

7

Popular Memories of 'La Violencia'

Without forgetting it is quite impossible to live at all. (Nietzsche 1980:10)

It may be imprecise in some details because it is based on two memories (his and mine), and then over long distance human memory is an erratic instrument, especially if it is not reinforced by material mementos and is instead spiced by desire (again, his and mine) that the story be a good one. (Levi 1986:144)

Experiences, like tales, fêtes, poetries, rites, dramas, images, memories, ethnographies, and allegorical machineries, are made; and it is such things that make them. (Geertz 1986:380)

The War on Memory

The Denial of History

The entire history of *la violencia* can be read as a war against memory, an Orwellian falsification of memory,[1] a falsification of reality. The military state attempted to deny people access to truth, thus contaminating their morality and their memory. This has entailed the cultivation of 'historical amnesia', that is, the suppression and neglect of alternative and oppositional voices (Williams 1977) such as the voices of human rights groups, relatives of the dead and the disappeared, and so on. This kind of amnesia is a means of social control because it both "furnishes a base for undisputed triumph of official ideology, and because, by weakening the sense of personal identity (by negating people's own history), it deprives them of a sense of efficacy and, thus, the capacity to organize and initiate actions" (Pateman 1980:35). The military's interest in social control during *la violencia* and its desire to distance itself from the worst of its atrocities in its aftermath means that the army has been primarily responsible for historical construction and historical amnesia at the national level; locally this is translated by paramilitary leaders (civil patrol chiefs) and military commissioners[2] who, fearing prosecution, also want to negate their violent deeds.

The war on memory is sustained through a constant ritual[3] of persecution, disappearing, torture, harassment, and causing harm not only to members of society who refuse to conform but to randomly selected victims. Maintaining high levels of fear creates a divided reality, adding confusion to survivors' fears.

But people do remember against the military forces' direct and indirect mandates to forget and, at the local public level, their memories contradict paramilitary leaders' presentation of the official history of the past as a coherent, unified narrative which blames the dead men for *la violencia*. Remembering[4] in Emol, where leftist sympathies had been strong, therefore occurs against the official version, or 'the truth', which is that subversives need to be eradicated to protect others from armed rebellion and take over.[5]

Persisting unofficial memories can be studied as the 'politics of forgetting' (Zemon Davis and Starn 1989) or as forms of counter-memory (Foucault 1977:139-64). Counter-memory is composed of the residual or resistant strains which withstand official versions of historical continuity. The precise terms and definitions are less important here than the working principle that whenever memory is invoked, one should ask: by whom? where? in what context? and in relation to what?

The Option to Forget and the Inability to Remember

Fear silenced survivors who use various conscious and unconscious devices in response to the state's demands to forget; the same strategies are used to protect oneself from the pain of remembering. The mechanisms used depend on whom the social actors are (Favret-Saada 1991). Conscious devices include silence, mutism, negation, forgery, and confusion, all of which are used in El Quiché as far as I could see. A less conscious device for forgetting is repression (Favret-Saada 1991) and a similar, unconscious device is denial: both protect one from psychic dangers. People sometimes deny especially painful and disturbing aspects. For example, many Emoltecos' conscious rejection of the fact of their mistreatment by the authority figures on whom they depend interferes with their judgement of reality (cf. Shengold 1989).

The problem for many survivors is that they cannot access their memories effectively. In situations of terror, memory is affected by the rapid and drastic alterations of awareness within the person and in their relationships with the world (Shurtz 1988:171). I was told, "You did not know what your thoughts were" after *la violencia* began. People lost the ability to think about themselves in the situation in which they found themselves: *la violencia* was without precedence in their experience; they had no way of imagining it in advance or thinking about it while they were in the middle of it. Mental processes function in relation to something that happened previously, that has been felt, seen or heard; without this, the usual mechanisms of perception and memory (such as association) do not work and chaos results. The K'iche' express the idea that wisdom is based on knowledge and memory (and intelligence and feelings) in just one word: na'ooj. People feel that their na'ooj was rendered worthless by the events of *la violencia*; they speak of losing their na'ooj (xsach r nu na'ooj).

Chaos enters the memory as an impression of chaos, without taking on meaning. For traces to remain in memory, the experience must be structured: what is well-remembered is what is found in memory as organized units, and ordered memories hangs on ordered experience.[6] It could be said that the value the K'iche' place on ordered experience — the cultural emphases on conformity, obedience, harmony, etc. — makes the experience of chaos even more terrifying.

Events could not be kept in mind not only because they could not be integrated into cultural categories, concepts or codes of significance but because those familiar mental categories were themselves shattered by the unprecedented events of *la violencia*; the dramatic changes following in its wake destroyed people's social reality. A sequence of disorientation and numbness, denial, severe anxiety, and, finally, anomie or despair arises from personal loss and the destruction of one's familiar world (Wallace 1961:202-206): "The entire affective world, constructed over years with the utmost difficulty, collapses with a kick in the father's genitals..." (Timmerman 1981: 148). Paralysis, including that of thought, takes place with this collapse of a person's conceptual order. Victims could not find thought categories for their experience; since neither culture nor experience provides structures for formulating massive acts of aggression, survivors could not articulate their experiences to themselves. Much of knowing is dependent on language but many survivors found they could not grasp and recall their experiences by formulating them in words. They found themselves adrift with no cultural models through which to transform normal language for the articulation of massive unprecedented atrocity.

Almost all the factors which can annihilate the mnemonic register can also deform it. Panic and terror are followed by heightened distortion (Symonds 1976:30); that is, something might have been taken into the memory and transformed, remaining in mind in that state and not as the original experience. The incorrectly recorded memories often trespass into people's consciousness but cannot be laid to rest for they make no sense to the sufferer. Unless the world can be made whole again, even with a different configuration, these reactions can last and thus affect memory (reconfiguration, if it is achieved, can also affect the mnemonic record). For example, I heard of a soldier being haunted by a memory of a woman strangling a chicken. Later, in analysis, he remembered that the woman was actually strangling her baby, not a chicken; after this elucidation, his disturbing memory subsided.

The external assaults on memory interacted with social dynamics and psychic processes which inhibit or enhance individual recall. People have varying degrees of control over their memories. Some people attempted to defend themselves against burdensome memories by impeding their entry; it is easier to deny entry to a memory than to release oneself from it after it has been recorded. Despite people's best attempts to avoid dealing with the memory on a conscious level, they cannot resist its subliminal entry; the memory cannot be forgotten but neither is it in conscious, accessible mind because they could not cope with the experience in the first place. They cannot make sense of it; they cannot know it cognitively. Perhaps they will not be able to remember it, except as haunting, fragmented visual percepts that they cannot integrate actively into their personality. This raises problems with issues of attention, perception, and memory.

Another reason why memories were not 'processed' was because all attention was directed outwards — upon survival from one moment to the next: people's thoughts were oriented in the present during *la violencia*. In normal life they thought about tomorrow and about the months ahead, although even under normal circumstances the K'iche' never think as far ahead in the future as Westerners do. But during times of crisis, the daily struggle for existence meant that they had even less time for reflection. The detached sensibility essential to knowing — in the sense of articulation analysis, elaboration, and knowing — is destroyed in situations of horror (Laub 1992:3). Close to the experience, survivors are captive observers who can only repeat it.

Whether memory is obliterated by violence or terror prevents access is, in effect, an academic point in that violence and terror are both aspects of the same phenomenon: thoughts of *la violencia* prompt memories of terror and vice versa. However, it seems that certain types of memory may be forever irrecoverable (Levi 1988), though it is possible that the memory is still there but in a chaotic, unnarratable form.

People's memories flow behind the scene of forgetting. *Doña* Ana-María wanted to forget but admitted, "I always say that the only time when I shall be able to stop remembering this is when I too leave this world. Even if I pretend that I have forgotten, I will not have until that time." Another widow told me, "Although we want to erase it [the memory of the massacre] from our hearts, we are unable to...it always makes us sad." Memories work against coerced forgetting, albeit at their own pace, "a pace quite detached from any seizure of central power" (Foucault 1977:27).

'Silence' is pervasive but not total. *La violencia* comes up sooner or later in many conversations, not only in private but also in more oblique ways in public. Many things are said, despite reticence and repression, even about so-called subversives, although there is a great reluctance to discuss *la violencia* in any great depth. Explicit discussion is avoided in all contexts for fear of army spies *(orejas)*.

The Silencing of Women

War-widows are a major butt of local paramilitary violence and intimidation. It is not merely that having no men to protect them, they are easy targets; rather, their continued survival is a living testament to the local and national mayhem and murder that was *la violencia.* Civil patrol chiefs *(jefes)* and military commissioners are aware that the widows' memories have the potential to infiltrate history by providing access to hidden domains of a past long since obliterated by the official version of history offered for public consumption (Ariés 1982:111, 116-7); thus they threaten, control, persecute, and occasionally rape and kill widows (especially those involved in CONA-VIGUA, GAM or other human rights organizations) in order to ensure their silence. They are afraid the women's testimony could represent an "unburial, an unearthing of the truth that translates into an invasion of the space occupied by official history" (Sternbach 1991:94).[7]

The *jefes'* and the army's perception that women's speech is potentially very powerful carries the threat of death; so too, does their fear that widows will be heard and taken seriously. A few women are aware of the power accruing to their speech owing to its potent content and are prepared to use it as a lever to do forbidden things, such as visiting the clandestine graves of their murdered kin (chapter eight). Most widows are reluctant to speak; being female and monolingual entails various practices which render Indian widows mute (cf. Ardener 1986). They perceive themselves as lacking the authority to speak; silence is encouraged by a lack of 'symbolic capital' to endow their speech with authority and ensure that they will be heard (cf. Bourdieu 1977). This feeling is not confined to women; Luis told me:

> My mother has not been educated, she is indigenous *(gente natural)* and she is unable to understand...she remains confused. We don't talk about it *[la violencia]* but only talk about matters of day-to-day living...not the future nor the past...especially not about what happened, for we do not have the authority to talk about it.

The contradiction between the *jefes'* and others' fear of women's words and the women's own perception that their words lack power and authority is more apparent than real. Locally, the physical power over life and death remains with the *jefes*, who fear that the women and their stories will escape into the wider world which they cannot control and in which, being Indian, they have neither status nor power. Ultimately, both widow and *jefes* are subject to 'symbolic domination',[8] which has been described as an invisible power working in a way that those subject to it engage in "a kind of active complicity" (Bourdieu 1991), thus ensuring ongoing, insidious intimidation. The widows are affected by images of the dead which are constantly vilified in the context of the political theatre of national security; they are depicted as communists, rebels exorcized in a national cleansing of 'impure elements'; the *jefes*, in common with all Indians, are affected by the state's use of the dead to initiate and sustain a process of colonization of a national consensus about the importance of monitoring a 'communist/devil free' nation.

Locally, the message that one should 'forget' or at least not speak about the atrocities is reinforced by the impossibility of performing rituals to memorialize the dead (chapter eight). There are few reminders of the war dead in the social and physical landscape. Most of the war dead have had no funeral; nor do they have graves in the village cemetery; other 'natural' mnemonic devices or markers such as altars, photos, and rituals such as commemorative services, were forbidden for many years. Not all relatives wanted concrete markers for recovered bodies because they were afraid that this would raise the suspicions of one side or the other. Women refrain from wearing the widow's traditional black hair ribbons for the same reason. Relatives fear remembering and they fear voicing their memories; they even fear mentioning the names of the dead, particularly those suspected of being native guerrillas and communists. These fears, compounded by the large number of dead, mean that over time one atrocity merges all too easily into the next and memory of events, and even of the dead themselves, is impaired. Almost unbelievably, some people forget the names of their close dead or missing relatives. One woman, for example, provided seemingly insignificant details about a violent incident but could not remember her husband's name; she showed signs of relief when she eventually recalled it several seconds later.

Women's choice to be silent and hidden is a form of communication which is both a form of resistance[9] and a gesture of solidarity and friendship between themselves (Conteponi and Conteponi 1984). One widow referred to herself and her friends as the "the silent women", an acknowledgement of the fact that silence and forgetting are present absences or negative spaces shaping what is remembered. Silence and forgetting work themselves back into memory for they structure what is remembered. There is a communal aspect to this: one of the things which makes memories shared is that they are not said. These unverbalized memories can be seen as meta-texts given the tacit agreement about what is remembered, forgotten or just not said. Women's remembering and their forgetting of *la violencia* are two sides of the same phenomenon — the past in the present. There is also tacit agreement that one should not know, or seek to know, what another woman's husband had been up to in the early 1980s which might have lead to his death. Knowing what not to know is a major coping response to terror.

Creating a Space for Memories

The Sites of Remembering
Women exercise the utmost caution when sharing their memories with one another (or with me) because the gaze of the state extends into society's

most intimate areas. Women only speak in the least patrolled and most autonomous sites, in other words, within the world of women's work where they can speak as they go about their daily lives. Guarded conversation takes place in their houses, as they graze their sheep, tend their gardens, and in other locations considered relatively safe. The most private conversations occur when women accompany a female diviner (aj q'ij) to the secluded mountains to perform protective and healing rituals or in their sweat baths *(temascales)* in which up to four women can bathe at a time.

The creation of secure sites for hidden discourse does not require physical distance from assailants when linguistic codes and gestures — opaque to the dominant — are deployed. When women speak about the perpetrators of *la violencia* they use symbolic markers, for example, 'they' killed the men, 'they' kidnapped people from the market place, 'they' bothered the widows. Guerrillas are referred to as the 'people from that side', 'those of the other place', 'those people', and even 'the people with arms'. More explicit terms referring to the army include 'the green men' (a reference to soldiers' uniforms) and 'the men with big boots' — guerrillas are said to go barefoot (a metaphoric statement, as they wear shoes but not boots). Similarly, guerrillas are referred to as 'the people from the mountains/uncultivated space'[10] *(esos de la montaña/del monte)* or 'the brothers from the pasture' *(hermanos del monte)*. Opponents respond that guerrillas are bastards *(personas del monte)*. The phrase, which derives from the fact that illegitimate sons cannot inherit their father's fields, is also used by guerrilla sympathizers, in which case 'men without fathers' merely indicates that they are not tied to, or identified with, their village of origin. Occasionally, one had to know where a person's sympathies lay in order to know who they were talking about: some people use negative expressions such as 'enemy' *(enemigo)*, commonly used in relation to the army, to refer to the guerrilla.

But within groups, there is an unspoken consensus regarding the meaning of particular words and phrases; when a widow refers to 'those who make war' (aj ch'o' jiib'), everyone present knows who she is talking about. Idiosyncratic and innovative language use enables women to provide each other, through very few words, with a summary of events which conjures up complete scenarios of shared experience whilst avoiding the dangers of full or open discussion. This way of speaking also gives the speaker the illusion of safety, for the ambiguous discourse of 'they' and 'that side' obscures political sympathies and analysis (which is never considered neutral). Idiosyncratic understandings or interpretations of new vocabulary (K'iche' neologisms, Spanish loan words), coupled with tacit agreement not to convey overt meanings or explain what the situation was, makes conversation a potential minefield for the unwary.

There is a limit to this: some euphemisms reveal political opinion. The K'iche' phrase for 'bad people' (itzel winaq) usually refers to military and paramilitary forces, though its Spanish equivalent, *'mala gente'*, is used by the army and its supporters as a synonym for guerrillas and has been adopted into the K'iche' lexicon as a single word. Only the army and patrol *jefes* are referred to as 'the assassins' (ri kamisanelaab') or 'those who do harm' (anal k'ax). New expressions which refer to murderous *jefes* include 'the guilty' (ri xkeqaleej) and 'killer' (ri kamisaneel). Using these oblique expressions avoids the risk inherent in naming the guilty. This practice is not new: discretion as a means of conflict avoidance is habitual to the K'iche'; it is merely the dangers, and their source, which have changed.

I heard women relate their memories in all these social sites. At first the widows were wary of me but, as trust developed, I became regarded as someone who gave them permission to speak and remember. Women began to speak about events for the first time; they also began to reveal memories which were progressively more idiosyncratic and unelaborated, in contrast to the well trodden narratives of memories which were stereotyped and fixed. There were widows who never spoke to me about their memories. They told me that disappeared kin could return if one waited in silence, conveying the sense that if they said anything, something would be lost. I was never completely sure whether these women really believed the men would be given back if they 'behaved' themselves or whether they just didn't want to talk to me or in my presence.

Generally speaking, the smaller and the more intimate the group of close confidantes — family, friends, and others perceived to be on the 'same side' (*de la misma cabeza/*ju maaj wach') — the safer the women feel to express themselves freely. *La violencia* undermined trust in relatives and neighbours; suspicion was rife that they may have betrayed the women's murdered kin. Consequently, silence has been adopted as a mechanism of defence and survival in all but select groups. This echoes the silence which Mayan Indians have used for centuries to protect themselves from outsiders, especially *ladinos*. This type of veiling can be a form of class struggle (Hobsbawn 1973:13); it can also be seen as a form of resistance. Indeed, some widows are aware of their engagement in a disguised form of resistance. Although all K'iche's are practiced at occluding their behaviour, some people find having to veil their behaviour within their own communities unsettling beyond belief. For most villagers, however, acting secretively has become almost a cognitive style (Melzak 1992). When the widows speak, their voices are hushed and their tones conspiratorial — even when talking of mundane things like going on errands. Or so I thought. It transpired that sometimes this was yet another example of the widows' occlusion of their intentions; *doña* Eugenia's 'errands' took her to the departmental capital to solicit CONAVIGUA's help in exhuming her son's clandestine grave.

Triggering Memories

Events in the present sometimes trigger memories of the past. Reminders include suddenly recognizing the site of a violent event. Daily reminders occur more in social interactions than in the landscape because the army attempted to obliterate the evidence of its brutality. Few physical markers of disaster remain, other than the charred ruins of houses; these relics have special significance for the K'iche' as the home serves as a mnemonic device to remember the dead who traditionally die there.

Temporal markers, such as when their missing menfolk would have performed cyclical agricultural tasks, also provoke memories.[11] Each meal is a reminder that one is denied the opportunity of sharing food with missing relatives. "When he returned at eight or nine o'clock in the evening, I was always close to the fire waiting for him," said *doña* Flora; "I always think of him during that hour." More occasional reminders include anniversaries and life cycle ceremonies because at these times male kin would have arranged matters and ensured that everyone was well provided for. Women are also reminded of their menfolk when they are penniless and when they are threatened by the *jefes* who come to their house at night. More idiosyncratic reminders include, for example, a widow married to a violent man who remembers her former, gentle husband.

An unanticipated incident of further violence is the most dramatic precipitant of spontaneous memories. In this type of situation the memories evoked are likely to be more pristine and unelaborated and less likely to have incorporated past narratives on the event. One of the most powerful memory triggers I observed was when a bomb exploded in the outskirts of Emol in 1990. Villagers were shocked because bombs had ceased to be part of life in the present. They were reminded of both the destruction caused by previous bombs and the full force of *la violencia*; the event triggered memories which previously had not seemed to exist at all. The memories unleashed by the bombing illustrate how emotions in the present can trigger memories of events which occurred when they were in a similar emotional state in the past and which they would have been unable to access in a different emotional state[12] (the corollary is that women's omnipresent anguish is sometimes aggravated by emotions evoked from the memories they recall). *Doña* Flora appeared 'possessed' by her memories following this incident and began relating memories I had not heard before. The most frightening and grotesque events from which she had protected herself flooded into her mind. Previously she had alluded to them with considerable reserve (if at all) but now, in an emotional state, she revealed her memories in graphic detail. She described how soldiers dragged her husband naked from his bed and how he got on his knees to beg for forgiveness, her frantic trip to the nearby town to look for her son. Her ambivalence to the event itself surprised me: she expressed both excitement that the fight had not been given up and terror about further losses she might incur. In the subsequent weeks, her dreams became dominated by violent incidents and she related them to me in a more spontaneous way than on previous occasions. She told me that after a gap of some years, threatening incidents were again occurring at night: one morning she told me black-hooded men had surrounded her house during the night. Her fears, though valid, were based on past events.

The only other occasions when women's narratives appear disinhibited is when they drink. Inebriation produces more incriminating memories as the women know their words will be attributed to diminished responsibility. I doubt that their memories are released recklessly even then, for hyper-vigilance is second nature to K'iche' women.

Sometimes a single question triggered a flow of memory from woman to woman in a concatenation of revelations and reflections. On many occasions a complex kind of 'reversible continuity' seemed to establish itself in women's accounts. They moved from the past to the present and from the present to the past and future. Often, when recalling the crisis, women's conversations were deflected from past worries to present anxieties. For example, in the middle of speaking about her husband's abduction, *doña* Josefina suddenly began to talk about her present feelings of insecurity: long after she had agreed to my recording some of our conversations, she suddenly turned to me and, with notable (and understandable) anxiety, asked about the fate of the tapes. At other times, women's conversations suddenly switched to the future, such as their worries about fertilizer for the next planting season or to more temporally distant concerns such as whether their children will have sufficient land as adults (both traditionally a husband's responsibility). Part of the problem of 'reversibility' is that "one can think one is suffering at facing the future and instead be suffering because of one's past" (Levi 1988:71). The women's lack of opportunity to renegotiate or rewrite the narrative of the violent past and their inability to allocate it to a comfortable place in the historical past exacerbated this problem.

Once memories are triggered, women are sometimes possessed by them. They seem to return momentarily to the world they are trying to evoke instead of recreating it in the present. Their eyes turn inward and they are back in the hostile climate of *la violencia*. Women's anguish, as they wrestle with deep memories or painful or guilt-provoking events, is conveyed more by tone of voice than the content of their speech. Sometimes women find no language adequate to describe the atrocities they survived although it is clear they remember something in some form. Most women grapple for explanations which are absent or incomplete. One woman, after a phase of apparent mental struggle, confessed: "What I saw, when I looked at what they were doing to our men, was totally beyond me, totally beyond my experience."

Women face the problem of how to 'translate' ideas and sentiments into expression when there are no words to describe them adequately. Once, when speaking to me about her murdered son, *doña* Eugenia became lost for words; she asked her grandson to bring out the photos of his father to show me as if the picture could tell me more than her words could convey.[13] In these situations, emotional language is lost to memory and forgotten. This was also illustrated in another incident involving a photo: Bartola, *doña*

Flora's daughter-in-law, never spoke about Juan, who the family eventually admitted was buried in the village ravines. Bartola is not the most talkative woman at the best of times but she is completely inarticulate on the matter of her husband. She seems quite stoical when anyone else speaks about *la violencia*, although this impression probably results from the fact that I only spoke to her in mother-in-law's presence. *Doña* Flora tends to negate Bartola's suffering, telling me that it is she who has shed many tears over Juan. However, one day when she brought out a photo of her son which had been hidden away, her granddaughter seized it, ran into the kitchen, and thrust it under her mother's nose, whereupon Bartola burst into tears. She wept pitifully for some time but she became no more articulate about her husband.

Surrounded by as many memory triggers as older women, young widows and especially widowed daughters-in-law are prevented from expressing their feelings and narrating their stories by the traditional K'iche' norm of respect for elders. This is rigourously enforced by the group. Many widows find comfort in these traditional structures, deferring to the authority of *doña* Eugenia which is no less than she expects: being an elder entitles one to respect and gives one the limited right to speak one's mind, something which *doña* Eugenia maintains she has always done. Her status in the context of the widows' group is enhanced by the fact that she is the widow and bereaved mother of two of Kotoh's most respected modernizers. She encourages the women to exercise emotional restraint and the women do manage to relate the most gruesome events fairly dispassionately. They occasionally cry when telling their stories and it is usually *doña* Eugenia who sets them off, virtually giving them permission to weep. They cry for each other out of empathy as well as from their own sadness and frustration.

At other times, women recount memories about their anger and indignation, ending up fantasizing about the death of the men who betrayed and killed their husbands. One widow, pretending to sharpen her knife, exclaimed, "I am sharpening my knives ready to kill him [the patrol chief!" Another woman replied, pointing to her machete, "Yes, if they [the patrols] come to my house, I'd say, here is your father [her machete] and I'd kill at least one of them!" Vengeance fantasies are usually expressed in a jesting manner as little social opprobrium is attached to joking about intentions to harm. A widow remarked wistfully, "We **feel** like taking revenge but we don't **think**[14] of doing anything specific. We feel this way because we continue to see the faces of those who killed in our villages and so we feel a lot of pain."

The Reworking of Narratives

Narratives of the Past

The past is produced through private memory and, as such, can be distinguished from dominant memory which is produced through "public representations of history"; "everyone participates, though unequally" in the "social production of memory" (Popular Memory Group 1982:207). The distance between private memory and public representations is particularly wide in repressive regimes such as that ruling Guatemala during *la violencia*. Political repression encourages citizens to psychologically repress (that is, 'not see') the atrocious aspects of government which they may observe; if they do see them, it is better that they do not remember. Rather, they should accept the 'official memory' of *la violencia*, which is distorted by the variety of political and social purposes it is made to fit. The 'official truth' undermines alternatives, deliberately violating people's memories. The violence to people's memories, though less tangible than the physical violence from which it is not entirely separate, affects victims for years because the violence is internalized.[15]

Indian women's private, unofficial memories, on the other hand, articulate with their own versions of events relating to *la violencia*; through reworking unofficial, secret memories, the women turn private tragedy into narratives. Their oral testimonies are as much human chronicles as merely historical ones; both are human 'documents' which "are no more *given* than any other. It is the historian or agent of history who constituted them by abstraction as under the threat of infinite regress" (Lévi Strauss 1966:257; italics in the original). Members of Emol's widows' group are in the process of creating oral history, endlessly working and reworking their memories to fit known cultural templates and narrative structures in an attempt to wring meaning from their experiences (cf.Bruner 1986:147).

It is not my purpose to distinguish between what is 'true' and what is distorted by memory for whatever reason (which is impossible in any case) but rather to show that the women's memories are dependent on the social and historical conditions of their production and reception; memory processes internal to the individual cannot really be separated from external conditions. Factual errors and omissions do occur but are inconsequential in relation to the multiple layers of memory which give rise to the women's representations of the 'self'. That the meaning of endeavours is appreciated through hindsight, when it had not been clear to women in the past, does not undermine its significance in the present. The women and their memories reflect and represent a specific moment in the process of history.

Widows retell and rework their memories in an attempt to resolve them; 'rewriting' the story gives a boundary to their suffering. The traditional precedent for this approach is the practice of telling the story of a person's life and death during the night vigil which follows an individual's demise. The story is composed collectively by the community as the night progresses (and mourners become progressively more drunk) and then 'left behind' (chapter eight). In the restricted 'community' of widows, women attempt to assemble stories about their individual and collective dead; they try to understand what happened to their kin and why. In doing this, the women rework and relive traumatic events which dramatically changed their lives. Constructing narratives collectively is a means of coming to terms with the events of the past and integrating them into their lives in a way which makes sense in the present. This is a creative and healing process, which makes the unknown known and less frightening (see Schuetze 1976:159-160).[16]

Oral testimonies do not uncover 'real' truth in a pristine form because the memories they unearth are shaped by cultural understandings. Characteristic of memories of *la violencia* is the combination of elements from different periods. Widows are not necessarily searching for the historicity of their experiences nor the chronology of events, which I tried to establish without much success; there seems to be some (probably unconscious) awareness of the difficulty of putting the diffuse and chaotic experiences of *la violencia* into sequential order (cf. Leed 1979). The lack of chronological reckoning of violent events by the majority of people is striking.[17] Widows are less concerned with the past than with how this past relates to their present lives: it is in the context of the present that certain moments of the past are retained, while others are actively forgotten. The most relevant memories (and, for different reasons, the most disturbing) are worked and reworked. For example, *doña* Flora insistently retells her memory of her son joining village meetings to learn about 'the Word of God' (liberation theology). Faced with ever stronger accusations that the long-dead Juan had been involved in 'delinquent' (subversive) activities, *doña* Flora's progressively elaborated narrative about her son is an unconscious acknowledgement of the danger the *jefes'* accusations present to her remaining family.

Together, widows produce and alter drafts of the past, discarding one in favour of the other. There is never a final version because they are narrating events of a problematic nature such as unnatural or uncertain death. The lack of a funeral deprives the bereaved of a bounded context in which to create the story of the deceased's life and death; details normally included are also missing. The death cannot be integrated within survivors' lives and, therefore, nor can it be left behind; memories of the war dead cling tenaciously to the present. Popular memories regarding the uncertainty surrounding the war dead — what they were involved in, what actually happened to them — are the most guarded.

Every time a narrative is retold, the possibility exists for a shift of emphasis, sometimes providing new information, sometimes changing a detail. In the process of retelling, women incorporate into their own memories the details of other people's memories, even those details they may have denied earlier. A woman hearing another's narrative remembers, forgets, transforms, and retells it in her turn. The process of "adjusting the fit is an ongoing one" (Knapp 1989:5); people are concerned about the ill fit between what actually happened and received narratives of the past, whether the official truth or the discrepancies in stories recounted by different people.

Some of the women's images are based on "false recognition, in accordance with others' testimonies and stories" (Halbwachs 1980:71). They hear themselves and others and this feeds back into memory and what really happened becomes mixed up with what they hear themselves and others say. What a woman says is also determined by what she can remember, what she feels she can say, who is present (including memories their presence evokes) and her own frame of mind (which is affected by what is going on in her immediate environment). For example, my presence as a powerful person (being white and monied) is a reminder of *ladinos*; this had a cognitive impact as it could remind them of an encounter with the army and inhibit them from speaking freely. Sometimes they forgot about my presence, although they always remain watchful for passing *orejas*; in the middle of conversation, one woman will suddenly step outside to make sure no-one is listening.

Thus the retelling of narratives modifies memories of what is being told. Memory is constantly in flux, continuously transformed by changes in identity, social experience, and by membership of the group and the narratives produced therein. In turn, memory transforms the narratives, the social experience, and possibly even behaviour itself. Memories are better characterized as provisional rather than as fragmented (Halbwachs 1980). Memory is not only a personal, subjective experience but also a social phenomenon. Memories become whole only in social contexts, taking their shape according to group processes and the conceptual structures of certain groups, be they family, church or communal association (Halbwachs 1980:22-49, 75ff) and the cultural past. New groupings such as war-widows select different memories and narratives from the flux of images of the past. There is a certain amount of conscious and unconscious teleology involved.

In some cases, instead of remembering the past — gaining control over it by making an orderly story about it — the remembered self is swallowed up by the narrated self and compelled to repeat the past. The revision of the story in each successive telling represents the remembered self's attempt to reassert her authority by interpreting instead of repeating what she has repressed: later accounts include earlier, repressed versions. This memory is called up less because it is more comfortable and can be left to one side. One local indigenous Catholic priest helps women with this process (although this may have not be his intention) by speaking of memories of the dead in the same analogous way as he speaks of texts about the Christian saints. He literally tells women to leave their thoughts 'to one side', which some told me they manage to do.

Memories of the Massacre

For Emoltecos, the village massacre is the most significant event of *la violencia*. It marked a dramatic change in survivors' lives although over time, it became merely the first of the many incidents which Emoltecos have been told to forget or at least never to mention. One young man told me that when he returned to the village, the *jefes* warned him: "Never will you say anything [about the atrocities] to anyone anywhere about what we did here."

Yet people do speak about it or allude to it, despite the danger in doing so. This made me question the importance of telling and retelling memories of traumatic events which have been silenced. Over time, I learnt that memories of this type are protected by a collective secrecy.

The victims of the massacre were Kotoh men who had returned following a conditional amnesty: returnees had to join the patrols. Despite their compliance, they were rounded up by the *jefes* and killed (chapter five). Before they were assassinated, some of the victims were taken to their homes and humiliated in front of their families. Then they were taken to a ravine and made to dig a large, ominous hole before being led, roped together, to the centre of Kotoh. Word spread rapidly and villagers rushed to the square. Once all the captured men had arrived, the *jefes* forced on-duty patrollers to 'torture'[18] the men to the brink of death in front of the crowd which included family and friends. The men, barely able to stand, were then dragged away by patrollers. The *jefes* allowed no-one to follow. The men were taken to the ravine where they had dug their own graves and thrown in.

This is the skeleton of a story which I heard many times in private. Although there is considerable uniformity in widows' accounts of the massacre (and other events), each version varies: the victims were buried alive, beheaded or slashed by machetes. Years later, the exhumation of the victims' graves (chapter eleven) proved all accounts correct: in a gruesome imitation of the mutilated, unrecognizable corpses dumped by death squads (chapter four), patrollers had attempted to deface their still living victims with their machetes and then thrown them, still breathing, face downwards into the grave. They had attempted to behead one man, *doña* Eugenia's son Gilberto. When I met the widows, these were not known facts; they were merely hearsay of a terrifying and incomprehensible kind.

The massacre was shocking in the extreme. Given that the event was named, interpreted, and stored as something different by different individuals, people's memories of it vary. When the memory is called up and retold, it is reinterpreted in the light of subsequent experiences and information which change the person and consequently their interpretation of their past:

Doña Eugenia:
> The men were tied up. They had thrown them on the ground like pigs who are about to be slaughtered.

Doña Candelaria:
> They were on the ground with their faces bloodied. Some shouted, "Please forgive us" out of devotion and because they were suffering so much.

Doña Flora:
> They asked the patrols to forgive them. Many of the murderers were evangelicals. After the killings they told people that those assassinated "had begged us, asking our pardon and our help to convert to our religion".

Doña Eugenia:
> But I know everything that happened and they [the dead men] didn't say anything like that... In fact, many didn't even utter a word. They couldn't even if they wanted to, because they were hurt so badly that they couldn't talk at all.

Doña Candelaria:
> Perhaps a few of them said a few things but nothing about that.

Doña Eugenia:
> Only my child said something when they first captured him. He said, "Mother, ask the *jefe* of the patrols to get help to free me. Tell him I have not done anything wrong." So I went to Mr. Justice [one of the *jefes*] and I asked him, "What did he do to make you take him? Why not let him go?" But he didn't respond; he just ignored me. I followed him until we reached the centre of the village. He didn't stop there, he just continued on a path which led to the ravine where they were digging the pits where the men would be buried. This is what happened. And, I tell you, I heard nothing about what you said, about conversion. That's all a big lie... Indeed, what they [the *jefes*] shouted was that the men they had rounded up were to be slaughtered because they had left the village and become 'organized'. They accused them of being guerrillas.

Doña Candelaria ended her narrative with a remark which prompted *doña* Eugenia to rethink her own interpretation of the event:

> We were all there sitting in the school waiting... And when they had buried them, they all returned to the school to threaten all of us. They warned us, "None of you had better utter a word about what you have just seen. And if we should learn that one of you has, then what you have just seen will also happen to you and you'll go with them!"... Because of this, I realized that the *jefes* themselves decided to kill the men [i.e., this was not ordered by the army].

In the process of sharing memories women create a shared identity and a feeling of trust, even with widows from other places who are ordinarily viewed with some suspicion. The knowledge that their male kin had been killed by the same side contributes to the feeling of camaraderie between them. For example, *doña* Ana-María, whose husband was killed in the massacre, discusses the event with her friend, *doña* Candelaria, whose husband was killed in a separate incident; both men had been prominent in Catholic Action. Between them, they try and impose order on this traumatic event:

Doña Candelaria:
> I do not remember well but they tell me that the first to die was Tin Ros since they thought that he was the subversives' sorcerer [i.e., the most dangerous].

Doña Ana-María:
> Ah! he was the first. You see, I do not remember because by the time we arrived [at the square] we were no longer people.[19]

Doña Candelaria:
    Oh God! But who wasn't like that on that day?

Even when they have already heard what happened in another locale, women still engage in conversations, repeating and reworking the past. *Doña* Eugenia and *doña* Flora came from different Emol hamlets and, although their husbands had been involved with the 'organization', the two women are not completely cognizant of events in each other's hamlets because the *jefes* put considerable effort into trying to keep widows apart:

Doña Eugenia:
    They took him [another Kotoh man] with my son and they killed them both in front of the school...they are both together [buried] in the ravine.

Doña Flora:
    There are many over there.

Doña Eugenia:
    Yes, there were many from our place too, twelve of them.

Doña Flora:
    They did the same to us [in Emol Central], they kidnapped twelve of them. But they say that one escaped.

Doña Eugenia:
    Is that so?

Doña Flora:
    Yes, he was a young man. Actually, just now he returned [to Emol]. He's just come to pay his turn [in the patrols] from the border of Mexico where he works. I would like to go and ask him about what happened, what he did in order to escape while our husbands perished.

The Reconstruction of the Self

The Struggle Against a Diminished Self

Through the vehicle of re-membering, women together recapture a morsel of the dignity destroyed in the public demonstrations of their failure as mothers, wives, and daughters as, immobilized, they were forced to witness the slaughter of their menfolk. When witnessing unprecedented violence, an individual's complex, symbolic, abstract identity, with its various commitments, loyalties, ideological beliefs, and sentiments, breaks down; people who did nothing to prevent it (whether or not this was actually feasible) feel they have renounced their family loyalties because the meanings of these concepts lose their reality in the face of so much pain. The

'self' and personhood of a parent who sees a child tortured is most profoundly violated; it is an experience which is culturally 'thin'. Subjectively, the
world seems to shrink to one's immediate surroundings, the here and now,
and the 'self' shrinks to the body; the loyal, committed, meaningful 'self'
disappears, leaving only the body and its suffering (Scarry 1985). How this
is explained and compensated for, how it is expressed, and how people
reconstruct themselves following such a violation, is cultural elaboration.

That women feel guilty about their inaction is apparent in the memories
they call up. *Doña* Ana-María, who witnessed the public beating of her husband before he was taken away to his death, told me, "When they were killing my husband, I was unable to say anything otherwise they would have
killed me too. I only said to myself, this would never had happened if had we
never returned." *Doña* Flora and *doña* Eugenia also attempt to resolve their
guilt and justify their actions:

Doña Flora:
Because we didn't want to abandon our little [unimportant] things *(cositas)*
and our houses, they killed all our men. If we had fled, then perhaps our poor
men would have survived.

Doña Eugenia:
If I'd fled, then perhaps they would have burnt my house because the woman
who lives behind the school, she fled and they burnt her house. They burnt
everything including her [stored] corn cobs *(mazorcas)*, her clothes which she
left behind, everything. Those of us who didn't leave didn't suffer this. We
didn't know this before, but my husband didn't want to leave in any case. He
said, "If they kill me, they kill me, I have no crime to my name." So we didn't
leave. Anyway, where would I have gone? I have my animals, my *mazorcas*
and all my possessions and why should I have abandoned them?

Victims of terror often exhibit a certain amount of wandering memory,
as can be seen in *doña* Eugenia's description of her confused thinking as she
tried to absorb what was happening to Gilberto. Her feeling of guilt was evident as she explained why she could do nothing to save him:

We didn't know what to do... I was able to leave the scene [before the massacre actually began]. But as I was walking, I did not know what to do. I asked
myself, "Should I go to the town [to report what was happening]? But what
would happen if I did? I could return to bring my son a blanket." But they [the
jefes] were watching me. I was already well on my way when they caught up
with me. They grabbed me and asked where I was going. I replied, "Nowhere"
and that I was only looking for my sheep. They took me and locked me in the
school with the rest. Then we were unable to do anything.

Women altered the focus of their memories as an unconscious means
of coping and of avoiding the guilt engendered in certain actions which

otherwise lead to a diminished self.[20] I observed women rousing memories among themselves, or telling them to third persons, choosing to contemplate moments of recess and strange, idiosyncratic details. One woman, when recounting the day when everyone from the market place was kidnapped, chose to tell me that dogs went into the houses and ate *tortillas* off the griddles. Although this did happen, the story is also an allegorical reference to their own helpless (in that they were unable to protect themselves from the animals which were supposed to protect them) and to the predatory incursions into their homes by local *jefes* (whose ostensible purpose is to protect villagers).

Women deal with the most painful aspects of events superficially; they hardly mention the disappeared or what may have become of them. They avoid elements not called up willingly from the layers of memory and therefore, with time, such memories tend to take on a more amorphous form. This is because typical memory processes such as condensation and association result in the simplification of memory's records. Some speak about macabre events in an almost exaggerated form such as throwing their babies ahead of them down the ravines when fleeing from the army. Sometimes, rather than referring to horrendous facts pertaining to *la violencia*, women prefer to remember and to speak about how they personally experienced this time. By focusing on their feelings of fear, perpetual anxiety, helplessness, and loneliness, which have salience in their own right, they deflect attention away from more painful memories.

The women's harsh self-criticisms also lead to diminished self-perceptions with which their memories and their continuing every day 'self' must contend. *Doña* Ana-María retrospectively judged herself for being part of the passively complicit audience (in the sense that she did nothing to stop it, the fact that intervention would have led to her own death notwithstanding). *Doña* Flora's remark that a 'good Christian' would have denounced the killings and abductions, which she herself did not do, in effect describes her retrospective perception of her own failing. This 'self' judgement led to a diminished self-perception with which her everyday 'self' must contend.

When recounting their reactions to the atrocities, women say they felt as though they were 'dead' or 'no longer human' (*doña* Lydia told me she 'lost her thoughts' (xsach nu chombal) and that she was like a 'pure wolf, howling, howling' when her husband was kidnapped). *Doña* Ana-María explained that she had been unable to talk or walk upright, adding,

> I was so afraid that I was no longer a person... I was unable to think or coordinate actions or understand what was occurring around me.

Doña Eugenia:
> They hit them in the mouth and they bashed them in the face. Oh God! Oh God! how they made them suffer... This moment was the most difficult that we lived through...we lost consciousness and it was as if we too had died.

Doña Ana-María:

> I felt as if my feelings and my thoughts had died during this time. You see, not
> only my husband died but many, many of the members of my family died.
> First my brother, and then they got my father-in-law; then my daughter and
> then my mother. OOH! God, no more! no more! I thought. Yes, many were
> taken in that way. And because of this I felt as though my feelings had died
> and I lost my memory completely.[21] It seemed like an attack *(un ataque)*. I did
> not know what to do and I lost my feelings. It was as if suddenly I was drunk,
> drunk, drunk!

*Doña*Ana-María was recording not only a mental and emotional numbness or the 'psychic numbing' (cf. Lifton 1986) endemic to the circumstances and place; nor was she only referring to her impaired thinking
because of tremendous grief or the death of a part of herself, her identity,
which was abruptly altered during 'that time': she was also referring to a
totally foreign atmosphere inhospitable to responses which for the K'iche'
are 'the right thing to do', including things that normally define a human
being. The resulting disunity alienated widows from their own conception
and personhood[22] as it operates in the present and as it had operated before
finding themselves in the midst of *la violencia*, a time when it was impossible to operate according to known codes of conduct. When external
events compel one to endure a crumbling milieu, as happens to victims of
violence, human personhood must be damaged. Indeed, when Emolteco
women speak of 'not being human', they refer to the fact that their personhood had broken down.

For the K'iche', personhood centres on social roles; failing to fulfill
one's legitimate roles in life presents considerable difficulty because they are
so clearly prescribed: "[L]iving within such strongly qualified horizons is
constitutive of human agency" and hence, "stepping outside these limits
would be tantamount to stepping outside what we would recognize as integral, that is, undamaged personhood" (Taylor 1989:27). Widows violently
deprived of their roles as wives and mothers found their social personhood
rescinded; it was not merely that they no longer considered themselves
whole persons but nor did their neighbours (Harris 1989).[23] They view themselves as failures and they express their self-perceptions as inadequate carers
obliquely through, for example, their statements that they can no longer keep
their animals alive. "Now my pigs die on me," said *doña* Eugenia. "They
don't live any more?" asked *doña* Flora. "No," replied *doña* Eugenia; "none
of my animals do. Only a short while ago I bought four foreign chickens and
they have already died." "They died?" "Yes," replied *doña* Eugenia; "and
then I went to buy four more and they died too." "Oh my child," commiser-
ated *doña* Flora, "it also seems that we have lost our power *(fuerza;* kowil)
and our will." This is a more acceptable allusion to their self perceptions of
negligence towards their families arising from their inability to fulfil the
quintessentially female function of nurturance even in circumstances which

made this impossible. This is also expressed in women's preoccupations about their traditional skirts *(corte)*, a metonym for Indian women in aj q'ij's prayers, being violently removed; the implied exposure reflects the public nature of this appalling indignity, the loss of ownership of the status of motherhood. The women's failures are built upon to the present: the woman continues to see herself, in the eyes of her children, her dead husband, and bystanders, as continually failing to consolidate her family's lives after a period of national and personal trauma.

The Creation of Fictitious Identities

> *When memory goes out to pick up dead wood, it brings back the faggot that it likes* (Mossi proverb).

The idea that each individual has a separate, unique identity is new to the K'iche'; although for their very different reasons, both 'new' Catholic missionaries and the national army have tried to encourage individualism, this way of thinking about the self has not really taken root — especially among women. Their socialization as 'conservers of tradition' coupled with *ladino* chauvinism means they have been less exposed to either catechist or military rhetoric on the subject.

Women construct a sense of themselves as widows, daughters, and mothers of the dead and disappeared through social interaction and sharing memories with 'people from the same group who understand' (ju maaj wach). They construct a self-image or 'face' (Goffman 1955) which can only be constructed, deconstructed, and reconstructed socially or intersubject-ively. The widows' self-image is sometimes a fictitious one. It needs to be in order to counter not only the image painted of them by the forces of re-pression but also their own image of themselves and to create a sense of continuity. Constructing fictional identities protects the suffering person by minimizing the need for radical shifts in self-concept and by providing a sense of continuity with the past (Charmatz 1992:76).

In devastating situations there is a certain amount of rejection of an intolerable truth and the construction of a different one. The process of re-elaboration of the past overshadows the actual event more than in ordinary situations. The extreme emotional impact on an individual is such that in memory, the actual event can become exaggerated in its minutiae: certain aspects may be exaggerated or completely fabricated; the omission of per-tinent detail becomes more likely, as does the fragmentation of memory and the insertion of fiction.

Over time, K'iche' women changed their accounts of their lives es-pecially from the time before to the time after *la violencia*. Previously im-portant family quarrels are now considered trivial and forgotten. In their place women create and recreate other stories of how they survived in the

face of the atrocities and the aftermath of *la violencia*. They speak of a heroic quality, usually attributed to the murdered men but now attributed to
women. Stories are told by the 'heroic' women themselves or by others who
marvel at their acts. The village massacre is one of the most common themes
discussed when they represent themselves this way; for example, *doña* María
narrated how, a few days after the massacre, she went to uncover the clandestine grave to see if the dead were there, saying to herself, "If they speak
to me, than I will know that my days are numbered and, because of this, I
thought that it was better to go alone." She returned to tell the others that she
had found them and, only one week after the burial, a group of women went
to visit their dead.

Similarly, *doña* Eugenia presents herself as taking a leading role in
countering the abominations. Her story that, when patrollers brought her son
Gilberto to her house before the massacre, she stepped forward and offered
them money if they would let him go, provoked a certain amount of horror
not only because of the danger implied by such behaviour but because, as a
woman and an Indian, she had 'broken the rules'. According to *doña* Eugenia, the assassins responded predictably by hitting her with their rifle
butts, shouting "<u>Xo</u>!" which is how one normally addresses an unruly animal. *Doña* Eugenia is not the only widow to portray herself as a 'disorderly'
woman who, in some way, is able to overturn gender roles, although the idea
is more commonly illustrated and discussed with reference to biblical characters — "the heroines of the old testament such as Ruth, Ester, and Judith",
as Petronila, the young K'iche' catechist who introduced Emolteco widows
to CONAVIGUA, puts it. Some women cultivate the very disorderliness
with which the *jefes* taunt them. The importance of widows' self-representa-
tions lies in the symbolic rather than the simply reflective character of representations and, at the same time, in the recognition of their potential influence on forms of behaviour.

This type of oral testimony draws a veil over more tragic elements —
the beaten men who were buried alive or chopped up into pieces 'like a
pumpkin' *(chilacayote)* — and brings out the symbolic and, to some extent,
actual overturning of order: it represents an infraction of the upside down
code which regulates women's relationships with the male *jefes*. *Doña* Eugenia's symbolic overturning of order (against local *jefes* associated with the
army and, hence, *ladinos*) in a society oppressive of women and Indians,
marks the beginning of the positive reconstruction of an identity for themselves. This is partly due to radical changes in the women's apperception of
both their 'selves' and their surroundings, which in turn creates new experiences and interpretations of the past. This initially happened without their
realizing it: widows had had to assume new responsibilities (including men's
tasks) in order to survive; by the time they began to assess what they had
done, their view of the world and their own place in it had changed, undermining the earlier, stable core with its assumed continuity of the self. Under

these circumstances, resocialization to a reconstructed self-conception accelerates (Charmatz 1992:74): "Motherhood and family life do, of course, have a very real practical and symbolic importance after a conflict, in that they re-establish stability and promise a future for people" (MacDonald 1987:10).

Doña Eugenia's narrative about challenging the *jefes* represents her struggle to maintain a sense of continuity within the chaos of her own identity. She re-affirms that, within her family, she conforms to K'iche' values of working hard and being a good mother; she simultaneously presents herself as 'a bit of a rebel', the same words she uses to describe her father, thereby identifying with the nonconformist tendencies of her family and staking a claim for continuity and order. The reference to her long-dead father also indicates her perception of a persisting *status quo* in the situation which, she told me, "One must endure *(tiene que aguantar)*"; life has always been hard. Therefore, while the disruption of relationships and the taking on of reconstructed identities is acknowledged, continuity is restored. This is fundamental for "life to go on" (Marris 1975:24).

The re-establishment of continuity is only partial, for women also speak about a disconcerting sensation of disjuncture in their lives. *Doña* Josefina remarked sadly, "The life I lived before and the life I live now are entirely different." This typical self-observation not only relates to the different types of action, roles, and responsibilities widows claimed to, and sometimes did, take on during *la violencia*, but is a comment on the moral space in which they now live. Identity or knowing who you are is "to be oriented in moral space...where questions arise about what is good or bad, what is worth doing and what not, what has meaning and importance for you and what is trivial and secondary" (Taylor 1989:28). The arrival of *la violencia* needed novel and unconventional definitions of 'self' in order for the person to operate at all. Women could not act according to customary definitions of morality without putting their own lives at risk. This pertains to situations where, for example, they did not go in search of their lost kin, including their children. Circumstances and not values determined their behaviour; values such as parental care lose their relevance in situations which preclude their expression. Therefore the establishment of identity had to find other anchors in the past; only in this way could the discontinuities in their identities be filled in.

Memories change as the women themselves change: their lives had changed dramatically and they had learnt to cope with that change (chapter six). As they changed, many widows felt the need to render a consistent account of their past and present life; they remember selectively and rewrite their personal histories to conform to their new images of themselves and of women generally.[24] The present serves to change the meanings of occurrences in the past. When suffering is initially caused by meanings, altering meanings can reduce the suffering. By rationalizing or reinterpreting one's inaction during *la violencia*, one may escape from a sense of guilt about it.

Doña Flora's story of her own heroism in challenging the *jefes* demonstrates this process. Using her *machete* as a prop to illustrate her narrative, she said,

> He [the *jefe*] asked me if I heard that they would come to the houses here. I told him that I had. He threatened me, saying that they were in the process of deciding which houses they would visit. I replied, "Let them come, let them come, because here is their father," I said, moving from side to side the *machete* in my hands [in a threatening manner]. You see, they got used to killing...they killed our men...now they want to kill us. This is what I said. I was hardly aware of what I was saying [she implies that she could not control herself]. I believe that because of what I said they did not come. But at the time I thought that they might come... Perhaps it would have been possible to injure one of them... If I had been there, when they came, I would have opened the door, quickly, and...!

It is unlikely that this incident occurred as *doña* Flora describes; she left Emol shortly after being threatened. Her narrative combines the basic reality of intimidation with what she wished she had said and done, thus creating a story which is more in keeping with the way she would prefer to see herself in the present. The fact is that most people at this time were petrified. A more characteristic reaction, as in their former lives (before *la violencia*), is passive endurance. This raises queries about what areas of freedom people actually retain and whether a person "does not adjust but instead manipulates the new environment according to his needs, and to which degree his frozenness prevents him from doing either" (Bettelheim 1986:39). *Doña* Flora's paralysis stemmed as much from the values and attitudes imprinted in early life as fear. Terror situations are anticreative, in that people cling harder than ever to known ways because of the rupturing of their world and the need to attain steadiness. Much later, *doña* Flora reframed the incident in order to maintain or create a certain narrative about the event which allows her to establish and maintain, at least some of the time, a positive image of herself in which her behaviour appears non-conformist and creative.

I am not suggesting that women never had the choice to perform heroic acts. In 'reality' some did, but only very occasionally. Heroic acts in the most extreme conditions prove that apathy can be overcome and irritability suppressed: "Man [and woman] can preserve a vestige of spiritual freedom, of independence of mind, even in such terrible conditions of psychic and physical stress" (Frankl 1964:61). Survivorship depends on the ability to preserve some area of independent action (cf. Bettelheim 1986:147).[25] Although the importance of independent action is, perhaps, more important among individualistic people than among the K'iche', the women still feel it is still important for the women to maintain their integrity and the perception of autonomous action (such as standing up to the patrols).

The tales of heroism which women recount to one another can be seen as memory, as a social construction or as a reconfiguration of the past. These processes act to form an identity which works against despair and the perception of a diminished 'self' (Halbwachs, cited in Hutton 1988). The women's self-constructions and reconfigurations of themselves work against the identities diminished as a result of their loss of traditional anchors of identity — family members, traditional relationships, and behaviours. The situation of *la violencia* did not allow the luxury of doing the 'Christian' thing (which is perhaps an ideology rather than a social fact, even in ordinary times). This does not prevent women, in their retrospective glances, from condemning others as a way of lifting themselves or, in more candid moments, from condemning themselves directly for not operating according to the morality of better times.

The widows' stories of heroism are a symptom of the disruption of known patterns of relationships which created a situation in which women are more free to take up novel positions, especially in relation to men. This is where many widows draw most strength. In reformulating her world and establishing a narrative of this version of the 'self', she does not seem bound by the traditional structure of her society.

Oral testimonies do not always flow between the selves which women describe. The discontinuities are different from the multiple selves which any person maintains which are usually integrated although not simultaneously operational in any one context. Women move between a traumatized self and another self — the woman who stood by and watched her son assassinated and the brave woman who stepped forward to try and prevent the assassination. The resulting disjuncture remains in memory if not in daily fact as desperation, even though this mental state rarely eclipses their present life altogether. This is because the need to work harder than ever prevented too much reflection. It was not only *la violencia* which changed the women's lives; it was only the beginning of the dramatic change, particularly in widow's lives (chapter six) following the loss of male kin and the shattering of world views. Because of this disjuncture, the period of *la violencia* maintains biographical relevance to the present.

Reconstructed identities can be considered, at some level, as fictional identities as they are based more on remembered past actions and future identity claims than on present pursuits. The women are unable to locate themselves in unmitigated reality (the lived present) and can only locate themselves in managed re-presented reality, that is, fiction. Some women's sense of themselves is no longer of someone real but of something 'other'. Not excluding the possibility that this stems partly from the counterfeiting effect of living behind a lie (the official truth) for several years, this feeling may arise with their constructions which protect the 'self' at a time of disruption, loss, and failure. The issues that people face in these times are a magnification of those which people face in less drastic situations when it is easier to maintain their 'ordinary masks' (Giddens 1979). That is, the discrepancy between the way one perceives oneself to act and the 'reality' is not so great. In dire situations there is an even greater need to protect the 'self' by minimizing the need for radical shifts in 'self-concept', providing a sense of continuity with the past. There is also a necessity to insulate themselves from the intrusive negative labelling of 'outsiders' (e.g., 'wives of the guerrilla'). Women reject this label as harmful to their sense of self; they see themselves as oriented towards the 'good' fundamental to the K'iche' value system. This labelling is important because names do more than reflect and classify; they also create experiences (Ardener 1975; Gell 1979; Rosaldo 1980; Heelas and Lock 1981). Being social, new metaphorical language creates not just new references but new "forms of life" or "events" (Parkin 1982:xxxiii). The new language pertains to the woman's 'self' definition and the new form of life is her own.

Discourses containing fantasy are also simply a means of covering up terrible events which are extremely painful to the narrator. The widow attempts to protect herself with 'cover-memories' (Freud 1899) not only from the events themselves but also her own retrospective self-criticism for not acting according to pre-existing values. Other war phenomena associated with everyday routine which were rehearsed over and over again, such as the many bodies found daily along the road or fleeing from the army whenever the bells tolled, are more difficult to cloak in this way. Thus the terrorized widow remembers against less than heroic memories of her failures in order to maintain a certain image of herself. Widows become hidden from themselves and so, in this way, what is public to whom is a vital domain with the potential to open or close.

As a way of dealing with unbearable guilt, shame, and anger, women also choose, consciously and unconsciously, not to speak and not to remember. Their guilt is a complicated guilt, an ambiguous guilt which is more than the 'survivor guilt' which is evidenced in women's statements that the order of her own and her men's deaths had been reversed: "If he had not been killed, then I would have died before him" (cf. Lifton 1967). It is a guilt which arises from the paralysis which prevented parents from acting to protect their children as they witnessed them being murdered. Most people feel guilty whether they were actively or passively involved; extremely few Emoltecos have been able to free themselves from this feeling by identifying themselves with K'iche' heroes such as Tecúm Uman, the last K'iche' king to be conquered and killed by Pedro de Alvarado.[26] Unlike 'natural' disasters, over which people perceive they have absolutely no possibility of exercising control, the violence unleashed by other human beings specifically against kin is continually exposed to interpretive understanding by victims burdened by the question of their own role in it. K'iche' women's guilt and shame is exacerbated by the fact that they cannot not fulfil their obligations to the dead. Perhaps the only way to deal with these intolerable emotions is by forgetting.

Violence forces shared discourses onto the person. People who stood watching and did nothing need a shared discourse in order to remember in a positive way. More often than not, these memories are elaborated; they appear more uniform and stereotyped than the idiosyncratic, unelaborated memories which an individual does not share with the group. Elaborated memories which attempt to negate guilt have already been shared and work-ed many times before; they are reconditioned and shaped differently from raw memories which nevertheless are already conditioned by the cultural and personal history of a woman's experience. The countless elaborated narra-tives and representations serve to lessen the diminished 'self' resulting from women's own recollections of the self-assessed 'amoral' (but in reality prag-matic) way they were forced to act during *la violencia*. In this way, women deal constructively with what happened to them as an inner experience.

Continuity with Women in the Historical Past

Identity depends on the memory state, that is, a 'self' that remembers its earlier states; it also depends on memory, on the narratives that construct (and deconstruct) identities by comparing the 'once upon a time' with the 'here and now' (Zemon Davis and Starn 1989:2).

In recent years the widows's group CONAVIGUA has fostered positive reconstruction of identity through connections with history in the more dis-tant past. CONAVIGUA was formally established in 1988, following a mass for widows requested by Petronila in May of the previous year. The date Pet-ronila chose for the mass was significant: Catholics dedicate the month of May to the Virgin Mary whose primary importance among the K'iche' (or at least Emoltecos) is as a wife and mother. The mass for widows was ad-vertized on the radio and thousands of women turned up; some had walked for days to get there. Women poured into the church in Chichicastenango, spilling out onto its steps and into the square; many got to tell their stories about their losses during the service. Thousands more heard the mass over the radio. The mass caused a major sensation in all sectors of society and the young indigenous priest, Ventura Lux, who conducted it was expelled from the municipality; he was later killed in car crash which few people believe was accidental.

Petronila has an eclectic approach to interpreting *la violencia*. She finds parallels with biblical characters which resonate with rural Indian women *(campesinas)*, such as the fact that the Virgin Mary and the *campesina* didn't go to school or speak Spanish; Mary became a girl from the cornfields (aj k'aleb). Petronila relates both the Virgin Mary and the widows to the mother of the twins Hunahpu and Xbalanqué who, according to the sixteenth cen-tury Mayan Counsel Book, *"Popul Vuh"*, also sacrificed her sons.[27] In her characteristically quietly spoken but direct manner, Petronila explains that it was not men who sacrificed their lives: "The women were those who made the sacrifices," she told me; "they sacrificed the lives of their men." One consequence of Petronila's approach is that the women she addresses begin to see themselves as heroines, celibates, and virgins (and therefore, to some extent, holy) (cf. Fiorenza 1983:344); instead of idealizing[28] their dead kin as martyrs (chapter nine), they have begun to portray both themselves and their dead kin as heroes. This enables women to reject the pejorative labels which have criminalized their late husbands as 'enemies of the state' and 'guerrillas' and themselves as 'wives of the guerrilla', thereby diminishing their anxiety; it also encourages them to think that they had been selected because of their specialness and, "like Christ", their suffering protected others. They derive comfort from seeing themselves as worthy and from thinking that their kin do not suffer in the afterlife (chapter nine). As Petronila speaks to the women, who identify with her as the Virgin and recognize themselves in her speech, a side of their personalities fragmented by the violence clings to the chance to become cleansed.

The link Petronila makes between religious, historical (mythological), and living mothers is especially potent: "it was this essential relation, that of a mother to her child, that quietly erupted within the space of death as a single most indelible tie of the disappeared ones to society" (Gregory and Timmerman 1986:71). It was this mother-child connection which propelled GAM into becoming a major symbol of resistance.

An important consequence of Petronila's novel combination of different strands of thought is that past, present, and future are joined through characteristics and events shared by both ancient and modern heroines. But ancient battles are not merely the initial stages of a historical process which culminates in something akin to modern feminism (although there is certainly the beginnings of a feminist proclivity to this group).[29] These historical struggles resonate with those facing K'iche' women in the present. The critical element, as with women's reaching back into their own personal histories, is the creation of a sense of continuity which links past, present, and future via historical sequence and analogy (Knapp 1989:130). By referring to heroines of the past who had sacrificed their men, the killings, public massacres, and other atrocities are given more than a very personal significance (Jones 1995). This added a converse process whereby these personal disasters "are suddenly perceived in *all* their historic significance" (Jones 1990:15; italics in the original). *La violencia* was the beginning of a violence which is not going to stop; in some ways, it was also a re-emergence of an old war brought by the Spaniards five centuries ago. (A *costumbrista* aj q'ij from the departmental capital, Santa Cruz, made the same connection when he announced that Tecúm Uman had returned to earth "to bring justice to Guatemala"; he is said to have brought two million 'warriors' (guerrillas) with him, though they are only allowed to enter the fight two or three at a time.) The surviving women are "suddenly thrown into history and forced intimacy with previously avoidable political realities" (Jones 1990:15). It is this which seems to create a turning point. In these processes, confrontation, reordering, and renewal are clearly observed (Lifton 1987:67). There is a confrontation with negative aspects (old fears, guilt feelings, and anxieties) of the self; re-ordering required a re-examination of these aspects; renewal resulted in an increased sense of purpose and responsibility which provides the framework for subsequent action.

Conclusion

There are political, social, and psychological reasons for both forgetting and remembering the events of *la violencia*. Memories have no reality as pure memories; they exist for individuals only to the extent that they resonate within them and can be borne. Memories becomes 'real' as social fact only to the extent that they are articulated and disseminated within the group. Just as there is no pure memory there is no pure recall. Rather, re-membering *la violencia* is an act of reconstruction, based as much on the memory of narratives of a past event as the past, as the event itself. Many questions remain, for example, about the narratability of violent events and the ability to recall what cannot be narrated.

What is re-membered is remembered against conditions created by 'the repression' and its aftermath. Terrorization and the imposition of the official 'truth' obliterates or at least distorts memory. Under conditions of terror, the elaboration of an individual's memory cannot be located in the landscape (because evidence of atrocity has been effaced) but within the social group; it is a social act that is realized between different groups, in this instance, women.

Women's refusal to accept the official version of events, which effectively silences them, is to be found in their popular memories, private narratives, and 'self'-constructions, for example, of themselves as heroines and their dead kin as martyrs. There is a tendency to glorify the fate of victims because "in doing so we cope with our distorted image of what happened, not with the events the way they did happen" (Bettelheim 1982:92). Petronila, on the other hand, does not necessarily react against this tendency but prefers to see the women as martyrs as well. Perhaps her concern is not with the events as they 'did happen'.

These behaviours immediately confronted the military government's assumed agenda and thereby turned private thoughts into political acts because these actions reinterpret, whatever the person's intentions, the political domain. Knowingly or not, through trying to understand and rework popular memories of atrocity, women employ strategies which can release Guatemalan history from its uni-dimensional official definitions, allowing it to become a malleable space of vying interpretations.

But the official 'truth' continues to harass positive efforts to re-establish an acceptable identity; it hinders attempts to re-establish continuity with the past. The problem of interface remains when the selves of the present cannot access those of the past; the trauma caused considerable alienation from constructions of the 'self' which operated up to the time when they were confronted with situations in which they were forced to act according to a different morality, a morality which has been left behind since 'that time'. Those memories which are connected with those disassociated aspects of the 'self', frozen in 'that time', are of events that are perhaps memorable in some form but not necessarily accessible or speakable which in the end, can neither be remembered nor truly forgotten.

Notes

1. A Swedish representative to the United Nations remarked that the rhetoric of General Ríos Montt's government (1982-1983) reminded him of Orwell's novel *"1984"*: "When they mean war they speak of peace and when they mean repression, they speak of freedom... Guatemala is the same" (Simon 1987:114).

2. See chapter four, note 8.

3. cf. Gregory and Timmerman (1986) for an explanation of the 'ritual-like' aspects of torture.

4. I have added a hyphen here to emphasize the nature of going over and over the different parts of a memory fragmented by violence in order to construct and reconstruct something whole.

5. cf. Masiello (1987:12-13): the authoritarian Argentine state articulates a uni-dimensional theory of reality, according to whose norms all dissent is described in metaphors of illness. The cultural field is then divided between 'us' and 'others' by the official discourse which employs the first person plural in an attempt to elim-inate opposition, the sense of otherness and ambiguity of thought.

6. cf. Lévi-Strauss (1966:257): memory, like history, must be chosen, severed, and carved up in order to avoid chaos.

7. Sternbach refers to written testimony about the disappeared in Argentina.

8. Symbolic domination is "that through which relations of domination are de-ployed into the culture and daily life of the other, dominated group" (Bourdieu 1991).

9. This should be distinguished from the 'secrets' pertaining to the details of their communities which the K'iche' have chosen as a strategy of protection of their culture (cf. Burgos-Debray and Menchú 1984:9). These are "largely public 'secrets' known to the Quiché and kept from us as a gesture of self-preservation" (Sommer 1991:33).

10. *El monte* refers to uncultivated space close to habitation which people use for pasturing their animals, collecting firewood, etc. It is a liminal area between the place of the living and the place of the ancestors (mountains).

11. Women also date events by the agricultural calendar. They say, for ex-ample, "Oh yes, this happened when the cornfields were being weeded", or "It was when the corn was high" or "It must have been November because they corn was ready for harvesting". However, many women are unable to say which year it was.

12. I owe this observation to John Morton (London School of Economics, Academic Seminar April 1992).

13. Photographs are significant markers of personal and collective identity; they are perceived as extensions of the individuals represented in the visual frame. Photos are 'pieces of the individual' and salvaging them entails a form of reconstruction and reintegration of the self. As such, photos are also objects through which symbolic violence was expressed towards the individual represented.

14. The word used here indicates a general desire to do something without any specific intentions to do anything.

15. This term, commonly used in psychoanalysis, means the process whereby inter-subjective relations are transformed into intra-subjective ones (internalization of a conflict, of a prohibition, etc.).

16. Survivors' need to construct various scenarios in their minds by which the outcome of trauma could have been changed has been recognized as the classic syndrome of obsessional review (Lifton 1967). However, there did not seem to be an obsessional quality to Guatemalan widows' concern with the traumatic.

17. Gestalt theory pertaining to memory suggests that when our surroundings do not change, we lose consciousness of time (Gurwitsch 1966). Therefore, the time spent in the ravines without growing corn and other markers collapses into a single image or brief evaluation — as did the soldiers' time in the trenches during WWI (Rosenthal 1990).

18. The word *torturado* (tortured) is another word which has entered the K'iche' lexicon along with other words such as 'disappeared'.

19. *Doña* Ana used the expression 'na oj ta chi winaq ri oj' which refers to a loss of control, a condition viewed as non-human.

20. Many survivors of wars or other complex and traumatic experiences unconsciously filter their memory (Laub 1992).

21. *Doña* Ana used a metaphor from corn planting: 'Xsach ri nuna ooj', which means 'I am not sown well'.

22. cf. Poole (1982:103): personhood involves basic concepts of "human nature" and is fundamentally related to ideas of corporeal (and noncorporeal) capacity, process, and structure and also to notions of gender.

23. "...moving through the moral career, the human being may or may not become fully a person. Even if he or she does become a person, personhood may be partly or fully rescinded later. A person's agentive capacities is bestowed or removed, confirmed or disconfirmed, declared or denied" (Harris 1989:604).

24. This is a process which I believe occurs all the time but is most apparent when people retrospectively edit their past to fit new meanings, including new ways of perceiving themselves.

25. The same applies to those patrols *jefes* and commissioners who helped people instead of complying with army orders.

26. This is a positive identification as it is believed that Tecúm will physically return to free indigenous Guatemalans.

27. The evils of the military state are also contextualized in terms of Mayan mytho-history. *"Popul Vuh"* refers to an evil power in the form of gods called Xibalbá who reside in the underworld; Petronila believes that evil is "when repression came to the Quiché... These men, those soldiers who killed us...that is what we call Xibalbá" (Carmack 1988:69).

28. This may also be due to the psychological process of idealization of the lost object (person) which is now 'within' the survivor in the form of memories (images, anecdotes, affective and auditory sensations) (cf. Parkes 1972). The bad object which is 'outside' is similarly idealized as the repository of all that is negative.

29. Petronila's feminist vision stems partly from her childhood when her mother travelled everywhere with her father (an aj q'ij) and the general equality expressed in their relationship. These ideas were built upon in her catechist training although she says many male catechists did not put the ideas into practice in their homes. Her ideas of equality grew from the abject poverty in which she grew up while viewing the lives of rich *ladinos* in the town.

8

The Dead, the Disappeared, and Clandestine Graves

A funeral rite, is a social rite par excellence. *Its ostensible object is the dead person, but it benefits not the dead but the living.* (Firth 1951:63)

Once again he sees his companions' face
Livid in the first faint light...
Tinged with death in their uneasy sleep...
"Stand back, leave me alone, submerged people,
Go away. I haven't dispossessed anyone,
Haven't usurped anyone's bread.
No one died in my place. No one.
Go back into your mist.
It's not my fault if I live and breathe,
Eat, drink, sleep and put on clothes."

(The Survivor, Primo Levi 1986)

K'iche' war-widows were generally prevented from burying their murdered and abducted relatives. Clandestine burials deprive them of the bodies of the dead; abductions deprive them of the certain knowledge that a relative has actually died. They have been deprived of the ritual which organizes and orchestrates private emotions surrounding death (cf. Hertz 1960), of mourning in the traditional manner (which has positive forgetting as one of its goals), of ceremonies of propitiation, and, finally, the rites of passage to widowhood. For most war-widows, widowhood, as an arrest of life history dramatized in a rite of passage, remains frozen in time in its liminal stage (Turner 1967:93), leaving women feeling separated from society and culture.

To understand the repercussions of the 'unnatural' treatment of both the dead and surviving kin during *la violencia,* one needs to contrast this with normal circumstances. For the sake of simple exposition, I shall reconstruct the usual course of events[1] pertaining to a death in a 'pure' Catholic (*cos-*

tumbrista) household, including the funeral and the rituals performed on the Day of the Dead *(Día de los difuntos/muertos)*. These events follow a set sequence which varies in elaboration according to the deceased's status, the family's economic standing, and the emotional involvement of the living. Underpinning these rituals are concepts of 'good' and 'bad' deaths and beliefs concerning the continuing 'life' of a person's spirit after death.

The Costumbrista Death

'Good' and 'Bad' Deaths

The relentless ideology of complementarity makes it difficult for the K'iche' to think in terms of opposites. Thus, while they do not make a dichotomy between 'good' and 'bad' deaths, their exegesis reveals that they have definite notions of which types of death are safer, or more dangerous, to the living. A good death is one which occurs with warning, at home: the dying person has sufficient time to settle his or her affairs and settle outstanding debts; the family is able to prepare for the event with traditional ceremony. A bad death occurs suddenly with little or no time to settle spiritual and temporal accounts.

The concept of a bad death refers to a human exit which is ill-timed and so fails to satisfy normal expectations associated with natural death (Metcalf 1982:254-7). Bad deaths are those which "most clearly demonstrate the absence of control" and which do not result in regeneration (Thomas 1975, cited in Bloch and Parry 1982:15). The death passes from human control and therefore cannot be reactivated as new life. There is a residual concept of the recycling of souls among the K'iche', who believe that the living come from, and return to, the after-world.

Dying away from home is considered a terrible fate and so the dead or dying are brought back to the village for interment if at all possible. If a hospital patient is thought to be dying, relatives will smuggle the person out so that he or she can die at home surrounded by family and neighbours. This is in keeping with the K'iche' value of remaining together before, during, and after death; many people told me they try to collect all the members of the family together because, "If we have to die, then we should die together in the same place". Behind these actions is the belief that if the soul is unable to return home for the living to help it on its way, it will be excluded from the after-world and condemned to a living death in the liminal space between physical death and the concluding burial ritual (Hertz 1960). Condemned to wander the earth as a lonely, malicious ghost, such restless, unhappy spirits haunt living kin who should have been responsible for its safe passage to the after-life. This is a recurrent theme throughout the funerary process.

Accidental deaths, despite being ill-timed, are considered in a less negative light than murder though both are thought to occur before the person's predestined hour of death. Murder is considered a heinous sin and neither murderers nor their victims are accepted by God/the ancestors. The spirits of such 'bad people' become night creatures (bibinaq) who frighten the living (Wagley 1949:64). This is connected to the idea, promoted through K'iche' language and grammar, that the act of violence not only involves both actors but unites them. The act of inflicting physical harm on another person is described using specific verb forms which contain the type of instrument or body part with which pain is inflicted within the meaning of their action. The violent act involves two specific persons, mediated by a specific type of object, for example, "he gave him a hand" (he slapped or hit him), "he gave him a foot" (he kicked him), "he gave him a *machete*" (he attacked him with a *machete*) bounded by a mutual understanding of place; subsequent details reveal whether the attack resulted in injury or death.

The disordering of time is also transcribed in the non-integration of death within the life cycle. The violent death of a young adult and the absence of ritual preparation which accompanies sudden death are central to the notion of bad death. Relatives of the war-dead bear a heavy burden because their kin had no opportunity to resolve their affairs before death; whilst sons are most likely to inherit a father's lands and property, it is the widow who is most likely to inherit her husband's moral debts.

The Rituals of Death

The good or bad fate of the deceased's soul or spirit *(alma* or *ánima)*[2] is determined by the collective obsequies performed by others after death rather then the deceased's own actions in life. It is in survivors' interests to meet their obligations in ensuring that the disembodied spirits of the dead go to their place of repose without delay: the idea that restless spirits bring misfortune to the living retains its potency despite conversion to newer religions.

The news of an impending or actual death spreads rapidly through the village and surrounding area. Although the immediate family are responsible for the well being of its deceased kinfolk, every household in the village has the right and the obligation to attend and contribute to the funeral process (funerals involve village households to a greater degree than ceremonies surrounding marriage and birth). Dying well, like living well, is not a solitary activity: other people are needed to help the spirit on its way to the after-life, where it becomes assimilated into the general category of ancestors[3] to whom the whole community pays homage on the Day of the Dead (Farriss 1984:328).

The process begins with a diviner (aj q'ij) performing traditional rituals *(costumbre)* over the dying person. Both men and women share the task of caring for the body. K'iche's seem comfortable about the bodies and possessions of the dead; they are able to view and touch them with little or no sign of disgust or fear and seem neither to be in any hurry to get rid of them nor to want to keep them beyond the time that tradition specifies they should hold onto them. Women wash the dead person's clothes; the head is washed and body clothed[4] and placed in a coffin bought by surviving male kin. The coffin, which is made to size by the village's coffin maker, is brought to the house with its wood shavings still inside. It became apparent to me that these shavings should not be removed and when I asked why I was told, "It is the custom *(Es costumbre)*".[5] Men bring the cloths to cover the face, light the candles which are left to burn at the body's head and feet (to signal its presence to the ancestors) and arrange flowers. They collect wood and water (usually a woman's task); women prepare food.

A night vigil or wake is held at the deceased's house. Family menfolk receive the guests who, prior to the advent of 'new'catholicism, included members of the saints' brotherhoods *(mayordormos/cofrades)* in full regalia (cf. Bunzel 1952:153).[6] That this did not happen at any funerals I attended is probably due to the collapse of Emol's saints' brotherhoods *(cofradia)* during *la violencia*: despite being revived, the *cofradia* now have a limited constituency, no authority, and little prestige. Since *la violencia*, patrol chiefs *(jefes)* and military commissioners are invited to avoid the possibility of causing them offence; the village mayor is also routinely invited. Today, those attending a funeral are blood kin, close neighbours, and friends belonging to the same political or religious groups (such as widowed members of human right groups such as GAM and CONAVIGUA, and patrollers belonging to CERJ, although their affinity is hidden because of the danger it implies). Relatives with different affiliations, who are ordinarily fairly distant from one another, rise above these differences at times of death: these rituals emphasize not only the importance of the house and generational continuity but also village harmony, an important K'iche' value which these days is more honoured in the breach.

Guests enter the darkened room where the covered corpse lays in its coffin. After praying over the body, visitors place a small sum of money on the metal plate resting on the corpse's chest. Each visitor also brings a token amount of food, such as sugar, to contribute to the food which is being prepared in abundance in the name of the dead person by female relatives. Female guests usually join the women preparing food in another room or on the patio; they serve food and a non-alcoholic corn beverage *(atol)* during the night. Men serve rum *(aguardiente)* or a home brewed, bootleg rum (kuxa) which is served without songs.[7]

Visitors make conversation with relatives and friends already sitting around the room. Everyone usually stays awake all night. People "spend the whole [time] talking about the dead person, about his life, remembering him" (Burgos-Debray and Menchú 1984:202). They construct a narrative about his life and also his death, which helps mourners to integrate the crisis of the death into their lives. Family and friends make comments such as, "He encountered a good life here on earth and surely he returns happily"; altern-

atively, they 'remember', 'with sadness', the dead person's failures, expressed in remarks such as, "He suffered much in his life and surely he will have
returned sobbing". When someone dies through an accident or homicide,
visitors talk about similar occurrences. Guests also chat and gossip about
other matters.

The atmosphere is usually one of restrained mourning with silent weeping; I saw little crying. The calmness of vigils is striking. Most people end
up drunk, 'in order to drown their sorrow' *(para quitar su tristeza)*. Whilst
all this is going on, an aj q'ij, who assumes religious responsibility for the
dead person and is referred to as his or her 'father' *(padrino)*, burns incense
over the body and calls upon the spirits of the dead to tell them that their
'child' is coming to join them. The aj q'ij is also responsible for accompanying the corpse to the grave and ensuring that the deceased's soul or spirit
accompanies its body to the cemetery (mukaan).

On the day following the wake, the deceased's mother (or other close
relative) advises the elder appointed to care for the body which clothes the
dead person should wear on the journey to the other world. Wearing appropriate clothing puts the dead person in the form of the ancestors (ka nimal,
old person); without the proper attire, the dead are said to wander about in
the spirit realm void of any form. Food and the 'big plates' on which the person ate daily are also placed in the coffin; this is said to assist the ancestors
in determining where a person comes from. Money is included because "the
dead may have to buy something upon arrival". Men are buried with their
machete and hoe; women with their best traditional woven tops (huipiles),
necklaces and comb; children with their (minimal) toys. Such accoutrements
are said to aid the ancestors in assessing what the person did during their
life. If the family can afford it, the corpse has a good pair of new shoes as
they "may have to walk far" (most children go barefoot while alive and they
go barefoot to the world of the dead). A candle is placed in the corpse's right
hand to light the way into the after-world. Finally, a crown and bracelet of
flower petals are placed on the corpse's head and wrist so that they will be
recognized as newcomers.

Whilst the body is being prepared for burial, male kin and friends leave
the house to dig a grave in the village mukaan. This is located at the village
perimeter to prevent the dead from returning to frighten the family; in contrast, clandestine graves (mukaniil)[8] are scattered throughout the village, hidden in the deep canyons which permeate the area, desecrating the boundaries
between the realms of the living and the dead. When the grave is ready, the
men return to the deceased's house and everyone is served a meal. The coffin is then brought into the courtyard and the top is temporarily nailed shut
for the journey to the cemetery. The coffin is made with a little hole in the
lid so that the spirit can escape — hopefully straight to the other world.

People standing in the doorway signal to the mourners inside the house
that the coffin is ready to be taken to the graveyard. Sometimes dramatic

scenes occur at this point. At one child's funeral, a sick child inside the house 'began to die' and the women flew into a flurry of activity to rescue him. They explained that 'wind had entered his heart' because of his 'sadness' on his sibling's departure. The child was indeed critically ill but this activity was more an expression of the women's panic: it diverted their attention from the pain of separation as the coffin left the house. Some relatives are too distressed to join the funeral procession to the graveyard, saying they would not be able to bear it *(aguantarlo)*. For example, at the funeral of a twenty-two year old Catholic man, the mother clung to the coffin and wailed as it was torn away from her; she remained in the house in the company of other women.

The newly dead person's spirit is also seen as grieving at the separation from living family members; it is said to be loth to leave them. The spirits of the recently dead are conceptualized differently from the spirits of people buried in the village cemetery who are seen as settled in the after-life; the newly dead are 'displaced' and temporarily homeless, often upset, angry, and vengeful. In order to prevent the spirit remaining in the house to haunt them, the dead person's *padrino* (the aj q'ij) beats the floor and the corners of every room in the house, the courtyard, and the pathway to ensure that the spirit does not linger. Attempts are also made to ensure that the spirit cannot find its way back to the house by rotating the coffin several times in front of the church so 'the soul loses its way'.

At the cemetery, the coffin is opened and a few last items placed inside. A soft drink (usually a bottle of coca cola) is opened and put in with the rest before the lid is finally nailed firmly shut. The coffin is lowered into a deep grave next to other members of the patrilineage (a widow is always buried near her husband). Everyone then contributes to the burial by throwing a fistful of earth onto the coffin. Men take turns to shovel the rest of the earth and other bones and belongings from previous burials. These items are passed around, inspected, joked about, and speculated upon before being thrown back in the grave. This stage of the funeral provokes the most laughing and joking although none of it seems particularly sombre.

When the interment is over, the aj q'ij invokes the dead person's ancestors and beseeches them to receive their child's spirit. Mourners remain kneeling until the praying has finished. At this point, people used to set off rockets to facilitate the spirit's way to the after-life. Today, there is no-one left in the village who knows how to make fireworks (they had been killed in *la violencia*) and people can no longer afford such extras anyway.

Most mourners then return to the deceased's home and proceed to get very drunk. Drinking alcohol is said to help mourners release their feelings in a cathartic manner and so bear their grief. Though the K'iche' generally attempt to avoid experiencing and expressing intense emotions, wailing and crying are encouraged at this stage of the proceedings because the expression of grief is thought to be beneficial to the bereaved.[9] A balance must be reached: a person who does not cry may be susceptible to illness, yet excessive crying is thought to have an injurious effect on one's own health and a pernicious effect on the dead. Eventually, when sober enough to walk, guests make their way home.

Despite the various rituals of separation on the day of interment (which may represent vestiges of the ancient Mayan belief in multiple souls), the soul or spirit does not disengage from the body until the nine day ritual (the *novenario)* is completed (García 1987). During this ritual, people pray rosaries; family and friends visit the house and church to pray and burn candles, particularly on the first day. This is a liminal period when the soul is an undesirable member of the household (García 1987:17), having returned to the house at some ill definable point (or indeed, never having left). On the last night of the *novenario*, Emoltecos lay a straw sleeping mat *(petate)* exactly where the person died, for the spirit to sleep on before leaving for the world of the dead, hopefully for good. People promise the dead that they will not remember, or cry over, them any longer because it is said that if they do, then the life of the dead in the after-life will be painful.

Three days after the death of a child or nine days after the death of an adult, a small procession, like that of the funeral, goes to the cemetery to place an uninscribed wooden cross at the head of the burial mound. In some areas, the spirit is believed to leave for the cemetery with the cross (García 1987:20) which in this situation probably represents the ancient Mayan symbol for the 'Tree of Life' rather than the Christian crucifix; individuals at the same funeral will 'read' the symbol in different ways. Emoltecos, however, do not make this connection; for them it is the flowers (a type of marigold known as 'the flowers of the dead') which are the ritually important element (cf. Vogt 1976:44). The raising of the cross marks the place of the dead and the end of the funeral. If this last phase of the funeral is not performed, then separation from the family is impossible and the spirit stays to frighten those living in its former home, appearing in relatives' dreams and so on. Some people believe that final separation occurs on the first Day of the Dead following an individual's death. Whichever point in the process people believe marks the spirit's departure, there is no guarantee that it will leave (García 1987:19).

All Saints' Day (pac q'ij)

The K'iche' commemorate their dead at the beginning of the dry season with a first fruits festival centering on the harvesting of the first ears of corn, a festival which predates the 'Christian' festival of All Saints' Day (*Día de los santos;* pac q'ij) to which it is now tied (1 November).

Preparations begin the day before All Saints' Day (31 October). Women spend the day cooking and cleaning. The special meal for the spirits of the dead is prepared: *tortillas* made from the first of corn of the year (aj wa) from the men's fields and home-grown pumpkin and chayote *(guiskil)*[10] from the women's gardens. Plentiful *aguardiente* is an important part of the offering to both collective and individual dead.

The room containing the family altar is prepared to receive the spirits of the individual family dead. The path leading to the room is decorated with pine needles; an arch of the yellow 'flowers of the dead' marks its entrance. Inside, the family prepares seating arrangements for the dead: chairs for men and a *petate* on the floor for women. A bowl of water is left in the room so the dead can wash their hands before eating. Candles are lit so the spirits can see the house; they are said to visit the saint statue housed in the local church on the way. An aj q'ij is called to make an offering to facilitate the spirits' visit.

In the evening, the family goes to the cemetery to clean and decorate the graves for the morrow. They weed and re-pile the grave mound, repaint crosses and sprinkle pine leaves and marigold flowers over and around the grave; men stay by the grave all night, watching over it.

The next day (1 November) is All Saints Day. People arrive from different villages to pray on the graves where the souls of the dead, the ancestors, and the saints descend from heaven. Living and dead family members then share the meal of 'first fruits' and copious alcohol; the ancestors consume the moral sentiment of the offering. The K'iche' celebrate that their dead have returned and are with them momentarily to share the products of the household. *Costumbrista* families ask an aj q'ij to visit the grave to evoke the spirits of the dead so that they can be offered gifts. Unlike other days when candles are lit as a form of penance, today candles are only for gift giving, a means of giving thanks to the ancestors and the spirits of the dead for the fruits of the land. People who can afford it pay for brass bands to serenade the dead, although celebrations are less obvious in poorer villages; in towns, gatherings in cemeteries are more like parties with fireworks and several bands all playing at once. At the end of the celebration, the saints return to heaven. Most people go home, but a few keep vigil in the cemetery for a second night.

The following day, 2 November, is is the Day of the Dead *(Día de los muertos)*. Also known as the Day of the Spirits *(Día de los ánimas)*, this is the more important day of the festival; at the end of the day, the spirits return to their place, taking the spirits of the recently dead with them. I was told "the Day of the Dead interests people more than the Day of All Saints because the saints do not have the same significance as the dead." The influence of the Catholic concepts can be seen in the observance of this day: "The day is a reminder of the Day of Judgement; the dead are mourned and the living do penance for their sins and offer candles and prayers on behalf of the souls in purgatory, to shorten their suffering" (Bunzel 1952:273). It is a day of grief and penance, when all Indians (except evangelicals) communicate with the dead.[11] Today, the emphasis is on appeasing the malevolence of the many spirits unable to make the final transition to the after-life.

The Fate of the Soul and the After-life

The syncretism between Mayan and Catholic ideas of the fate of the soul is evidenced by the various interpretations of the after-life/heaven which I collected in Emol. People seem to believe in both systems, linking them at different points. For example, some people's language use indicates a linkage between ancestors and saints; both come in large numbers and share the same position in the hierarchy in relation to God. The link is the saint statue in the local Catholic church which has replaced the stone idols (camawil) and sacred caves venerated in pre-Conquest times (cf. Wilson 1995).

The spirits and the ancestors are traditionally considered as living members of and actors in the K'iche' social universe; they are omnipresent and can effect the lives of the living for better or worse. The current emphasis on their negative aspects is probably of pre-hispanic origin as the K'iche' have seen no need to adopt Christian concepts of a separate purgatory and hell: in the traditional schema, everyone buried with proper ritual in their village cemetery, regardless of whether they were good or bad in life, enters the after-life and eventually becomes an ancestor and hence part of the living, sacred landscape. Spirits not accepted by the ancestors are condemned to remain among the living, causing havoc among them by trying to attract attention to their predicament (by visiting misfortune on their kin) or company in it (by causing further deaths). These ideas have coloured local perceptions of the Christian heaven: everyone, good or bad, goes there; it just takes some people longer. In the meantime, the person who experienced a bad death and /or was improperly buried lives in a kind of purgatory, the location of which is identical to the whereabouts of traditional, rejected spirits. One has to pray for them a lot in order to get them into heaven.

The Christian idea of Judgement Day has also been grafted on to the traditional schema: people say everyone will go to heaven after the final judgement. Some people say only God lives in heaven, which is often described as high in the sky, the implication being that it is above and beyond and definitely distinct from the 'world' inhabited by living and dead K'iche'. Others claim that children, who have no place in the traditional after-life because they are incomplete (unmarried) persons, go straight to heaven. *Doña* Eugenia, whose favourite great-granddaughter died in the measles epidemic, told me children were chosen by God to be little angels *(angelitos)*, "especially if they are intelligent". The K'iche' have only adopted those parts of the Catholic concepts of heaven, hell, and purgatory they can use; the traditional Mayan concepts concerning the dead and the after-life retain their validity and power.

The mechanics of the soul's transition from the dead person to the world of the dead is of little concern to most K'iche'. Aj q'ij explained that the dead entered the world of the dead *(los mundos)* through its doors and windows, i.e., the sacred caves and 'holes' at high points on the landscape known as r'k'u'x (heart or essence). These sacred sites retain their potency for aj q'ij but, for most *costumbristas*, the church has taken over as the focus for prayer.[12] An aj q'ij told me that there are many *mundos* situated 'above and below', north and south, east and west, as well as in houses and sweat baths *(temascales)*. All are addressed in aj q'ij's prayers and offerings.

Mundo (literally, the world) is a Spanish loan word which has been transformed into mundt. In some areas, this has come to mean 'heart of the skies' (Bunzel 1952:264).[13] The word is used to refer to the ancestral landscape, the sacred mountains and distant volcanoes *(dueños)* which literally and figuratively dominate the landscape, the sacred caves and potholes which connect the world of the living with the world of the ancestors where people leave offerings. When used by aj q'ij, the term refers ancestors.

Responses to my enquiries about what life after death is like varied according to people's role in life, religion, education, and so on. *Costumbristas*, especially aj q'ij, have the most elaborate concept of the after-life but it is still rather vague. One told me, "We know a bit about what goes on in the other world from those people who die for twenty minutes or half an hour and then when they are resuscitated, they return." This is said to happen because their name is not on the list held by the 'judges in the skies'.

For the K'iche', a person's spirit *(ánima)* is an almost tangible reality[14] with a life of its own in the other world. Despite some gaps in their concepts of the after-life, it is generally seen as a replication of their own world. This also applies to the temporality of events. An aj q'ij said, "I have been told that if one builds a house here then they build one there at the same time." Another aj q'ij told me:

> We are only able to see outside the windows but not inside their world but we know that the ancestors live inside. We know that they are not dead for they are talking and living over there; in fact, they are more alive than the living. We are able to call them and we know that their spirits come to the edge of the *mundos* but we are unable to see them.

Some people have a rather idealized image of the 'other life', such as 'a garden which grows well'. Others had a more negative image, as a place where "You must work hard, even the oldest of people, even the original Mayas, because the overseer *(caporal)* orders you to". When I asked an aj q'ij for more details of the type of work people performed in the after-life — do they plant corn fields *(milpa)*, he replied, "Who knows what they do?" Then he joked, "When you die, you had better take a bit of *milpa*!"

The dead are dogged by human-like emotions. Ancestors experience pain, anger, greed, and sadness. Spirits who have not been properly expelled are said to be most vulnerable and least able to transcend human frailties, remaining susceptible to the actions of the living. Through consultation with a diviner, a person may discover, for example, that their tears are causing their dead kin to be beaten by the *'caporal* in the sky'; they may be told that their indecorous behaviour is causing problems for the dead. Alternatively, the living may learn that their present life is being affected by the their dead kin's current life in the other world or past life in this one. Spirits may be jailed in the after-life because the dead person failed to resolve their problems (such as marital disharmony) before death. It is said that the dead need the living to 'liberate them from jail' and requests by the dead were explained as follows:

> Some of them are in pain because they are incarcerated in the other world. This is why they solicit help from their children and grandchildren who are here on their land with their animals. They send messages asking for their help via illnesses or dreams. And the recipient of the message then goes to the aj q'ij to discover its meaning.

Whatever the cause for their unhappiness, spirits — whether accepted into the after-life or not — make problems for the living who remain in the family home. Theoretically, the difference between them is that excluded spirits are malicious rather than merely capricious; in practice, the effects are often the same. An aj q'ij explained that the living can cure problems such as sickness, crop failure, and disputes by making offerings; only in this way would the dead leave the living in peace.

The spirits of the dead can also reciprocate human generosity, normally only after their descendants have made copious offerings. They can help the living, most importantly by leaving them alone or at least not judging them too harshly for their failings. Serious sins, such as acting 'without respect', abuse of women, adultery, and feeling too much hatred are all believed to prompt the spirits of the dead/ancestors to call the guilty to the after-life. Serious, repeated sins can also result in the death of the guilty party's offspring; the child becomes the scapegoat and a substitute for the sinner.

The living should continually assure the dead that they have not been 'forgotten' otherwise disasters such as death, crop destruction, the occasional earthquake, and war may arise (chapter nine). This does not imply a literal forgetting but the moral sentiment of remembering the ways of the ancestors (the promises not to remember made at the end of the funeral refer to the disorganization of strong, personal emotions) and maintaining traditional codes of conduct. Descendants should also lavish appreciation and abundant offerings upon the ancestors. It is not that they should literally be remembered because the K'iche' do not easily forget their dead.

Death During 'La Violencia'

Burying the Dead

When the first few people were killed in Emol, their families held full funerals. More households than usual were represented, reflecting the solidarity which grew at the beginning of *la violencia*. One villager told me the entire village attended the first burial, regardless of religious or political affiliation. There was still a semblance of social solidarity which was threatened by such atrocious and bad deaths. Everyone was deeply shocked and frightened, but it seems that each subsequent death became less bad as, with time, such atrocities came to be expected and 'normal'. What constitutes a bad death shifts in a changing context.

As *la violencia* progressed, chaos and terror intensified and village solidarity collapsed. Holding full funerals for people killed by the military or the *jefes* exposed relatives and friends to accusations of subversion, especially if they buried their relatives face downwards as is the custom for those who die a violent death. This is done to prevent the malicious spirit from calling relatives and friends to join them when they return to the spot where the violent death occurred (later, it transpired that the *jefes* had themselves buried massacre victims, to whom some of them were related, face downwards). This previously rare form of burial brings malicious gossip and rumour (*chismes*; ta juntziij pixaab'),[15] drawing attention to survivors. Surviving kin had to choose between temporal and spiritual dangers: burying the body the wrong way up brings dangers from the spirits yet burying them face down brings dangers from the *jefes*.

Mainly for security reasons, any interment following an assassination was generally rushed and reduced in size and complexity. During *la violencia*, necessities such as coffins, incense, and food for guests were often unobtainable; if food was unavailable, then the ritual was curtailed. Financial and time restraints dictated that if more than one member of a family was killed simultaneously, then coffins (if used) were often shared; if two people from the same family died on consecutive days, the second corpse was interred without a vigil in order to avoid preparing a second meal for visitors. More worrying for survivors was the fact that aj q'ij were not available to perform *costumbre*. Funeral gatherings shrank to whoever was available or brave enough to attend; few people stayed to perform vigils. People were afraid to host large gatherings at their houses for fear of being accused of holding a subversive meeting. Villagers stopped attending funerals in other villages because passage between them also came to be viewed as a seditious activity.

At the height of *la violencia*, people became accustomed to 'burying the dead from one moment to the next' for fear of being caught by the military. Two widows recount their experiences:

> My child died in the afternoon and my husband prepared a little coffin for her. We still managed to hold a night vigil but we were terrified for the army were living in the village. The following day, we rushed to the cemetery, where we left her without detaining ourselves.

> My mother died 'under the mountains' and we buried her the next day. We didn't carry out a night [vigil] in the house because we were in hiding but we managed to hold one under the shelters *(champitas)*. We did it like this in order to hide from the army. The problem was that while we were making the coffin someone shouted that the soldiers were coming and everyone ran for their lives. Once the soldiers withdrew, we buried her but without a coffin because we couldn't wait for them to finish making it.

Worse than these makeshift funerals was the fate of victims of violence whose bodies were collected by volunteer firemen *(bomberos voluntarios)* or removed from the village under the supervision of military personnel *(oficiales)*: the corpses were taken to the morgue in the departmental capital, where they were disposed of, or, as villagers describe it, 'thrown away'. Victims of local massacres come in the same category of awfulness. Relatives were rarely allowed to see the dead after massacres; depriving survivors of the bodies of their kin was a deliberate insult to their customs and beliefs (fear of being reported to the authorities came later). Sometimes dazed villagers were forced to bury their dead in a mass grave, actively involving survivors in the 'forgetting' of their kin.

The sheer frequency of death meant that people became desensitized to its potency. The heterogeneity of the dead — the difference between the death of a husband, a son or a father — was transformed into a homogeneous mass of improperly buried, inadequately mourned dead. During the course of *la violencia*, the community was socialized to the repeated occurrence of abrupt violent death.

Commemorating the Dead

During *la violencia*, many 'new' Catholics and *costumbristas* converted to protestantism which does not advocate the performance of rituals for the Day of the Dead. Change in ritual practice has also occurred among Emol's 'new'Catholics and *costumbristas* because of the nature of the deaths during *la violencia*: families cannot be sure that relatives who met un-timely deaths and were not buried correctly will return on this day. Even if the spirits do return, they are thought to return to the family home and not the cemetery because, obviously, they are not buried there: such a spirit may be able to visit its family but not join the rest of the community of living and dead K'iche' in the village graveyard. Thus, year after year, the lost spirit fails to be taken away to the after-life by the departing ancestors and saints. This interpretation is more common among people who still feel guilty about their inability to bury their dead. *Doña* Josefina makes offerings in the local cemetery for her mother, who died of natural causes and was given a conventional burial, but waits in her house for the spirits of her murdered husband and abducted grandmother; after eight years, she is still uncertain of her grandmother's fate but puts out food and *aguardiente* for her in case she is among the visiting spirits. She says their spirits spend the night in her house and then, as they have not been helped on their way to the after-life with a funeral, proceed to wander around again; her mother's spirit returns to her grave in the village cemetery. This interpretation of the visiting habits of the dead is relatively new even though (despite claims to the contrary) a small proportion of every generation of Emoltecos die from natural causes and are buried outside the village, most commonly on the coastal plantations *(fincas)* or on the road; death in the lowlands is an occupational hazard for highland labour migrants. The repercussions of these deaths are nothing like as fright-ening as the consequences of losses attributable to *la violencia*; although the spirits of the dead harass the living in both cases, in the former the dangers associated with place of death and burial are missing. I gained the impres-sion that labour migrants who died of natural causes were not necessarily excluded from the after-life; some people include them with the general collectivity of the dead. But the victims of *la violencia* are differentiated from the collectivity of the dead just as their surviving kin are differentiated from the community of the living.

The uncertainty of a spirit's return is increased in the case of the dis-appeared whose status is unknown. *Doña* Candelaria, once a fairly puncti-lious 'new' Catholic, told me that she stopped celebrating All Saints' Day following the abduction, assassination, and clandestine burial of her hus-band. By not visiting the cemetery on the Day of the Dead, she avoids facing the additional loss of being unable to celebrate the return of his spirit. She has relinquished this cyclical ritual which links between the living and the dead: his abduction was from a different time and a different world. *Doña* Candelaria prefers to try and forget her family's ordeal. She has no altar in her house; she says all her photographs of her husband were taken by the *jefes* so that witchcraft *(brujería)* could be performed to facilitate his death.[16] Without such representational objects, into which memories and thoughts about the dead can be projected, memories are more fragmented than usual.

The Disappeared

...the continuity of life cannot be re-established until the nature of the dis-ruption has been made clear. The loss must be insisted upon, otherwise the value of the lost relationship may seem disparaged, threatening all such relationships which still survive; but it also must be made good, and the bereaved must be led to re-establish themselves within society...for while the dead must be dismissed, the values they represented in all their relationships must be preserved (Marris 1975:34-35).

Families who have not performed any interments include those who claim not to know the whereabouts of their missing kin. Many simply don't know; some seem not to want to know; others have heard that their kin are dead and buried elsewhere. Denial arises not only because of the risks involved in kinship with the dead and disappeared but also because of people's fears about the imagined state of the remains, whether buried or not (chapter four).

Families of the disappeared fear that rumours concerning the abduction of their relative(s) will mean their own death. Most did not search for their kin because they were too afraid to do so. Woman generally did nothing to recover the bodies of sons, husbands or fathers, even when they knew them to be dead. The common response to my enquiries about this was, "What can we do? *(¿qué hacemos?)*"; their answers indicate their feelings of guilt about not looking for their kin as this precluded bringing them home and sending them on their way to the after-life. A few unusually brave and determined women did search for their kin.[17] Accompanied by other widows, they combed fields, visited army barracks and hospital morgues full of mutilated bodies, threats from soldiers, *jefes,* and military commissioners not with-standing. Their descriptions evoke a picture of desperation. Realizing the dangers of probing 'matters', many women gave up the search for the sake of their surviving children. Other families who did nothing at the time of ab-duction searched for their kin when *la violencia* abated. One woman ex-plained:

> After *la violencia* we went to look for him where he used to work. The other workers told us that after a year he went elsewhere to look for new employ-ment but some neighbours say that he was taken away in a helicopter.

Doña Lydia had been stupefied with shock for three days following her husband's abduction from his street stall in Guatemala City. She never searched for him; she didn't know where to go and was too afraid to ask. Friends *(campesinos)* who shared her rented room told her that he had been taken away in a car. She eventually returned to the village to wait for him; when he had not returned after three years, she finally entertained the idea that he might be dead and decided to celebrate a mass for him. She told me:

> I think that my husband will never return now...we don't know if he is dead or alive...only God knows... I am sure that he died as I heard that when they took him away they threw him into a car and plain clothed policemen *(judici-ales)* squashed him with their knees...he must be dead as they folded him in half and tortured him... Who can withstand such torture? Because of this we say he must be dead. And who knows where they left him... At first I thought that he would come back, then one year passed, then two years and they still told me that he would come. I thought that he would come after two to three years but now I think that the *judiciales* killed him as they were mixed up in *la violencia.*[18] Now six years have passed and I think it unlikely that he will return.

As *doña* Lydia discovered, it is very hard psychologically to mourn without a corpse. Death in the abstract can never be as convincing as the body of dead kin. Where death is witnessed, it becomes a personal reality. Abductions, and especially unwitnessed ones, are more complicated: there is the loss of the body as an object to be mourned. Without a body, the social and psychological processes contingent on death and its expulsion are severely and irreparably disrupted: the individual cannot be placed within the wider, collective tragedy because, owing to the secrecy surrounding political killings, the timing or even the occurrence of death (or abduction) of relatives is not mentioned.

For women who have not seen the bodies of their dead, grieving is extremely problematic: "in the total absence of the body, there exists for the bereaved a terrible struggle between the need for certainty, to allow an ending, and the inevitable irrational hope" (Stewart and Hodgkinson 1988:12). Without seeing the body, doubt exists:

> ...whereas denial is an unconscious defense which gainsays the facts, doubt has a conscious, logical edge... Doubt is the main element in the difficulty in accepting the reality of the death...this 'questioning syndrome' appears to be typical of inhibited grief (Stewart and Hodgkinson 1988:13).

Even *doña* Eugenia, who knew, on an intellectual level, that her son was dead and even knew where he was buried, was unable to accommodate this on an emotional level. She had seen him beaten almost to death but had not seen him die; his death only became completely 'real' for her when his body was exhumed more than ten years later.

Grieving is even more difficult for the wives of the disappeared. Some women wonder if their missing husbands had decided to leave of his own volition; a wife might think her husband had eloped with another woman or joined the guerrilla (as the army claimed). Two women whose husbands were kidnapped express their uncertainty about the men's fate:

> Only God knows if my husband lives in the military base [is in detention] or if they killed him[19]...or if he still lives... If he is alive, what could they be doing with him?... What I want to know is if he will ever return from the base or not!

> I would say that they killed him...or perhaps he lives with the military [is in detention]. I do not know exactly...he could be alive or dead...

The widows' efforts to resolve their grief were hampered by official denials that anything had happened to the disappeared. Denials operated on two levels: the official and the unofficial. The military high command denied responsibility for the disappearances and sought to annul the reality of their occurrence; local officials at military bases also denied any knowledge of the whereabouts of the disappeared to any relative who had the temerity to ask.

The army line was that if the men were missing, they were subversive. Relatives were told that the missing had taken to the mountains (joined the guerrillas) or left had the country (being a refugee is also considered a subversive act). Although women did not really believe this, the insistent, official 'truth' fed into their faint and, as most accepted, unrealistic hopes that their menfolk were still alive; it also exacerbated women's uncertainty about what their relatives had got up to in the past, leaving them confused in the present. The illogicality of army explanations — that the men had been disfigured beyond recognition when a bomb meant for the military went off prematurely, for example — had the same effect. Occasionally, relatives were told that their disappeared kin had been executed by the guerrilla as traitors.

The more time passes, the more likely the missing are to be presumed dead, though the progression to certainty is never steady or final: women's thoughts fluctuate from moment to moment. A mother told me, "Now it has been seven years since they took him away...I think he must be dead", while on another occasion she said:

> My son died in 1983... I mean I don't know if he died but he has not returned since then. When *la violencia* came he was no longer able to make visits here to his house from his place of work. Since his father was unable to communicate with him, we don't know if he was killed or kidnapped. But we think that he's dead because we went to look for him and couldn't find him and never saw or heard of him again... I simply don't know what happened to him...

Women's conviction that their men are dead is sometimes reflected in their beliefs about the form in which the men now exist. One woman told me that her husband had presented himself to her in a dream: "He told me he was dead," she said; "he also told me who killed him and where he was buried." Although rumours from independent sources confirmed the existence of a clandestine cemetery in the place indicated in her dreams, she has not verified whether or not her husband is buried there.

Not knowing the fate of the dead and disappeared increases the trauma for the living who need to redefine themselves in the light of these events because "with losses people lose aspects of the self, aspects of social and personal identity" (Oliver-Smith 1986:184). Although there is a growing body of evidence indicating that people who view the bodies of loved ones killed in disasters have less difficulty in coping with their loss, the situation in a genocidal or civil war is not so clear-cut: survivors may want to know what happened to their kin but, as they have seen more than enough mangled corpses, they are terrified that their missing relatives may have suffered a similar or worse fate. They want to know their kin's status but do not want their worst fears confirmed. The 'wives of the disappeared' sometimes admit their desperation and some confessed that they wished to die, even though such desires are considered sinful.

More typically, women understand that their kin are dead from the presence of their spirits in dreams. They then consult a spirit caller (aj mes) who ascertains the dead's whereabouts through interpreting the widows' dreams:

> After a month I went to the aj q'ij to try and find out if my son was alive. The aj q'ij said that he was alive and that he would return. But I was not sure if what he told me was true, I thought only God knows... I thought that the aj q'ij really does know because he is a wise man *(sabio)* and he gets signs *(señas)*... After a week I went back to the aj q'ij who again told me that my husband would return...so I waited... After one month to the day after my husband was taken, I dreamt that God spoke to him...then I thought that he must be dead... but I still waited...

Most women's concerns about their kin's whereabouts relate more to the location of their spirits than their physical remains: it is important for them to know if the spirit has been permitted to enter the after-world. Survivors consult an aj q'ij to ascertain whether the judges in the after-life consider their kin to be someone 'who spoke the truth' or a 'sinner'; in this context, 'sinner' means someone who betrayed others under torture or in a vain attempt to save his own life. The influence of the concept of Judgement Day can be seen here: while the assimilation of the spirits of the dead into the amorphous mass of ancestors is still believed and spoken of, albeit vaguely, many people now believe (or at least hope) that the fate of the soul depends on the ancestors' judgement rather than on the collective funerary rituals carried out by the living. An aj q'ij told me, "*Los mundos* have their hierarchy" and explained that the ancestors work in conjunction with a hierarchy of judges to assess the fate of the dead: when the new spirit enters the other world, an ancestor hands the judge an account of the person's sins. These are written records of the person's behaviour in life and, I was told, "they cannot be changed". Recorded sins can, however, be transferred to someone else, for example from murder victim to murderer.

Other women came to the conclusion that their disappeared male kin were dead by retrospectively reviewing 'signs' they had received before their kin went missing. One woman said her kin had appeared in her dreams to say good-bye; another saw herself alone and in trouble. A few women told me that they began to think that their male kin were dead following some action on the part of a spirit. One widow only realized her husband was dead when a family member became ill. The aj q'ij had told her that the illness was sent by her dead husband as a sign that he should be helped to be 'liberated'; she promptly asked the aj q'ij to perform *costumbre* to assist him.

Notwithstanding these signs, events sometimes occurred which threw women into doubt after they had more-or-less accepted that their missing kin were dead. One woman had been virtually convinced of her son's death after finding some torn clothes in the village ravines which she thought were his.

Then, a year before my arrival in Emol, an incident occurred which made her doubtful again. Two unknown *ladino* men came to the village in a big black car, bringing a photograph of her son; they told her he had been working as a nurse in the refugee camps in Mexico. With the photo in her hand, I asked her if she was sure it was him and that the story was true. She replied, "Who knows? *(¿Saber?)*." This perpetual vacillation in beliefs about the fate of the disappeared ones leaves the anomalous living kin in perpetual states of liminality (cf. Turner 1969). Their existence is suspended, especially in the beginning, although this state may continue for many years. The unplanned, involuntary, yet uncertain removal of a person is echoed by the lack of certainty of either their return or their death. The liminal state is replete with ambiguity, marked by undefined identity in those transitions, existing and yet not existing as social persons in society.

The Missing Funeral

Spirit Dangers

For most of the bereaved, the lack of ritual to expel death from the village is profoundly disturbing. K'iche' beliefs have always stressed the importance of *ánimas* and it is the fate of these spirits which is at issue here.

There is no consistent opinion concerning the meaning of the violations of the usual treatment of the dead. Some people told me there are no detrimental consequences to practicing delayed, rushed or abbreviated funerals at an unappointed time without suitable materials or rite if this was caused by the war conditions of *la violencia*: what matters (so far as avoiding ancestral wrath is concerned) is the willingness to perform the rites. The psychological repercussions are probably more difficult to contend with as it is the actual carrying out of ritual, rather than an intention to do so, which is therapeutic.

No ritual at all is more problematic than abbreviated rites because this is considered to indicate a lack of the important element of moral sentiment. *Doña* Consuelo, whose husband was abducted in Guatemala City where the family had fled during *la violencia*, refutes this notion. Combining traditional beliefs about the dead with 'new' Catholic concepts, she said:

> Since I do not know where my husband is I cannot celebrate this day [the Day of the Dead] but I 'remember' him through praying. I do this whenever I remember him. I have to call his spirit just through praying. And since God knows where he is buried, praying and a Mass is enough.

Other people retain their traditional beliefs that not burying kin means they are not sent to the divinities of the dead. This idea, harnessed to traditional beliefs that people who meet unexpected deaths experience extreme difficulty in entering the after-life and that murder victims are unable to gain admittance at all, makes the victims of *la violencia* extremely dangerous to the living.

Nowhere is completely safe because people were killed and dumped or buried anywhere and everywhere, violating K'iche' concepts of cultivated and wild areas,[20] of inside and outside, of the domain of the living and the domain of the spirits. The spirits of the war-dead move among the living, defiling the organization of space. *Doña* Eugenia, talking about the death and burial of her grandson's father-in-law, explains:

> Among the worst things was the place where they buried him. It was in a place of cultivation (sq'ulbal) and now it's a clandestine cemetery. This is really terrible. Now it's wild with only weeds growing there.

Doña Flora concurred, but was more concerned about the condition of the bodies, many of which had been buried without so much as a *petate* in slipshod, shallow graves:

> Yes, that they did it in this place is absolutely dreadful...Jesus! If you go there now all you see is that little by little they are being excavated [through weathering] and you can see their bones and lots and lots of hair. AEEEH! It's the hair of these poor people who remained there without a proper burial.

People's everyday movements are affected by the vengeful spirits of the unburied or improperly buried dead. They avoid the ravines where most of the illicitly killed are clandestinely buried because their unsettled, suffering spirits pace up and down there. Fatal accidents resulting from encounters between spirit beings and the living are said to occur at these places with a hitherto unknown frequency. People are more afraid than ever to go out at night, not just because of the patrols but because of the innumerable wandering spirits. The spirits appearing where people were killed create a continuum of defiled space which collapses diachronic difference (Feldman 1991).

The forced abandonment of funerary and commemorative rituals for the dead is seen to affect both the community at large and individuals in particular. *Doña* Josefina attributes the numerous deaths from the 1990 measles epidemic to the unburied dead. Individuals are told, through the voice of a medium (not of a grieving spirit or ghost), that their tremendous suffering is brought about by their abandonment of the dead. One woman who consulted an aj q'ij was told that her physical pain was caused by her neglect of her disappeared father: he had 'grief in his heart' because he was not 'remembered' by her which, together with the wrong done to him, made him a vengeful and aggrieved spirit. She had expected his spirit to come back because he had been left unburied; only through making offerings and (though this is less common) sacrifice could she relate to him and show him that she 'knew' (recognized) him, thus appeasing him but not ridding herself of his tormented presence. Such messages can be seen as projections of the feelings and experiences of the bereaved, for whom the certainty of death has not been established. Being bothered in their dreams by restless and unhappy spirits can also be similarly viewed. Several women told me of dreams in which their male kin appeared, sometimes crying. Recurrent dreams of the deceased, so much a part of grief work, take on a particular meaning to the K'iche'. Women interpret their menfolks' presence in their dreams to mean that their souls are wandering and/or tormented because they had not been allowed entry into the other world. Although sad and lonely (bis), a 'good' man, even in death, is described as protecting his female kin by encouraging them to carry out protective rituals to prevent themselves from being drawn into joining him (as most unhappy spirits are reputed to do). This is also a statement of the men's innocence: the spirit of a 'sinner' (someone who had betrayed fellow villagers to the army) could not deliver such messages. Yet some women gain no comfort from their dreams of the dead:

> I'm unable to sleep when I go to bed. Then when I finally fall asleep I feel that the bad spirits are disturbing me. These are the people who had been killed during 'that time'... Who knows if my father and brother are among them. They come because they are unhappy and lonely. They never visit in a pleasant way but are always very bothersome. Because of this I have suffered from fright *(susto)*... This fear never leaves...

The increased presence of the spirits since the advent of *la violencia* is attributed to the sheer frequency and randomness of violent death within a limited space and time. In folk explanation, the negative activity of spirits is the inevitable result of the defilement which emerges from the flooding of social space with death and the unburied dead. Local theory assumes that there is a natural balance between the quantity of death and spatial and temporal dimensions; the death toll of *la violencia* broke this unspoken understanding, upsetting the classificatory order and allowing the future to leak into the present (in the warnings of spirits) and the return of the past in the present: wandering spirits and the dead as ghosts.

Grief

The Suppression of Grief

As *la violencia* progressed, it became increasingly impossible for survivors to admit that they had incurred losses. Death was denied. For widows, this perverse echo of traditional attitudes to widowhood, when elders expected widows to behave as if the conjugal relation had never existed (chapter three), distorted the reality of their experience. Denied their only culturally sanctioned opportunity to mobilize the expression of their grief, their grief reactions are further restricted by the K'iche' cultural idiom for communicating distress. One mode is popularly known as 'the attack' *(el ataque)* or 'nervous attacks' *(ataques de nervios)*, a label given to behaviours ranging from epileptic type fits to more subtle sensations like the 'throat becoming thirsty' (a desire to drink liquor). Regular drinking to escape grief and other suffering is fairly common among women, despite the fact that this is condemned by 'new' Catholics and especially charismatic Catholics and Protestants. *Doña* Flora drank for a year after her husband's abduction in order to 'take away the sadness' *(quitar la tristeza)*. She is ashamed of this and criticizes acquaintances who continued to drink for a longer period.

Alcohol is also involved in the open expression of the pain of loss which often occurs at a daughter's wedding; it is more acceptable to show overt grief at the departure of a living daughter than at the departure of the dead. At one wedding, the befuddled mother of the bride displayed intense grief, emitting heart rending sobs; she flung herself against the door from which her daughter and the marriage procession departed for the groom's parents' house. I was rather surprised to see women crying upon my departure and I assumed that, having spoken a considerable amount about their lost kin, my departure symbolized the re-departure of these nominally unmourned men. The departure of the living, rather than subsequent funerals which are harder to manage, provokes the melting of their frozen grief.

It is difficult for the bereaved to bring out emotions and concretize them when there is no corpse over which to articulate and give form to their feelings. Emotional outpourings are mostly confined to hidden spaces (except for the occasional drunken outburst, which the authorities generally attribute to the person's altered and unreasonable state). Here they often weep with frustration as they realize they have no access to interpretations of events or the possibility to act. They have been reduced from complementary partners in an ongoing social and economic enterprise (the household) to the social equivalent of children. The widows' position in the new structure impedes their grief; this interacts with their feelings of guilt about their inability to perform funerary rituals, which seem to intensify over the years.

Women report that they feel 'dirty' since *la violencia*; they are concerned to present themselves well but show a preoccupation with being literally dirty. Some women who have been unable to bury their dead describe themselves as 'cemeteries' (cf. Sternbach 1991), as embodying the pollution of the bodies of the dead; this sentiment is the one most likely to intensify with time. Both they and their improperly buried kin are anomalous beings: even in ordinary times a corpse and his or her living spouse are between classificatory boundaries (it is no longer a person but not yet a spirit; the surviving partner is no longer a spouse but not yet a widow/er). Deprived of a funeral to mediate the transition from one category to the other, the war-dead and their living kin remain between classificatory boundaries indefinitely and hence the sensation of pollution and danger remains (Douglas 1966).

Widows' feelings of liminality are exacerbated by their inability, even among and for themselves, to construct a narrative about the life and death of their kin. Their efforts are fraught with uncertainty owing to the official and unofficial versions of the truth (cf. chapter seven). In official discourse, the dead and missing have been marked as 'bad people' (guerrillas). In opposition to the official 'truth', women construct their own narrative in which they speak of their kin's innocence. But their portrayal of the dead is inconsistent, reflecting women's confusion resulting from their ignorance of what exactly their men were up to. In several senses, the women perceive themselves to be (and, in a real sense, are) 'betwixt and between' social realities. This open-ended quality compounds the ambiguity of women's lives and identities over time. Catholic widows (and younger *costumbrista* women influenced by catechist religious or political ideals), face a deep moral dilemma when they remarry for economic or social reasons, because remarriage is associated with betrayal.

The Somatization of Grief

Although unusually resilient, the widows' repressed pain, grief, guilt, and anger is manifest in a deterioration of their health.[21] Psychic pain is often somatized in cultures which traditionally inhibit the expression of emotional distress in a psychological idiom (Lipowki 1988) as the K'iche' do. Forced to 'forget' the episodes of violence they witnessed and experienced and to repress pain caused by their losses, the women's pain re-emerged as physical pain. Their bodies have become repositories of the painful experiences they have been unable to articulate as a result not only of being silenced but also because of the non-narratability of atrocious experiences. The images women used to convey their pain included descriptions of changes in the form of different parts of the body, new sensations in various body parts and the action of things such as sharp objects on the body (stabbing pains). Extreme pain, usually traced to *la violencia*, is often spoken of as 'a thorn in the heart'.

Some knowledge of local theories of disease etiology and the cultural forms they take is necessary to understand the women's symptoms. The most important concept is that of 'life force' (*fuerza*; kowil), which is located in the heart, the brain, and, in men, the testicles. If one's life force, which animates a person's individual essence (k'u'x), is taken, then the person will die. The K'iche' speak as if they have a limited amount of essence which can be depleted in a particularly arduous situations such as *la violencia*. As one woman said, "My essence is all used up because of this *[la violencia]*." Other women spoke of temporarily losing their essence: "I lost my essence (xs sax k'u'x) — I did not know what to do or where to go and it was no longer important if there was light or it was night time, I lost my mind and became uncontrolled."

Local understandings of loss of *fuerza* or k'u'x underpin another widow's description of the day her husband was killed:

I don't remember when they killed my husband but it was the day when we were putting the cross for my father-in-law. We were all together in the house when they [the army] arrived but I cannot remember the details. I just remembered hearing something and then suddenly they were in the room. We were all shocked. I felt that I was on the point of dying. But although I was ready to die death did not come. Only my blood moving in my body, jol, jol, jol, jol, [the sound of her blood] told me that I was going to disappear from the world.[22]

Doña Ana, who lost several members of her family to *la violencia*, talked to *doña* Flora about how she felt when her baby died of starvation, their conversation underpinned by a common understanding of *fuerza*:

Doña Ana:

My milk dried up in *la violencia*. My breasts were merely skin. I was unable to feed my baby because I was so sad[23]... I could only give my child water and because of this she died. My heart was very tired and I was extremely weak. I felt that my heart could tolerate no more. I felt that when I exerted myself the life-force left my stomach. We were no longer resilient because of the blows [of fate]. All this has made me forgetful. I am just not involved and I'm very absent-minded.

Doña Flora:

Yes, man, we are no longer strong as we used to be because of all the shocks we had during 'that time'. Now we are like a rat that you encounter in your latrine *(agujero)* over there.

The women refer to their 'weak' *(debil)* or insufficient *(falta)* blood, or to a weakening or 'cooling'[24] of the blood, which is associated with loss of essence (k'u'x) and eventual death; they say they felt as though they had "no life force (kowil)". They associate these phenomena to their experiences during *la violencia*. It is not always clear if these sensations are caused by real or "magical fright" (Gillin 1948:198). Explanations of 'soul loss' caused by magical fright need not refer immediately to social or psychological causes (cf. Rubel 1964:280; Uzzel 1974:372-3); the latter may be more important when fright (*susto*; xib') and death are spoken of in relation to real fright as in instances such as running from the army. Real fright may be unrelated to magical fright, given that when fleeing from the army, people often ran to liminal areas where encounters with the spirits were more likely.

The essential nature of the individual (k'u'x) is associated with the heart (uanima') which is regarded as the strongest organ of the body. The heart is the centre of intentions, disposition, and thoughts, all of which are considered 'mental force' and are expressed literally as 'force of the heart' (u chu k'ab p ranima') and contrasted with physical force which is referred to as 'force of the bones' (u chu k'ab pu bäkl). Wishes and other feelings are reflected in expressions which refer to the heart or essence: examples include utz ranima', a general expression meaning 'best wishes' (literally, 'good heart'); utz uk'u'x is a good-hearted person (literally, 'good essence'), and nimaal uk'u'x a patient person (literally, someone with plenty of essence). Itzel uk'u'x is a bad person, aaq uk'u'x, a rebellious one, and so on.

The heart (uanima') or essence (k'u'x) is the seat of the emotions. Troubled emotional states are referred to as, for example, 'swollen heart', 'wind in the heart', 'broken heart', 'words leaving from the heart' (someone 'whose words do not leave their heart' (na ke'eek ta uk'u'x), on the other hand, is a calm person). A child, an old person, someone unable to 'tolerate many things' such as anger and sadness, or someone weakened by the 'bashing' *(golpes)* they received during *la violencia*, are all said to have 'a little heart' (ch'ti'n ranima'); such people are said to cry for any reason.

K'u'x (essence) is closely linked to, if not a part of, the concept of *ánima* or spirit (the linguistic link is through the word for heart, uanima', which is derived from the Spanish *ánima* (spirit), an early loan word).[25] K'u'x is also used to refer to the essence of an aj q'ij's divining beans (tz'te); r'k'u'x, the umbilicus, is literally a hole in the sacred landscape where offerings are made to the ancestors. K'u'x is also used to refer to the essential part of an ear of corn and seed corn;[26] it is the place from which life emanates and has connotations of reproduction. Some people locate k'u'x in the belly. Thus, when widows use k'u'x in a phrase meaning stomach ache, they are using a metaphor which links them to the key elements of their culture — corn, essence/spirit, ancestors: they are expressing, in a condensed form, not only the disequilibrium of their lives in the present but also the consequences of widowhood: barrenness, the household's inability to produce corn, and so on.

The strong, negative emotions which deplete essence are said to physically affect the stomach (pam). It is common for women to refer to their stomachs when speaking of their reactions to extreme duress during *la violencia*; for example, "We ran and ran [from the army] until our stomachs fell." In a similar vein, another widow described how her essence left her stomach, even going so far as leaving her mouth — as the spirit does at death — before returning to its proper place: "It was as though a ball from my stomach or somewhere left through my mouth and then came back again." Narrating terrible memories sometimes precipitates stomach pains: once, when *doña* Flora was relating her story of her son's ill-advised return to Emol and his subsequent disappearance, she suddenly reached the limit of her narration, stopped, and began talking about the pain in her stomach.

Loss of appetite is another physical symptom of emotional upset which is frequently associated with a loss of essence arising from sadness, grief, and fear. Many women told me that they did not have any desire to eat "for an entire year" after a close relative was disappeared or killed, and that "food had no taste" during this period. Widows sometimes measure their emotional upset by the number of *tortillas* they could eat:

The saddest thing is that we did not see what became of him as we were in the capital when he returned to the village. We were all so sad that when we went to buy thirty *centavos'* worth of *tortillas*, we could not eat them, we could not finish them, we were unable to eat anything. It was a lot if we ate one *tortilla*... But since we couldn't eat anything...we were almost lost. This contrasts to the time when my husband was alive and one *quetzal* [100 *centavos'* worth of *tortillas*] was not enough for us.

Anger (aiwal or oyowaal) particularly affects the abdomen: there is a stomach illness called ja chapam which is said to be caused by anger, as is another common stomach ailment, allam. Most of the widows' complaints about their bodily aches and pains refer to the abdominal area (pam/k'u'x). Anger is an emotion which is usually attributed to men, because it has to do with issues of dominance and submission; women speak more readily about their pain (k'ax) and sadness (bis). A person's admission of sadness is said to create compassion in others and this is reflected in expressions of consolation such as "My heart breaks for you (kapax nu k'u'x chawe)" and "There is pain in my heart for you (k'ax nu k'u'x chawe)".

'Sadness' (bis), with its connotations of loneliness and isolation, is the local explanation of many symptoms which are classic indicators of depression as defined by Westerners — the concept does not exist among the K'iche' (cf. Schieffelin 1985). Widows ascribe loss of appetite and weight loss to bis, although these symptoms also reflect their poor diets resulting from their inability to generate sufficient income; they interpret their sleeplessness and bad dreams as being visited by spirits; they attribute their various aches and pains to loss of essence, though these are partly due to their extra, and extremely heavy, workloads. These and various other physiological symptoms are perpetuated by living in constant anxiety. Most symptoms tend to last for at least a couple of years after they lost their relatives but their headaches (k'ax nu jolom; literally, 'my head hurts') and other bodily pains persist to the present.

Most widows attribute their symptoms to their experiences in *la violencia* and the losses they suffered; the most common way of mentioning them is after speaking about such events. Some women did not make this connection and it was only after I had asked when the symptoms began that I was nearly always told that they had indeed begun during *la violencia*, usually after a specific appalling experience, the description of which was usually brief and vague. It was as if the deep alterations which occurred in their lives during this time had been recorded in their bodies, which remember events which have not been verbally remembered. Perhaps such extreme experiences of pain evade language. Indeed, the unique inexpressibility of pain is linked to "its lack of referential content" (Scarry 1985). The message conveyed through the 'silent-space' of the disappeared and unburied dead is so dreadful that it cannot be accommodated within the normal social dialogue and cultural metalogue (Scarry 1985).

There is considerable variation in K'iche' people's response to loss. Some appear stoical and can stare death in the face; others are more emotional and fear that they would be unable to bear facing the improper state in which the dead now lay. Sometimes a widow admitted, "I can't bear the loss of his death (nu k'et ranima' la ucämnak)." I was told many times that death or madness resulted from intolerable loss. *Doña* Candelaria told me, "A woman I know lost her reason during this time. Now she just wanders to and fro and does not think." This could well have happened but *doña* Candelaria's relation of the story could also be a projection of her own feelings; I saw very few women who had lost touch with reality.

Reclaiming the Dead

Symbolic Burials

After *la violencia* abated, *doña* Josefina began to perform symbolic, retroactive burials for the missing, thus attempting to reincorporate the dead in their proper place in K'iche' society. She showed me the importance of the placing of the dead and their belongings by performing these rituals for relatives who are 'sad' because they have not had the opportunity to bury their dead or their possessions. Since the deceased's belongings are normally buried with the corpse, keeping their possessions takes on a special significance; while surviving kin do not have the body, they do have their clothes and other symbolic bits of the person. *Doña* Candelaria told me with some despair that she still has her husband's clothes and belongings. Even though she knows he is dead, she cannot quite believe it because she has not seen his body. She described how his things were kept pretty much as they had been when he was taken.[27] *Doña* Eugenia reveals the importance of burying the dead symbolically through interring their belongings:

> When my husband and only son died I cried for two years. I saw their clothes and could not bring myself to touch them. You see, the clothes are usually buried with the person and it was almost as though the corpse was there with the clothes.

Doña Josefina interprets family afflictions as arising from the fact that the dead and their possessions have not been interred. She takes families to the calvary (the Stations of the Cross at the chapel attached to the cemetery) to call the spirits. The family then prays for nine days. At the end of this 'work', *doña* Josefina advises them to ask the village mayor for permission to bury objects such as clothes, tools, and photos of the dead and disappeared and to place a cross bearing their name in the cemetery to signal to the authorities in both worlds that a particular person has died. She feels it is important to advise the saints and the ancestors as well as village authorities (especially the *jefes)* about this so that relatives can perform *costumbre*, unfettered, in the cemetery. In this way, *doña* Josefina reverses the effect of abduction which "symbolizes and reifies the body of the victim not in physical death but in destruction of the body as an object to be mourned, buried and remembered" (Gregory and Timmerman 1986:68).

Once symbolically buried, the spirit is said to cease wandering although I was told that in some cases they still roam. When death breaches all cultural notions about a good death, the bereaved cannot simply take refuge in the conventional patterns or rituals of burial and mourning. Nevertheless, through symbolic burials, aj q'ij such as *doña* Josefina aid mourners by providing them with a *"language"* with which "unexpressed and otherwise inexpressible psychic states may be immediately expressed" (Lévi-Strauss 1963:198; italics in original).[28] Here, the concretizing of the event in a nonverbal medium (although it is also verbal) is considered to be just as important. Both verbal and non-verbal forms make "it possible to undergo in an ordered and intelligible form a real experience that would otherwise be chaotic and inexpressible" (Lévi-Strauss 1967:193-194).

At a time of chaos and incompleteness, the symbolic manipulation of objects, space, and the corpse itself in the ritual processes of burial, serve to transform the present experience of confusion and loss, placing it within the context of a set of meanings which resonate throughout the entire cultural system. This method of reburial tends only to be solicited by families who have no idea about the whereabouts of their kin and not by those who believe their dead kin lay in specific clandestine graves.

Clandestine Cemeteries

One of the subterranean secrets which pervade the K'iche' countryside, as well as the minds of its people, is the clandestine graves beneath its surface. Knowledge of where bodies are clandestinely buried is actually fairly widespread. Efforts to locate missing relatives by checking local body dumps is so common in some areas that when an Amnesty International delegate asked an Indian in a remote area for directions to a hidden burial site, he simply replied, "Oh. Are you looking for relatives?" and gave directions to the nearest site known to him (Amnesty International 1991).

At the end of the 1980s, very few people dared to reveal the location of known clandestine cemeteries to human rights agencies. Fear, illiteracy, and ignorance of the lengthy legal processes involved deterred all but the most determined. Successful petitions were often thwarted by frightened killers who removed the bodies, leaving relatives to find freshly dug earth and empty graves.[29]

In most villages, no-one refers to these graves unless in the company of close kin or friends with whom they have a relationship of trust. Emolteco widows did not mention clandestine graves in front of me for many months. Some women whose relatives were killed by local men know that their kin are buried in the village's deep ravines and a few of them know exactly where their dead are buried — for instance, one young man executed by the *jefes* was buried adjacent to his mother's land. She has never set foot in the vicinity of his grave; like most people who know the location of clandestine cemeteries, she refuses to go anywhere near it for fear of punishment. The *jefes* are hyper-vigilant over the graves, knowing that their discovery can, in theory, result in their conviction and imprisonment.

Women gather information about the whereabouts of their kin's graves through rumour and hearsay, the drunken boasts (or confessions) of local killers, and, in a few rare instances, from their own investigations. Several years after their kin's abduction, women continue to obtain further clues from one source or another — such as an article published in a daily newspaper in May 1990 which revealed that thirty-five clandestine cemeteries had been found in a village in an adjacent township *(municipio)*. I was told that Emoltecos had suspected that this had been the destination of the trucks into which the army had thrown everyone kidnapped from the market place in June 1982.

Reclaiming the Day of the Dead

Although they have been warned never to mention the massacre they witnessed in 1982 or the clandestine cemeteries "or else something will happen to your children and grandchildren", four years later an unusually determined group of Kotoh women approached Mario, the village's most feared *jefe*, to tell him that they knew the location of the massacre victims' graves. Taking their lives in their hands, they threatened to report him unless he allowed them to visit the graves on the Day of the Dead. Echoing their husbands' words, their attitude was, "If they kill us, they kill us". *Doña* Eugenia described the event:

> Although we knew where they [the dead] were, we could not make this known publicly, so mourning became a private affair. In secret, we went down to their clandestine grave on the Day of the Dead to perform *costumbre*. We threatened the killers that if they prevented us from going, we would report their sins.

By this time, a civilian president had been installed and the army's hold on the national psyche had weakened, leaving *jefes* feeling rather insecure. Fearing that the graves would be revealed to the civilian authorities, Mario was forced to agree to the women's request. He imposed conditions which the widows accepted: they were to be discreet about their visits, tell no one about them, and only go once a year, on the Day of the Dead. Not all the women whose kin lay in the clandestine cemeteries visited them; some sent their children and grandchildren in their place. *Doña* Eugenia no longer went herself because she could not bear the 'sadness' stemming from the fact that the dead were not in their place in the village cemetery but set apart.

I accompanied the widows on their third journey down the ravines to two clandestine cemeteries, each containing six bodies. The women took all the paraphernalia that K'iche' people normally take to family graves on the Day of the Dead: bundles of pine branches, the yellow flowers of the dead, candles, food, and *aguardiente* (kuxa). The widows' children and grandchildren helped to carry the goods and flowers. Everyone was dressed in their best clothes for the occasion. Only one man, a widow's new son-in-law, joined the groups of women 'for protection'.

Once at the graves, which were about a hundred yards apart and appeared indistinguishable from the rest of the ravine, the women busied themselves decorating them as though they were normal graves in the village cemetery. The atmosphere and conversation did not differ much from that at ordinary graves until a considerable amount of alcohol had been consumed. Only then did women begin to speak about the events which landed their kin in this inappropriate spot, sharing memories about the fatal day of the massacre (chapter seven).

One woman, who knew her son to be in the clandestine grave, suddenly plucked up courage to ask her friend's new son-in-law, "And my husband, don't you know where they left him?" The young man replied, "No, I don't remember." The widow then asked, "And your dead father, where does he remain?" He answered, "Ah! him, the truth is I haven't a clue where he is. I only know," he said, pointing, "that that is the general direction of his whereabouts." The conversation continued. The woman asked the young man again, "So you never found out where they put your dead father?" He replied, "I remember that it was over there down the ravine. I think it was there they left him but, you see, I was not with the others when they came here."

Doña Vicenta, *doña* Eugenia's daughter-in-law, recalled how young her son Martín had been when his father was killed and how the patrol *jefes* had involved him, as a fourteen year old patroller, in his father's 'arrest' and then made him watch him being beaten almost to death. Then she instigated a conversation about the graves' location:

Doña Vicenta:
Well, you know that they say that they divided the dead between these two holes so that there are six here and six over there.

Doña Rosa:
Yes, yes, this is what the old one [a derogatory reference to the jefe] said, they left six in each hole.

Doña Vicenta:
Yes, he showed no shame in admitting this.

Doña Rosa:
> Apparently he was drunk when he said this. Had he not been drunk, then perhaps he would have kept quiet about it.

Doña Ana-María:
> Yes, if he had not been is such a state I probably would not have learnt where my husband was either, for when he was like that he told me, "Your dead husband is down in the crevice with Gilberto and Pablo, while your child is in the other hole."

Despite the sombre content of the conversation, the occasion itself was rather jovial. The women, creating a sense of support and social closeness between themselves, advised one another on how best to lay the flowers, candles, and so on. They bemoaned the fact that the *jefes* were likely to steal the metal pots which they used as vases; they knew the *jefes* would invade the space and desecrate it, as they had already desecrated their lives. As was often the case, dramatic and painful moments alternated with the comic. One woman made the others laugh when she said, "And the dead would say to them, 'Why are you taking and destroying what does not belong to you?' I am sure they [the *jefes*] would be very frightened."

They continued to joke as they took swigs of *aguardiente*, sharing it with the dead by pouring it onto the burial mounds which were covered in a luscious blanket of pine leaves, petals, and numerous burning candles. As the liquor seeped into the earth, *doña* Elena exclaimed, "Look, they [the dead] are drinking it!" When the liquor began to seep more slowly, she continued, "He says that he doesn't want to drink it all." This provoked *doña* Rosa, becoming serious for a moment, to ask her, "Is it true that your papa [husband] has still not returned? Do you think he will return?" *Doña* Elena answered, "No, now he will not return."

Doña Elena, returning to banter again, speculated about what she would do if the dead began to talk to them. Continuing to oscillate, the conversation turned serious again when *doña* Petrona recounted to the others how she had discovered the site of a clandestine cemetery: she had suddenly heard one of the dead saying, "Thank you for coming to visit...we are all here in this spot." *Doña* Vicenta began to wave incense over the graves and, pretending to be an aj q'ij, asked the ancestors to pardon the women's sins.

Doña Petrona then related how the *jefes* 'ate' (killed) their relatives: "There were so many of them [who were being killed] that I began to ask the old ones *[jefes]* how they wanted them prepared, fried, or in a sauce!" This reference to the belief that sorcerers (with whom *jefes* are identified) steal people to make *tamales* of their flesh (cf. Manrique 1967:716) made the women laugh. It was the laughter of the politically impotent, a symbolic compensation for their inability to protest against their situation. The symbiosis between violence and laughter displayed in their narratives on this special day is also fairly typical of other occasions pertaining to *la violencia*.

The conversation turned to gossip relating to the context in which they found themselves. They gossiped about the death of a woman who had had many affairs and had fallen to her death close to where they sat talking. Once their tongues were loosened by the *aguardiente*, the women's conversation turned to sensitive issues which are otherwise rarely discussed. More than anything else, they wanted to give those inside clandestine graves a proper burial in the village cemetery. They speculated about the number of years which would have to pass before they could exhume the bodies and they decided the time must be about ripe. They were exhumed two years later (chapter eleven).

Petitioning Exhumations

Doña Eugenia told me that it was important to her to give the dead a proper funeral so that she can lay beside her husband and son:

> What I would like to do more than anything is to exhume their bodies. I wanted to do this last year but some people from the village warned me that if I did this then the assassins would finish me off. I'm afraid that if I go to report the graves [to CONAVIGUA or GAM] and as a result they [the *jefes*] are jailed, then their accomplices would take revenge by killing my grand-children. So because of the threats I have not done anything yet...

She was shortly to change her mind. Most villagers are too frightened to avail themselves of their legal right to petition for the exhumation of clandestine cemeteries. People whose jobs bring them into contact with petitioners receive death threats: examples include civilian officials involved in successful legal exhumations; a local judge who had finally allowed an exhumation in El Quiché go ahead after prolonged petitioning, suddenly withdrawing consent; a forensic expert present at another exhumation who resigned her post after receiving similar threats. Lawyers and forensic scientists, fearing for their personal safety, refuse to act for petitioners; civil servants procrastinate, taking an average of five months to process petitions which, by law, should be answered within three days.

Behind the threats and delays is the military, which is clamourous in its opposition to exhumations. In April 1990, the Guatemalan press reported that the Minister for Defence, General Héctor Alejandro Gramajo, had publicly labelled as 'subversive' anyone claiming that clandestine graves actually exist. Immediately contradicting himself, Gramajo then claimed that the dead buried in clandestine graves had all been killed by 'subversives' and "that is why they know where the bodies are". At local level, military commanders attack clergy and human rights workers who support peasants' requests; patrollers are coerced to demonstrate against visits by GAM representatives. An Emolteco told me that after the exhumation of five bodies in Pacoc, Zacualpa, El Quiché, in June 1988, the civil patrol responsible for the killings tried to kidnap the person who instigated the process (cf. Amnesty International 1991). In these circumstances, widows show great bravery in appealing to GAM (or CONAVIGUA) to reveal the cemeteries.

Some very determined Emolteco widows have not been deterred by GAM reports that few exhumations have been properly conducted or allegations of inappropriate behaviour during exhumations. For example, during one exhumation in El Quiché, local officials who should have been supervising showed little interest in the proceedings and stood some distance away while volunteer firemen, who actually exhumed the bodies, laughed, joked, and played football with one of the disinterred skulls; in this instance, no official action was taken to determine the cause of death of those exhumed or to establish responsibility for their deaths and secret burials. In properly conducted exhumations, the forensic team determines cause of death (where sufficient evidence remains) and the perpetrator: it is easy to distinguish army bullets from those used by the guerrilla. No evidence has yet been found in the many graves containing women and children carrying baskets and babies to support the army's claim that the guerrilla were using women as couriers for weapons and other supplies. This information is valued by mothers who feel it is important for their children to know that they, their long dead fathers and other murdered kin really were innocent. The motives of other women, including the widows of Emol's massacre victims, are different: their primary aim is to regroup their families in sanctified ground where they belong. They want to mourn their dead properly and re-enter society as less anomalous beings. The importance of these concerns can be gauged by the danger widows knowingly face in order to achieve them.

Yet despite the women's personal and culturally driven motives, exhumations invade the space occupied by official history. The unburial and reburial of the dead takes on political meanings, regardless of whether or not the women are aware of it. The more politicized widows are aware that the suppression of exhumations arises from the fact that the dead and kidnapped can be used in acts of political mobilization. Political ideologies can be articulated on the bodies of the dead; depending on one's perspective, the dead are linked to past heroes or modern villains. Whichever is the case, the elements of a political ideology are structured in terms of both the behaviour and the symbolic force of certain key individuals. The dead can thus be used by both sides to symbolize complex ideological issues.

Conclusion

For K'iche' society, death ritual encapsulates the very principles or beliefs and values which are most under threat at the time of death. The particular way that the boundary between life and death is managed is critical to the fostering of a sense of cultural continuity in the face of the loss of society's individual members. The soul and social *persona* of the deceased are structured in the private realm and it is here that the social consequences of death are organized. While the private world of the bereaved emphasizes the non-material features of social being, the material presence of the corpse provides a unique occasion on which social, religious, and political identities are effectively synchronized in order to refresh and rejuvenate the communal and cultural worlds of the living. Kin relationships, religious beliefs and ritual, political interests and sentiments are re-awakened and handled in the presence of death and nowhere more explicitly than in their absence: funerals for the political dead are usually prevented from happening because the body has been appropriated. For the assassinated and abducted, there is no opportunity to collectivity "triumph over death" (Bloch and Parry 1982 :4); kidnapping is discontinuity personified. When K'iche' society most needed the power to express and recreate central values, the vehicles to do so were least available. Consequently, the central belief system is no longer experienced as given, unquestionable, and enduring (cf. Hertz 1960). Everything is thrown into question in times of war.

Killing and abduction followed by a prohibition on funerary ritual represents a reorganization of the social landscape through death. Like unforgotten but inaccessible memories, the dead structure what goes on in the present as a sort of presence *in absentia*. The dead cannot be remembered properly; they are left unmourned and their kin are unable to release their grief. Survivors are unable to forget their ineluctable, wandering, and malicious spirits, left in a liminal state of living death, haunting the living and threatening society with further death. The victims of state terrorism, having internalized violence, are caught in the ultimate contradiction between life and death, returning to terrorize their own people (see Sallnow 1989:33). The armed forces literally expelled people from the world of the living but, as death was not expelled, the spirits cannot not be disposed of — they form a new sort of patrol, becoming another terrifying presence, persecuting the living just like the local *jefes*. The sense of persecution is pervasive.

Notes

1. The data for this comes from my own observations which took place after *la violencia*. It is difficult to know how much procedures have changed.

2. The words *alma* and *ánima* are often used interchangeably; however, *alma* refers solely to the Christian concept of soul whereas *ánima* refers to traditional Mayan concepts of individual and collective spirits, living and dead.

3. Ancestors and guardians are, in most respects, interchangeable. Ancestors are generally considered an amorphous collectivity whereas guardians tend to be individually located in time and space; both are related to the landscape. The K'iche' can be said to live in a deified landscape. Sacred landscapes are a means of legitimating domination (by Mayan elders in the not so distant past) and also a means of resisting it (for the indigenous person in the present) (cf. Sallnow 1987:267). There is likely to be a shrine to the ancestors wherever a natural formation or

even cultivation has emphasized a geographical spot — a mountain peak, a cluster of trees, a spring or a promontory overlooking a valley. Every mountain has its (named) guardian or owner *(dueño)* (Wagley 1949) who is generally described as a *ladino*, "with light hair and light skin" (cf. Siegel 1941:67; Oakes 1951:93; Adams 1952:31). Mountain spirits or guardians are frequently described as being dressed like nineteenth century German coffee planters responsible for the previous major expropriation of Indian land). Sometimes guardians are described as wearing plumes in their hats and clothes like the "dancers in the Dance of the Conquest"; the person contained in episodes of meetings with guardians is not the ghost of the distant dead but rather someone who has been dead for twenty years, "a friend of my father's or my own grandfather" (Wagley 1949:55-64).

4. In the case of a Catholic or *costumbrista* child, this is done by the original midwife and/or the child's godmother *(madrina)*.

5. The body and its accoutrements were traditionally wrapped in a straw mat *(petate)* and it is only in recent years that the K'iche' have begun to bury their dead in coffins. I do not know when this change came about; I was merely told that the practice began because *ladinos* insisted that the Indian practice of burying corpses in a straw mat was 'unhealthy'.

6. A number of myths show how clothing functions as a symbol for its wearer and the community. Ceremonial clothing is often used a metaphor in myths for the power it symbolizes, implying that the power of the civil-religious office is vested in clothing rather than the office holder.

7. Songs are only sung at Catholic and Protestant burials. At Protestant burials, songs are sung to the accompaniment of guitars and accordions. Catholics drink *aguardiente*; Protestants do not.

8. Literally, 'it [the corpse] is hidden in the earth'.

9. This is connected to ideas about 'heat' and 'coolness'. Ordinarily, the expression of 'hot' feelings can cause the evil eye in another person, but it is best to release these feelings after being bereaved (see Neuenswander and Souder 1977).

10. This south American vegetable is a member of the cucumber family.

11. Only aj q'ij and a few *costumbrista* elders retain the traditional custom of institutionalized, daily interaction between the living and the dead, burning incense and praying in their houses at the family shrine.

12. That village churches (as buildings) replaced the cave as a focus of prayer and power probably contributed to the isolation of aj q'ij from the civil aspects of the *costumbrista* hierarchy (chapter two). cf. Wilson (1995).

13. cf. Bunzel (1952:264) who found the rarer term juyu'-tiqaj (mountain-plain) which appears "sometimes with, sometimes instead of, the more common mundo". She suggests that this "refers not merely to the varied surface of the earth which plays an important part of Quiché ritual, but stands for the concept of the synthesis of opposites in totality which runs through Quiché pantheism". I found that local aj q'ij used this term — pronounced slightly differently, juyub-taqaj (hill/mountain-coast/plain) — and also nim juyub, nim taqaj (big mountain, big plain) and xa(...)knul juyub (volcano).

14. cf. Vogt (1969:371): "The ethnographer in Zinacatan [a Maya community in Chiapas, Mexico] soon learns that the most important interaction going on in the universe is not between persons nor between persons and material objects, but rather between souls inside these persons and material objects".

15. Literally, 'I heard a word'.

16. Taking photographs is associated with the stealing of a person's life essence or soul which is physically relocated in the photographic image: "A bright light (the camera flash) shines at the moment the soul leaves the body" and the soulless person is said to feel poorly and die soon afterwards. During *la violencia*, this idea was exploited by the military and their henchmen. PAC *jefes* were the suspected culprits when photos disappeared from people's houses; they are believed to have given them to sorcerers who took them to the cemetery and burnt them as part of their witchcraft practices.

17. Ultimately, culture determined their behaviour: women who searched for their kin were rare, not only because doing so involved behaviour contrary to their socialization as women (i.e., they should not leave the house unaccompanied by a husband or other appropriate in-law) but because in times of crisis, most people are more 'conservative' than usual.

18. Village men went to the capital, associated with the city police, and disclosed the identities and whereabouts of other villagers hiding there to the police.

19. The woman used the word *'ejercitando'*, which means 'practicing'. This colloquial usage derives from *el ejército*, the army. What she actually said is, "Who knows if they have 'armied' him", i.e., done to him what the army does to people. By this she means that he may have been tortured and/or killed, his body dumped or clandestinely buried.

20. See Watanabe (1992) for a description of cultivated and wild spaces.

21. This is confirmed in research on victims of violence elsewhere (Cliff and Noormahomed 1988; Diekstra 1988).

22. The blood (kik') is said to 'talk', indicating to a person what their state is and its felt movement in a particular part of the body can act as a sign *(señal)*: aj q'ij diagnose spirit loss by taking a person's pulse. cf. Nash (1970:147); Wilson (1995: 147).

23. Several women spoke of passing their sadness to their babies via their milk.

24. According to the K'iche', the balance between hot-cold and wet-dry is important for good health; coldness is associated with weakness/ill health (Neuenswander and Souder 1977). Notions of hot and cold are also documented in other areas of Mesoamerica although the meaning of each caloric system changes with indigenous grouping and linguistic area (e.g., Redfield 1934, 1941;Wisdom 1974 [1940]; Ingham 1986; Wilson 1995).

25. Spirit co-essences (anhual) are part of the same matrix of pre-Christian ideas. See chapter nine.

26. Other words which refer to both humans and plants include ruixie (the roots of both a person and a plant) and wach (the face of a person or plant, i.e., the fruit). Children are said to grow like 'green corn'.

27. This is reminiscent of Gorer's (1965) concept of 'mummification'.

28. Lévi-Strauss (1967:193-194) discusses the importance of the transition to verbal expression in connection with a shaman providing a sick woman with a language.

29. As the peace process progresses, an increasing number of people are petitioning for exhumations; now, the EAFG cannot keep up with petitions.

9

K'iche' Theories of Causation and the Reconstruction of Meaning of 'La Violencia'

In order for a person to engage in both primary and secondary control, to change the world and change the self, people construct a set of assumptions about the world which make life seem predictable. Gross misfortune violates these assumptions, throwing ontology open to question and rendering one's sense of reality tenuous, thereby making one feel vulnerable; a broad feeling of powerlessness ensues. *La violencia* called many basic beliefs into question: "How can one explain all the massacres? What happened to our protective spirits?" (Manz 1988:92).

This was the situation in which Emoltecos found themselves when *la violencia* descended upon them with shocking suddenness. They had not witnessed any brutalities connected with the political violence in El Quiché province in the 1960s and 1970s; to them it had been an abstract phenomenon. Emoltecos say that the reality of *la violencia* descended upon them as unexpectedly as a tornado and that its course was even less predictable and even more destructive than anything they had ever known, worse even than the devastation of the conquest.[1]

In order to restore a sense of an orderly world and the belief that one is capable of dealing with it, the K'iche' attempt to find meaning in *la violencia*. Known theories proved inadequate; moreover, the continuing violence did not permit the degree of detached sensibility necessary for analysis of their experience. With time and access to a variety of discourses, degree of detachment and some cognitive understanding were achieved.

Framing 'La Violencia'

Emoltecos attempt to set *la violencia* within an over-arching frame in terms of traditional, religious or political concepts. Few people found any one discourse adequate to explain what happened; most resort to several discourses to explain both the phenomenon and the events which comprised it, swapping from one to another for a variety of reasons.

The tools used to reconstruct past exegeses about violence were facilitated by the reflections of specialists. Meaning was negotiated during visits to the diviner (aj q'ij), Catholic priest, or representatives of organizations such as CUC or CONAVIGUA. Personal and public statues of the saints *(imágenes)* also act as mediators between people and the ancestors and are instrumental in the process of constructing meaning: they serve as mirrors to reflect unarticulated meanings which, until the moment of 'conversation' with the object, had eluded the speaker (chapter ten).

Theories and their applications are all means by which the malignancy and contingency of evil can be comprehended and made simultaneously universal and impersonal. The universality of the suffering provided certain guarantees that the crisis was not brought about by any particular failing of the victim but by an impersonal force which is seen as indifferent to whom it selects or spares. In contrast, other explanations relate to particular atrocities within *la violencia* rather than to *la violencia* as a general phenomenon.

Most people, especially in the initial, ambiguous stages of *la violencia* when events were unfamiliar, tended to interpret equivocal events according to folk descriptions of disasters in an attempt to extract information from the event itself. One aj q'ij contextualized *la violencia* in cyclical time as only one disaster in a long list of calamities which extends back and projects forward in time: "Last time, it [disaster resulting from ancestral retribution][2] was an earthquake," he said; "we'll see what the next one brings."

Women also attempted to understand and assimilate new experiences into what they already knew:

> It was only when *la violencia* was upon us that I remembered what my grandmother had spoken about years before. Then she had warned us, "They will eat among [kill] us and we will fight among ourselves. It will be the end of the world."

Others remembered warnings delivered through stories or passages from the Bible, saying ,"We think that *la violencia* came because of God...it has been written in the Bible... God wrote that *la violencia* would come."[3] This idea is reinforced by priests who, when trying to explain *la violencia* in their sermons, use the Bible as reference point.

Women also told me that although they had forewarning of *la violencia*, they could not understand them because they were obscure and disconnected from the context at the time. Women spoke of dream-like visions in which they had been visited by their kin before their death or disappearance; the women retrospectively realized that this was a sign of their immanent departure from this world. The vision, the foretelling, is constructed retroactively and then retrospectively confirmed. People did not lament their failure to read signs but attempted to gain a sense of mastery by reinterpreting them. *Doña* Petrona said:

> I had no idea that *la violencia* would happen before it actually did. It was only once I saw the burning and smoke that I began to realize what this *violencia* was. Then I said to myself, "So this is *la violencia* that they had been talking about." In retrospect, I realize that when they had spoken of *la violencia* I had not understood anything they said.

Women's lack of forewarning of *la violencia* produced anxiety about the future: the world had become a less predictable and more punitive place. Anxiety was reflected in constant interpretations of present events as signs pertaining to the return of *la violencia*. But this was not the only source of women's anxiety: their world had been irretrievably altered by events for which they had been unprepared and did not understand at the time or in retrospect.

Costumbre

Costumbre has been in decline since the 1950s (chapter two); the authority system dominated by elders has been supplanted by a more fluid and competitive field of catechists, pastors, health workers, and, of course, the army and patrol chiefs *(jefes)* who educate and organize the K'iche' in new ways. Yet many people, including some 'new' or charismatic Catholics and nominal Protestants, still adhere to their beliefs in fate *(suerte)*, the fulfillment of prophecy or ancestral retribution *(castigo)* and ideas of evil *(el mal)* perpetrated through malicious envy *(envidia)*, of which witchcraft *(brujería)* is the most extreme form of locally solicited supernatural powers: these were the main exegeses people used to explain *la violencia* to themselves, other people, and to me. These discourses relate to different aspects of K'iche' thought: people either blame themselves for the misfortune which befalls them (i.e., their behaviour has solicited supernatural punishment) or other people (malicious gossip, rumours, witchcraft).

Suerte (fate). Through the overarching cult of the ancestors and the belief in their omnipotent power, a person may be reconciled to a harsh fate. *Suerte* is not so much an abstract, general notion as something which is said to cling to each individual person as he or she passes through the universe.

Fate is a quality of the nahual or anhual[4] (alxik/spirit double) which shares the same life and destiny of its living counterpart (Foster 1944; Vogt 1970); it is part of a system of 'multiple souls' (cf. Burgos-Debray and Menchú 1984: 39). In Emol, only aj q'ij were able to tell me anything about anhuals; the general population know nothing about it, although aj q'ij say that people are nevertheless controlled by their anhual. *Doña* Josefina told me that the anhual is a companion animal which protects the individual and that it is a vital part of one's character (cf. Bunzel 1952:274): whether a person is angry and aggressive, a good worker or a person-eater (killer), etc., depends on the anhual an individual is born with. That in turn depends on one's day of birth: every day in the Mayan calendar has a named anhual (Wright 1991). Thus, although *suerte* is a quality of the anhual, obviously it is also a person's fate to have a particular anhual, otherwise fate would have decreed that a person be born on a more auspicious day. Thus, physical violence as a stable personality trait is associated with an inauspicious anhual rather than with the circumstances in which *jefes* practiced their violence. Uncharacteristic violence is considered an invasion by bad spirits and is viewed as a temporary state. This can also be attributed to an inauspicious anhual, though of a different kind: not being able to withstand spirit attack implies that the person has a 'small heart' (is weak).[5] A person easily swayed by others (such as men who commit atrocities while on patrol duty) is some-times described as having this type of anhual.

The *suerte* incorporated in one's anhual which "is given by God when one is born" (Wagley 1949:66); it determines the length of one's life (Gossen 1975) — death from natural causes is normally attributed to *suerte* — occupation, special duties, and so on. *Suerte* has a powerful effect on be-haviour yet *doña* Josefina told me that it can be influenced by making offerings to God and by the way children are disciplined.

The theme of *suerte* provides a clue to attitudes towards good and evil. Whether one is good or evil depends on the *suerte* one is born with; sooner or later one's true colours will reveal themselves. In this sense, God is seen to will evil to be done. There is a confusion of world views here: the Christ-ian doctrine of free will implies that people can choose between good and evil, irrespective of the *suerte* they are born with, and be judged accordingly by God.[6] Most people hold a syncretism of both of these views; for example, they say that since *la violencia* was written in the Bible, it was bound to happen because it was their destiny.

The course of *la violencia* is not necessarily seen to be determined by *suerte* but whether or not a person was assassinated or kidnapped often is. Two widows illustrate how the concept of *suerte* is used in relation to *la violencia*:

Doña Rosario:
    I ask myself whether the people were assassinated by their own neighbours because of their *suerte*... Was it their destiny to be condemned by their own community? I don't think so, for they were young and I'd say it was still their *suerte* to live. Who knows? Perhaps God made their *suerte* this way...

Doña Petrona:
    I thought, "If they take me, they take me, and if not, not." You see, I thought,

"If they kidnap me, there is nothing I can do about it. If my time is up, then it's up."

The world is essentially a mystery to the K'iche', with insight granted to only a few. *Suerte*, which can be revealed by aj q'ij (who are the strongest proponents of fatalism), provides people with a self protective mechanism against too much introspection. When asked by a client about the fate of the dead or disappeared, aj q'ij generally reply, "They were killed because their time was up. It was quite simply that their hour of death had arrived and God decided that they should perish in this manner."

Aj q'ij also use the concept of *suerte* when advising people not to investigate a death or look for the disappeared, thus steering them away from the harm which may befall them if they look into sensitive matters. "You should not do bad things," they say, meaning that the bereaved should not try to discover those responsible for their relative's death because this implies judging them and seeking vengeance; instead, mourners should respect their parents by performing *costumbre* because, "Only in this way will we improve the face of the earth..."

There is an element of prediction in the concept of *suerte*. It can be seen as the process whereby the imagination manufactures the idea of fate in order to protect itself from the ravages of random circumstance. Some people turn to the predictive spirits, a version of common memory, hoping they will impose meaningful sequence on the details of one's life. Thus, instead of suffering great psychological stress over such circumstances as losing the entire male presence in their family, there is self denial and self-effacement and a kind of resignation to the fate of enormous loss. What befalls a man depends on his *suerte*. This is linked to the attitude of passive resignation of "what comes, comes". This, as well as "only God knows", "only God is in charge", and "if God wishes, God sends it", were stock responses that I heard over and over again. Yet despite acceptance of God's will, people sometimes communicate immense suffering.

The theme of *suerte* is also tied to ignorance which, in turn, is tied to the precariousness of one's immediate fate. This ignorance is also attached to wider matters: many widows had little access to the media or to information regarding the political motivations for *la violencia*. Women complain of being treated as 'ignorant' creatures or 'like an animal'; this perceived absence of information creates a frame of mind in which it is difficult to expect any national, political or historical contextualization of *la violencia*. Women are more likely to refer to *suerte* than someone who is *au fait* with the political situation.

On the other hand, some women, politicized by their losses and subsequent discussions with the women of CONAVIGUA or GAM, deny or at least question the role of *suerte*. *Doña* Flora said:

It *[la violencia]* was ordered by people, not by God. If it was an illness, then it would be God but, since it wasn't, then no, it is not because of God... I do not know if it was his [her husband's] *suerte* [to die] or it was simply because they wanted to kill him.

Another widow also saw *la violencia* as the violation of a person's *suerte* rather than an expression of it:

I had a dream that he had been murdered. I saw him crying and he carried a candle in his hand [to light his way to the after-life] but I could not unmask what was going on, I could not understand why he cried. Perhaps it is because his time had not come because, you see, he died because of *la violencia* and not according to his *suerte*.

Castigo (ancestral punishment). Opinion differs about the extent of the ancestors' involvement in the actual course of *la violencia*. Some say its vagaries were independent of, although not unrelated to, the ancestors. An aj q'ij said, "*la violencia* was all part of *una violencia* which our ancestors sent." The ancestors are said to punish people who maintain anti-social attitudes (particularly adulterers) by seizing their spirits, causing them illness or even death. Thus, spirit loss illnesses are engaged as a mechanism of social control.

Aj q'ij facilitate the creation of meaning around *la violencia* as ancestral punishment, encompassing it within notions of disaster (yabil) and pain/suffering (k'ax) or extreme pain/suffering (k'ax k'ax). They claim to read the course of both *la violencia* and illness through 'signs' *(señas)*; recovery from either is determined by the spirit guardian *(dueño)* of the illness and *suerte*. The use of the term yabil reflects that the speaker believes the causative agent of *la violencia* is the ancestors or God. Yabil and its connection to ancestral wrath is, then, a statement about the perceived moral degeneration of K'iche' society. For *doña* Ana, *la violencia* was itself a sign:

I wonder, in retrospect, if *la violencia* was a sign sent to earth [by the ancestors]. It was like other signs of the past only its form was different from previous ones such as earthquakes and floods. This time its form was people's fighting and killing each other with *machetes*.

People say that *la violencia* was caused by the K'iche's' immoral conduct, and that this is what God wants to change through *la violencia*: "*La violencia* happened because we are not loyal to God. People no longer think about (pray to) him nor about their elders." In this exegesis, *la violencia* is just action by the ancestors on behalf of a society which has gone wrong. It is a discourse from the cultural present where traditional explanations of ethical and unethical conduct prevail: "*La violencia* came because we hate each other...it happened because of our sins." Instances of self-blame go far beyond simple errors in judgement or deed which led to being affected by *la violencia* (such as not fleeing from the army). Rather, these people feel that their lives were not being lived properly and hence they deserved correction from the ancestors. I was told that 'it' *(la violencia)* "was sent by the ancestors who wanted to slaughter the men who fight and those with more than one woman".

La violencia as yabil is the result of some other wrong;[7] it is suffering which has grounds in some other unacceptable behaviour and, as such, can be contrasted with *la violencia* as the evil itself with its potential for further suffering. Yabil *(la violencia)* and yabil (illness),[8] though both forms of extreme suffering, are not necessarily the same, as I discovered during the measles epidemic in which over one hundred Emolteco children died. Nevertheless, *la violencia* is referred to as yabil because it is seen as a form of potentially lethal punishment sent by angry ancestors for the sins of the living. One woman remembered that 'the brothers' *(hermanos)*, by which she meant radicalized members of Catholic Action, had told villagers "that a day would come when the men would kill their fathers and fathers would murder their sons". She interpreted this as a threat and blamed the *hermanos* for *la violencia*, saying, "I suppose it was because of this that *la violencia* came."

During consultations with an aj q'ij, people are told that they have "created their own problems"; one aj q'ij tells his clients, "Our people provoked this situation where there is no respect." Aj q'ij explain that both *la violencia* and illnesses occur because of the "abandonment of the our customs" (including respect behaviours, agricultural work, and 'pure' catholicism). An aj q'ij told me:

> The elders [ancestors] say that when we change our customs *(costumbres)*, illness, death, and even war results, because our *costumbres* are something sacred. They are like laws but, in fact, they are even more than this.

Fictions of deservingness are employed in the K'iche' victim's construction of an illusion of justification. That the world is just is a generally held belief in K'iche' society; justice is seen as the response of a personified, deified agency to an individual's moral conduct and his or her relationships with supernatural powers. These beliefs translate into the idea that people get what they deserve: suffering is seen as punishment for one's faults and misdeeds. The self-blame inherent in the concept of ancestral punishment makes people more susceptible to the blame cast their way by the military and the *jefes* who manipulated K'iche' concepts of sin (mak) and their predisposition to hold themselves or their kin responsible for the problems they encounter. For example, *doña* Rosario said, "My brother was kidnapped because 'they' [the *jefes*] told us we were 'bad people' (itzel winaq)." Her use of this expression, which carries specific connotations in terms of traditional values, is unusual as it is more commonly used as a synonym for the army.

Patterns of self-blame permit individuals to believe they can avoid further their misfortunes if they avoid repetition of the deed. People do not feel morbidly guilty because, although somehow answerable for something going wrong, convention obliges them to perceive misfortune as ultimately stemming from the ancestors. The denial of control removes the connection to current or future suffering and eliminates responsibility. Ancestor-worship provides "an institutionalized scheme of beliefs and practices by means of which men can accept some kind of responsibility for what happens to them and yet feel free of blame for failure to control the vicissitudes of life" (Fortes 1959:29); the belief that ultimately whatever the ancestors proclaim is just also relieves them of some of their anger (cf. Fortes 1959:31).

People who visit diviners are fortunate because "they had the immediate relief of knowing which agency caused their troubles and in the case of a supernatural agent, which ritual steps to take" (Fortes 1959:10). These traditionally include visits to aj q'ij to make offerings and to confess their sins (mak),[9] which may well be a pre-Christian, Mayan religious practice. Whole families come to confess[10] their moral transgressions against other people and the ancestors; during these occasions the aj q'ij elicits their sins directly and also indirectly through the use of divining beans (*piloys*; tz'te'). The aj q'ij, both the 'worker of sins' (aj mak) and the 'settler of accounts' (aj toj) then decide on an appropriate penalty. Adults may be whipped by the aj q'ij with a spindly branch, mostly a symbolic gesture which inflicts psychic, rather than real pain; they may also pay a fine *(multa)* or be charged a specific fee — 100 *centavos* (known locally as a roban) or 25 *centavos* (mul); some of this money goes towards the aj q'ij's expenses (candles, incense, *aguardiente*). Other expiating behaviours include traversing the length of the room to the altar on one's knees.

Appealing to a diviner is similar to applying to an oracle to discover witchcraft: oracles "do not in fact enable men to master their fate...they merely help to reconcile men to its ineluctability" (Fortes 1959:5). The same can be said of the aj q'ij's divination in relation to the ineluctability of violence perpetrated by the *jefes*.

Thus, instead of feeling overwhelmed with rage about army assassinations or patrol massacres, people see the deaths as retribution by God and the ancestors and merely ask their pardon. But the matter is not that simple: an aj q'ij may, for example, tell a person that a problem is due to both ancestral punishment and an attack by a sorcerer *(brujo)* motivated by *envidia*.

Envidia (envy). *Envidia* (titk'iil) means 'bad feelings which one has for not being equal to another'. An elder told me that *envidia* "is created among the poor who have nothing". As I unravelled this concept, the meaning broadened; I found that it reflects related sentiments (such as hate and hostile competitiveness). *Envidia* is the most frequently cited cause of *la violencia* both as a national, general event and as a specific event affecting the speaker. Through resorting to this concept, *la violencia* is represented as an internal matter within society.

Suspicion and enviousness *(envidia)* are characteristic of the K'iche'. This is partly because they live in a world in which the goods people want exist, or are perceived to exist, in limited supply: one person's fortune is believed to be at the expense of someone (or everyone) else. A person who is simultaneously experiencing bad luck will automatically assume that another's fortune has been gained at his expense, that he has been harmed by witchcraft solicited by his richer neighbour or that the ancestors have 'punished' him after receiving false reports about him from this unaccountably lucky person. The implication is that all fortune is illicit, a form of stealing. In order to defend himself, the unlucky person visits an aj q'ij and asks him to inform the ancestors of the spuriousness of the reports they may have received; he also asks that the ancestors punish the thief with the same damage done to him (Schultze-Jena 1954:43). As economic stratification had already begun to occur prior to *la violencia*, *envidia* was rife even before the violence created a situation of greater deprivation than the usual conditions of 'limited good' (Foster and Rubenstein 1965). The disintegration of the *cargo* system added to village rivalries, resulting not only in increased competition but in the need to gain some sort of power to define one's self merely to have enough to survive.

Envidia seems to pertain to every aspect of K'iche' life; the term expresses every day theories of causation of enmity. The common denominator in all instances of *envidia* is its relation to perceived threats to the balance of power. Discrepancies in wealth (or, more accurately, poverty), prestige, and popularity are the most frequently cited reasons for *envidia* which is expressed through malicious gossip and rumour *(chisme*; ta jun tziij pi xaab') and witchcraft. The threat of both discourages conspicuous display. Post *la violencia*, *envidia* is also expressed through slander *(calumnias)*, false accusations, and betrayals.

Envidia expresses something which is not so much a feeling but has more to do with relationships between people and the strong value placed on conformity, so that no one gets ahead of anyone else or, alternatively, falls appreciably behind. *Envidia* is said to be the motivation behind the death of anyone who stood out in Emol, such as *doña* Eugenia's husband Antonio: "They had *envidia* because he was advancing, so they killed him." *Envidia* was also given as the motive for the assassination of her son, Gilberto, who had helped to build the village school and, in the face of parental opposition, had encouraged children to attend. Someone else said *envidia* had been aroused because Gilberto had been responsible for bringing the road to Kotoh; it traversed the land of another man, who then decided to betray *(calumniar)* him. One of his sons also attributed his father's death to *envidia* because he had been the village health worker and had made many friends through his work. Gilberto had been involved in establishing language and literacy classes which some believed were being used to spread 'subversive' ideas; he was a wanted man. Talk of such men's subversive activities is always mixed in with accounts of *envidia*.

In another instance, the operator of the Emol Central's only electric corn grinder was killed; again *envidia* is cited as the cause. The man's sister said the military commissioners who abducted him claimed he had written a 'subversive note' (death threat), but she believes the real reason was that someone else wanted his job: "There was no subversive note," she said; "it was something that they did out of *envidia*."

Envidia as a rationalization of killing carried out by fellow villagers illustrates that being nonconformist and non-compliant is considered dangerous. I was never sure whether the men were singled out because of local troubles or because they were on army death lists for their political activities: local events were grafted on to national events by reason of contiguity. Some women insist that local competition was of overriding importance. *Doña* Candelaria believes that "Even if my husband wasn't in 'the organization', they [the *jefes*] would still have killed him, for he was intelligent and he worked for the community."

Envidia as an internal problem arose over other issues such as land rather than a person's activities. *Doña* Rosario explains:

> If you have a large plot of land, then they will *envidiar* you by accusing you of being a guerrilla. They want you to die so that they can take over your land. Perhaps they [military commissioners] thought that when María's children die [their mother had been shot dead], they can appropriate their land... In fact, they even admitted that.

Doña Rosario reiterated her conviction that *envidia* is perpetuated by fellow villagers when she explained why she did not go into hiding:

> It is not the army that kill, it is the very same people from our community who go and bring the army and afterwards they say that it was the army. This is a lie. We don't know what these people want from us, perhaps they want us to leave our lands free so that they can take over our land. I do not know what they want. But we have to remain firm and not leave our lands and that way they can't do what they want to do.

Envidia also revolves around vengeance. The major issues for which revenge are sought are traditional rivalries and discontentments. Instead of resolving problems such as, say, adultery, in the traditional manner through asking a *brujo* (the mediator of the devil) to kill the adulterer and or their lover, some people now prefer to betray or denounce them to the *jefes* (the mediator of the military). Sometimes people seeking revenge step entirely outside local cultural boundaries and hire a 'gunman'. Whichever is the case, the resulting murder(s) are attributed to *envidia*.

People say the expression of *envidia* increased during *la violencia*. The civil patrol system is also seen to be responsible for exacerbating *envidia*, throwing an idealized past into relief. *Doña* Flora claimed, "Before they instituted the patrol system there was no *envidia*. Everyone lived in their house safely with a feeling of tranquillity. We all co-operated with one another." Other people see *la violencia* as a continuation of existing enmity within communities; this is traditionally expressed through *brujería* which is normally viewed as being motivated by *envidia*.

The concept of *envidia* is also applied to clashes between groups. *La violencia* was played out along factions extant both within and between villages, townships *(municipios)*, and so on. This is reflected in statements such as, "The Protestants had *envidia* for the Catholics, so they killed them". In this interpretation, *la violencia* is seen to be perpetuated on behalf of a whole community even though the perpetrators comprised only a group within it.

Several women gave me the impression that it was common to settle old scores during *la violencia*. *Doña* Eugenia says her husband Antonio was denounced by a "woman who had wanted to marry him many years ago"; *doña* Rosario claims personal reasons lay behind the assassination of her father and spoke of the *calumnias* which incriminated him:

> We tried to find out what inaccurate information they had given about him because we thought that perhaps they deemed him to be a 'bad person' (*mala gente* [guerrilla]), which was not true. I think they killed him because of this false information.

Many deaths resulted from personal quarrels; one party denounced the other as a subversive or army informer. *Jefes* also settled old scores of their own; as far as their selective killings are concerned, envy and competition may well have been the motivation. The national evil perpetuated by the army is seen to alternate with, and be grafted onto, local-level enmity, feuds, and vendettas expressed as *envidia*. This primarily personal interpretation is largely confined to the K'iche'.

Locals are seen to have got caught up in or, worse, to have taken advantage of a situation in which killing — whether by local *jefes* or by villagers in pursuit of some personal grievance — took place with impunity, despite an accumulation of feelings of vengeance. Sometimes virtually everyone seemed to be settling some old or new score. This impression reflects the deep mistrust which developed within the community after friends and fellow villagers *(compañeros)* gave the names of supposed collaborators when being tortured or bribed (enticements are said to have included taking over land, goods, and even the wives of people they denounced). The deteriorating relationships within the village crystallize the meaning of national events for women.

Some women convey the sense that almost the entire community is responsible for violence, either directly or indirectly, through betrayal; this impression annuls accounts of friends and neighbours' help and protection. Without wishing to gainsay the veracity of these statements, some women know and many others suspect that their kin were betrayed by other villagers. The search for reasons precludes acceptance of the idea of random, arbitrary victimage.

Envidia is also employed as an exegesis in the face of a paucity of other interpretations. Sometimes a person revealed their incomprehension, saying, "Who knows? *(¿saber?)* ...I suppose *envidia*". Women use *envidia* to explain most problems pertaining to violence and resort to this concept when they have no idea why their male kin were killed or abducted. The concept is used out of habit and the lack of a more satisfactory inference. *Envidia* is the most common explanation given for 'ordinary' deaths such as sudden, unexpected death in the night or inexplicable, incurable illnesses; it explains the ills which befall a person and, as with most other acts of aggression between people, *envidia* must also be behind the senseless, evil deeds of *la violencia*. This application of ordinary language to extraordinary circumstances is a way of rendering the incomprehensible comprehensible. Perhaps, taking this further, the application of everyday terminology allows the person to apperceive aspects of the world of *la violencia*. The extraordinary experience is thus grasped through this classification by ordinary language, although different people may be more or less convinced.

Attributing events to *envidia* is also a means of masking political experiences whilst revealing them to a listener who shares the understanding of the way this term is being employed in the present. When I pursued the meaning of *envidia* in instances where the semantic content of this concept appeared flimsy, I found that the speaker thought the particular violent act was politically motivated.

> I think that they [the military commissioners] abducted the men because of *envidia*...
>
> [What do you mean exactly by *envidia*?]
>
> Well, they had *envidia* for my husband because he went into hiding in the woods *(el monte)*...because of this they were hostile towards him.
>
> [Why should this make them hostile?]
>
> They suspected that he had gone with (joined) the guerrillas in the mountains.

Together with "who knows" and "only God knows", *envidia* is a protective expression of political neutrality. By explaining everything by resorting to *envidia*, the concept becomes meaningless and tells one nothing about the victim's political alignment. Such statements imply that *envidia* was the motivation even for killings by the army (i.e., suspicions of the victim's 'subversiveness' were based on personal, non-political affairs). I asked *doña* Rosario why her father was killed, rather than someone else:

> Because the people said that my father was sowing the pain (k'ax) [planting 'subversive' ideas] in the communities.

[Who said it?]

> The military did. They accused him of teaching people 'bad things'. They also did *calumnias* on us because we have land, because we plant onions and we usually have good harvests. This is why the people were against us. This is the main reason that they had *envidia* for my father. Also there was a Judas who was a traitor who supplied his name [to the army]. Because of this they killed him because they were told that he was a member of the guerrilla.

[And was he really one?]

> No, they made this up. They accused him because of his land and the fact that he was a worker, so they accused him...

[Who did?]

> Friends, friends accused friends and *compañeros* accused *compañeros*. They did it because they were forced to do it...or who knows... He wanted to remain an independent person. This created a problem in the community because most people went with one side or the other; so they got annoyed at him. This became an enormous issue. I can't explain to you just how enormous the problem became... But in any case, I tell you that my father did not want to accept either the organization of the guerrilla or the organization of the army, so they killed him.

[Was it the guerrillas who killed your father then?]

> No, it was the army who killed him.

Christianity

Some women told me that many of the men killed and kidnapped were victimized because of their own or their relatives' work as catechists or merely because they were active members of Catholic Action groups:

> They took them because they were Catholic Action people...because they spoke about the truth, the truth that people *[ladinos]* didn't want to hear.

> I don't know why [they kidnapped her son], perhaps because of a religious accusation. Actually, they wanted to kill his father [a catechist], but they killed

the boy instead. Those who worked for the struggle *(la lucha)*, when they were
kidnapped and asked who their *compañeros* were they didn't tell. Martyrs are
those who died without accusing anyone. They are those who were tortured.
One of my *compañeros* said, "If they kill me, they kill me" and they did. He
is a martyr.

The idea that their kin were martyrs is a common one. *Doña* Flora
claims her son is a martyr "because he didn't betray anyone"; *doña* Eugenia
agreed, saying, "Our sons and husbands died as Christ did, with blood-
stained faces, having been tortured." Catholic priests encourage this view of
la violencia and the dead. *Doña* Eugenia's grief over the deaths of her husband and son diminished after visiting the local priest who advised her to
'put her grief to one side'. He had explained, "They killed him like they
killed Jesus Christ, for speaking the truth."

Another widow commented on the connection drawn by the priest
between the dead and the village's patron saint, *San Sebastián*, with whom
villagers strongly identify.[11] "The priest helped us so much. He drew parallels between our dead sons and husbands who had given their lives in the
Word of God [to the catechist movement], with *San Sebastián*." The connection in women's minds between the saints and their martyred husbands
is so strong that at times it was not clear to me whether speakers' statements
referred to the saints or their dead kin. One day, *doña* Flora asked me if I had
seen *San Sebastián*; I said I hadn't. "You really should," she replied, and
went on to talk about something else. Suddenly she said, "He is very special.
He was an exceptional person but they tortured and killed him." "Who killed
him?" I asked, slightly at a loss; she replied, "The soldiers, they shot him."

The innocence of dead male kin is spoken of directly, although in-
frequently, in women's private discourse;[12] they were the 'good men', the
'good Christians' who were killed through no fault of their own. Women's
explanations and views of their husbands as martyrs are not necessarily consistent; they have ambivalent memories of the dead because they have never
been mourned (chapter eight). When in touch with one fragment of herself,
a widow may see her husband in an idealized way, as a martyr; when accessing another fragment, she wonders whether he was a 'sinner' (traitor):

Doña Josefina:
He [her husband] must have suffered great pains over there [in the after-life].
They told him, "You have been called here early because you've sinned and
now you've abandoned your children [by dying]." I heard him cry. I also
heard them tell him off every time I cried, saying: "You know your wife is
unhappy." I know all of this because I went to call him in the ptan ceremony
with the spirit caller (aj mes).

[Who is it that tells him off?]

Doña Josefina:
> The spirits of our ancestors, the elders who died before.

[In what way do they reproach him?]

Doña Josefina:
> By making sure that he remembers all of the sins that he committed in his life. I don't know what his sins were, but over there they do.

This type of vacillation is less present in *doña* Flora's view of her son, who she consistently martyrizes. This is connected to her feelings of guilt: she had encouraged him to go to the meetings; she is the one to blame. She is more ambivalent about her husband who she had also encouraged to go, but this has more to do with the way he abused her within their marriage.

Many Catholics are more able to accept their misfortunes as having positive value because of the resemblance to the suffering of Christ and the saints. The saints are characterized as "very good people who were tortured and killed for no good reason", thus reflecting the events of the women's recent past.

Martyrdom and sacrifice are an extreme form of placing positive value on death. The idea of religious martyrdom, in imitation of Christ, appeals to some Christians; political martyrdom appeals to those who identify with heroes such as Tecúm Uman, the martyred Indian hero of the Conquest. By linking the deaths of Christ, the saints, and Mayan heroes, the war dead are linked with an undifferentiated time of heroes, origins, and myth in order to re-invent tradition, or to connect present events in the past. This connection provides history and hence meaning (cf. chapter ten): seeing one's suffering as part of a script with high moral value probably makes it more tolerable.

Women's views of martyrization persist beyond the eclipse of Christian doctrines, such as in folk beliefs that sacrifice constitutes the best path to virtue which will be rewarded in the after-life. Women explain that the sins of male kin have been erased because they died for 'speaking the truth'. Comfort is also derived from the belief that killers will be punished for the sins of the war-dead who would then be 'liberated'[13] from any sins they may have accumulated during life. The expression of these traditional beliefs reflects women's constructions of their kin's innocence. Catholic converts express the same idea when they claim that the murderers will be penalized by being deprived of salvation.

The 'Organization'

As people become politicized, they are more likely to link *la violencia* to the 'organization' (politics) and the armed forces than the ancestors. In this interpretation, *la violencia* is seen as resulting from the malevolent effects of greed for *ladino* resources[14] and the military's assassinations as punishment *(castigo)* for the error of collaborating with 'subversives'.

While some K'iche's understand the wider problem through the teachings of popular organizations and the guerrilla, they also see that their association with local radicals and their ideas does not get them anywhere but, instead, makes trouble for them. Ultimately, they blame the people who involved them in new ideas *(ideas)* (chapter two) which only resulted in mass destruction. Their discourses reflect retrospective glances condemning their involvement with the popular organizations. Others still believe in the popular organizations such as CUC (if not the guerrilla cause) but are too afraid to voice their views, let alone act upon them. While perhaps holding newer political explanations in mind at some level, they often yield to more ingrained explanations.

Women are largely excluded from political discourse although a few had 'awoken' (become politically aware). Any woman who has an assassinated or disappeared relative became politicized to some degree. Women do not, for example, use Marxist-Leninist ideas to interpret their situation. The closest many women come to political explanations are quasi-political understandings of current events reached through biblical analogies:

> I think that God allowed this to happen to us because he too gave his spirit and his body and his soul on the cross. They crucified and killed him so that we could stay on this land. Perhaps it is because of this that our relatives suffered in the same way that Christ suffered... They too were like a representative of God. They were tortured and kicked to death too. Their blood poured out from their faces too. Isn't this what they did with the Son of God before [he was crucified]?... Perhaps God gave our men the idea to work with the people of their community. But it is this that did not go down well with the people. They did not like it when they spoke of equality.

This type of explanation reflects the way in which women heard about *la violencia* in the first place: through catechists, who translate the events of 'the struggle' *(la lucha)* so that they make sense to locals. Women also use their own folk explanations: the rich getting richer and the poor poorer, or being 'pushed aside'. The ethnocidal aspect of national level violence was dramatized in the transformation in local level relations: the 'poor Indians' *(naturales)* are oppressed and abused nationally by *ladinos* and locally by *jefes* who like to think of themselves as *ladinos*.

The idea of ancestral condemnation is conflated with political reasons for assassinations, indicating the transition in politicized women's thinking:

> Perhaps we were judged [by the ancestors] because we didn't carry out the unity. It is true that we organized but we didn't let everyone join and some committed [unspecified] errors when *la violencia* came. Perhaps because of this *la violencia* came and affected everyone.

Some women regret that they did not do more within the popular movements; at times they believe their failure was not due to the organization itself but to their inability to make it succeed. One woman blames their lack of success on their forefathers who had not educated them or given them any *ideas* (chapter two). *Doña* Flora conjectured: "Perhaps we *indigenas* could not tolerate the things relating to 'the organization', the fact that they talked in a different way... And because of this, they [the army/*jefes*] tarred us all with the same brush."[15]

I heard several women question the wisdom of having involved themselves with 'the organization'. Women who accept the blame cast their way by the army express remorse and blame themselves and their kin for their troubles. Other women, for whom being 'organized' means to speak about issues such as equality, only sometimes blame themselves or their menfolk: such women never hold their husbands responsible for *la violencia* on these grounds. Women are more likely to blame people who objected to the ideas put forward by the organized about improving their lives: such people, they told me, are 'lazy people who did not want to improve themselves' and 'rich *ladinos*' who had killed in the village. This phrase, generally used to ridicule people who are 'too big for their boots', gains a sharper edge when applied to *jefes* whose association with the army provides them with wealth and power.

Giving involvement in the organization as an explanation of a relative's death is very rare. In some instances, this reflects reluctance to mention it for reasons of safety; in others, this is how the death is actually seen. Most women do not seem to know if their husbands were involved with the guerrilla, *per se*; they say their menfolk were involved with the Catholic Church and held meetings to discuss issues such as equality. As the Guerrilla Army of the Poor (EGP) took *sub rosa* advantage of Catholic popular organization, it is possible that women had little idea that some of their catechists and health workers were part of a revolutionary network (cf. Stoll 1993). Even the wives of such men were sometimes unaware of their activities.

Some women allude to their spouses' 'bad' behaviour; they make a distinction between their husbands and themselves on moral grounds, thus explaining to themselves why they were protected. *Doña* Josefina maintains that, unlike men, "Women were not murdered because they are more religious; they are more attentive to the ancestors." *Doña* Candelaria also believes that women's moral behaviour according to K'iche' principles overrid political activity:

> God helped the women and not the men who were annoyed and drunk and who do not pray. We admitted to God that we were organized but we also told him that we did not steal and that we always worked to serve the lives of women and men. There were, in fact, many women who were kidnapped during this time, but not us because we asked for God's help.

Women are more likely to blame those immediately and directly responsible for the events: they saw the *jefes* carrying out massacres and therefore blame them and not the army behind the scenes.[16] This is a strategic choice as it centres directly on those human agents who are feasibly within their range of social action (cf. Scott 1985:182). Women's testimony shows resistance to army and patrol rhetoric and indicates that they believe *la violencia* stemmed from attempts to counter villagers' efforts to improve their lives ('organizing'). Oppression is defined in both ethnic and class terms:

Doña Candelaria:
> The reason for *la violencia* is that people were asking for their rights.

Doña Flora:
> *Ladinos* and our people, *indigenas* who are like the *ladinos* in that they don't want to organize, claim that it was our fault that their husbands died. They say that they died because we were organized. But I think it is because they didn't like what we were talking about...things like equality... You see, they wanted to remain rich while the poor continued to eat shit.

In this scenario, punishment *(castigo)* for 'organizing' is sent by the military and their accomplices who are now the omnipotent authorities in this world. The army and their accomplices indoctrinate people to believe that their kin were guerrillas and their pursuits immoral; only the army can save the community. Many people told me that the army and local *jefes* did the killing, but the guerrilla was responsible because "if the guerrilla had never come, then the army would not have come to kill". *Doña* Helena echoes the army's version of events:

> It was our fault that we suffered from *la violencia* because we allowed the guerrillas to enter the village. If the whole world had refused to speak to the guerrilla, then all the problems we have lived through would not have arisen...

This statement is typical of many I heard. It reflects women's tendency to communicate in terms of ancestral anger and 'sadness' (here meaning loneliness resulting from abandonment) rather than their own 'bad' feelings. Ancestral wrath is viewed as a 'punishment for the living', in this case for the women's bad thoughts and actions. At times women convey a sense of overwhelming 'badness', that is, they see the atrocities which arose with *la violencia* as an affliction in response to their own evilness. Women's feelings of evilness stem from their desertion of *costumbre* for catholicism, not burying their dead, and so on.

Interpreting 'La Violencia'
People's explanations about the causes of *la violencia* are not static but

operate according to several exegeses simultaneously with one interpretation not necessarily being more accurate, complete or final than another;
each is a version of the truth as understood at the time. Several currents flow
at different depths in K'iche' statements, as they invariably do in anyone's.
What appears to be a reduction of exegeses and confusion is partly due to
K'iche' tolerance for alternative explanations; it is also partly due to the fact
that every event at the national level is not only an event at the local level but
is frequently seen as a supernatural event as well. Apparent inconsistencies
also reflect the need to negotiate and renegotiate the meaning of *la violencia*;
the grafting of several levels onto each other allows women to constitute an
event in terms of several categories.

People vary their exegeses of the same phenomenon depending on context, to whom they are speaking, and the level at which they choose to pitch
their interpretation. Explanations depend on changeable aspects such as a
person's mood, whether they are afraid or what is happening in their lives
at the time (for example, another death, a clandestine grave exhumed). Exegeses also depend on the speaker's psychological state: women resort to different exegeses to explain *la violencia* and their dead relatives' part in it
depending on the point they have reached in the grieving process. The category of the perpetrator and that of the victim also affect exegeses. Attributed
meanings also depend on the nature of the specific event: an unwitnessed
abduction is more likely to leave relatives uncertain about the reason for the
disappearance[17] yet they feel more free to speculate about alternatives and to
project their worst fears into empty space.

My questions and their assumptions about who I was and what I was
trying to pursue also influenced women's definitions. When I tried to elicit
more specific explanations, I found that people who had given political interpretations resorted to a different discourse, such as supernatural causes. In
some instances, there was an element of changing the subject, of refusing to
take a line of reasoning further than they wanted to go (for reasons of safety,
for example). For most women most of the time, explanations are not distinct
or separate; they operate simultaneously at different levels.

The holding of a satisfactory interpretation (or not) is not an absolute
occurrence; it is not that one person holds a full explanation and another has
none. Exegeses are generally partial. Several women, for example, have a
partial understanding of *la violencia* as a general phenomenon as well as
others pertaining to specific incidents. They offer several possibilities in one
breath regarding the murder or abduction of their male kin: they might realize, say, that their kin had been targeted because they had attended meetings (which may or may not have been political) or were involved in literacy
programmes, yet a certain amount of vacillation and confusion often arises
when trying to explain why a particular person was victimized.

A person's experience of, or identification with, the events comprising
la violencia also results in divergent explanations. Exegeses are readily

available according to the source of the derived meaning of events. People
resort to alternative modes of explanation, depending on cultural meaning
which, in turn, depend on factors such as a person's political affiliation, religion, gender, monolingualism, and other internal issues such as the capacity to mourn. People involved in religious or political activities (there are
surprisingly few of the latter) relate to and interpret incidents differently
from uninvolved, conservative members of society. For example, when a
married couple were disappeared, the wife's brother, an aj q'ij, told me this
had happened because they fought excessively and the ancestors had therefore decided to bring them to the after-life; however, a neighbour and the
jefe both explained their disappearance as part of the army's campaign to rid
the community of guerrillas.

Vested interests also affect interpretation of events. Some people attempt to cast themselves in a good light and the other, including the dead, in
a negative one. I was told of a teacher (probably employed by the army's
psychological warfare branch) who taught children who had returned from
the mountains that guerrillas, and not the army, had murdered their parents
in order to take over their land. The military's relentless repetition of the
'official truth' blinds the indoctrinated to the illogicality of their claims.

People have a vested interest in interpreting the death or disappearance
of kin: the cause of, and responsibility for, a death can affect land inheritance. Women also have a vested interest in maintaining certain images of
their kin for their own peace of mind. Some take comfort in thinking that
their husbands died as martyrs rather than as the result of ancestral reproof.
The way women understand the innocence of their dead affects their own
identity: they can be the widow of a martyr or of a 'sinner' (traitor). But
feelings towards dead kin, especially husbands who are no longer there to
protect them or to beat them, are ambivalent: one moment the dead are martyrs, the next moment they are 'guilty'.

At different times people perceive the situation and those present (including myself) as threatening. The K'iche' deftly employ deflective devices
and tend to be reticent about explaining *la violencia*. At times people feigned
ignorance, answering "Who knows? *(¿Saber?)*" to my questions; at other
times they felt compelled to give me some kind of answer for fear that I
might suspect they were hiding something. *'Saber'* is the safest answer to
give an interlocutor who is either not clearly marked politically or viewed
with some suspicion. This response reflects the wish to minimize the risk of
being perceived as sympathetic to one side or the other. Rather than reflecting a vacuum of meaning, *'saber'* can be a statement of neutrality.

Saber also reflects a deeply discouraged view of things, expressed as
an abdication of responsibility: who knows when this took place, when this
began, what is true and untrue. *Saber* is also the least presumptuous answer;
for the K'iche', presuming to know such answers is like playing God. Only
God knows what is true and just; only he can act; only he knows what is

going to happen, *"Sólo Dios...sólo Dios"*. Here, God is very distant from the person. Other factors which have a bearing on this response are the proliferation of both army and guerrilla propaganda and rapid religious conversion.[18] Exposure to different ideologies resulted in conflicting explanatory frameworks. Some people see the vacillation itself as an explanation for the degradation of moral values, leading to confusion and, ultimately, to killing.

The Reconstruction of Meaning

K'iche' people explain *la violencia* by means of a variety of categories of causation, most of which are employed for explaining why things happen in normal times. Through *la violencia*, the military have come to be included with other worldly institutions such as ancestors and *jefes* with local level figures such as *brujos* and ordinary villagers.

Interpretations became guiding forces to action: people who believe in God's and/or the ancestors' anger or their protective powers firmly believe that prayers save them and they pray morning and night; those who believe that they are afflicted by witchcraft and ancestral wrath visit aj q'ij to solicit protection and appeasement respectively; people behave as modestly as possible to avoid *envidia* and *calumnia* and tend to trust very few people with important information about themselves. Belief in *suerte* leads to little positive action though it stops some people from dancing to the tune of intimidating forces as one's time of death is predetermined.

Employing familiar exegeses which obscure what really happened sets the experience in a familiar context. Exegeses of normal causation erase the violent intent of the military and attribute a knowable cause of death, placing social action (assassination/abduction) in parentheses. The garbing of murders in a false cloak of naturalness makes them manageable to some extent, although the causal accounts of death are unsatisfactory attempts to come to terms with the uncontrollable, violent, and relatively unknowable aspects of human agency. All these explanations preserve the *status quo* by obscuring substantial political/economic and historical issues. The very inappropriateness of these exegeses to describe political killings underlines the difficulty of finding a vocabulary of comparison for incomparable atrocity. Their use also reflects people's need to protect themselves from further atrocity.

Some comfort is derived in the repudiation of responsibility by thinking that everything is in the hands of God or the ancestors. This explanation does not provide the benefits of a sense of empowerment afforded by exegeses containing at least the remnants of political causation for *la violencia*. Enlightenment at this level is helpful even though — depending on the level at which explanations are pitched — people who acquire this new understanding continue to resort to supernatural explanations.

These transformations of reality allow the experience to be assimilated in a way which is less possible for those who do not adapt known interpretations of causation. The least fortunate are people unable to incorporate *la violencia* into old explanatory frameworks or to create satisfactory new ones. Some people lost their religious faith; their exegeses about God, appropriate for normal times, broke down in extreme disaster. They saw that God did not protect them and that their corn still grew when circumstances prevented the performance of ritual. People who lost faith in the ancestors stopped consulting aj q'ij, depriving themselves of the opportunity of ascertaining 'cause of death' (*suerte*, ancestral punishment or *envidia* or any combination of these) and establishing the dead person's innocence; instead, such people commonly resort to *envidia* to express their kin's blamelessness.

People who suffer from a loss of meaning also lose the sense that the world is a predictable place. Some of them are left with feelings of profound insecurity and the sense that *la violencia* might suddenly return at any moment (a real threat at the end of the 1980s). They attribute causation of *la violencia* to contiguous events (such as the clergy leaving El Quiché in the early 1980s) and, when similar events occur in the present (a priest forced to flee a nearby *municipio*), they fear that *la violencia* is about to return.

Among those left without an adequate way of explaining the loss of their dead kin are people who were forced to forget, as advocated by the military and their local supporters. People whose explanations are inadequate (or non-existent) for them to assimilate the experiences brought by *la violencia* are left with a separation between agency and event, between the loss of a husband or son and assigning responsibility. For some, that loss is a source of lasting confusion: "My own fault, or it was God's will... *Saber.*"

Individuals unable to escape suffering are isolated within their own physical and emotional conditions, deprived of any vehicle through which their experience can be made meaningful and, therefore, sufferable. The grief experienced by people who cannot explain an ordeal is more intense than that of others who can explain and thus integrate their past. Grief is more likely to be resolved when the cause of death makes sense to the bereaved and when they can have peace of mind about the event (Eisenbruch 1984:331). Commonsensical systems of thought are insufficient because "the events through which we live are forever outrunning the power of our ordinary, everyday moral, emotional, and intellectual concepts to construe them, leaving, as a Javanese image has it, like water buffalos listening to an orchestra" (Geertz 1968:101). In the case of the drastic changes brought about by *la violencia*, the K'iche's' experience of the situation was perhaps even less comprehensible.

Notes

1. cf. Wilson (1995:206). The common element, apart from the death, destruction, and invasion of Indian communities, is the invaders' attempts to re-organize indigenous society in its own image.

2. The tendency to interpret disaster as punishment is not confined to the K'iche' nor does it need the endorsement of aj q'ij to be felt. A psychologist's study of natural disasters has shown that victims tend to react to them as if they were punishments; there is a desire to detect moral agency in non-human causes. In the moment of being struck by an overpowering force, victims often have a feeling of an agency which acts with intent (Wolfenstein 1957).

3. The Bible is still used as a means of warning people of dangers; e.g., the army is denounced through reference to Roman soldiers (Wilson 1995:250).

4. *Nagualismo* is the phenomenon of 'transforming witches' or 'wizards'. In Chichicastenango, a *nagual* is a person's 'destiny animal' (Bunzel 1952:431).

5. Having a 'small heart' is also associated with old age, the ills of which are ascribed to depleted 'essence' and hence an inability to withstand spirit attack.

6. Some Protestant sects emphasize predestination (which is seen as akin to *suerte)* rather than free will. I was unable to ascertain the prevalence of this belief among K'iche' sects because of the political situation.

7. The Maya believe that all illness, affliction, and death are caused by sin (mak); the army plays on this notion, saying *la violencia* was its victims' own fault, a sickness they brought down on themselves.

8. A distinction is made between lethal, epidemic diseases (such as smallpox and typhus) and chronic, endemic diseases and misfortune. The former are classed as general disasters (yabil) sent by the guardians (ancestors) or God as a punishment to society at large; the latter are seen as individual punishments *(castigo)* sent by the same agents to persons who commit any one of a multitude of sins or, if they do not demonstrate appropriate corrective action, to their children (cf. Wagley 1949:76) or other close relatives.

9. Messages of repentance are also delivered by both Protestant and Catholic evangelicals.

10. A Catholic priest told me that *costumbrista* confession is more effective than the one-to-one Catholic confession after which a person can go home and carry on as before because the rest of the family has not heard it.

11. *San Sebastián* is generally depicted at the moment of execution, tied to a tree with his hands above his head and a quiverful of arrows embedded in his naked chest. It seems that Indians see parallels between this popular saint and their own situation (tied to the land, perpetually attacked, etc.).

12. In contrast to women's private discourses referring to the moral behaviour of the dead, men tend to refer to the wider, national, political, historical scene. Men who had been actively involved (and especially those who had joined from ideological commitment), experience and identify with the events comprising *la violencia* differently from women and uninformed, conservative members of society.

13. Subordinates (e.g. prisoners) have an incentive to comply when faced with a vision of their own liberation (Patterson 1982). But the widows' vision involves the liberation of the dead, not themselves. This phenomenon is connected to the fact that they are women, which is other-oriented in their culture (as it is in many others). It is also a sort of psychological compensation due to their guilt for surviving.

14. The problem with wanting things and services most *ladinos* take for granted is that the entrenched belief in 'limited good' implies that the introduction of the

new will result in the loss of something already owned. Thus people who want these things are dangerous.

15. The expression *doña* Flora used was the more aposite 'they burnt us all' *(nos quemaron todos)*.

16. cf. Warren (1993:38): "Political violence is not enacted solely by outside institutions but is also locally authored".

17. "When Ixils from northern El Quiché use the indefinite 'they' to assign responsibility for killing, further acquaintance usually reveals that they are referring to government security forces; when Ixils blame guerrillas, they do not hesitate to say so. Where Ixils seem genuinely uncertain is in regard to individual homicides for which witnesses are lacking" (Stoll 1993:328, fn.27).

18. Evangelicals tend to deny 'real' events and emphasize the hoped-for better after-life. Their sects are attractive to people who wish to escape (psychologically) from the intolerable events surrounding them.

10

The Cultural Construction and Reconstruction of Danger

"Caslic (Still alive)?"
"Mi xej awib (That fear should not be with you)"
Common K'iche' greetings

K'iche' cultural constructions of danger resonated with the new perils which arose with *la violencia*; these reverberations coloured ways of perceiving where danger lay and, in turn, changed the reality of threat in K'iche' existence. K'iche' symbols of authority and danger have been manipulated and changed by the army and its various local level cohorts; they have also been reinterpreted, with varying degrees of success, by the K'iche' themselves. The reconceptualization of danger is not complete, uniform or fixed and this serves to fragment community response.

Prior to *la violencia*, the K'iche' lived in a decipherable, if ambiguous world: people held common beliefs in *communitas* (Turner 1969:96), yet were riven by fears of witchcraft (*brujeria*; itzel). The resultant endemic mistrust generated by the actual or suspected use of *brujeria* is socially, economically, and politically crippling. Nevertheless, 'we' (inside) was separated by clearly defined frontiers from the 'enemy' (outside). Army rhetoric worked on this model, resulting not only in a proliferation of frontiers between 'we' and the enemy, but a redefinition of the enemy itself (devil, subversive, thief, non-patroller, member of a human rights group).

Preparation for the Recognition of Danger

Perceiving and understanding dangers requires both learning and a complex process of assimilating and integrating knowledge, a process which extends far beyond any inborn predisposition towards fearing certain aspects of the environment. Through inculcating appropriate behaviours, the K'iche'

together construct the meaning of dangerous agents, their socialization practices, and their fear. As a result, the cultural communication of a sense of
what is dangerous becomes all the more crucial for defending a person from
both palpable and impalpable threats. This process takes place in the socialization of the vulnerable infant and child and, to some extent, in the resocialization of the adult.

Among the K'iche', the preparation for scenarios of danger begins with
parents' fears of their child's vulnerability to spirit attack. Child mortality is
extremely high in the highlands and parents equip neonates with amulets and
bracelets of red stones to ward off the evil spirits held responsible for their
deaths (the widows sent me some of these when they heard that my child had
been born). Fear of the spirits is inculcated through parent/child interaction
where a spirit such as the q'ol q'ol (chapter nine) is invoked to frighten a
child; the idea that one is only safe in one's own home is enhanced by warnings that the cemetery and other uninhabited, uncultivated spaces are full of
murderers and spirits (Wagley 1949:30). Then, as a preliminary to the moral
lesson of respect, children are encouraged to fear unfamiliar villagers and
strangers who approach their homes. Showing respect to elders and significant others is one of a parent's first expectations of a child; also stressed is
the importance of greeting everyone they meet. Both are anti-conflict devices
and children are socialized to perform them from an early age. Yet inculcating fear of outsiders is not merely a socialization techique; K'iche's are
genuinely fearful of others' motives and intentions.

Children are taught to fear the anger of others, be they living K'iche'
or spirits. In developing this sense of fear, elders attempt to engineer desired
behaviours: fear, respect, and shame are what a 'good' person feels. A person who has no fear *(no tiene miedo)* or behaves 'without respect' is warned
that the ancestors may call him or her to the after-life; such reprehensible behaviour usually refers to some violation of social relationships rather than a
person's individual qualities. The K'iche' family is a complex behavioural
environment with prescriptive rules for interaction based on generation, age,
and sex, within which children learn the hard lesson that their spontaneous
feelings, hopes, and wishes have to mesh with the desires of those in authority. At an early age, children learn to take many things into consideration
before they embark on any course of action: the overt deeds and words of
others plus the underlying motives and needs that these convey; ideals of
group harmony and filial obligations; and, lastly, personal needs for self-
respect. The importance of the traditional notion that the household (and
after that, the community) takes precedence over the individual is emphasized in a variety of ways; for example, children are warned against stealing
before they begin to talk and undergo certain rites to purify their hands to
prevent them from 'taking from the community' (cf. Burgos-Debray and
Menchú 1984:32).

Advice, rather than physical punishment, is the main means of socializing correct behaviour in children within the family. Advice operates as a potent check on K'iche' behaviour; people are accustomed to receiving advice from others well into adult life, especially from diviners (aj q'ij) and elders who are said to 'orientate' them in terms of the correct behaviour for different circumstances. The need for orientation is understandably heightened in unknown situations where values have been violated. In the face of the demoralization of the old power structures, the army and local patrol chiefs *(jefes)* prescribe and proscribe correct behaviours: one does not, for example, openly offer food and clothing to the guerrillas or even to people labelled 'guerrillas' by association (such as the widows and children of the war dead) if one wishes to stay alive. A few people manage to keep on good terms with both sides.

The result of this socialization process is that the K'iche' constantly monitor their own (and others') behaviour. They live not only with the expectation that others will take offence but with the fear of the consequence of that offense. People go to great lengths to avoid giving offence and will immediately apologize and quickly compensate others for unforseen problems or accidents.[1] In a small, almost face-to-face community like Emol, actions soon become common knowledge, yet disapprobation of another's behaviour usually takes indirect forms: disapproval can be expressed through a joke or 'indirect words' (sarcasm) or, covertly, through witchcraft. Such obliqueness leaves the K'iche' uncertain of others' evaluation of their behaviour, resulting in great individual concern with one's own appearance of personal correctness but also greatly preoccupied with others' real or imaginary responses. This insecurity translates into suspicions that others harbour envy or have solicited witchcraft against them.

The Things Most Feared...

K'iche' people fear socially empty space, which they associate with night. People avoid being on their own (referred to as a 'sad' situation), even in their own homes. They are wary of going anywhere alone, particularly to other townships *(municipios)*, which are traditionally viewed with hostility and suspicion and of being out at night for fear of encountering spirits. This all-pervasive notion is also reflected in attitudes towards incoming strangers, ideas, and things.[2]

Strange People, Places, and Things

Fear of others' intentions splinters social life, causing neighbour to avoid neighbour; close neighbours are considered more dangerous than more distant ones because of boundary disputes. Merely being observed by one's neighbours can be threatening; they may spread rumours of illicit activities or subversion which could end in death. After many instances of betrayal during *la violencia,* the K'iche' are even less sure of others' intentions and thoughts. This alienation is frequently expressed as 'every head is a different world' *(cada cabeza es otro mundo)*.

A stranger who intrudes on known territory is considered dangerous. Every villager keeps a scrawny dog with a vicious sounding bark and a bite to match; when it barks, a child is usually sent to investigate. Hoping to reassure those inside, the visitor calls out, "Don't be afraid (mix nxbij)". Nowadays, instead of consulting an aj q'ij about an unfamiliar visitor's intentions, the hosts themselves ask, "What will happen to me if I speak to you?" or, "How do I know if you have come with good intentions?" A straightforward answer is rarely completely accepted and hidden agendas are usually suspected.

To counter potentially malevolent intentions and create a sense of intimacy, a visitor is invariably asked to share food. The recipient often feels apprehensive about accepting; people are discouraged from eating food 'from outside' *(ajena)* as it may be poisoned. The food is therefore offered with many assurances 'to eat with confidence'. A visitor's apparent reluctance to eat is seen by the host as a welcome sign of respect and good manners; outright refusal indicates mistrust or displeasure and can be dangerous. The visitor, knowing how sensitive the host is likely to be to any sign that his offering (a symbol of non-aggression) is unacceptable, repeatedly thanks the giver throughout the meal. However, the K'iche' are conventionally reserved and may become suspicious of an over-complimentary guest.

Apparently, people have 'never' really appreciated unexpected visits because, to the K'iche', and especially to women, the house is their haven. Unfamiliar, feared or disliked visitors are usually greeted at some distance from the house, preferably across the corn fields. Even in heavy rain, guests are seated under the veranda. One reason for this is that people fear exposure to envy *(envidia)* should others see their possessions, even though goods of any value are stored inside the house, covered with cloths *(pañuelos)*.

Fear of the presence of others increases when someone comes to stay for an extended period through marriage, adoption or, in the case of the anthropologist, prolonged squatting! Apprehension is felt both by the inhabitants of a home and the newcomer, who is expected to conform to the household's ways; they have to achieve a delicate balance between trust and respect which is renegotiated as they become more familiar.

Unclassifiable outsiders, again including the anthropologist, inspire some of the most dramatic proclamations of all types of fear. In an attempt to make the unknown more familiar, people classified me within various known categories, including *gringa*, *ladina*, guerrilla, and army spy (xikin). I was jokingly called 'k'u'xnelita' (literally, 'person of essences', meaning 'little person eater' i.e., killer) by my adoptive family, who laughed when I referred to myself in the same way; however, there was a certain amount of fear behind it. Fear is sometimes expressed in a playful, amusing, and inventive manner, even in the presence of the anxiety provoking agent. While people are terrified of the deadly effects of the worst kinds of evil, at times they can joke about it and make humorous parallels (Freud 1960).

After centuries of oppression, villagers have a pathological mistrust of foreigners, *ladinos*, and any outside authority. *Ladinos* (mo's) frighten the K'iche', who shoulder the brunt of their racist attitudes and actions. Being friendly with a *ladino* can be dangerous for an Indian, arousing suspicion and envy among those who suspect that they are getting something from the *ladino* in a dishonourable fashion. Indians aspire to raising their standard of living but acquiring wealth through immoral means is reprehensible. Many women told me of their frightening dreams of *ladinos* and foreigners which reflect their ambivalent attitudes towards these categories of people. *Doña* Josefina told me of a dream in which she had been seduced by a blond *(rubio) ladino*. In *Doña* Ana's dream, she was killed by a *ladino* with a *machete* and then resurrected as a *ladina*.

Gringos (who may also be referred to as mo's) are also considered dangerous. At best, *gringos* are thought to have 'no respect'; at worst, they are believed to abduct children, cut off their genitals and turn them into curative medicines. So-called progress, particularly that introduced from 'outside', is often similarly viewed. Electricity is a prime example: electric light is implicated in human deaths because human heads are said to be needed to generate electricity. The motorized corn grinder *(el molino)* is said to 'kill' the maize, making those who eat it vulnerable to illness (there is some truth in this, if the corn is over milled); in contrast, hand-milled maize remains 'alive' and the people who eat it stay healthy. Electricity is also needed to run the TV and video player recently brought into the village: *doña* Flora once told me, "They show the raping of women and killing of children in Guatemala City [on the TV]." Another woman merely exclaimed, "It's all very frightening!" They are referring to the nightly video shows for men and boys only: action movies, martial arts films, the Rambo series, and such like. Mothers worry about their sons' addiction to this seemingly harmless form of entertainment but as these fictional representations provide normative and behavioural models thus (to some extent) constituting reality (Chaney 1979), they have reason to be concerned. The young men identify with James Dean, Rambo, and other violent characters: one young man told me that when the army grabbed him for military service, he managed to escape by throwing himself from a truck using a Ramboesque stunt.

Cross-gender relationships also give rise to fear. The opposite sex is a relatively unknown quantity because it is considered dangerous to violate the traditional taboos which separate the sexes. Girls are socialized into being 'ashamed' in front of groups of boys and will usually rush past them in a group, covering their mouths with their shawls, giggling nervously. Women fear men's authority and potential violence. Wife beating has always been fairly common and, since *la violencia*, women have also had to contend with other types of abuse from *jefes* and military commissioners.

Women often speak of being afraid when they venture to unknown places beyond the village perimeter. When passing unfamiliar places, people fear becoming the object of *envidia*, gossip, and rumour (*el chisme*; <u>ta jun tziij pi xaab'</u>). Here, too, they are more likely to meet another's fearful, malevolent or critical gaze: criticism can endanger one's public image or lead to witchcraft *(brujería)*. Fear increases if the other person is thought to be angry, drunk or menstruating; they are said be 'hot people' (cf. Wilson 1995: 132) with 'strong blood', which enables them to give the evil eye (*mal ojo*; <u>rawinak</u>), harming plants and animals and causing illness and sometimes a child's death. <u>Aj q'ij</u> explain that it is the person's <u>nahual</u> (companion spirit) which actually gives the evil eye to the other person, causing them to become ill (cf. Tranfo 1974:232). The evil eye, then, is an attack from the spirit of a living person.

Other fears of contact with people outside the village relate to racism. *Ladino* racism is a fact of life for the K'iche': from childhood, they are intimately familiar with the exploitation of their parents on the coastal plantations *(fincas)* where they were robbed of their full salary one way or another; they are also frequently exposed to racial abuse and violence from *ladinos* in the town, especially in the market. Women's fears relating to racism are sometimes expressed in the idiom of dress, which is part of their ethnic identity: for example, a widow, confronted with the possibility of going beyond the town, asked me, "Will they tear off my skirt when they see me?"

These views of the world beyond the village are reflected in beliefs concerning the landscape. According to local conventions, the more unfamiliar, less-frequented the landscape, the more potentially menacing its supernatural landlords or guardians (*dueños*; <u>witz</u>) become. Steep, inaccessible areas beyond the cultivated fields[3] are considered frightening and remote from daily life. The location and boundaries of these spaces remains constant, although the cultural meanings associated with them vary according to the time of day. Night transforms the local landscape into a different world in which the strange and uncanny prowl the village streets. Like the remote mountains, each with its *dueño*, night holds unknown possibilities.

Few people stay up late and no one leaves the village after nightfall; to be up and out after dark gives rise to suspicion. Traditionally, night is when *brujería* is performed; more recently, it is the time when people 'organize' or are disappeared. At night, spirits leave the remote, liminal areas where they reside during the day and wander around the houses. More recent demarcations of dangerous space include the civil patrol and army bases which, though located on the village perimeter, are considered to be 'outside'.

The saints, like living K'iche', leave the night to the unseen denizens who know it best. As the dangerous spooks (<u>mib'inaaq</u>) and demons retire at dawn, the realm of the saints comes to life once again, reestablishing the proper relationship between spatial categories, supernatural domains, and human experience and knowledge.

Drunkenness; Verbal and Physical Abuse

Violence is almost always preceded by the consumption of alcohol. Though the K'iche' are more prone to tears than anger when drunk, brawls do break out: men swing punches at each other, women pull hair and hurl insults. Such outbursts, especially in public domains, were traditionally referred to the village mayor *(alcalde)*. The most common form of interpersonal violence is wife beating by drunken husbands.

The strict norms of respect which operate to maintain harmonious social relations dissolve when people are drunk, leading to potentially explosive situations. This is a particular risk at *fiestas* when many normally reserved villagers get drunk, becoming assertive and even abusive. Drunks are feared because they have neither fear nor shame *(no tienen miedo ni vergüenza)*. Their lack of fear can have serious repercussions for others: a drunk may admit to his own or someone else's activities; he may become explicit about community tensions or avenge a previous insult aggressively; he may even break the silence which *jefes* have imposed regarding their atrocities.

Since *la violencia*, drunkenness among women has become less rare. Women have been known to take verbal revenge when drunk: *doña* Josefina told me she chased the *jefe* who had killed her husband, "all the way to his house. I was shouting at him, 'Murderer!...assassin!'" Some women seize the opportunity to make accusations, knowing that their actions should be attributed to their drunken state. Sober spectators fear for her life; relatives also fear for their own.

Should violence break out, sober men are portrayed by both genders as the protectors of women and children. Women are anxious when men are absent, even temporarily, from the household; they fear drunken *jefes* and commissioners in combative or amorous mood at night; assaults on women are more common than they were in the past. Direct violence between sober people, especially kin and neighbours, though rare, is nevertheless seen as a worrying possibility.

Verbal violence ('painful words'), particularly if vociferous, is perceived as sinful and usually only occurs when the offender can avoid retaliation from the living. For example, Teresa, the vice-president of her village CONAVIGUA group, had fled when her friend, the group's president, was shot dead by the village military commissioner in May 1990. When Teresa returned to visit her mother a few weeks later, the whole village, including members of CONAVIGUA, was forced to turn out and jeer at her, accusing her of having 'stuck her ass' (fornicated) with the human rights procurator. There was nothing Teresa could do to defend her reputation. Later, her CONAVIGUA colleagues privately apologized: they had complied with the hated commissioners and *jefes* because they were afraid.

Malicious rumours and gossip are another form of verbal violence. Gossip networks are powerful in a village which lacks newspapers and has few radios: they can influence an individual's standing in the village or even cause his or her death; there is little victims can do to prevent it, though they usually attempt immediate corrective action. To be seen gossiping is just as dangerous as being gossiped about: both bring vengeful actions. These days, a group of gossiping women can be accused of 'organizing'; it is also believed that informers have been planted to report on *los chismes* reflecting alignment. Recently, villagers have become more wary of both gossip and rumours, which they believe are increasing; *doña* Lydia lamented, "The problem with people is that we have become accustomed to gossiping, rumours, and the lies *(mentiras)*." 'Not to tell tales' is now the most important advice given to children.

La *violencia* took shape through gossip and rumour. In this chaotic and life threatening situation, information was either non-existent or ambiguous: rumour and gossip were the only source of news of events in the extra-local world. As *la violencia* increasingly disrupted the everyday order of K'iche' life, fear and rumours came to dominate people's perceptions of the world; gossip arises "when order gives way to confusion and incoherence" (Haviland 1977:180). Politically charged rumour came to be seen as autonomous and volatile, able to spark off violent acts; eventually, the rumour or gossip itself came to be seen as dangerous. Hot tempered and envious people inspire fear in others because, as well as giving the evil eye, they are the most likely people to gossip.

Spirits, Spooks, and Demons

The drama of the spirits in El Quiché has historically communicated that the anger of spirit or human others should produce fear. The spirit domain can represent both the danger of problems, such as illness, and its eradication. Spirits embody the contradiction between nearby frequented and known space and the socially dormant night (Watanabe 1992).

Generally, spirits are the souls of the dead who roam the wilds and haunt deserted parts of the village; murder victims are the most dangerous and are a major concern following *la violencia* (chapter eight). Some spirits are poltergeists who throw stones or call out to passers by on lonely paths; some are disembodied voices, weeping inconsolably, and others are bodies without voices (cf. Watanabe 1992). *Doña* Eugenia told me about a spirit of the dead known as an aj tol who enters the house and violates women without them knowing it; it then opens the door to the kitchen (usually a separate building) and eats the food, again without the woman realizing what has happened. She also told me about the *llorona,* the silent spirit of a deserted wife which appears late at night on deserted paths, wearing K'iche' women's dress but with loose, unplaited hair. An encounter with a *llorona* invariably presages bad luck. One man told me he had seen a *llorona* shortly before his wife died. Another man, after an evening's drinking with friends, followed a *llorona*, thinking it was a living woman: one of his godmothers *(comadres)* died soon afterwards. The *llorona* is anomalous and symbolically appropriate as a mediator between cultural categories, in this case, categories of space (cf. Douglas 1966:34-60).

People are not hostile to the spirits although they fear them. They attempt to minimize contact (by avoiding liminal places, never being alone or venturing out at night) and flee from those they see. Spirits are omnipresent, unlike people (such as foreigners) or events (such as earthquakes). They have innumerable faces and are therefore perfect objects to house and express the plethora of K'iche' fears; they can be seen as multi-functional, operating on several levels simultaneously.

Spirits personify danger; they replace the image of other dangers which are intangible or too dangerous to acknowledge openly (it is safer to advise someone not to go out at night because of the spirits than to warn them of possible army or guerrilla attack); they can be seen as the targets of K'iche' anguish caused by their helplessness after being subjected to one source of aggression or manipulation after another. Tales about spirits also refer to the dangers inherent in certain social situations. Themes include unfulfilled family obligations, husbandless households, deceit, adultery, temptation, and being alone, particularly at night when spirits are especially prevalent.

As a generality, spirits are ambivalent beings who share human motivations and traits; unlike humans, spirits are free to act out all the emotions, frustrations, and desires which living K'iche's are culturally constrained from expressing. Thus spirits are considered more likely than humans to intend harm and cause fright; the lack of social compulsion renders them capricious, mischievous, and malevolent. It is not merely that people project into the spirits those malevolent traits which they know best because they exist in themselves (cf. Bettelheim 1986) but that this understanding of spirit behaviour implicitly reinforces K'iche' constructions of the best way to be.

Only the devil, known as *el malo, remalo* or itzel (evil), is unwaveringly malevolent. There is some category confusion here in that itzel is a generic word for spirits, who are generally described as 'bad' but classified as ambivalent. The association between traditional Mayan spirits and the Christian devil, first posited by Spanish missionaries five centuries ago and reinforced by Catholic missionaries over the past forty years — together with Indians' greater need to project feelings related to the abuse they received from the Spanish invaders and their successors the *ladino* army — seems to have led to an emphasis on the spirits' negative characteristics.[4] Thus, over time, the meaning of the term aj itz (*brujo*; sorcerer) has changed from 'worker of the spirits' to 'worker of evil'.[5] Traditionally, contacting the spirits (itzel) through an aj itz was illicit because help was sought by and for the individual: putting the self above the community is contrary to traditional mores and it is this which is evil rather than the spirits themselves, who remain ambivalent. (That individuals approach aj q'ij for rituals of protection against witchcraft does not contradict this: counteracting *brujeria* benefits the whole community). The spirits' ascribed capricious, if not malicious, nature 'encourages' them to co-operate with individuals who seek to harm others.

The most common form of 'contact' between the worlds of the spirits and the living occurs in dreams. Traditionally, spirits, ancestors, and guardians communicate with elders, letting the dreamer know what the future holds. One villager told me that his uncle, an aj q'ij, had a dream where he saw 'the situation' *(la violencia)* unfold before his eyes; he went blind and died shortly afterwards. The aj q'ij described his nocturnal, supernatural visitor as a white-skinned figure dressed in old-fashioned European clothes.[6]

During and after *la violencia*, dream communications between spirits and ordinary mortals became common. Some of these dreams are terrifying, leaving the dreamer afraid for some time afterwards. As the domains of illness and dreams are not enclosed within the self, spirits can enter these arenas freely and influence the course of events.

Other dreams are seen as portents.[7] Many widows told me they had been forewarned of *la violencia*; others told me that their husbands had informed them of their imminent demise and instructed them on what they must do, and not do, once they were gone. Some spirits are even more helpful: *doña* Flora told me how one man's dream had saved him from the army:

> There was a man, José, who they abducted along with my son Juan. They took them both to the army base in [Santa Cruz del] Quiché but unlike my son, José managed to escape. When the time came, he bolted. He ran for the road and he jumped over the cactuses. He ran and ran, like a plane, faster than the cars. And when night fell, the rain poured in buckets, drenching him. Then, when midnight came, he felt very sleepy. José wanted to go on but he didn't know which way to go. He just decided to go one way and eventually he came to a ravine. Then he changed directions and came to another one. He was stuck. Suddenly his eyelids began to droop and an elder in white trousers [an ancestor] appeared. He said, "Look José, here is the path." And when José woke, there was the path before him which led him back to safety.

Other omens of death sent by the spirits include the eagle-owl *(tecolote)* and cats which yowl near one's house at night. The recipient of these signs becomes frightened because these night-time creatures' activities indicate that they are emissaries of the devil. People are also grateful for these warnings, for they give them the opportunity to settle their affairs before death (chapter eight).

Witchcraft and El Bin

K'iche' culture is infused with fears of *brujería* because the spirits, whether summoned by a *brujo* or acting on their own behalf, can harm, kill, and disappear people. *Brujería* should not be directed at kin although members of the same family do sometimes plot to kill each other through this medium. I was told of a young man who thought his brother had received a bigger share of their father's land; he is said to have killed his brother through *brujería* and taken over his land. In another case, a man who fell in love with his cousin is said to have killed her the same way when she rejected him.

Until recently, *brujería* was the most popular and common form of premeditated aggression; it represents an alternative to direct violence and is believed to be just as harmful. For example, if someone falls seriously ill, relatives' first thought is to attempt to identify the source of the sickness; if witchcraft is divined, it is seen to stem from a specific hatred aroused by the ailing person and is not considered to pose any further threat to kin (a child's death does precipitate direct vengeance sorcery because the attack is thought to be aimed directly at the parents). Some people believe that direct violence is empowered by *brujería*; most Indian soldiers are afraid of *brujos* and some believe that *brujería* enables killing to take place.

Although aj q'ij have largely fallen into disrepute in El Quiché, *brujos* are still seen, even by sceptics of the old beliefs *(creencias)*, to wield hidden influence. Even Catholic and Protestant converts surreptitiously resort to an aj q'ij if they believe that they have been harmed by *brujería*. They travel far in order to escape detection, especially by the intended victim (*brujería* can rebound on the sender). At shrines also visited by aj q'ij, they work with the sorcerer to concretize their revenge in the form of *brujería* or the evil eye, using a variety of objects such as dead toads, black or blue candles, and objects belonging to the victim.

There is a hierarchy of *brujos* about which, unfortunately, I found out very little; *brujería* is not something people talk about freely. It seems that *brujos* are ascribed different powers in different areas; in Emol, *brujos* are said to be able to transform themselves into the physical form of their spiritual or animal counterparts (nahual).[8] Sometimes the *brujo* is invisible (or at least unperceived by his fellows), his presence only recognized retrospectively, following an incident involving an animal. A woman told me:

> One day my brother-in-law got drunk in the presence of a *brujo* at a *cofradía's* house. My brother-in-law began to abuse the people there, so the *brujo* warned him that he should be careful or something bad would happen to him. But he didn't take any notice. Then, exactly on the spot where he had misbehaved, a snake came and bit him. He fell on the floor in a stupor.

At other times, someone is recognized as a *brujo* because of something aberrant in his or her appearance or behaviour. This type of *brujo* is known as *el bin* and is said to come from 'the evil one' *(el maligno)*. In real life, *los bines* look like ordinary people but a second glance will reveal that a female *bin* has, for example, wrapped her *corte* the wrong way round; she may be extraordinarily beautiful but walk with her head cast down. *Los bines'* heads may be twisted round or missing altogether; they do not greet people they

meet. They are described as being rather 'timid', 'unintelligent', and unintel-
ligible ('speak ugly').[9] *Los bines* have the ability to transform themselves.
After somersaulting in the air three times,[10] the soul *(alma)* or spirit *(ánima*
or nahual) abandons the human body, usually taking on the form of a predatory animal which also has something amiss about its appearance. As animals, *los bines* perform evil deeds at night, such as stealing livestock and
children, cutting off men's genitals, and raping women (cf. Saler 1969:25).
Until spirit re-entry, the *bin's* human body remains motionless in the place
where his or her soul converts. Re-entry can only be prevented by pouring
cal[11] into its orifices, putting salt on its head (Redfield 1934:179) or burning
clothes left behind by the transforming person (Oakes 1951:174). The preferred local option renders the malevolent spirit impotent and leaves the
brujo in animal form for ever. Attacking the animal form also affects the
brujo; if it is killed, the human *brujo* also dies (cf. Tranfo 1974:239). In
some areas, however, it is believed that the transforming *brujo* (nanahualtin)
cannot be harmed by a knife, a gun or stones because of his secret defensive
power (Lewis 1951:280). In others, it is believed that the transformed *brujo*
is only vulnerable to a greater evil: the devil or, as some people claim, his
modern incarnation — the army.

The Manipulation of Concepts of Danger

The K'iche' have experienced conflict and its associated problems for
centuries but *la violencia* was different from previous conflicts not only
because of its severity but because it was intra-communal rather than inter-
communal. 'Outside' dangers became indistinguishable from those within:
both external forces (the army, who wanted to control the population) and
internal forces (villagers who wanted to settle personal scores) operated
through local civil patrols and *brujos*.

Guerrilla-devils

Military tactics have a psychological proclivity to involve the reconceptualization of the nature of danger. For the army, the enemy/outsider was the
guerrilla/subversive/communist/human rights worker. These were not only
new words for monolingual K'iche' speakers (which included most women)
but also new concepts for the non-politicized (which again included most
women). Most villagers were therefore unable to assimilate these new but
fearsome agents; the words themselves came to be seen as dangerous and
their use avoided for fear of giving the impression that the speaker had
knowledge of these matters. As their insecurity increased, so did their
suggestibility to new information (cf. Sapir and Crocker 1977).

With the help of the army, the unknown was made known through slot-
ting the new concept of 'guerrilla' into a series of familiar categories: other/
outside = guerrilla = devil = evil = danger (see Figure 1). The rarely seen

guerrilla is spoken of in terms of the familiar, malevolent spirits: as an unknown, invisible, powerful, evil, all-pervasive force, superhumanly cunning and cruel, living in dangerous places and operating at night. The K'iche' have no concrete evidence with which to refute the army's linkage of the spirits with the guerrilla, yet the combination of invisibility, ambiguity, and danger is all the more fear provoking. The unknown which threatens one's life is much more frightening than the known, even if the known is terrifying: "we cannot forget it, so it dominates our mental life as conscious or unconscious terror" (Bettelheim 1986:230).

More readily understood is the army's order to the civil patrols to attack any foreign elements in the community, which resonated with K'iche' notions of stranger-danger. Making analogies between new concepts and established, fear provoking beliefs is an efficacious means of instilling fear of the unknown, which becomes known in the process. The fear evoked is thus a deeply instilled one.

Analogies are made through the telling and retelling of stories in which the malevolent spirit is simply replaced by a guerrilla: "narrative structures serve as interpretive guides...that transform the alien to the familiar" (Bruner 1986:147) and sense is made of a situation which initially presented itself as a constellation of 'signifiers' (Barthes 1973). In the following narrative, similarities can be seen with *el bin*. A young man who works in the city recounted a story told to him by his ladinized friends (who are army sympathizers) to explain guerrilla actions:

> At night, unbeknown to her husband, a woman got up and went outside. There, somersaulting three times, she transformed herself into an animal, like a coyote.[12] Her human body remained motionless in the place where she converted herself. As a coyote she went from house to house, killing the sheep and eating the meat.[13] Once her belly was full, she did not return home. She went to an abandoned house, where other 'bad people' (*mala gente* [guerrillas]) awaited her visit. She climbed a ladder to a secret hideout in the attic. Then she regurgitated the meat. Her *compañeros* were well pleased because they ate well that night.[14] The coyote then returned home before dawn and, somersaulting three times again, she re-entered her human form. She got back into bed with her husband who remained fast asleep and completely unaware of her actions.

The army directly exploits the concept of *el bin*. When setting up patrols and, later, when attempting to keep the system active, army *oficiales* tried to convince villagers that guerrillas were lurking everywhere and that neighbours and kin had, like *los bines*, double lives, despite their apparently normal appearance in 'real life'. The army constantly warns villagers to protect themselves from these perilous villains who have the potential to take over the village and its inhabitants, an idea which resonates with K'iche' ideas of being taken over by spirits unless one is constantly on one's guard.

Acting on army orders, the *jefes* portray guerrillas as non-humans and devils who live in the underground worlds (caves) scattered throughout the village, thus reinforcing the connection between guerrillas and the ancestors and guardians, to whom the caves are sacred. Like the *conquistadores* before them, the army has attempted to demonize the sacred Mayan landscape, whose *dueños* — mountains and distant volcanoes — dominate the community literally and figuratively; they have also linked *costumbristas*, for whom these caves were the main focus of prayer and sacrifice, with the guerrilla. The mayor of the local town, a *ladino* Christian Democrat who collaborated with the army in intimidating villagers, also tried to convince people that guerrillas permeated the countryside. On one occasion in 1990, at a time when several civil patrol units wanted to disband, he announced that underground caverns, still warm from guerrilla occupation, had been found in the village.

Another army ploy is depicting guerrillas as devils disguised as angels, wandering between angels/saints and men, befriending people and enticing them into sinful acts (i.e., becoming a guerrilla), thus causing their souls to be invaded by the devil. Allegories are made of wolves (guerrillas) befriending humble people *(humildes)* only to steal their chickens. Guerrillas are described as immoral beings whose behaviour is contrary to social norms: they are violent, deceitful, lazy, thieving atheists who live like animals in the mountains. There are many people who hold similar views about the army.

Soldier-saints

Apart from 'playing God' by deciding who lived or died, soldiers attempted to become 'saint-like' by associating themselves in the most concrete way with objects the K'iche' view as representations of the saints. Having equated the guerrilla with the devil, the army represented itself as friend and 'provider' (the army competes with NGOs to appear as the best provider and a potential source of progress) and even saviour/saint/God. This is particularly clear in the flyers distributed throughout El Quiché, in which the army is associated with the divine, protecting people and the church from the guerrillas (the devil personified) via the civil patrols (see Figure 2). The army's association of itself with the saints is especially significant, given the danger associated with being a Catholic during (and since) *la violencia*. Being Catholic is sufficient grounds to be labelled a subversive; many catechists and some priests were army targets during this time. The military's success is shown by the fact that some people now approach the army rather than the saints for favours and advice.

Saints are the most sacred personages in K'iche' life and are considered to participate directly in their daily lives. Their assumed proximity and ritual accessibility makes them ideal bridges or mediators between people and God (a concept which has its roots in Catholic doctrine) although others say that, for the Maya, the saints are pure representations of God. For the K'iche', God

Figure 1: "Soldier Saints"
Flyers distributed in K'iche' villages

Figure 2: "Guerrilla Devils"
Flyers distributed in K'iche' villages

is concrete and speaks; a local priest told me, "The saints are something palpable for the Indian; they are something they can touch."[15]

Literally, saints are wooden images kept in Catholic churches, *cofradía* houses, and people's homes. In many parts of the highlands, these images are bedecked in local Indian dress which constitutes an obvious and important marker of ethnic identity. That Indians identify strongly with these icons is shown by the frequent comment that an image 'looks just like (say) an Emolteco'. In some areas of El Quiché it is said that village patron saints gave the people their unique costume and language. The saints are also place markers: each of Emol's hamlets has a named patron saint who is an intimate member of the community. The patron saint presides over the congregation in church (tjaa dios; the 'house of God') and over the whole community when it sallies forth during religious processions to survey the boundaries of its domain. The importance of the village saint is evidenced by the fact the tjaa dios is often referred to as the house of (say) *San Sebastián* (tjaa *San Sebastián*). It is the village patron saint, said to have been erected by long-forgotten ancestors, which is believed to provide the community with protection. Where communities still have them, processions are still accompanied by (ostensibly disarmed) patrollers.

The K'iche' do not see any Spanish connection to the icons, which are viewed as the same as Mayan idols; they are old Mayan gods dressed in the Catholic guises of the conquest period (cf. Farriss 1984:312) and are viewed as indigenous *(naturales)* like themselves. This is evidenced by fact that the saints, like the ancient Mayan gods and living K'iche', have to be married in order to be considered full persons: a Chimalteco reported that the icon of *Santa Ana* was married to the icon of *Santiago*, next to whom she stood on the church altar; in a well-known story reflecting a common problem in a society in which arranged marriages used to be the norm, *Santa Ana* had an illicit affair with *San Sebastián*. When her infidelity was discovered, *Santiago* beat her and threw her in jail and ever since then he watched her closely — "for like all women, she is very loose" (Wagley 1949:53).

As putative social beings, these personages demand that the K'iche' relate to them in certain ways. These conventions also articulate concepts of the sociality, linking not only mortals with gods but mortals with mortals (Watanabe 1992). Saints can be viewed as the conventional embodiment of unquestioned authority sanctifying the propriety of local social relations. Appropriate behaviour accounts for one's closeness to the saint and also for one's true membership in the community. Failure to conform to local conventions engenders the social and ethnic distance epitomized by the physical remoteness of the devil (or *dueño*) and by the amoral behaviour of outsiders.

Indians display some of their most expressive behaviour before icons. The K'iche' show their devotion, both in saints' brotherhood *(cofradía)* houses and the church, by traversing the length of the room towards the icon on their knees. Sometimes, in drunken states,[16] they converse with them warmly and familiarly, gesturing, appealing, even crying, and listening as though they were real people. During one procession, I noticed that the patron saint's nose was broken; the account of the accident was related to me as if the saint had experienced human emotions at the time. Icons' human qualities are also illustrated by the answer given to anthropologist David Stoll who had asked why two soldier figurines flanked an icon in the church: "I saw him run away" (Stoll, personal communication).

Interactions with icons are two way: K'iche' not only project their thoughts and feelings onto the icons but also internalize what they hear is said to them. As the psychotherapy client accepts what the authoritative voice of the therapist tells them about themselves and mirrors the postures and jargons (which are salient to them), so the Indian does the same with the powerful and guiding saint.[17] They internalize the physical and behavioural qualities they perceive in the images. Villagers told me that the icon of Jesus of Nazareth, which shows Jesus hanging his head forlornly, is 'the worker of sadness' (aj bis); I saw K'iche' people imitate this posture when pensive during church services or when praying in front of this icon. "Indians pay more attention to the gestures of the saints than their histories as written in the Bible," a priest working in El Quiché told me; "they will often not know the characteristic of a particular saint, when he died, and so on, and they might not even know its name."

Against this background, at the height of the military's control of the countryside, the army dressed church icons in their uniform[18] in order to create a positive association between themselves and the saints. The army hoped to harness the power of these revered authorities, thereby penetrating the community, winning K'iche' hearts and obtaining omnipotent control over the people.

The usurpation of indigenous symbols is part of a process of undermining Indian morale and rebuilding a new consciousness in which people identify themselves, the army, and the saints in the same image. This process also has the effect of manipulating K'iche' sites of memory: the army breaks the bond of identity with the ancestors, saints, and God and locates itself in its place. Dressing icons in army uniform not only associated the saint with the army in K'iche' eyes: it also associated the K'iche' with that which the army represented to them and also that which these authorities attribute to them. But a saint dressed in army fatigues does not have the same associations for everyone. While the army had one idea in mind, most K'iche' had another. Indians' own agenda meant that icons became something other than what the army intended; at best, they represented both what the army intended and something else. The army was not altogether successful in associating itself with saints; Indians have not forgotten the army's treatment of icons during the destruction of churches and *cofradía* houses during *la violencia*. People say that the damaged icons had been maimed and tortured. Emol's principal saint, *San Sebastián*, is said to have given his life for the 'truth', just like the women's husbands, sons, and fathers. In villagers' eyes, the saints have shared their experience; they acknowledge the saints' anger while repressing their own.

Another reason for the army's lack of success stems from their inability to control people's interactions with the icons on their domestic altars. These are handed down from generation to generation; they are individually named according to personal associations or for the tasks they are seen to perform — certain saints are imbued with powers over specific crops or periods of growth (cf. Ingham 1986:99), for example. *Doña* Eugenia told me about the icon she inherited from her in-laws: it was of the Black Christ of Esquipulas, which is one of the most common images of Christ on home altars, although rare in local churches. She told me, "He is a *costumbrista* and able to perform miracles, therefore we have corn *(Es de costumbrismo...es miliagroso ...por él tenemos maiz)*." In this regard, icons are like the ancestors and mountain spirits (dueños) (cf. Wilson 1995:60); the identification is enhanced by the fact that like the generality of K'iche' spirits, icons are "imbued with human attributes and human faults" (Wagley 1949:53) which are not necessarily those of living members of the household. Unlike other supernatural entities, icons are considered active members of K'iche' households, with distinct personalities. Sitting close to a woman's altar one day, I asked her the names of her children; she retorted, "You ask me the name of my children but not the name of my saint!"

Yet another reason for army discomfiture is that icons have their own, personal significance: one saint is not miraculous in the same way for everyone. Saints are different things to different people at different times; how people relate to them also varies. Sometimes they relate to them as intermediaries and at other times as the saint or deity itself; a person may go from one mode of relating to another within the same 'conversation' with the icon.

Community icons have been reclad in Indian or *ladino* dress; it is now the living who wear khaki or camouflage clothing (women even wear PAC caps). In El Quiché, the army did not attempt to change local concepts of God or the saints with whom they partially succeeded in associating themselves.[19] Unaware, at least initially, that Mayas assert one vision of God and the *ladino* state another, the result has been not what the army intended: it has linked itself to the ambivalence of the saints. In K'iche' eyes, both the army and the saints have the potential to be malevolent or benevolent; the saints grant fertility to the earth,[20] the smooth running of a business, and so on. However, both saints and army are perceived as capricious and able to wield power to harm, the saint by 'sending' illness and crop failure and the army by destroying villages and crops. Thus, by associating themselves with the saints and attempting to appropriate the symbolism of their powers (cf. Wilson 1995:241-242), the soldiers are more likely to have Indians internalize their demands, not through love, but through respect and fear. This echoes the Mayan conquest experience when fear led Indians to transform the guardians into Catholic saints: "If Indians did not at first accept the saints out of love, perhaps they learnt to do so out of fear — or desperation" (Watanabe 1992:233, n.10).

The army use both sides of the religious constructs of the devil and the saints or *dueños*, little realizing that *dueños* can be both. They also employ the sentiment of antagonism between local residents and outsiders to express, in comprehensible forms, their own position in the Indian experiential world. The manipulation of this conventionalized dichotomy dictates what the K'iche' can expect, not only from their 'saints' (now the army), but also how they should relate to one another and to outsiders (guerrilla-devils). In doing this, the army has assigned the powers of the disembodied spirits to individual and collective living people, imposing their own interpretations on the growing tendency for Indians, through "increased contact with the *ladino* world...to transfer characteristics once ascribed to the witz *(dueño)* to actual human beings, both *ladinos* and Indians" (Wagley 1949:56).

Powerful, ambivalent figures, whether corporeal or spiritual, are likely to become the focus of competing interest groups who try to manipulate them or their practices in a way which resonate in the object of manipulation. An effective area in which one can gain control over a person is that of confessional space, which includes forced denunciations and confessions under torture. Here the person becomes vulnerable; they are in a liminal state and more susceptible to the power of the figure to whom confession is made (cf. Franco 1985), be it diviner, saint image, saint icon, psychiatrist or torturer.

The Reconceptualization of Danger

Notions of Evil

The militarization of the countryside, the institution of the civil patrols and the army's attempts to 'get closer to the Indians' by trying to communicate with them in their own languages and not negating the existence God, all contributed to Indians' reconceptualization of danger. The army's task was facilitated by its power to commit horrendous atrocities: villagers soon discovered that denying army authority was likely to result in numerous deaths. The sense of danger built upon and altered existing K'iche' fears.

The K'iche' did not necessarily assimilate the army's message as they were intended to;[21] thus, while all villagers feared being killed or kidnapped, not everyone feared that they would suffer this fate at the hands of the same agent. Some, convinced by relentless military and paramilitary propaganda that there was a genuine need to guard their village from guerrilla attack, fear the rebel forces and are more than ready to comply with the army's exhortation: "Don't let the communist thieves into your village." Despite remembering how they had suffered at the army's hands, they fear that this monstrous entity described by the military could be even worse.[22] Others are more able to resist state-sponsored manipulation and continue to fear the military. The extent of people's receptiveness to the army's message depends on several factors, including their own agendas, preconceived notions of agents of evil, suggestibility and their exposure to army rhetoric and/or consciousness raising. People attend to different aspects of the discourses (at different times and in different contexts) and thus make idiosyncratic sense of them. Manipulation is therefore only successful to the degree to which particular resonance is actually achieved. A big stumbling block was the army's use of the concept of 'evil'; to the K'iche', this is not an absolute concept. Members of popular organizations, guerrilla groups, and various categories of sympathizers have a different, more positive image of 'evil' (as defined by the military) and perceive the agent of evil differently. Even women who had been sheltered from guerrilla teachings and who might therefore be expected to be more 'neutral', had negative views of the army because of their direct experience of the arbitrary death and destruction it brought in its wake.

Most women are shielded from direct army propaganda not only by language barriers (most soldiers speak Spanish) but because they tend to be confined to the home; they are usually the last to receive indoctrination. Army rhetoric often reaches them through gossip (which, when spread by people who are trusted, has more influence on women's thinking and behaviour than direct communication from the authorities) or a series of rumours; like Chinese whispers, the original message is likely to become distorted. Women are, on the whole, more conservative and less willing to be persuaded by novel rhetoric, whatever its source. At the end of the 1980s, the army attempted to reach illiterate women through distributing leaflets (Figure 2) with which they hoped the women would identify. The army's means of delivery was often counterproductive: for example, almost immediately after an army massacre in a nearby town, I found some of these leaflets on an idle bus in the bus station; on other occasions, villagers terrified by the sudden reappearance of army helicopters, found themselves merely showered with thousands of pieces of paper. Later, this type of leaflet was given to schoolchildren, with the message that they should give them to their mothers. But most women were unaffected by the pictures; they are impervious to the army's cover-up of their crimes because of their partial success in not having their memories eradicated (chapter seven).

The Spirits

People often make parallels between the army and known frightening spirits. The military, who arrived in the village with a death list and taken people away, are likened to devils leading condemned souls to hell. One village woman told me:

> During *la violencia* the soldiers took the place of the spirits. They were the ones who killed. At times they found children who had been left in their ham-

mocks when their mothers fled out of the house to hide and, without shame, they smashed their heads or they simply left them hanging in a noose from a tree...

Another woman simply said, "Previously we had the spirits, now we have the army." Women told me stories in which the army, like the spirits, appear in liminal areas such as rivers. One man who told me a fairly well known legend in which a spirit, the saq'xol, appears dressed in Mexican clothes, dances around, and then throws itself into the river and disappears, went on to tell me:

> My brother told me about a man whose wife told him to go and work in the corn which was very tall. So he went and there he encountered soldiers who had appeared from the river bank. They took away his hoe and took him away.

K'iche' anger and anxiety is often deflected and projected on to the spirit world; talk of increased spirit numbers and unhappiness, reflecting insurmountable fear of the army, is projected on to this more acceptable target. Talk of spirit violence has a psychological function, helping to avoid the real possibility of intra-communal violence (some villagers are looking for an excuse to avenge their dead and abducted kin).

People feel more vulnerable to unpredictable, inimical, forces since *la violencia* because of the conflation of fears of the army and/or *jefes* and the spirits. This is exacerbated by the fact that people's ways of dealing with death, and hence the spirits, were violated. Appropriate ritual *(costumbre)* was impossible during *la violencia*: fear drove many aj q'ij to give up their practices; others were killed. The performance of *costumbre* lessened for other reasons such as Protestant conversion and loss of faith because "innocent people were not protected by the ancestors" during *la violencia*. This shattering of K'iche' world views about protection left people with a profound sense of insecurity at a time when they were still afraid of the potential dangers of both supernatural and military forces.

The *jefes* are seen by some as the devil personified. *Doña* Candelaria said:

> Now the devil [the collective *jefes*] is constantly bringing evil and we are constantly suffering from it... They wanted to eat my husband alive...they wanted to kill him little by little so that he would feel it...they have the soul of a pure devil.

Many people, particularly widows, associate *jefes* with *brujos*, who have a well-known predilection for human meat (cf. Redfield 1934:179); in contrast, diviners (the *brujos*' 'good' counterpart) are associated with anti-state activities, thus turning the state's analogy between *brujos* and guerrillas upside down. In the villages, it is clear that *jefes* have functionally replaced *brujos*: both spy on others, harm them, and disappear them (cf. Madsen 1967 :630); both have the capacity to inflict damage 'invisibly' and both play dumb to any consequences of their evil actions. The traditional proclivity to intend harm via *brujería* made people more liable to denounce a threatening neighbour to the *jefe*; the sentiment is identical in both cases.

The difference between traditional and non-traditional dangers is in the directness of the violence. Bullets are more predictably fatal than the implements of *brujería*. *Jefes* are endowed with special powers, not because of their destiny but because of their less than imaginary guns. I am not suggesting that people do not continue to fear *brujos*; even *jefes* are afraid of them. However, some people conflate the powers of bullets and witchcraft. I was told, "If someone wants to do harm, then they enter the patrols where the devil goes and then they call the devil to do the bad things that God does not allow." *Brujería*, like malicious gossip, is seen to be even more widespread and terrifying than before *la violencia*. People feel very vulnerable to it, especially those who have lost their faith in the protective power of the ancestors. An additional problem is that few aj q'ij are willing to offer rituals of protection without which the life of every innocent man, woman or child is seen to be at risk.

For some, both aspects of itzel (spirits and witchcraft) are bound up with the equivocal forces of nature which have been defeated. Such people transfer their allegiance to the army and the *jefes*, believing that they are less likely to experience retaliation after soliciting their help than a *brujo's*. The belief that their secret is safe with the *jefe* may be naive but the realization that *jefes* and hit men (unlike *brujos*) are protected is accurate: it is extremely rare even for known murderers to be prosecuted.

Other villagers, while appearing to have been taken in by army rhetoric, view the *jefes* and the army itself to be the real danger. People fear the *jefes*, who are said 'to hold the law' and to 'make their own justice'; their 'justice' was seen to contradict the 'real' laws of the ancestors and those written in the constitution, the existence of which is only known to a minority.[23]

Doña Josefina:
> The *jefes* have been given the law...they call us subversives...meanwhile, after killing, they then go around raping women and stealing land and trees.

Doña Flora:
> Before the patrols we were in safe... But then the patrols started. With guns in their hands, they felt taller and above the rest of the people [i.e., like *ladinos*] and they wanted to kill.

Contrary to the military's objectives, it is not necessarily the guerrillas but the *jefes* who are perceived as murderous, treacherous, and dangerous. *Doña* Josefina remarked, "The way that Mario [the *jefe*] did the betrayals *(calumnias)* was by accusing ordinary people of being subversive. "The *jefes*

are also equated with general delinquency and given ironic titles; for example, Emol's most dangerous *jefe* is referred to as "the criminal Mr. Justice
(don Justicia)".

New Dangers

Some villagers are not taken in by either army or guerrilla propaganda.
They feel caught in the middle and are fearful of both aggressors, regardless
of whether or not they associate either or both with supernatural forces. As
one villager told me, "One thing is for sure and that is that we always feel
afraid because the guerrillas killed and so did the soldiers." Another Emolteco concurred: "The truth is we are afraid of the guerrillas and those who
are trying to make us turn against them. Neither the soldiers nor the guerrillas are in our favour...because whatever happens, something always
happens to us."

One man claimed, "Both sides came to kill." Yet the vast majority of
killings was carried out by the army which committed massacres and mass
kidnappings, including those of women and children; these crimes were then
blamed on the guerrilla. One astonishing army claim is that a Jesuit priest,
who had allegedly joined the guerrillas, was responsible for the Spanish Embassy massacre in 1980.[24]

Others reported that 'unknown people' *(desconocidos)* came to kill and
that the army blamed the guerrillas or, sometimes, Indians as a generality.
María, a K'iche' woman now living in the capital, told me: "The soldiers
always hide their faces and make out that the general population do these
things." It is not always easy to identify killers and kidnappers: armed groups
are often described as taking pains to disguise their identities in order to
mislead people about who they really are (cf. Manz 1988):

> Soldiers came to the village and stole people's clothes. They removed their
> own uniforms and donned the peasants' clothes instead. They pretended to be
> the guerrillas and asked villagers for the names of the religious people who
> they subsequently killed.

It seems that guerrillas and the army are variously named by people depending on where their sympathies lay and how they want to present themselves to those with whom they are conversing. People who identify guerrillas as the culprits are generally army supporters, although some villagers
make this attribution simply because it is the safest answer to give in the
current circumstances.

The Repercussions of the Proliferation of Danger

The army associates the dangers of guerrillas with communists and
Catholics and, in recent years, with villagers who abandon the patrol system.

The proliferation of 'enemies' continued until the entire Indian population was included. This, together with increasing mistrust among villagers, results in a situation where everyone fears the potential enemy in everyone else, leaving everyone feeling totally surrounded from outside and within. Villagers know there is a genuine likelihood of being afflicted by vengeance *(venganza)* or envy *(envidia)* — of which fear of witchcraft is only an extreme expression; no-one is uncontaminated by *la violencia.* The degradation of ideals of self-restraint and non-violence resulting from a combination of army indoctrination and the establishment of different norms and values in order to survive in a hopeless situation have increased fears of witchcraft and *envidia.* Recent violations of cultural norms have left people unsure of what is permissible behaviour on both moral and legal grounds.

The objects of fear have multiplied in everyday life and fear has become more intense. People feel there is no escape from the violence owing to the disintegration of relatively safe spaces within the community. The sanctuary offered by safe communal spaces in general and by the home in particular has been appropriated, in different ways, by both guerrilla and para-military organizations (cf. Franco 1985).

A lack of consensus about where danger lies has led to the inclusion of family and neighbours in perceptions of the dangerous 'other'. In the circumstances, it is not hard to imagine that rumour and fear dominate people's perception of the world. The rumours are revealing for they clearly express partly developed but usually unacknowledged collective fears. In their rapid development and dissemination, they represent a kind of instant mythologizing in which terrifying new experiences are reinterpreted in terms of more familiar constructs.

Conclusion

La violencia was not the point of origin for clashes of interest or *envidia,* lack of support between villagers or some people's ability to transform themselves into malevolent forms. But *la violencia,* together with other recent social changes, created massive tensions which not only intensified and channelled conflict but altered the directions and patterns of violence. It brought the coercive powers of the state and its political opposition — expressed in the capricious powers of soldiers, spirits, and guerrillas — into everyday life to such an extent that they could no longer be ignored. Internal violence erupted across hamlets and religious/political factions and raised the stakes of social criticism and political action.

Rapid social change in Emol brought "new values and norms into conflict with indigenous ones" which, together with "the creation of new relationships and the fundamental modification of old ones" resulted in "an increased preoccupation with beliefs in sorcery and witchcraft" (Marwick 1965:247-8). In these circumstances, the stories of *el bin* have particular resonance in a community where people live together and consider themselves to be the same but fear others' concealed interests.[25] The proliferation of internal enemies in times of upheaval and rapid social change frustrates the need for community; the elaboration of the malevolent aspects of the spirits as an outside agency of danger has become not only something around which to crystallize tangible fears but also an alternative 'other' around which some sense of community can be formed. Comments such as "You can't do any-thing" are indicative of thwarted communal efforts to survive.

Notes

1. One woman told me that when she heard that her cow had eaten corn from a neighbour's field, she immediately went to find out how much compensation she had to pay for the damage.

2. Fear of strangers (including ethnographers) existed well before *la violencia*. Oakes (1951) reports how local people in Todos Santos, where she conducted fieldwork in the 1940s, initially treated her (and other strangers) with suspicion. She was unable to develop a relationship of trust with the villagers.

3. cf. Watanabe (1992:64): "Chimaltecos associated socially empty or unfamiliar space with distant quotidian time — that is, with the dormant period of night — regardless of the absolute location or relative distance from the *pueblo*".

4. In some areas, elements of the witz (*dueño*; mountain guardian) persist in the very real, but more ambivalent, figure of the devil (Watanabe 1992).

5. In Santiago el Palmar, El Quiché, the *brujo* is called a win (Saler 1969). In Santiago, Chimaltenango, people describe two types of *brujo*: the xhwiin and the ky'aawil (Watanabe 1992:191).

6. See chapter nine, note 2.

7. Not all dreams are believed to be caused by the spirits. Some women recount frightening dreams about the army in which there are no signs of spirits. These are, nevertheless, viewed as premonitory. No woman I ever asked remembered dreaming about the massacres of their menfolk (cf. Bettelheim 1986:128, fn.10)

8. In some areas, everyone is believed to possess the power to take the shape of their animal counterpart (Kaplan 1956:365-7) but in Emol, most people are not even aware that they have one. In some areas, part of a person's inner soul is thought to wander from its human body at night — during sleep, when a person is sick, has sexual intercourse, feels strong emotions or is dying. In others, ancestors can punish individuals by knocking out part of an individual's inner soul and releasing their animal counterparts from the safety of their special sanctuaries (Vogt 1970). In yet others, only powerful elders and aj q'ij have animal spirits which they can use to bring individuals as a punishment for social transgressions (Villa Rojas 1947). These beliefs about the nature of the self are variations on a common Mesoamerican theme; the capacity for humans to convert themselves or to have spiritual counterparts is basic to ancient as well as contemporary Mesoamerican mythohistories and religions (Tedlock 1985, Erice 1985, Musgrave-Portilla 1982). Scholars have traced these beliefs to pre-Conquest cultures in Central Mexico and to the interplay of Mesoamerican and Spanish understandings of indigenous cultures

(Foster 1944; Tranfo 1979).

9. Although it might seem that the developmentally delayed are the most obvious candidates for *los bines*, the concept also reinforces the high value placed on behavioural conformity.

10. In the Maya village of Chan Kom, *brujos* are said to somersault backwards nine times to facilitate transformation (Redfield and Villa Rojas 1934:179).

11. Limestone which is boiled with dried corn to soften it.

12. This is a reference to the Mesoamerican god Huehuecoyotl, whose name means 'the old coyote, the nahual (spirit essence) of this particular god'. Like the transforming *brujo*, Mesoamerican gods transform themselves, taking on the disguise of their special nahual (Musgrave-Portilla 1982:6-9). The element of chicanery is emphasized for the K'iche' listener by the reference to the coyote, the ultimate trickster figure.

13. cf. the story of a shepherd who lost many sheep to coyotes: he climbed a tree to guard his flock and from that vantage point, watched an Indian family remove their clothes and turn into coyotes (Oakes 1951:173). Considering how loth Indians are to say anything which may disturb community harmony, this could well be an allegorical account of plain sheep stealing.

14. This sexist story implies that the mother coyote is teaching her cubs to be guerrillas. Women are 'other' oriented in K'iche' culture, in-marrying 'strangers'.

15. Referring to the images of the saints, one Q'eqchi' catechist said that the elders "believe more in what's here on earth than what is in the sky" (Wilson 1995: 181). In El Quiché, elders and 'pure' Catholics (and many 'new' ones) also revere the images.

16. Alcohol brings people into communication with spiritual beings. cf. Allen (1988); Harvey (1991).

17. I make this analogy because I think that the saints are like psychotherapists for the K'iche'. In neither case does the person emulate these aspects as they 'are' but as they are perceived (ie. through the meaning attributed to them by culture). This, in turn, changes the icons themselves in the eyes of the K'iche' and so on.

18. During the 1850s, dressing Catholic icons in indigenous clothing was one of the main features of the War of the Castes in Yucatan (Villa Rojas 1978:100).

19. cf. Wilson (1995:320-1): In areas where demonizing mountain spirits proved unsuccessful, the army changed tactics, reshaping them in order to insinuate itself through traditional forms of imaging. The contradictions in this approach undermined army attempts to turn Mayans into nationalistic Guatemalans. Indigenous catechists also utilize the concept of mountain spirits as a vehicle to enhance ethnic identity rather than to recreate traditional communities.

20. During planting, the Q'eqchi' petition all the gods who might help them, including the saints. This is done not so much to propitiate fearsome powers but is a practical activity to ensure life, not that these aims are mutually exclusive (Wilson 1995).

21. I do not wish to over stress the intentional aspect because I believe that the army's actions are not necessarily always conscious.

22. A repressive regime can so disintegrate the personality of adults that they can "firmly believe what they would know to be false if their anxiety permitted them to know it" (Bettelheim 1986:290).

23. Awareness of the existence of the Constitution and people's rights under it has increased since the creation of MINUGUA in 1995. Today, several human rights agencies also work towards raising awareness of the Constitution and the Peace Accords.

24. See chapter four, note 18.

25. They also deal with women's subversion of male authority and other aspects of gender relations.

11

The Exhumations and Beyond

Returning to Emol

I returned to Guatemala in August 1993 to find that much had changed. Three years previously, escalating violence had brought the country to the brink of a repetition of *la violencia*; not only had this not happened but there was a new, tentative acknowledgement of the concept of plurality, be it on political, religious or ethnic grounds. Two events the previous year had focused attention on indigenous rights: first, the continental campaign '500 Years of Resistance' protesting against the official celebrations of the quincentenary of the 'discovery' of the Americas and second, the award of the Nobel Peace Prize to an indigenous Guatemalan woman, Rigoberta Menchú.

There had been a dangerous moment for Guatemala's fledgling democracy a few months earlier when President Jorge Serrano Elías (1991-1993) at-tempted an *'auto-golpe'* (self-authored *coup d'état*) in May; the military's response was an expressed wish to appoint a new president of its own choosing. Popular organizations, backed by the international community, rejected this possibility and named the former Human Rights Ombudsman, Ramiro de León (1993-1995), as President. The appointment led to an in-creased presence for Mayan organizations in the national political sphere. Three months later, the Mayan Peoples' Assembly (*Asemblea del Pueblo Maya*; APM) was formed to ensure and promote Mayan participation in on-going political discussions regarding the transition to fully democratic rule. The Civil Society Assembly (ASC), whose members deigned to support the army or the rebels, also began demanding inclusion in the peace talks between the government and the Guatemalan National Revolutionary Union (URNG) which had begun in 1991; the talks, which eventually led to the Peace Accords signed on 29 December 1996, became a vehicle to articulate Mayan demands. These range from increased rights and political autonomy to the broader process of national political and institutional reform (Bastos and Camus 1995). Voicing such demands had been unthinkable in 1990.

President de León Carpio had been office for just a few months when I returned to Guatemala in 1993, yet political change at the macro level was almost palpable. His government included several Mayans, thus furthering indigenous demands within the state and paving the way to the 1995 elections when political parties not vetted by the army were at last allowed to put up candidates. The New Democratic Front *(Frente Democrático Nueva Guatemala)* fielded some very famous candidates from the national human rights sphere: Amílcar Méndez and Nineth García (the founders of GAM and CERJ respectively) and Rosalina Tuyuc (the current head of CONAVIGUA), all of whom were elected to the Congress of Deputies. These political changes increased the possibility of both symbolic and material defiance (cf. Rollins 1985:126).

As I travelled to Emol by bus, I wondered how much of the burgeoning change at national level had percolated down to the local. We passed a patrol base where patrollers stood, guns in hand. The next patrol base was deserted; its wooden doors were shut and the blue and white Guatemalan flag lay like a crumpled, dirty rag on the roof. This juxtaposition of manned and deserted patrol bases proved to be typical: patrol units, hamlets, and entire villages made different decisions on whether or not to continue with the patrols. What was really new was that people were less concerned about being attacked by other villages' patrols than at any time since the system was inaugurated (which is not to say that they had dismissed the possibility altogether; anything but).

The bus stopped at the bottom of the hill leading to the patrol base in Emol's main square, which I had to pass to reach the hamlet where I was going stay. I asked the driver to take me to the usual stop. He refused. My initial thought, that the new bus stop represented a loosening of control, was hopelessly wrong: former patrol chiefs *(jefes)* had threatened to kill any foreigner looking for more clandestine graves. Clearly the driver had heard about this and, for safety's sake, insisted I get off. I found myself outside one of the five Protestant churches built in Emol since 1990 by North American missionaries who give up their summer vacations to bring their particular brands of Christianity to this remote highland village.

Physically the village looked much the same (except for the new chapels) but there was something different in the air. The market, closed following a mass abduction in 1982, had still not re-opened; only one man was sitting under the arches of the administration building, selling his apples. As I watched him, I was surprised to see that the mayor's office was open and even more surprised to see Julio, a former military commissioner, enter it; he had been elected mayor *(alcade)* earlier in the year. People are happy with this arrangement as they now have someone to whom to take their problems who can arrive at a more peaceful resolution of disputes. The reopening of this small office, the lowest rung on the national, civil administrative hierarchy, is an important, if symbolic, token of the lessening of local impunity.

In Emol, 1992 was the year when the clandestine graves of the village's massacre victims were exhumed and the patrols ordered to turn in their guns to the army base in the departmental capital; about half of Emol's patrollers immediately walked away from their hated duties. *Doña* Flora told me that men were patrolling one day and gone the next. Two hamlets (including Kotoh) disbanded their patrols completely; two kept theirs. In the remaining two hamlets (including Emol Central), about half the men decided to continue to patrol, which effectively dissolved the system; it also created new splits in the community. One of Kotoh's less guilty *jefes*, frightened by the loss of his powerful position and fearing vengeance witchcraft, converted from 'pure' Catholicism (*costumbrismo*) to protestantism; another *jefe* fled to the coast for a while. Mario, Emol's most hated *jefe* and the head of all the village's patrols, remained in the village as always. He and 'continuing' patrollers continue to exert a baleful presence; their illicit power continues, if in a muted form.

Despite the lessening of impunity represented by the reopening of the civil administration and the disarming of the patrols, trouble continues in Emol as it does in other villages. Following the exhumations, some former *jefes* and patrollers — including Mario, his brothers-in-law, and their cronies — stepped up their intimidation of the local population, especially widows. The exhumation created a precedent and they fear that more could follow; that there have been no more testifies not only to the effectiveness of their intimidatory tactics but to continuing impunity. Their fears of being formally identified as the perpetrators have less to do with the possibility of prosecution under national law than with fears of local retribution and vengeance. On the other hand, local perpetrators fear that just as people learnt to manipulate them as agents of revenge (chapter five), they will learn to use the *'ladino'* judicial system[1] in the same way against them. Although some victims' relatives are learning about their legal rights from human rights agencies such as CONAVIGUA, GAM, and CERJ (and latterly, the promotion of the Peace Accords), the vast majority have little faith in a legal system which has failed them in the past. Nevertheless, *jefes* continue to target members of these organizations even though most of their members, like the majority of Indian survivors, are too scared to take any action against them. The *jefes'* paranoia has led to further killings even though there is in, in fact, very little action their opponents can take. For example, in May 1993, in San Pedro Jocopilas, patrol *jefes* are believed to be responsible for the deaths of eleven community members they described dismissively as 'thieves', a common synonym for guerrillas; they were probably patrol resisters. Such occurrences are more common in more militarized areas (cf. Jay 1993; Solomon 1995; Popkin 1996).

Most indigenous people, whether they have a story to tell or a story to hide, remain ignorant of many of the implications of the decisions being made at national level. The bold and the fearless with a tale to tell tended to support GAM's campaign, which began in 1988, for an objective investigation into human rights abuses in Guatemala. This was taken up by the ASC but rejected by the URNG for fear of jeopardizing the peace negotiations; the URNG's Political-Diplomatic Commission even acceded to the army's demands that the proposals to establish a Truth Commission be removed from the Comprehensive Human Rights Accord signed in March 1994. This concession was essential in order to secure the agreement, which came into immediate effect. (The Guatemalan Bishops' Conference was so outraged that it formed its own 'truth commission'— officially entitled 'The Recovery of Historical Memory Project' (REMHI) — which would name the perpetrators and the victims the politicians seemed to want to forget.) Shortly thereafter, the URNG changed its position and, in June 1994, signed an agreement with the government to establish a 'Commission for the Historical Clarification of the Violations of Human Rights and Acts of Violence Which Have Caused Suffering to the Guatemalan Population', known as the 'Commission for Historical Clarification' (CEH) or 'Truth Commission' for short. Its stated objective is 'to clarify with complete objectivity, equity, and impartiality, the human rights violations and acts of violence which have caused suffering to the Guatemalan people and which are linked to the armed conflict' between 1960[2] and the signing of the Peace Accords in December 1996. The Commission was to be established immediately thereafter and sit for only six months, although the agreement does allow for its operation to be extended to twelve months. It was eventually established on 1 August 1997. There was one advantage to this delayed start: it gave the REMHI time to collect 5,000 testimonies and evidence of 300 mass graves, all of which they handed over to the official Truth Commission.

Five months after the agreement to form a Truth Commission was signed, the U.N. Mission for the Verification of Human Rights in Guatemala (MINUGUA) was established in November 1994. Although a joint invitation was issued to the U.N. by the URNG and the Guatemalan government following the 'Comprehensive' agreement in March,[3] this is a separate initiative from the Truth Commission: MINUGUA is concerned with current human rights abuses, whereas the Truth Commission deals with those in the past, a distinction which makes little sense to the survivors of *la violencia* for whom the atrocities of 'that painful time' continue to be part of the lived present. Indeed, a separation between 'then' and 'now' is meaningless and incomprehensible to people who are still being terrorized by the perpetrators of 'past' atrocities. A further difference between MINUGUA and the CEH is that the former can (and did) indite individuals who commit human rights violations in the present whereas the Truth Commission can neither name nor punish those guilty of human rights violations during the 'armed conflict' between 1960 and 1996. Deciding what is and what is not part of the 'armed conflict' in what was largely a 'dirty war' is extremely problematic. Even the perpetrators are confused. Initially reassured by MINUGUA's decision that institutions, not individuals, will be held responsible for the crimes of *la violencia* (which has eerie echoes of Mayan beliefs concerning spirit invasion),[4] they were frightened by the news that, shortly after its creation, MINUGUA indited *jefes* and patrollers from Joyabaj, El Quiché, for the murder of the local leader of the movement to disband the patrols; they have not been reassured by the fact that government agents have yet to execute the arrest warrants. Local perpetrators would have more cause for concern if they realized that the patrol system, and especially the atrocities its members were encouraged and sometimes forced to commit, were designed to be 'deniable'. This legal fiction means that, if politically expedient, local killers could, at some future point, be offered to the public as the ultimate perpetrators of *la violencia*.

In the meantime, the intellectual authors of *la violencia* remain part of the military and political elites, protected by the decision regarding the placing of blame which was confirmed in the Law of Reconciliation (the Amnesty Law) which came into effect in January 1997. This law had the URNG's consent even though it violates the anti-impunity clauses of the Comprehensive Agreement on Human Rights signed in March 1994. Leaders of the human rights movement opposed the amnesty; they claim, with justification, that the combination of this law and a weak Truth Commission[5] protects the instigators and perpetrators of the atrocities committed during *la violencia* and its aftermath. Being able to avoid accepting personal responsibility for past political crimes means that impunity persists and the rule of law remains remote. There is, then, an air of unreality about the killers' fear of being tried, judged, and imprisoned.

There is little unreality about many villagers' continuing fears of their *jefes* — the current threat is, "Just you wait until MINUGUA has gone, then we'll get you." Patrol resisters and human rights workers who campaigned for the withdrawal of military bases, especially from areas of refugee repatriation, showed great personal courage in increasing their demands for an end to the illegally enforced participation in the patrols as well as an end to conscription. Although these aims have now been achieved, protesters' troubles are not over: in the claustrophobic world of the highland village, they are still defined in terms of 'otherness' with all the dangers this entails (chapter five). Petitioning for exhumations before the Peace Accords were signed indicates courage of almost foolhardy proportions; in some areas, it still does.

The Exhumation in Emol[6]

Widows' Motives

The prime mover behind the exhumation was *doña* Eugenia. She had dreamed for years of reclaiming her son Gilberto's body from the ravine and re-interring it in the village cemetery so that when her time came (which, at over seventy years of age, she supposed was imminent), she could be laid to rest beside him. *Doña* Eugenia explained why it was so important that Gilberto should be helped on his way to the after-life:

> I wanted him [Gilberto] to see me. I wanted my son to be there [in the cemetery], but nothing. But if he had seen me, then I would have died too because it would have spooked me because he was dead and so, if it was he who looked at me, then I would have died.
>
> [And not now?]
>
> No, there are no ghosts because he is in the cemetery.
>
> [And your husband can't spook you?]
>
> No.
>
> [Why not?]
>
> Because I did not feel he was there. I **had** felt that my son was, but not any more.

Another reason for *doña* Eugenia's desire to rebury the dead in the village cemetery was that she was frightened of two of Emol's most violent *jefes* (Mario and his Kotoh brother-in-law) who spied on the women when they visited the clandestine graves and then threatened to kill them. On a more mundane level, *doña* Eugenia's arthritic knees made it difficult for her to visit her son in his inappropriate grave.

As Director and, more importantly, the eldest woman in the widows' group, *doña* Eugenia set the agenda and she wanted to exhume the bodies of the men killed in Emol's first massacre. Her close friends within the group supported her desire to exhume Gilberto's grave, even though none of their husbands was buried with him; they empathized with the beliefs which motivated her — that is, that the bodies are the repositories of the spirits of the murdered men whose corpses have to be reburied with appropriate ritual in order for their spirits to finally make the journey to the World of the Dead. Also among her supporters were women who wanted to see the killers get their come-uppance.

To the perpetrators of this atrocity, the bodies were evidence of crimes they wanted to hide (unfortunately for them, the burial of victims of later murders and massacres were so slipshod that corpses are sometimes exposed following heavy rains or landslides; *don* Juan told me that when this happens, patrollers either remove the bodies or chop them into little pieces *(machetearlos)* with their *machetes*). *Doña* Eugenia therefore had to keep her plans secret to prevent the bodies being removed before they could be exhumed, which has been known to happen at other sites. She showed considerable pride in the fact that she had managed to work on the exhumation for three years unbeknownst to the *jefes* (and for that matter, me; she had begun working on the exhumation whilst I was still in Emol). She told me she had not even discussed the matter within her family:

> I said nothing to the woman [Vicenta, her daughter-in-law] because she drinks and she could have said something. So I said nothing. Only with Saturnino and Martín [her grandsons] did I speak, warning them not to breathe a word.

Saturnino and Martín are *doña* Eugenia's main confidantes. They have always been supportive of her; they had encouraged her to join the widows' group and supported her CONAVIGUA activities from the outset. They also supported her efforts to exhume their father's grave, although Saturnino asked her what she thought the outcome would be:

> She said that they [the widows] would succeed in putting the killers in the jail. She said that they would do the exhumations and then they [the killers] would go to jail. I asked if this would really happen, and she said, yes, she had gone to the people of CONAVIGUA and they had told her that it was possible. So then I said, "Well, if it's possible, then O.K., go ahead and do it, but if it's not, then it would be worse if another problem in the community arose", and that she had to consider this. But she told me that they had done exhumations in other places and that with CONAVIGUA it would be possible, that they would arrange the exhumations and that in this way the people would see what happened and who did the massacres. So this is how she began to process the papers that were needed.

When I asked Saturnino if he had been worried about how his grandmother would cope with seeing her son's body, he replied immediately, "Yes, yes, because imagine seeing..." He could not continue. Saturnino also admitted that he had been concerned about what could happen if his grandmother had not been successful:

> Well, what would happen if she didn't manage it or the people of Emol heard about this and they came to kill again, because the patrols are[7] still there and, instead of doing the exhumation...we fell into their hands again...there would be more problems. But she told me not to worry, that it was in her hands.

Practical support came from *doña* Manuela, the daughter of her niece *doña* Consuelo. Although they collaborated — *doña* Manuela wrote the letters, composed the petitions, did the paperwork; *doña* Eugenia made the endless trips to Guatemala City — they also compete in their claims as to who was the prime mover in the project. *Doña* Manuela admitted to me that

it had not been her idea to begin the process; this had been planted by
CONAVIGUA. She had agreed to help once the women decided they
wanted to go ahead. People told her she was mad to get involved, especially
as she was not among the 'wives of the cadavers'; her own husband was
buried in the cemetery (mukann). *Doña* Manuela's motives were mixed: her
education had brought her greater 'consciousness'; she was also sufficiently
angry about her own experiences during *la violencia.* Her parents had fled
to the city, taking the children with them. She told me,

> The patrols who did this were the same ones who burnt our house. They took
> everything we had. We had chickens and turkeys and they stole them as well.
> They were the same ones who did this. This is why we went to participate in
> the exhumation. Because they did this to us too.

Doña Manuela's father, who had been President of Kotoh's Catholic
Action group, was assassinated in Guatemala City; she believes that Emolteco men betrayed him to a death squad. She wanted justice to be done; she
wanted to free the living widows from the calumny bruited about by the *jefes*
that the women themselves were responsible not only for the deaths of their
own menfolk but also all other 'unnatural' deaths in the village. The bottom
line is that she helped because *doña* Eugenia asked her to; she could not
refuse her mother's aunt.

Doña Eugenia also received support from *don* Juan, a former CUC
activist who lives in Kotoh; he helps the widows as best he can and encourages them to join CONAVIGUA. Although his wife's brother was in the
same grave as Gilberto, *don* Juan's reasons for supporting the exhumation
were neither personal nor religious: he wanted it done for "the experience,
for history". He wanted people to see the awful things that had been done in
the community and to think about them, which is the last thing most villagers
want to do:

> We thought it was better [for people] to see that there are things that should
> not be done and that's that. If they [the bodies] were in the ravines and one of
> us dies tomorrow, then they [the dead] will never be taken out [exhumed], so
> it's better to take them out so there is a record *(historia),* so people won't do
> it again. It will awaken their sorrow and they will realize that it's not worth
> while to do these things because it was written in the newspapers *(prensa)* etc.

Achieving 'justice' was a commonly expressed aim. *Doña* Eugenia, for
example, believes not only that the killers should go to jail for their crimes
but had expected that this would follow automatically when she began soliciting the exhumations. She was completely unaware of the legal processes
involved; she was (and remains) incognizant of the concept of impunity,
despite living with its consequences all her life. This is not unusual; the average indigenous woman just does not know the structures whereby the guilty

can be brought to book. *Doña* Eugenia and her friends thought that CONA-VIGUA had all the answers and the power to move the process along so that the *jefes* would be at least removed from their post.[8] *Doña* Eugenia's understanding of the situation led her to make repeated trips to the CONAVIGUA office to find out when this would happen; she told me that they repeatedly told her 'to be patient'. Time was something the widows did not have, especially seventy-two year old *doña* Eugenia: at that time (1990-1992), the longer the process took, the greater the threat to their lives as the perpetrators became increasingly convinced that nothing would happen to them.

The Forensic Team Arrives

Doña Eugenia's house in Kotoh became the base for the forensic team, who took their meals there. Kotoh widows rallied round to cook for them, rather in the style of any major life crisis event.

As the long-awaited and long-hoped for exhumation began, the solidarity of the widows' group flew apart. The women's common purpose in seeking the exhumation had hidden the fact that they were as riven by factions, suspicions, and rivalry as the rest of the community, despite being marginalized by it. They had never reached a consensus on the proper way for a woman to conduct herself in the new situation of war-widowhood; there were almost as many ideas as women. Presented with the new and harrowing experience of the exhumation process, they floundered in a welter of conflicting responses and emotions.

A major split occurred between the widows of Kotoh and Emol Central on the first day of the exhumation. *Doña* Flora, who lives in Emol Central, had been invited to *doña* Eugenia's house to participate in the exhumation. She was eager to go because, apart from wanting to participate in the event, she had finally gathered sufficient courage to reveal that she knew where her murdered son was buried and wanted an opportunity to talk to the CONAVIGUA representatives about it. *Doña* Eugenia had been keen for her to do this and suggested that she bring other women from Emol Central to do the same; *doña* Flora brought fellow-widows' group members *doña* Josefina and *doña* Ana. The CONAVIGUA representatives were unresponsive to *doña* Flora's approach, scolding her irritably for thinking she could get an exhumation done without 'working for it' (following the proper procedure). Other Kotoh widows echoed this view: "You can't just take them out on the road, just like that, it isn't a game!" Worse still for *doña* Flora was the silence which greeted her admission that she came from Emol Central; it seemed to her that the CONAVIGUA women thought she was in cahoots with Mario. She felt deceived by the Kotoh widows, especially *doña* Eugenia and *doña* Manuela; for their part, they were angry with the widows from Emol Central. It was hinted that the Kotoh women were annoyed because the Emol Central widows did not make a financial contribution to the meal. It is more likely that the Kotoh women's intense feelings got the better of them at the moment when they realized that the exhumation was actually going to happen, right now, triggering feelings of 'ownership' of the grave: all the men in these clandestine graves were from Kotoh (as were the men who killed them). Kotoh residents tend to blame their traditional rivals in Emol Central for the deaths and it is true the village's most violent *jefe* and the instigator of this massacre (Mario) lives there. Even Kotoh's most aggressive *jefe* can be associated with Emol Central as he is Mario's brother-in-law, friend, and supporter. With feelings running high, the Emol Central widows found themselves categorized by where they lived and felt distinctly unwelcome. *Doña* Flora and her companions declined to stay for the meal prepared in *doña* Eugenia's house and returned home. The relationship between the widows of Kotoh and Emol Central broke down. When I spoke to *doña* Flora about this incident, she used the obfuscating mode of speech K'iche's employ to avoid admitting to conflict, despite our close relationship.

Within days, the solidarity of the Kotoh widows' group also collapsed. The competitive claims of *doña* Eugenia and *doña* Manuela began it all. Watching her niece translate for the forensic team, *doña* Eugenia felt her 'ownership' of the process was being usurped by the younger woman whose husband was not in the grave. *Doña* Eugenia bridled at this lack of respect. Nevertheless, *doña* Manuela stayed with her great-aunt when, a few days later, a dispute broke about between *doña* Eugenia and another of her nieces, *doña* Candelaria (whose husband was not in this particular grave either). I never did find out what the argument was about but it was serious enough for the Kotoh widows to split into two groups, one of which remained based at *doña* Eugenia's house while the other stayed with *doña* Candelaria in the school building — her sons Santos (a policeman) and Esteban (a soldier) forbade all mention of the exhumation at home. Establishing a centre to provide food and rest for grieving widows in the village school was *doña* Candelaria's last act for and on behalf of the widows' group with which she had been involved since its inception. Relations between *doña* Eugenia and *doña* Candelaria became very strained and although they have since improved, the camaraderie which existed as they secretly planned the exhumation has gone for good. Despite all this friction, several women, including *doña* Manuela, insist that the widows continued to support and console each other through the agonizing experience of the exhumations.

The widows were unable to contain their intense pain when the bodies were exhumed. The condition of the corpses revealed a level of humiliation which they had been unable to imagine before seeing it with their own eyes. It remains incomprehensible to them. Hands tied behind their backs, feet tied together, the beaten men's faces had been mutilated with knives before they were buried alive, creating images which could not be assimilated into cultural categories of death — these were 'bad' deaths beyond people's worst nightmares. Years of frozen grief poured from the women. *Doña* Flora told me that during the exhumations, Kotoh widows in *doña* Eugenia's house had got drunk, screamed and cried, and thrown themselves on the floor.

The exhumation exposed a reality far worse than any the women had anticipated even though they had heard and discussed the rumours which had circulated the village for years about how their men had died (chapter seven). The bodies testified to the extremes to which humans, their own neighbours, can go to defile another human being, leaving survivors with increased anxiety. The only way to make sense of it was to conclude that the perpetrators could not be human. But these people still remained in close proximity; coming face to face with what these men were capable of doing was something that survivors could not put behind them. Saturnino:

> Until then, we had only wondered how they might have been [killed], but to see them made one feel something inside which is very strong. At times, one wonders what type of people could have done this and one thinks that they cannot be human beings to have been able to do this, this is the reaction that one has, the way that one thinks about it.

Foreign observers at the exhumation say that *doña* Eugenia's pain when she witnessed the exhumation was almost palpable (this is not something that the K'iche' would ever admit to); they told me that when she saw her son's remains, she had emitted a scream which was primal. Other widows told me she had been on the verge of dying of 'sadness'. A year later, she described the exhumation process and her pain to me:

> They were here for eight days taking them out.

> [And how did you feel during this time?]

> I was crying. I went to buy my two measures [bottles] of local rum (*octavos de guaro*: kuxa) but I didn't drink it. When they took them out, my rum (kuxa) was still there. Gilberto was the first [body] which came out *(salió)*. The six [corpses] were like this [she gestured how they lay], one on top of the other, face downwards *(boca abajo está)*.[9] I recognized his clothes. I told them that this was my family. I was crying. They had chopped his head with a *machete*, on the head, like this [she indicated the back of her head] — not the others, their bodies were whole. They had chopped off a piece like this [showing me again], only his little face *(carita)* remained.

> [And it did not frighten you to see him like this?]

> I was not afraid but I had pain because it was still my body and he had his clothes. He was tied up [like an animal] and he was face down, he was face down, he was. When they took off his clothes, you could see that he [the *jefe*] had cut him across the back.

[This must have been extremely painful for you to see.]

It was painful, but what can I do?

[And it's not more painful now than before?]

No, now I'm forgetting the sadness a little.

The bodies were taken away to a hospital morgue in the provincial capital where the forensic team carried out analyses of bones and artifacts found in the graves in order to identify the remains and ascertain cause and time of death. Some women, including *doña* Eugenia, went "to visit the corpses in hospital where the doctors are attending to them" in the months between exhumation and reburial in an attempt to normalize and universalize the process, but the healing of both the contorted and defaced corpses and the women's pained, diminished selves could not be achieved.

It was eight months before the bodies were returned for reburial. The widows had not expected this long time lapse and were disappointed that massacre victims could not be commemorated on next the Day of the Dead (1 November). A communal mass was said to mark the event instead (*doña* Flora attended this mass but had 'not had the time' to visit her former friends in Kotoh since). Martin told me that when the bodies were eventually reburied in the village cemetery, "All the wives, how they screamed and cried." Ten years of blocked anguish, when local power holders had effectively banned the expression of grief, offers of condolence or help, funerary ritual and memorial services, led to huge outpourings of pent up pain.

The funeral had taken place only a few months before my return and emotions were still raw. Women said that the massacre victims' spirits were appeased by the funeral and that they now leave the living alone; they were looking forward to being able to share in the collective commemoration in the village cemetery on the Day of the Dead in a few months' time (see chapter eight). This is an important consequence of the exhumation, as one of *doña* Eugenia's grandsons explained:

> I would say it was good to do the exhumation because we all visit the graves on All Saints Day and our custom here is that we do this together; it is not appropriate for us to have to go down the ravines in order to do this because God has told us that we have our place. If we die we die, but we have to stay in one place only. Even animals shouldn't been thrown away just like that, they must be buried. And our having to go and pray in the ravines is no good. We should go like everyone else to the cemetery to do this. Because we can now, we are happier... Well, we are not happy, but at least we know that my father is in the cemetery.

Doña Eugenia told me that she felt calmer knowing that the men were in the cemetery and not in the ravines, partly because she is now able to visit them whenever she feels like it:

> I still feel the loss of my child, although less so now that he is in the cemetery. I am a little happier because of this. Not like before when he was down in the ravines. I was so unhappy then, so sad. I couldn't go and visit him there but, now, I am able to go and visit him; I am free now to visit him unlike before when I was afraid that if I went down the ravine to his grave then they [the *jefes*] would come and kill me. I did go down the ravine to visit him, but I went covertly, looking around me on all sides. I only went there to leave a few little candles for him and then I fled back to my home, hoping that no one noticed where I had been. I went about four times; we went as a group, none of us dared to say a word to one another as we crept down the ravine, we went in silence, we told the children not to utter a peep and we prayed that the dogs would not bark to signal what we were doing. But now if we want to go and leave a candle we can.

Being able to celebrate the Day of the Dead with the rest of the community 'normalizes' massacre victims' social and spiritual fate. *Don* Juan explains:

> They can adorn their graves and so on on the Day of the Dead. Now things are out in the open so they can go to the cemetery without fear, they can go to the place where God says they [the dead] ought to be left. They know where the bones are.

For some, the fact that the dead are properly reburied marks the end of their mission. For other survivors — usually the more politicized — the mission is only half accomplished because the perpetrators are still at large and justice has not been achieved. Some women feel their mission has barely begun; there are still so many missing bodies.

After the Exhumation

Belief in the exhumation process has grown slowly because of continuing threats from *jefes* and military commissioners; in many places, the abolition of their posts (in 1995 and 1996 respectively) has not deprived them of power. Yet confidence grows with each successful exhumation and, although there have been no further exhumations in Emol to date, *doña* Eugenia's success in exhuming the victims of the massacre which marked the introduction of intra-village terror has contributed to local confidence in the process. By 1996, the Guatemalan Forensic Anthropology Team (*Equipo de Antropologia Forense*; EAFG), a Guatemalan NGO, had more work than it could handle. They exhumed seventeen mass graves in 1996 and now that they have three teams conducting this work, anticipate being able to carry out a further twenty in 1997. There are literally hundreds more graves which could be exhumed.

In Emol itself, there had been no public mention of the massacre or its victims, let alone the possibility of exhuming them, until the exhumations actually began. Some villagers are still reluctant to mention the matter; they believe the army will exact its revenge later, as well it might. Their fears are based on the current behaviour of former and continuing *jefes*, who resumed their campaign of intimidation against widows immediately the outside experts and foreign reporters left. As a social category, war-widows are extremely vulnerable to male violence both within their communities and beyond, and they know it. They are a living testament to state and state-inspired atrocities and their very survival is a constant reproach to the military who still influence Guatemalan politics. The existence of MINUGUA has made little difference to their situation: Emol's most hated *jefe*, Mario, continues to terrorize war-widows and other nonconformists but, as ever, is smart enough not to do anything which MINUGUA or the civilian authorities could verify. It remains to be seen whether talks initiated by President Arzú Irigoyen (1996-) regarding the role of the national army in civil society will have any effect on men such as Mario who are, in Guatemalan terms, small-time killers.

Women prominent in local widows or human rights groups are still singled out for harassment. *Doña* Manuela told me that during the 1995 election campaign, former *jefes* threatened that she would be the first to die if their preferred candidate, General Ríos Montt (the former dictator who unleashed the patrol system on an unsuspecting public), won the presidential elections.

> All of the ones who went to take their husbands [from the clandestine graves] are now receiving threats. The men are saying, "If one of us goes to jail, then you will see what we do with you." This is what they are worried about and this is why they are threatening us and now we are afraid... Now we are all so frightened because we do not know if the whole thing will happen again. The patrols are saying it will happen, this is what they are saying!

After the excitement of achieving the exhumation faded, *doña* Manuela's fear of the patrollers reasserted itself. She feels particularly vulnerable as she is convinced the *jefes* hold her responsible for the exhumation because she is literate. Kotoh's most violent *jefe* is particularly menacing. *Doña* Manuela knows that patrollers do not need guns in order to kill; Kotoh men never had any and this particular *jefe* had forced patrollers to kill with their bare hands, rocks or their *machetes*. She is afraid of what the *jefes* might be up to, confessing, "I'm too frightened to find out!" After former *jefes* threatened to decapitate CONAVIGUA members, she decided to stop participating in demonstrations and to curb her participation in widows' organizations;

since seeing Gilberto's remains, she and the other women know that the men are capable of doing such things. This causes her considerable conflict because she had begun 'organizing' in memory of her father. On another occasion, she said she had to continue, even if she experiences the same fate.

Yet despite her own fear of the *jefes*, *doña* Manuela joins in *doña* Eugenia's criticism of *doña* Flora for not participating in the exhumation and for fearing that the *jefes* will kill her if she attempts to have her son's remains exhumed. *Doña* Eugenia even claimed, "If they [the *jefes*] lived closer to me, I still wouldn't be afraid." Despite *doña* Eugenia's bravado, her disparagement of *doña* Flora is hardly fair: the patrols have been completely disbanded in Kotoh (where they were never particularly gung ho) whereas *doña* Flora lives close to Emol's most feared *jefes* (including Mario), from whom she has received death threats since the exhumations. *Doña* Flora's anxiety increased when she heard them asking in a threatening manner, "What do they want with those bones anyway, they haven't got any meat on them any more!" Her agitation intensified following her humiliation by her former friends and escalated further when reports of their scorn reached her. Although she had been guilty of the same displaced self-flagellation, she was too fraught to recognize that *doña* Manuela and *doña* Eugenia were using her as a vehicle to criticize themselves for not locating their other missing menfolk.

The long interval between the exhumation of the bodies and their return for reburial created a sense of anti-climax, especially for those whose kin had not been in what is, in Guatemalan terms, a small clandestine grave. *Doña* Manuela's feeling of achievement rapidly dissipated, to be replaced by chronic fear of the *jefes* and anxiety about her father's fate:

> Whereas the women could see what happened to the cadavers of their relatives, we do not know what happened with my father, whether he was buried or merely chucked into some ravine somewhere. This is why we began a sadness too...we were most sad when they did these exhumations because, unlike the women who know where their cadavers are and that their bones are now buried, we do not. We have no idea where they took my father... Even if we found a little bit of bone, at least we would know where he was but we don't know and this is what is most difficult; this is why we have suffered so much sadness since the exhumation.

[And your mother [*doña* Candelaria] feels this way too?]

Yes, she got ill from it all.

[What happened?]

She got an excruciating pain in her head and a pain in her heart which was because of sadness... She still suffers from it today.

Yet when I asked her whether she has any regrets about the exhumation, *doña* Manuela replied:

> No, I think it was better that they did it; since we are human, it is better that
> we put the dead in their proper place and that we know where they are. Had
> we been dogs, then you can bury them in the ravines but since we are people
> then you can't bury them there. We can't think that we are buried, as humans,
> in the ravines. We need to know where we are going to be buried when we
> die, not in the ravines in whatever place. However, in *la violencia*, people
> were buried just like that in the ravines like animals. But according to my way
> of thinking, it is better to take the bodies out and put them in the cemetery
> because it's our house.

Doña Manuela's ambivalence — the endless switching from the sense of achievement resulting from participation in the process to fear of the consequences of that involvement — is typical. Unlike *doña* Eugenia and other 'wives of the cadavers', she achieved no lasting, personal benefit because her father was not among those exhumed. Many other widows and 'wives of the disappeared' also found the exhumation unhelpful; they have been deterred from exhuming their kin because, as *doña* Flora said, "I'm afraid of seeing the bodies." Although obviously excited by the exhumation — it was the first thing she mentioned to me when I asked her what had happened in the past three years and, to her, was much more significant than the disappearance of the patrols — she cannot bring herself to petition for the exhumation of her son's body. This is partly because she wants to retain her last image of Juan as a healthy and whole living person and partly because she believes her petition will not garner other widows' support: Juan was not a prominent member of the community and he is buried in a solitary grave, which suggests to *doña* Flora that she would have to bear all the costs herself. "A lot of journeying and money," she said (bus fares are expensive for indigenous widows), with no guaranteed outcome. She has been overwhelmed with anxiety at the prospect of reactivating village hatreds (which flared up following the exhumation, prompted various re-alignments, and then calmed down again) and the possibility of reprisals, yet she envies *doña* Eugenia's increased peace of mind since she achieved her objective.

Doña Eugenia herself told me that her emotions were 'calming' now that she has exhumed her son; she is now able to 'remember' him without so much sadness. She also describes with glee her new found confidence, how she walks proudly into Emol Central, her head held high. She claims she is no longer afraid of the former *jefes*:

> Before I was afraid to go to Emol, but not anymore. Now when I go there,
> they turn their heads away from me and I stay looking at them.

[How was it before?]

Before they make such a face, they get angry, what a big face they make *(me hacen cara, bravo se ponen, que caron hacen)* [she speaks in the present tense]. Now I watch him [Mario] and he moves away without so much as a hello. This is how it is now that the cadavers have been taken out.

Doña Eugenia's ambivalence is echoed by her grandson Martín. Although he had experienced an overwhelming sadness when viewing the condition of the corpses, he too appreciates the benefits of the exhumation; he is also concerned about its implications for the fate of the disappeared:

We are saddened by seeing the condition of cadavers in the graves. This has also made us wonder about my grandfather. We don't even know where he is, only God knows where he is. We have seen my father but not my grandfather. No one knows where he is...the state of the cadavers has made us wonder where he is and what they did to him. I expect that they did the same thing to him as they did to my father. The exhumation has made us sadder because we still do not know where my grandfather is... He was an old man, he was more than seventy-five years old and they still took him away. This is a big sadness for me because he was an old man. This is a big sadness.

Doña Eugenia's pleasure in the outcome of the exhumations is also tempered by thoughts of her husband:

Only I can't find my husband, so what can I do with him? It is not that I am neglecting to take out [exhume] his body, I just don't know where it is. It would be good if the two of them [father and son] could be together, but it isn't possible. They don't tell me where he is, so what can I do?

She has no idea where her husband has been 'thrown away' and tries to console herself with the thought that she has done everything she can in relation to both her menfolk; she has even visited a medium in a nearby town in an attempt to communicate with them. She therefore feels protected from the judgement of God and the ancestors — at least on this score.

For most people, the exhumation re-opened festering wounds caused by the silencing of trauma. Martín's memories are particularly distressing: as an under-age, fourteen year old patroller, he had been on duty that day and had been involved in rounding up its victims and roping them together. He had seen his father beaten almost to death from close quarters, although he did not see his death and burial. The exhumation caused him to relive the trauma which he describes in terms of experiencing a 'video' which has been 'engraved in his head' ever since. Martín told me he has never mentioned this to his family because of the overwhelming sadness of it all; the 'video' still plays in his head and continues to disturb him.

For Martín, the confirmation of his memories has been extremely painful. For people who had come to doubt their memories as a result of living with impunity and the concomitant play on reality, the exhumation, despite its awfulness, confirmed their memories of what actually happened. The exhumation validated people's own truth to themselves, just as it immediately invalidated the 'official truth' they had had to accommodate for the past decade. It also released people from their self-judgements of their own guilt and collusion with the perpetrators which had arisen because fear had prevented them from doing or saying anything against the atrocities.

What people, especially widows, had seen during the exhumation intensified feelings of revenge. Although some women share the common K'iche' view that justice is inseparable from retribution, most widows fear their own urges towards vengeance, which has to be kept in check or projected onto the *jefes*. For example, *doña* Eugenia is still beset with feelings of anger and revenge; she remains angry about the *jefes*' continued liberty:

> They remain content...in their homes with their wives and kids while we remain afraid and poor[10]... One can't remain like this, the men have to go to jail, they have to go to jail!... Then we will be equal... But who knows if justice will be done.

Doña Eugenia's concept of vengeance encompasses the perpetrators' entire families; she wants them to know what it is like to live in poverty without a grown man in the household. Thoughts of vengeance certainly cross the minds of her grandsons, but they are loth to perpetuate the cycle of violence: they believe that if they avenge their father and grandfather, the perpetrators' children will avenge themselves on their (Saturnino's and Martín's) children and grandchildren. Saturnino gave me some insight into the women's vengeful feelings when he told me:

> I realize how sad some of the other widows are when I meet them on the path and I stop and talk with them. They are unable to talk about anything except this [the exhumation], this is all that they can remember [think about]. Now even though it [their pain] is a little less than before, some widows are thinking of taking revenge; when they are drunk they think about taking revenge for all of this. When they are sober, however, they do not talk about it.
>
> [If they were serious, how would they do it?]
>
> Perhaps through one medium or another or perhaps by putting them in jail.
>
> [What do you think about the possibility of putting them in jail?]
>
> If there was a possibility of doing it, it would be O.K.

Saturnino then told me that even if justice were done, it would not resolve the problem for him:

If they [the killers] go there [to prison], this would not resolve the problems because my father and grandfather are dead. If we put them in jail, we would still have the problem that they would still be dead. If we put them in jail, this would not make them come back, so we wouldn't really gain anything by putting them in jail.

Children as Symbols of the Future

Once the exhumation was over, conflicts and jealousies emerged with a vengeance within the widows' group. Renewed death threats and the withdrawal of the NGO which had worked with widows for over a decade — the widows' group it established had been taken over by CONAVIGUA[11] — provided excuses for its collapse but not reasons. The group dissolved because it had achieved the objective *doña* Eugenia (encouraged by CONAVIGUA) had set for it and, in so doing, had exposed the differences which had developed between the women over the years since the group was inaugurated. It was as if having recognized and then ignored the differences between group members in terms of aspirations, temperament, circumstances, and experiences of loss, no further evaluation of difference had taken place for several years. In the interim, the women's children had grown up, pulling them in different directions. Children (especially boys), always a symbol of hope for the future, became the means through which widows framed that future. The children's survival into adulthood is the most visible symbol of the fact that the widows coped with *la violencia*; women say this gives them a sense of achievement which helps to alleviate their grief.

Despite their children's moral and financial support (which not all women received), widows are unable to leave the past behind. Families of the war-dead are noticeably poorer than other villagers (especially army supporters); their poverty is not only a daily reminder of their losses but also a cause of resentment. One of the things which particularly annoys *doña* Eugenia is that everyone now takes the road which her son had built for granted; (comparatively) rich villagers drive their trucks along the road which, according to one exegesis about *la violencia*, it cost her son his life to build.

In some widows' families, sons and grandsons counter the looming presence of the *jefes* who represent a more negative future, especially in terms of the traditional Mayan world view. In others, boys identify with a more militarized model of manhood; this is more common among boys who were very young when their fathers and other male relatives were killed, leaving no-one in the family to teach them what it is to be a K'iche' man.

As fatherless eldest sons (and, since *la violencia*, grandsons) grow up, tradition dictates that they assume the role of household head as soon as practicably possible. Many widows are happy to relinquish this role; a son's or grandson's assumption of the role 'normalizes' the household's status. The price women pay for this is the loss of their autonomy: 'normalization' revokes their hard won independence. They also find themselves identified in terms of their sons' different alignments and attitudes to life. This became blatantly obvious as the widows' group imploded. The experiences of the principals of the widows' group — *doña* Eugenia, *doña* Candelaria, *doña* Consuelo, *doña* Flora, and *doña* Josefina — are typical.

Doña Eugenia

Doña Eugenia is satisfied with the way her grandsons have developed and I never heard her utter one complaint about them. In fact, her main concern seems to be that through her husband's and son's premature deaths, her grandsons' education was cut short and their lives have been unnecessarily hard. Her eldest grandson, Saturnino, told me that his grandmother says that if Gilberto were still alive,

> ...we would not be as we are now. She tells me, "You would have been study-ing if he was here." She doesn't say this so much nowadays, she hasn't for the last three or four years, because now she can see that she has help. Although she is still sad, she doesn't worry so much about household necessities, such as the corn; she sees that we can maintain the corn fields *(milpa)*. She is there-fore not terribly worried about this.

Doña Eugenia receives considerably more support from her grandsons than, for example, *doña* Flora does from hers; the ten year difference in their grandsons' ages is significant. Saturnino and Martín were in their early teens when their father and grandfather died and had received considerable guid-ance from both men, who were community leaders; the young men retain positive images of them which are reinforced by comments made and stories told by their grandmother and others who supported the way the men had worked for the community. Many people speak of how their father had en-abled the community to develop and how their grandfather was often called upon to settle disputes. With this heritage, it is not surprising that five years after the worst of the violence, the community turned first to twenty year old Saturnino and then his younger brother Martín when seeking someone to fill a leadership role. As it was still dangerous to assume any role not sanctioned by the army, the young men responded with fear and reluctance but gathered courage and, later, expanded their activities. Martín told me that they are motivated by the memory of their father:

> No one felt like becoming leader after the killings...but he [his father Gilberto] was determined to do the right thing and I have never forgotten about him. Because of this, we are determined to do more and more.

Saturnino became Kotoh's health worker and then President of its Improvement Committee. He handed over both jobs to his brother when he became one of the few Emolteco men to have a paid job in the capital, where he is a machinist in a clothing factory. Although he lives mostly in Guatemala City, Saturnino's seniority and obvious intelligence have made him household head; he returns to the village every few weeks to see his wife and children who, as is the custom, live in his natal household. He continues to assist his grandmother in whatever way he can. Often his family hardly see him during these visits because he resumes his leadership role when he is in the village and people continue to seek him out to ask his opinion on things. Like his father, Saturnino is also interested in Emol's youth: he participates in running youth groups with *don* Juan and he teaches youngsters about their Mayan culture, organizing special events in relation to this. For example, on Independence Day (15 September) he and like-minded friends take a political stance to create awareness among the young that indigenous people are far from independent.

Yet despite his commitment to the community and the high esteem with which he is regarded by many, Saturnino suffers from low self-esteem: he wants to be more like his father and feels he has failed Gilberto because he did not complete his education. Saturnino exhibits many of the symptoms of depression;[12] he told me that he expects his life will be cut short. Attacks against him have already begun; for example, his pride in the successful completion of an NGO-sponsored improvement project was destroyed by malicious rumours that he had embezzled money from it. He also has serious alcohol problem; he was so drunk at his daughter's naming ceremony in 1993 that he nearly dropped her.

Doña Eugenia's second grandson, Martín, is one of the many frustrated young men who have been unable to find regular employment in the capital, but she is happy to have an adult male around to help her organize the male-gendered tasks of the household; her *milpa* looks quite good as Martín chose a good *mozo* for her. His own *milpa* certainly looks healthier than Saturnino's, something he was eager to point to me as this is an area in which he excels in relation to his brother; it is also an important confirmation of the identity he has begun to take on for himself as a Mayan traditionalist. He and Saturnino are among the few young men in the community who have begun to excavate their Mayan heritage and have increased their self respect as a result. Martín has literally excavated a stone idol (camawil) from his garden. That he inherited the piece of land containing this important object is significant to him, reinforcing the messages to become a diviner (aj q'ij) he receives through his dreams. He has made contact with the growing national movement to return to the 'real' Mayan religion (which considers *costumbre* and the *cofradía* Spanish impositions) and is in touch with Mayan priests in other areas of the country, particularly Momostenango. Martín has little to do with *don* Ven, Kotoh's rather eccentric coffin-maker, who has already become a Mayan priest: *don* Ven has withdrawn his support for the widows on the grounds that their organizations only 'cause trouble' (because they are a conduit for new, non-traditional ideas, especially about the role of women; he has forbidden his wife to attend women's groups). Martín remains friendly with the two other men, *don* Juan and *don* Salvador (a former activist now resident in Guatemala City), who have always done their best to support Kotoh's widows even though they ridicule 'new' traditionalism. Drawing a single maize plant in the earth as we sat outside his house, *don* Juan explained the problem of new converts to old ways. Rubbing out some of the leaves of the plant he had just drawn, he said that 'new' traditionalists only want maize as their forefathers had it and that they do not want beans or pumpkin (both secondary crops climb up the tall bean stalks; the beans also renitrate the soil). Using the modern fields as an analogy, *don* Juan said converts only want the ancestors, not God or the saints. He is concerned that this claim for so-called religious purity could split the community further (despite its attempts to create a pan-Mayan identity), a concern which Martín seems to share despite his leanings towards the movement.

The third boy in the family was legally adopted as a baby by Vicenta; his mother was a friend of hers who died of natural causes after his father was disappeared. He was only a toddler when his adoptive father was killed. Raised by *doña* Eugenia and her grandsons, he has received more of a traditional education than most fatherless boys in his age group; he now works in Guatemala City in *don* Salvador's shop. *Doña* Eugenia also has two granddaughters who are now both married, which further 'normalizes' the household and reintegrates it into village life.

Doña Eugenia attributes the fact that she feels better than when I last saw her to the easing of her sadness (bis) and the support she receives from her grandsons who helped her with an important aspect of her life, enabling her to cope with the future more easily: "Before, without my husband and son, there was no one to care for me but now that my grandsons have grown up and I have taken out [exhumed] my son's body, I begin to feel a bit better." She also gains comfort from the fact that she can see resemblances to her son Gilberto in Saturnino's character and Martín's looks, creating a symbolic immortality.[13] Imbuing the younger generation with the characteristics of deceased members of the family is fairly common among the K'iche' (chapter six), although the young men themselves do not seem to feel the need to interpret loss in this way. Another reason for this ascription is that Saturnino and Martín have assumed the traditional roles of protectors.

After a decade of upheaval, *doña* Eugenia's household is the most successful in terms of retaining traditional values and mores. She herself is as vibrant as ever; she seems to have gained strength from achieving the exhumations.

Doña Candelaria

Doña Candelaria has prospered the most from her children's employment. Her eldest son has been a street trader in Guatemala City since childhood; he is firmly settled in the capital. Her second son, Santos, who once wanted to become a teacher, is now a policeman and a younger son, Esteban, is a soldier; she benefits from the extras they receive from their employment in these corrupt organizations. Her struggles to educate all her children have paid off in unexpected ways. When I visited her, she had just returned from market and was in her kitchen, unwrapping crockery and an abundance of all sorts of other goods which I had never seen an Emolteco widow indulge in. Although she is wealthy in village terms, she does not seem either healthy or particularly happy. She has grown rather fat, lost her teeth, and developed diabetes.

There is no talk of the exhumations in *doña* Candelaria's house. Santos had forced his mother to withdraw from CONAVIGUA even before I left the village in 1990. Unlike their father, Pedro, Santos, and Esteban are uninterested in community or church activities; they are more concerned with the 'good life' and the power attendant on being part of the military and the police. They took no part in the exhumations. Much as *doña* Candelaria loves her children, I had the distinct impression that she thinks her husband, to whom she had been happily married, was a better man than her sons. She is dependent on them and appreciates their generosity, so she says nothing.

Santos is how head of *doña* Candelaria's household: he is married, his wife and children live with his mother, and he is in full time work. Employment in the police force is pitifully paid but membership of this powerful *ladino* institution provides status and good, if not legal, perquisites. Santos' improved financial position means that his wife has taken a stronger position in the family. She had arrived in Emol speaking Spanish and wearing *ladina* clothes but has learnt K'iche' and adopted the traditional skirt and blouse.

The third son, Esteban, also began his working life on Pedro's street stall in Guatemala City. Once Santos had joined the police, he helped Esteban to join the army at a higher level than is normal for Indian recruits. The brothers opened a new shop in Kotoh (the one run by widows had folded due to poor management) and proceeded to drink away the profits their wives earned; by 1995, that too had closed, leaving Kotoh without a shop at all.

Their salaries and attendant 'extras' meant that despite their excessive drinking, they could easily afford the two day *fiesta* their mother held to celebrate the baptism of Santos' new baby. This was a family affair and *doña* Eugenia and *doña* Consuelo arrived together to help with the preparations, even though *doña* Candelaria had fallen out with them during the exhumation. *Doña* Eugenia took her usual honoured position, which was reflected in the fact that it was she who distributed the meat into bowls, while *doña* Consuelo served the liquid part of the soup. *Doña* Candelaria's brother, a former military commissioner who has made himself scarce since the exhumations, did not attend and may not have been invited, despite his nephews' current allegiances.

Before I went to the *fiesta*, Saturnino told me he no longer has anything to do with *doña* Candelaria's sons. He had once felt close to them, given their fathers were not only cousins but firm friends and had suffered the same fate. He warned me about the way they had changed since I saw them last, describing Esteban's character as 'very strong' *(muy fuerte)*, an expression which carries connotations of aggression. I did not recognize Santos and Esteban when they were brought to the party in an inebriated state by friends who had had to fetch them and help them cross the river; in their drunken state, the lack of recognition was mutual. I was surprised to see that in contrast to the modest dress of most villagers, Esteban was wearing a skimpy tee-shirt which displayed his well-muscled body. He flexed his muscles for me when he said hello, which is most unusual behaviour for a K'iche' man. Later he showed me series of photos hanging in the patio. Most were of him: in some he brandished status symbols such as large machine guns, in others he had *ladino*-looking girls on his arm. As Esteban showed off his new militarized persona, I remembered that he had watched his father being killed by the village authorities which included Emol's military commissioner and his uncle. I wondered whether his behaviour, a flagrant display of 'identification with the aggressor', reflected that he had not survived his ordeals during *la violencia* any better than his cousins Saturnino and Martín.

Doña Consuelo

Doña Consuelo has one son (aged fifteen in 1993) and six daughters. She and her husband had shared Gilberto's belief in the importance of education and had sent their eldest surviving child, Manuela, to school, believing that learning Spanish would open up new avenues of opportunity for her. An additional motive was her father's concern that Manuela would have no brothers to protect or provide for her. Her surviving siblings are considerably younger than she is; the long-hoped for son was only a toddler when their father was killed. After his death, *doña* Consuelo supported the family by making pottery (chapter one). There is a fairly regular demand for this and *doña* Consuelo's skills place her in a better economic position than most Emolteco widows, enabling her to send her younger children to school too.

Doña Consuelo genuinely misses her husband; of all the widows, she and *doña* Candelaria seem to have had the best marriages. Unlike other widows, she does not refer to her loss in terms of her husband's income generation: *doña* Consuelo is a highly capable woman whose abilities had been largely masked by the traditional interpretation of gender roles. Nor, thanks to Manuela's competence in Spanish, does she miss the male household head's traditional role of accessing, interpreting, and mediating with the outside *ladino* world. When I first met them, both women seemed happy about not having to submit to male domination.

Manuela had married a landless man at sixteen. Shortly afterwards, her husband was abducted by men he knew, beaten unconscious, and buried in a shallow grave from which he managed to extricate himself. This failed murder is referred to by perpetrators, victim, and family alike as a 'punishment'. *Doña* Manuela says he never recovered from his physical and psychic wounds. Two children and six years later, she was a widow; she supported them through teaching literacy classes and helping her mother. The worsening economic conditions of the late 1980s resulted in the closure of the class and she had to look for an alternative means of earning a living as she had to buy corn on a year round basis; her mother's land is inadequate to support her own dependent children, let alone Manuela's. She lived in a house belonging to her much younger brother, faced with the knowledge that he will reclaim it when he marries. Brought up in a home full of competent women, he has yet to show any signs of wanting assume the role of household head.

Doña Consuelo and her eldest daughter are very close and supportive of each other. Manuela supports her mother's involvement in CONAVIGUA: her education enables her to have a better understanding of its objectives than the average Emolteco woman. She became the link between *don* Salvador in Guatemala City, his friend *don* Juan in Kotoh and the hamlet's widows; she helped *doña* Eugenia with exhumation petitions. Yet despite her abilities and the power which accrues from genuine competence in the Spanish language, it was her mother who was elected president of the local branch of CONAVIGUA. *Doña* Consuelo is a very likeable, diplomatic, and nurturing woman whose nature gained her the trust of other widows.

Doña Manuela had remarried by the time I returned to Emol in 1993. Despite her continuing fear of Emol's worst *jefes*, she has left Kotoh and gone to live in Emol Central with her husband, a former military commissioner who accepted her children. Although being a military commissioner does not necessarily imply army sympathies, her marriage caused gossip in Kotoh. The story of Manuela's need for male protection, not to mention a roof over her head and someone to grow corn for the family, is told with considerable relish. Although she had told me with pride in 1990 that she had learnt to be much more independent and mobile through living on her own and had become less afraid to speak out and had even travelled to Costa Rica with CONAVIGUA, her own and her children's survival needs outweigh her ideological stance. *Doña* Manuela is nostalgic for the atmosphere of her childhood home; she told me that she believes life was better 'before' when the women did not get together because they were all with their husbands. Despite her education, *doña* Manuela has been unable to escape the fate of a K'iche' widow; ultimately, her education has been less useful to her than her illiterate mother's pottery skills. Her mother, on the other hand, quite likes her new life; she just wishes her husband was alive to share it.

Doña Flora

Doña Flora has mixed feelings about the development of her grandsons, whom she helped her daughter-in-law Bartola to raise. Fifteen year old

Eustaqio and his thirteen year old brother Apolinario were toddlers when both their father and grandfather were disappeared; the third child, Florinda, was born after her father's death. Little Florinda lives with her mother and grandmother, helping in the household. *Doña* Flora rarely mentions her namesake. This reflects K'iche' social norms *(doña* Eugenia barely mentions her granddaughters or great-granddaughters either) and does not necessarily imply that the girl is not valued or loved. She is, like all unmarried K'iche' girls, an implied presence who existence has to be read from others' actions.

Ever since I met her, *doña* Flora has frequently lamented that Eustaqio and Apolinario are badly brought up boys *(malcriados)*; she used to threaten them that they she would have to send them to the army to become soldiers if they did not behave. By contrast, *doña* Flora speaks about the boys' father in positive terms, mentioning both the way he behaved towards the household (the nearest she can get to teaching the boys proper male roles) and his contribution to the community; at the same time, she portrays a more ambivalent image of her husband. Neither man had been particularly prominent in the community and are not much spoken about by others; they were followers, not leaders.

Doña Flora feels a little more hopeful about the future now that both boys work; Eustaqio contributes twelve Quetzales (under three U.S. dollars) to the weekly budget. He works in a nearby town where he picks and packs fruit, loads the truck, accompanies the driver to Guatemala City's main bus station, and helps unload it. Apolinario, her 'angry' *(bravo)* grandson, works for the same *ladino* but, unlike his more 'understanding' older brother, does not contribute financially to the household. Nevertheless, *doña* Flora told me with some pride that neither boy goes barefoot anymore and she was touched by the fact that Eustaqio asks her to help him buy his clothes.

Although she is pleased that her grandsons have taken on the responsibility of work, *doña* Flora worries about them when they are away from home. She is afraid that something might happen to them 'on the road'; many men, including two of the boys' maternal uncles, had disappeared this way during *la violencia*, when people simply did not return from their journeys or were found dead. She also worries that the army might kidnap them for military service, as they had her son. Forced conscription is now illegal, but *doña* Flora is not convinced that it no longer happens.

Doña Flora is very disappointed in the boys' reluctance, when they are at home, to help with male gendered tasks around the house; neither has any interest in helping with the *milpa* and it has become difficult to get them to co-operate even in fetching the labourers *(mozos)* she has to hire to work her land. As children, they had helped the *mozos*; now they were working, their grandmother has to find even more money to hire a man to work her fields in their stead. *Doña* Flora had been unable to plant all her land in the last growing season for lack of funds; her savings, in the form of a little bull she had been raising for sale, disappeared when it died; the vegetables she had hoped to sell in the market failed. As she told me this, she began to cry; she believes her grandsons would have been better 'educated' if their father or even their grandfather had been around to guide them. She knows the boys will not return to the land but nevertheless hopes they will when they marry. This mixture of awareness and hope influenced her decision, in 1993, to allow their mother to remarry on condition that the prospective groom lived in her house on her land. The man refused, as he was not prepared to farm land which he had no hope of inheriting: as far as *doña* Flora is concerned, the land belongs to Eustaqio and Apolinario whether they want it or not.

Doña Flora feels anxious without her grandsons in the house, but insists that she is not afraid because neither she nor her dead kin committed any crime: "If they kill me, they kill me!" she says, identifying with the bravery of her husband who had remained in Emol when it would have been wiser to flee; "Like my husband, I say I am not afraid!" But she is afraid and alone; her upbringing prevents her from looking to her daughter-in-law for moral or emotional support. War-widows in Emol Central, unlike those in Kotoh, are fragmented: she says they are either too scared, too drunk or 'too busy' to join her; she had not even asked some of the widows she knows to accompany her to the exhumations, knowing that they blame the dead for the death and disappearance of their own menfolk.

Doña Flora's vulnerability is plain for all to see and she is scapegoated by people looking for someone to blame. She finds the increased animosity between segments of the community following the exhumations very hard to bear; some of it has been directed against her. She told me that an ex-commissioner's wife was demanding that now the Kotoh victims had been exhumed, the people of Kotoh should reveal her brother's grave; the woman claimed that he had been killed there and his body never returned. This is entirely possible but *doña* Flora is hardly the person to ask about it. She is also experiencing difficulties in her relationships with other women, such as the sisters of a man named Miguel with whom she collaborates in carrying out duties for the Charismatic Church. One sister blames *doña* Flora and the rest of the 'organized ones' for the murder of their brother and the subsequent murder of her husband who had been killed by hooded men when he returned from hiding. This woman went nowhere near the exhumations in Kotoh; her behaviour is a statement of her current alignment rather than the reality of her brother's, her husband's or her own loyalties at the time of her menfolk's deaths. Another of Miguel's sisters expresses her animosity towards *doña* Flora more obliquely; she is angry at her for not having undergone her Baptism of the Spirit, which is required by the charismatic sect. *Doña* Flora thinks this second baptism unnecessary but the woman warns her that her refusal to go through with this means she will go to hell when she dies (a threat that carries little weight to people raised in the *costumbrista* faith, which has no hell). Another, more culturally valid, excuse for these verbal attacks ('painful words') stems from the fact that spending time with a man to whom one is neither married nor related to is considered very improper.

The antagonism expressed towards *doña* Flora indicates her weak position in Emol Central. She stands out from other women because of her natural elegance and style; her former position in the widows' group brought her status; her role as co-ordinator of the Charismatic Church also brings her to prominence; men in leadership positions appeal to her for help when they want the widows' votes, etc. Standing out, for whatever reason, has always been and still is good enough reason to attack someone. Her humiliation at the hands of her erstwhile friends in Kotoh marked the beginning of her loss of status, always an important factor in K'iche' social relations. *Doña* Flora was keen to accompany me to *doña* Eugenia's house although it was not clear to me whether this was because she regretted falling out with them or because she wanted to relive the good times we had had together during my first visit to Emol. As we walked down the ravine which separates the two hamlets, we encountered the vicious dogs which Kotoh people keep to warn them of intruders: *doña* Flora scared them away with her stick, joking that she knew how to handle them with her 'gun' *(arma)*. Despite her woes, her sense of humour had not disappeared. Although *doña* Eugenia was pleased to see *doña* Flora, the differences in their current situations seemed to preclude a resumption of their friendship. *Doña* Flora became very demoralized by the loss of her friends and their support. When I last saw her in 1995, this had taken its toll; she had finally lost her optimism and had taken to her bed.

Doña Josefina

Of all the widowed household heads within the group, *doña* Josefina had fared the least well in the three years since my departure in 1990. If anything, she was worse off. Her drinking problem had worsened, which means she is less sought out for her services as diviner (aj q'ij) even though she performs her duties conscientiously. Her grandfather could no longer help with her *milpa*; he was on the point of collapse from the same cause. Her sons, only slightly younger than *doña* Flora's grandsons, did not work; she considered them too young to leave home. Her daughter, upon whom she relied for emotional and practical support, had married and left home.

The first time I went to visit her, her youngest son (who accompanies her almost everywhere) was playing outside the house; he ran over to tell me his mother was unwell and that I should return another day. On my next visit I found her grandfather bleeding copiously from a gash in his leg; drunk as usual, he had lost his balance and fallen over. I had to apply a tourniquet.

Doña Josefina was sober and pleased to see me. She happily showed me her baby granddaughter, the child of her adopted son Diego. He had been the least supportive of all the widows' offspring but had returned to the fold after marrying the daughter of *doña* Josefina's widowed friend, *doña* Ana. Diego feels much more committed to the household since his daughter was born and visits more frequently — like Saturnino, he works in a factory in the capital — and is much more diligent in attending the cornfields: he seems very attached to his daughter and wants to ensure that everyone is well fed so that they can attend to her needs. He is grateful for his 'mother's' care of his wife and especially his daughter and sometimes rewards her efforts with presents of small sums of money or, unfortunately, alcohol. Despite his regular income, his financial contributions are based on whim or his own alcohol consumption.

Another motive for Diego's increased diligence is that he is hoping for a share of *doña* Josefina's land. He may have a long wait as her sons are still many years away from coming of age. In the meantime, *doña* Josefina gives him corn in return for his help with the *milpa* and the small amounts of cash on which her little family depends. Her worries about her economic situation drive her to drink more.

Doña Josefina is very protective of the family she has under her care and authority. She is an affectionate woman who enjoys female company; now that her daughter has married, she is pleased to have another 'daughter' in the house and enjoys having a baby to look after. Her own daughter is childless, which causes them great concern; *doña* Josefina has been using her professional skills to help remedy the situation, so far with no result.

Doña Josefina was crushed by the treatment she, *doña* Ana, and *doña* Flora received at the Kotoh exhumation site. Unlike *doña* Flora, I never heard her mention the possibility of trying to petition for an exhumation in Emol Central. Diego did not offer her the same support as, say, *doña* Eugenia's grandsons, but then this cannot be expected given he is not related to either *doña* Flora or the dead in the village's known clandestine graves; he does not know where his own disappeared father is buried. He prefers to leave the past behind; he is less politicized than many other widows' sons.

Conclusion

Women and men, whatever category of survivorhood one assigns to them, have coped with their experiences over the past fifteen years with varying degrees of success. Many are still in mourning, not only for the dead and disappeared but also for the destruction of life-ways, the loss of previously occupied categories of person, of trust in themselves and in others, and of reputation. Other losses include deteriorating standards of living generally and of health and education in particular. People are still paying for the psychological, social, and economic costs of the disaster which befell them and are likely to do so for generations to come.

Emolteco men and women have been unable to create a satisfactory and satisfying explanation for what happened to them. They have therefore been unable to compose a story of their experiences and leave it behind as they do the stories they create together, as a family and a community, at traditional funerals following a village death (chapter eight). For many people, this story can only be told in its proper time and place, that is, during the funeral; however, the bodies of hundreds of Emoltecos have not been recovered. Most never will be.

The harassment by military and paramilitary forces created an environment which prevents people from resolving past violations (the official abolition of paramilitary organizations is of little benefit in this regard, as former members continue to live, unpunished, in their midst). Women face the problem of trying to recuperate from violence and the less tangible ideational manifestations of violent practices while the violence or, at best, only the threat of violence, continues around them. Yet women continue to struggle to find meaning in their experiences; they give significance to and cope with *la violencia* in diverse ways, albeit within a specific cultural idiom. This idiom has itself been damaged by the hectic change prior to *la violencia* and frantic, chaotic change during it, leaving survivors confused about the efficacy of traditional world views in explaining the present. Their inability to comprehend the incomprehensible exacerbates the sense of loss.

It is the struggle for meaning which has been the subject of this book, how people grapple with existing cultural categories of explanation, reshaping them, discarding them, recombining them, and so on, in the desperate search for certainties in an extremely uncertain world. In the process, the voices of Guatemalan Indian women, silenced both by their position in the local and national social structure and the threats of power holders, have been resuscitated and their version of history recorded: "in reading history we must learn to read silences, for the victim rarely gets an opportunity to record his or her point of view...the speech of the victim must occupy the central place in the narrative of the anthropologist" (Das 1987: 13).

There are provisos: firstly, the women only speak through my ethnography, meaning that they exist only as my representations of them (over which they have no control) and secondly, ethnographic revelations have been constrained by the persistent situation of terror and impunity in Guatemala. Yet surviving widows should not been seen as passive beings, completely controlled and moulded by the various institutional and symbolic processes of revictimization; whilst vulnerable, they are not so defenseless. They have learnt to adapt, to survive; some have begun to 'work' for justice (women who define this as putting the perpetrators behind bars have not lost hope of fulfilling this goal, the Law of Reconciliation notwithstanding).

The same can be said for K'iche' society as a whole. Recording war-widows' subjective experience of violence in every day life has resulted in a kind of history of fragmentation and realignment. According to people with long experience in El Quiché (such as missionaries), violence has severely damaged traditional forms of solidarity; the women's lamentations about the disintegration of their extended families are valid. There is a new emphasis on the nuclear family if not isolated individuals, which is completely contrary to the values the women were taught as children and which they in their turn taught their children. Faced with a present and a future in which different family members ally themselves with different political or religious groups, many people hark back to an idealized past before *la violencia*, a time when (according to their retrospective glances) the community was 'populated' (and therefore 'happy'),[14] unified, friendly, and relatively less poor. Such idealizations, together with references to the Golden Age before the Conquest, illustrate that people are still not at home in the present. The constant realignments are symptom of this.

The widows' greater sense of self-sufficiency can be interpreted as contributing to the erosion of social solidarity though it would be more true to say that they survived in spite of the increased emphasis on individualism. Although widows are socially isolated within their villages and forcibly separated from their extended family networks, they do not conform to either the state's vision of the future (in which traditional loyalties are replaced by individual loyalty to the national state which is fostered by protestantism) or to still-persisting traditional ideas of the appropriate way to live. Rather, using traditional concepts of solidarity as a guide, women regroup themselves according to religious affiliation and family ties — in places like Emol where nearly everybody is related to everyone else, one always has relatives to choose from, to regroup with. That said, rifts and splits have occurred down to the level of the household and this recent development is impossible to ignore. Also new is the extension of solidarity and sisterhood through organizations such as CONAVIGUA to women beyond the family, village or *municipio*. However, such is the tendency for splits and realignments that the new foci of solidarity have become the very sites around which fragmentation and realignment occur. Factionalism has always been endemic in Emol but prior to the arrival of the new religions and political philosophies, it was covert and muted; the new ideologies presented a vehicle through which to express existing factionalism. During *la violencia*, factionalism was expressed through overt and intense violence, shocking perpetrators, victims, and survivors alike.

All Emoltecos are now painfully aware of where open factionalism can lead. They have lived the horror of doing things to each other that they had previously believed only *ladinos* capable of. Worse, they know they could be made to do it again. Although villagers are currently enjoying a respite from military supervision *(control)*, no-one believes that this will be anything more than temporary. It is hard to reassure them as the likelihood of renewed violence is not so remote: impunity continues; the perpetrators — both the actual killers and the men who instigated the violence — remain at large. Many people would agree with *doña* Flora's prophecy: "An even greater hunger will come than we have known so far." Through this oblique reference to 'eating', the K'iche' metaphor for killing, *doña* Flora succinctly expresses her belief that the killers' appetite for death remains.

Notes

1. Most indigenous people feel that this Spanish-language institution is primarily used against them.

2. It was the army who chose the 1960 start date; they hoped to discredit the URNG and improve their own image by drawing attention to guerrilla atrocities of that era. However, even taking these into account, the army's aim of 'balancing' each army-attributed human rights violation presented to the Commission with a guerrilla atrocity would have represented a considerable distortion of the truth.

3. U.N. observers were invited for a three year term, commencing from the date of this agreement. Their departure has been 'imminent' since April 1997 but they were still in Guatemala in November.

4. Local perpetrators are generally unaware of or do not understand the distinction between post and post holder and so continue to issue threats to people who visit, or might possibly visit, MINUGUA offices (thus unwittingly bringing themselves within its jurisdiction). Whilst many of their victims' kin think of army indoctrination as being analogous with spirit invasion, *jefes* and others who for various reasons have given their loyalty to the army cannot afford to do so.

5. Truth Commissions in El Salvador, Argentina, and the former Yugoslavia name the guilty; in Argentina, the tribunal can (but rarely does) initiate prosecutions.

6. Details of the exhumation (dates, etc.) have been omitted to allow the village to remain anonymous.

7. The change of tense indicates Saturnino's belief that patrol groupings and loyalties remain in place.

8. In some respects, CONAVIGUA was ascribed the ancestors' powers of justice and retribution.

9. *Doña* Eugenia spoke using the present tense. This is partly due to the fact that this memory remains part of her 'present' and partly due to K'iche' constructs of time and the way this is expressed in the K'iche' language. *Doña* Eugenia has translated these concepts into the idiomatic Spanish typical of K'iche' speakers who (unlike her grandson Saturnino) have not been to school.

10. And hence, as she put it on another occasion, "We remain mute." cf. Ardener (1975).

11. The take-over of the NGO widows' group by an organization with more political objectives (CONAVIGUA) echoes what happened to the women's menfolk (with disastrous results).

12. It will be recalled that whilst one can diagnose depression according to Western medical criteria, the concept does not exist among the K'iche'.

13. See Das (1990:358) for use of this anthropological concept and her reference to Lifton's (1967) psychological use of it.

14. This is an oblique reference to the population loss caused by *la violencia*.

Epilogue

Further studies are needed not only to evaluate how culture affects responses to the various consequences of war, but also how culturally prescribed behaviour affects the individual experience of chaos, loss, and grief. For instance, although the K'iche' are socialized to suppress anger, the widows had to learn to suppress more anger and resentment than they had previously thought it possible to feel. Future research needs to compare socialization practices in different cultures and examine how this impinges on the impact of war; the data presented here suggests that caution should be exercised when applying western psychological theories to non-Western peoples.

While the present study focused on Guatemala, one third of the world's countries are presently engaged in war, and two thirds regularly practice human rights abuses in order to control their populations. Therefore it is evident that social scientists, no matter what their field of study, will in all likelihood confront some instance of socio-political violence in the field. Researchers who choose to focus on socio-political violence in any of its guises in other areas of the world need viable field methods and theoretical frameworks. The approach and questions raised here encourage a basic rethinking of the conceptual foundations that surround socio-political violence and the way it is played out in areas of the world beyond Guatemala. It represents an initial step in designing theoretical frameworks for studying violence which elucidate the lived realities and thereby enhance knowledge of its effects.

List of Acronyms

APM. *Asamblea del Pueblo Maya* (Mayan People's Assembly). Founded 1993.

ASC. *Asamblea de Sociedad Civil* (Civil Society Assembly). Coalition of non-aligned interest groups brought together to provide their input to the peace negotiations. Founded 1994.

AVANCSO. *La Asociacíon Para el Avance de los Ciencías Sociales en Guatemala* (the Association for the Promotion of the Social Sciences in Guatemala). An independent organization which sponsors and publishes sociological research. Formed 1986.

CDP. *Comité de Paz y Desarrollo* (Committees for Peace and Development). Current incarnation of PAC/CVDC. Renamed 1995.

CEH. *Comisión de Esclarecimiento Histórico* (Commission for the Historical Clarification of the Violations of Human Rights and Acts of Violence Which Have Caused Suffering to the Guatemalan Population). Known as 'Commission for Historical Clarification' or 'Truth Commission'. Accord signed June 1994. Commission actually established August 1997.

CERJ. *Comité de los Étnias,* <u>Runujel Junam</u> (Council of Ethnic Communities "We are all Equal"). Established 1988.

COMEGA. *Coórdinadora de Organizaciones de Mujeres Indigenas de Guatemala* (Co-ordinaton of Indigenous Women's Organizations). An umbrella group co-ordinating dozens of smaller groups. Focuses on education, grass roots organizing, media production, commerce, and analytical investigation. Formed March 1996.

CONAVIGUA. *Coordinación Nacional de Viudas Guatemaltecos* (National Co-ordination of Guatemalan Widows). Established 1988.

CONDEG. *Consejo Nacional de Desplazadas de Guatemala* (National Council of Displaced Guatemalans). Formed 1989 by displaced persons in Guatemala City and the south coast.

CPR. *Comunidades de Población en Resistencia* (Communities of Population in Resistance). Formed 1982.

CUC. *Comité de Unidad Campesina* (Committee of Peasant Unity). National Peasants' League formed among Ladino and Indigenous temporary and permanent plantation workers in the early 1970s.

CVDC. *Comité Voluntarios de Defensa Civil* (Voluntary Committees for Civil Defence). Name changed from PAC in 1988.

DM. *Defensaria Maya* (Mayan Defence). Deals with indigenous rights and encourages people to defend those rights. Founded 1993.

EAFG. *Equipo de Antropoligia Forense de Guatemala* (Team of Forensic Anthropologists of Guatemala). Formed 1992, this Guatemalan NGO exhumes clandestine graves.

EGP. *Ejército Guerrillero de los Pobres* (the Guerrilla Army of the Poor). Formed by dissident members of FAR and EGP in 1968. Renamed EGP in 1972 when re-entered Guatemala.

FADS. *Familiares y Amigos Contra la Delicuencia y el Secuestro* (Families and Friends Against Kidnaping and Crime). Founded 1996.

FAMDEGUA. *Familíarés de Detenidos y Desaparecídos de Guatemala* (Families of the Detained and Disappeared of Guatemala). Offshoot of GAM. Founded 1994 to search for whereabouts of remains of relatives. Conducts mass exhumations; works to identify those responsible for atrocities.

FAR. *Fuerza Armades Rebeldes* (Rebel Armed Forces). Formed 1962.

GAM. *Grupo de Apoyo Mutuo* (Group for Mutual Support); support group for families of the disappeared. Established 1984.

MINUGUA. *Missión de Naciones Unidas para la Verificación de los Derecho Humanos en Guatemala* (United Nations' Mission for the Verification of Human Rights in Guatemala). Established 21 November 1994.

ORPA. *Organización Revolucionaria del Pueblo en Armas* (Revolutionary Organization of People in Arms). Formed by dissident members of FAR in 1971 and renamed ORPA in 1979.

PAC. *Patrullas de Autodefensa Civil* (Self-Defence Civil Patrols). Established from 1981. See CVDC, CDP.

PGT. *Partido Guatemalteco de Trabajadores* (Guatemalan Workers' Party). The official Communist Party of Guatemala. Legalized 1951; banned 1954, since when it has functioned clandestinely. Formed its own guerrilla front (FARM) in 1962.

REHMI. *Recuperación de la Memoria Histórica* (The Recovery of Historical Memory Project). Alternative 'Truth Commission' founded by the Guatemalan Bishops' Conference in 1994.

URNG. *Unidad Revolucionaria Nacional Guatemalteca* (National Revolutionary Union of Guatemala). Formed 1982. Umbrella organization, diplomatic wing and military high command of Guatemala's various guerrilla groups.

USAID. United States Agency for International Development.

Groups Formed by Indigenous RefugeeWomen in Mexico
(now operating in Guatemala)

Ixmucané. Named after Mayan Grandmother Goddess. Formed 1993 by indigenous women of the Northern Return.

Mamá Maquín. Named after Adelina Caal Maquín, an indigenous woman killed in the 1978 Panzos Massacre. Coalition of Mayan women founded in May 1990. Work for women's rights, 'alphabetization' (literacy), and women's return to Guatemala.

Flores Unidades (Flowers United). Works to ensure women returnees' rights to own land and obtain credit.

Bibliography

Adams, R.N. 1952. *Creencias y Prácticas del Indígena*. Guatemala: Instituto Indigenista Nacional.

Adamson, James. 1992. "Patterns of Death: An initial geographic and temporal analysis of rural state terror in Guatemala". Unpublished paper presented at an International Symposium on Torture in Guatemala: Confronting the Heart of Darkness. Olivia Gowan Hall, The Catholic University of America. Washington D.C. November 13-15.

Alavi, Hamza. 1973. "Peasants and Revolution", in K. Gough and H. Sharma, eds., *Imperialism and Revolution in South Asia*. New York: Monthly Review Press.

Allen, Catherine. 1988. *The Hold Life Has: Cocoa and Cultural Identity in an Andean Community*. Washington, D.C.: Smithsonian Institution.

America's Watch. 1986. *Civil Patrols in Guatemala*. New York: America's Watch.

———. 1988. *'Closing the Space': Human Rights in Guatemala, May 1987-October 1988*. New York: America's Watch.

———. 1989. *Persecuting Human Rights Monitors: the CERJ in Guatemala*. New York: America's Watch

———. 1990. *Messengers of Death: Human Rights in Guatemala, November 1988 to March 1990*. New York: America's Watch.

Amnesty International. 1987. *Guatemala: The Human Rights Record*. London: Amnesty International Publications.

———. 1989. *Guatemala: Human Rights Violations under the Civilian Government*. New York: Amnesty International Publications.

———. 1990. *Annual Report*. London: Amnesty International Publications.

———. 1991. *Guatemala. Lack of Investigations into the Past Human Rights Abuses: Clandestine Cemeteries*. London: Amnesty International Publications.

Annis, Sheldon. 1987. *God and Production in a Guatemalan Town*. Austin: University of Texas Press.

Ardener, Shirley. 1975. "Language, Ethnicity and Population", in J. Beattie and G. Lienhardt, eds., *Studies in Social Anthropology: Essays in Memory of E.E. Evans-Pritchard*. Oxford: Clarendon Press.

———. 1986. *Visibility and Power. Essays on Women in Society and Development*. Delhi: Oxford University Press.

Arias, Arturo. 1990. "Changing Indian Identity: Guatemala's Violent Transition to Modernity", in Carol Smith, ed., *Guatemalan Indians and the State: 1540 —1988*. Pp. 230-257. Austin: University of Texas Press.

Ariés, Phillippe. 1982. *Un historien du dimanche*. Paris: Seuil.

Aulie, Wilbur. 1979. "The Christian Movement among the Chols of Mexico with

Special Reference to Problems of Second-Generation Christianity". Dissertation, School of World Mission, Fuller Theological Seminary.

Balderston, Daniel, D. W. Foster, T.H. Donghi, F. Masiello, M. Morello-Frosch, and B. Sarlo. 1987. *Ficción y política: La narrativa argentina durante el proceso militar*. Buenos Aires: Alianza Editorial.

Barnard, Chester I. 1968. *The Functions of the Executive*. Cambridge, Mass.: Cambridge University Press.

Barry, T. 1989. *Guatemala. A Country Guide*. Albuquerque, New Mexico: Inter-hemispheric Education Resource Centre.

Barth, Fredrik. 1981. *Process and Form in Social Life*. Selected Essays, Vol. 1. London: Routledge and Kegan Paul.

Barthes, R. 1973. *Mythologies*. London: Paladin.

Bastos, Santiago, and Manuela Camus. 1995. *Abriendo Caminos. Las organizaciones mayas de el nobel hasta el acuerdo de derechos indígenas*. Guatemala: Flacso.

Beals, R.L. 1966. *Community in Transition: Nayon-Ecuador*. Los Angeles: University of California.

Bettelheim, Bruno. 1980. *Surviving and Other Essays*. New York: Vintage Books.

———. 1986. *The Informed Heart: Autonomy in a Mass Age*. U.S.A.: Peregrine Press.

Bloch, Maurice. 1995. "The Resurrection of the House", in J. Carsten and S. Hugh-Jones, eds., *About the House*. Cambridge: Cambridge University Press.

Bloch, Maurice, and Jonathan Parry, eds. 1982. *Death and the Regeneration of Life*. Cambridge: Cambridge University Press.

Bohannan, Paul, ed. 1980. *Law and Warfare: Studies in the Anthropology of Conflict*. Austin: University of Texas.

Bossen, Laurel Herbener. 1978. "Women and Dependent Development. A comparison of women's economic and social roles in Guatemala". Ph.D. dissertation, State University of New York at Albany.

———. 1984. *The Redivision of Labour: Women and Economic Choice in Four Guatemalan Communities*. Albany: SUNY Press.

———. 1988. "Toward a Theory of Marriage: The economic anthropology of marriage transactions", in *Ethnology* XXVII:2(4):127-144.

Bourdieu, Pierre. 1977. *Outline of a Theory of Practice*. Cambridge: Cambridge University Press.

———. 1991. *Language and Symbolic Power*. Cambridge: Polity Press in association with Basil Blackwell.

Bowlby, John. 1961. "Processes of Mourning", in *International Journal of Psychoanalysis* 42:317-340.

———. 1969. *Attachment and Loss*, Vol. 1: Attachment. New York: Basic Books.

Bricker, V. 1981. *The Indian Christ, the Indian King: The Historical Substrate of Mayan Myth and Ritual*. Austin: University of Texas Press.

Brintnall, Douglas E. 1979. *Revolt Against the Dead: The Modernization of a Mayan Community in the Highlands of Guatemala*. New York: Gordon and Breach.

Broder, Tanya, and Bernard Lambeck. 1988. "Military Aid to Guatemala: The failure of U.S. human rights legislation", in *Yale Journal of International Law* 15(1):111-145.

Bruneau, T. 1979. "Basic Christian Communities in Latin America: Their nature and significance (especially in Brazil)", in D.H. Levine, ed., *Churches and Politics in Latin America.* Beverley Hills: Sage.

Bruner, Edward M. 1986. "Ethnography as Narrative", in Victor W. Turner and Edward M. Bruner, eds., *The Anthropology of Experience.* Pp. 139-155. Urbana: University of Illinois Press.

Buda, Blanca. 1988. *Cuerpo I-Zona IV. El infierno de Suárez Mason.* Buenos Aires: Contrapunto.

Bunster, X. 1986. "Surviving Beyond Fear: Women and torture in Latin America", in June Nash and Helen Safa, eds., *Women and Change in Latin America.* Pp. 297-325. Mass: Bergin and Garvey.

Bunzel, Ruth. 1952. *Chichicastenango, A Guatemalan Village.* American Ethnological Society, No. 12. New York: J.J. Austin.

Burgos-Debray, E., and R. Menchú. 1984. *I...Rigoberta Menchú: An Indian Woman in Guatemala.* London: Virgo.

Cabarrús, Carlos Rafael. 1979. *La cosmovisión K'ekchi' en proceso de cambio.* San Salvador: UCA Editores.

Carmack, Robert M. 1979. *Historia social de los Quichés.* Seminario de Integracíon Social Guatemalteco No. 38. Guatemala: José de Pineda Ibarra, Ministerio de Educación.

———. 1983. "Indians and the Guatemalan Revolution", in Jason Clay, ed., *Death and Disorder in Guatemala.* Cambridge, Mass.: Cultural Survival.

———. 1990. "State and Community in Nineteenth-Century Guatemala: The Momostenango Case", in *Guatemalan Indians and the State, 1540-1988,* C. Smith ed. Austin: University of Texas Press.

Carmack, Robert M., ed. 1988. *Harvest of Violence: The Maya Indians and the Guatemalan Crisis.* Norman and London: University of Oklahoma Press.

Certeau, Michel de. 1980. "On the Oppositional Practices of Everyday Life", in *Social Text* (3):3-43.

Chaney, David. 1979. *Fictions and Ceremonies: Representations of Popular Experience.* London: Edward Arnold.

Charmatz, Kathy. 1992. "Turning Points and Fictional Identities", in David R. Maines and Anselm L. Strauss, eds., *Social Organization and Social Process: Essays in Honour of Anselm Strauss.* New York: A. de Bruyter.

Ciencia y Tecnología Para Guatemala (CITGUA), 1987-9. 1989. Pp. 4-7. Mexico: CITGUA.

Cliff, J., and A. Noormahomed. 1988. "Health as a Target. South Africa's destabilization of Mozambique", in *Social Science and Medicine* 27:717-722.

Colby, Benjamin N., and Pierre L. van den Berghe. 1969. *Ixil Country: A Plural Society in Highland Guatemala.* Berkeley: University of California Press.

———. 1977. *Ixiles y Ladinos: El pluralismo en el altiplano de Guatemala.* Guatemala: Editorial 'José de Pineda Ibarra'.

Comité pro Justicia y Paz de Guatemala. 1985. *Informe Publicado con la Colaboración del Consejo Mundial de Iglesías, Guatemala.*

Conteponi, Gustavo, and Patricia Conteponi. 1984 *Sobrevivientes de la Perla.* Buenos Aires: El Cid.

Cook, Guillermo. 1985. *The Expectation of the Poor: Latin American Basic Ecclesial Communities.* Maryknoll, New York: Orbis Books.

Coser, Lewis. 1956. *The Functions of Social Conflict.* New York: Free Press.

Crónica, La. 1991. Weekly magazine. 20 September. Guatemala.

Dahrendorf, Ralf. 1979. *Life Chances: Approaches to Social and Political Theory.* London: Weidenfeld and Nicolson.

Das, Veena. 1987. "The Anthropology of Violence and the Speech of Victims" in *Anthropology Today* 4(3).

Das, Veena, ed. 1990. *Mirrors of Violence: Communities, Riots, and Survivors in South Asia.* Delhi: Oxford University Press.

Dassaint, Alain Y. 1962. "Effects of the Hacienda and Plantation Systems on Guatemala's Indians", in *America Indigena* 22(4):323-354. Mexico.

Davis, Sheldon H., and Julie Hodson. 1982. "Witness to Political Violence in Guatemala: The suppression of a rural development movement", in *Impact Audit 2.* Boston: Oxfam America.

Diekstra, R. 1988. *Psychosocial and Mental Health Problems of the Khmer Refugees in Site 2 and Site 8 on the Thai—Kampuchean Border.* Geneva: WHO Report.

Diocesis del Quiché. 1994. *El Quiché: el pueblo y su iglesia 1960-1980.* Santa Cruz, Guatemala: Diocesis del Quiché. July.

Douglas, Mary. 1966. *Purity and Danger.* London: Routledge and Kegan Paul.

Dunkerley, James. 1988. *Power in the Isthmus.* U.K.: Verso.

Economist Intelligence Unit. 1989. *Guatemala, El Salvador, Honduras: Country Profile 1989-90.* London: EIU.

Eisenbruch, Maurice. 1984. "Cross-cultural Aspects of Bereavement. II: Ethnic and cultural variation in the development of bereavement practices", in *Culture, Medicine, and Psychiatry* 8:315-347.

Elhers, Tracy. 1990. "Central America in the 1980s: Political crisis and the social responsibility of anthropologists", in *Latin American Research Review* 25(3): 141-155.

————. 1990. *Silent Looms.* Boulder, Colorado: Westview Press.

Erice, Ana. 1985. "Reconsideración de las creencias mayas en torno al nahual-ismo", in *Estudios de cultura maya* 16:255-270.

Estrada Monroy, Agustin. 1979. *El mundo Kekchi de la Verapaz.* Guatemala: Editorial del Ejército.

Falla, Ricardo. 1980. *Quiché rebelde. Estudio de un movimiento de conversión religiosa, rebelde a las creencias tradicionales, en San Antonio Ilotenango Quiché (1948-1970).* Colección 'Realidad Nuestra', Vol. 7. Editoral Universitaria de Guatemala. Guatemala: Universidad de San Carlos.

————. 1984. *Massacres in the Jungles. Ixcan Guatemala, 1975-1982.* Colorado: Westview Press.

————. 1988. "Struggle for Survival in the Mountains: Hunger and other privations inflicted on internal refugees from the Central Highlands", in R.M. Carmack, ed., *Harvest of Violence.* Pp. 235-255. Norman and London: University of Oklahoma Press.

Farriss, N.M. 1984. *Maya Society under Colonial Rule: The Collective Enterprise of Survival.* U.S.A.: Princeton University Press.

Favret-Saada, Jeanne. 1991. "Sale Histoire", in *Gradhivan* 10:3-7.

Feldman, A. 1991. *The Narrative of the Body and the Political Terror in Northern Ireland.* Chicago and London: Chicago University Press.

Ferguson, R. Brian, ed. 1984. *Warfare, Culture, and Environment.* New York: Academic Press.

Figueroa Ibarra, Carlos. 1980. *El proletariado rural en el agro guatemalteco.* Guatemala: Cuidad Universitaria Guatemala: Editorial Universitaria de Guatemala.

Fiorenza, E.S. 1983. *In Memory of Her: A Feminist Theological Reconstruction of Christian Origins.* New York: SMC Press.

Fortes, M. 1959. *Oedipus and Job in West African Religion.* Cambridge: Cambridge University Press.

Foster, George M. 1944. "Nagualism in Mexico and Guatemala", in *Acta Americana* 2:85-103.

———. 1979, revised edition. *Tzintzuntzan: Mexican Peasants in a Changing World.* New York: Elsevier.

Foster, M., and R. Rubenstein, eds. 1965. "Peasant Society and the Image of the Limited Good", in *American Anthropologist* 67:293-315.

———. 1986. *Peace and War: Cross Cultural Perspectives.* New Brunswick: Transaction Press.

Foucault, Michel. 1977. *Language, Counter-Memory, Practice.* Ithaca, New York: Cornell University Press.

———. 1979. *Discipline and Punish: The Birth of the Prison.* New York: Vintage Books.

Franco, J. 1985. "Killing Priests, Nuns, Women, Children", in Marshall Blonsky, ed., *On Signs.* Pp. 414-420. Baltimore: John Hopkins University Press.

Frank, Luisa, and Philip Wheaton. 1984. *Indian Guatemala: Path to Liberation.* Washington, D.C.: Ecumenical Program for Interamerican Communication and Action (EPICA) Task Force.

Frankl, Viktor E. 1964. *Man's Search for Meaning.* New York: Hodder and Stoughton.

Freud, Anna. 1937 [1936]. *The Ego and the Mechanisms of Defence.* English translation. London: Hogarth.

Freud, Sigmund. 1899. *Ueber Deckerinnerungen.* Gesammelte Schriften, 1, Band 1, S 465-488. Leipzig.

———. 1960. *Jokes and Their Relation to the Unconscious,* James Strachey, ed. London: Routledge and Kegan Paul.

Fried, Morton H., Marvin Harris, and Robert Murphy, eds. 1968. *War: The Anthropology of Social Conflict and Aggression.* New York: Doubleday.

Friedman, Susan Stanford. 1989. "The Return of the Repressed in Women's Narrative", in *The Journal of Narrative Technique* 19:141-156.

Friedrich, Paul. 1970. *Agrarian Revolt in a Mexican Village.* Chicago: University of Chicago Press.

Fromm, Erich. 1965. *Escape from Freedom.* New York: Avon Books.

GAM (Grupo de Apoyo Mutuo). 1997. *Annual Report.* Guatemala: GAM.

García, Enrique Hugo. 1987. "Análisis estructural de los ritos funerarios de San Miguel Aguasuelos, Veracruz", in *Palabra y el Hombre.* Universidad de Veracruz: Nueva Época, April-June 1987.

Geertz, Clifford. 1968. *Islam Observed. Religious Development in Morocco and Indonesia.* New Haven, Conn.: Yale University Press.

———. 1986. "Making Experiences, Authoring Selves", in V. Turner and E. Bruner, eds., *The Anthropology of Experience*. Chicago, Il: University of Illinois Press.

Gell, Alfred. 1979. "Reflections on a Cut Finger: taboo in the Umeda conception of the self", in R.H. Hook, ed., *Fantasy and Symbol*. London: Academic Press.

Gibson, J.T., and M. Haritos-Fatouros. 1986. "The Education of the Torturer", in *Psychology Today* 20:50-58.

Giddens, Anthony. 1979. *Central Problems in Social Theory*. London: MacMillan.

———. 1985. *The Nation State and Violence: Volume Two of A Contemporary Critique of Historical Materialism*. Berkeley, Ca.: University of California.

Gillin, John. 1948. "Magical Fright", in *Psychiatry 11* (November):387-400.

Glazer, Myron. 1970. "Field Work in a Hostile Environment: A chapter on the sociology of social research in Chile", in F. Bonilla and M. Glazer, eds., *Student Politics in Chile*. Pp. 313-333. New York: Basic Books.

———. 1972. *The Research Adventure: Promise and Problems of Fieldwork*. New York: Random House.

Gluckman, Max. 1963. *Order and Rebellion in Tribal Africa*. London: Cohen and West.

Goffman, Erving. 1955. "On Face Work", in *Psychiatry* 18:213-232.

———. 1956. "The Nature of Deference and Demeanour" in *American Anthropoloist* 58 (2):473-582.

———. 1961. *Asylums: Essays on the Social Situations of Mental Patients and Other Inmates*. New York: Anchor Books.

———. 1963. *Stigma: Notes on the Management of Spoiled Identity*. Prentice-Hall, N.J.: Englewood Cliffs.

Gorer, Geoffrey. 1965. *Death, Grief, and Mourning in Contemporary Britain*. London: Cresset.

Gossen, Gary. 1975. "Animal Souls and Human Destiny in Chamula", in *Man* 10 (3):448-461.

Government of Guatemala, National Institute of Statistics [Instituto Nacional de Estadistica de Guatemala]. 1991. Guatemala: Government of Guatemala.

Grafico, El. 1992. Daily Newspaper. 10 August.

Green, Linda. 1995. "The Paradoxes of War and its Aftermath: Mayan widows in rural Guatemala", in *Cultural Survival Quarterly*, Spring issue: 73-75..

Gregory, Steven, and Daniel Timmerman. 1986. "Rituals and the Modern State: The case of torture in Argentina", in *Dialectical Anthropology* 11(1):63-72.

Grele, Ronald J., et al. 1985. *Envelopes of Sound: The Art of Oral History*. Chicago: Precedent Publishing.

Guatemalan Church in Exile. 1990. *Official Documents of the Communities of Population in Resistance of the Sierra, El Quiché, Guatemala*. Mexico: Guatemalan Church in Exile.

Gurwitsch, A. 1966. *Studies in Phenomenology and Psychology*. Evanston: Northwestern University Press.

GVIS (Guatemala Geo-Violence Information System). 1993. A data base containing about 18,400 computerized cases of rural political violence which occurred in Guatemala between 1 January 1978 and 31 January 1985. Network in Solidarity with the People of Guatemala (NISGUA), 1314 14th Street NW, Washington, D.C. 20005.

Haas, J. 1990. *The Anthropology of War.* Cambridge: Cambridge University Press.

Halbwachs, Maurice. 1980 [1950]. *The Collective Memory.* New York: Harper Colophon Books.

Handy, Jim. 1984. *The Gift of the Devil.* Toronto: Between the Lines.

———. 1990. "Anxiety and Dread: State and community in modern Guatemala". Unpublished manuscript.

Harris, G.G. 1989. "Concepts of Individual, Self, and Person in Description and Analysis", in *American Anthropologist* 91:599-611.

Harvey, Penelope. 1991. "Gender, Community, and Confrontation: Power relations in drunkenness in Ocongate (Southern Peru)", in M. MacDonald, ed., *Gender, Drink, and Drugs.* Oxford: Berg.

Haviland, John Beard. 1977. *Gossip, Reputation, and Knowledge in Zinacantan.* Chicago: University of Chicago Press.

Hawkins, John. 1984. *Inverse Images: The Meaning of Culture, Ethnicity and Family in Postcolonial Guatemala.* Albuquerque: University of New Mexico Press.

Heelas, Paul, and Andrew Lock, eds. 1981. *Indigenous Psychologies: The Anthropology of the Self.* London: Academic Press

Hertz, R. 1960 [1907]. *Death and the Right Hand. A Contribution to the Study of the Collective Representation of Death.* London: Cohen and West.

Heusmann, L.R., and L.D. Eron. 1984. "Cognitive Processes and the Persistence of Aggressive Behaviour", in *Aggressive Behaviour* 10:243-51.

Hill, Christopher. 1993, revised edition. *A Nation of Change and Novelty.* London: Bookmarks.

Hinshaw, Robert E. 1975. *Panajachel: A Guatemalan Town in Thirty-Year Perspective.* Pittsburgh: University of Pittsburgh Press.

Hobsbawn, Eric. 1973. "Peasants and Politics", in *Journal of Peasant Studies* 1(1):13.

Hoyt, Elizabeth. 1959. "The Indian Labourer in Guatemalan Coffee Fincas", in *Inter-American Economic Affairs* 9:33-46.

Hutton, P.H. 1988. "Collective Memory and Collective Mentalities: The Halbwachs—Ariés Connection", in *Historical Reflections/Reflexions Historiques* 15(2): 311-322.

Infopress Centroamérica [IC]. 1988. Weekly News Magazine. 21 January.

Ingham, John. 1986. *Mary, Michael, and Lucifer: Folk Catholicism in Central Mexico.* Austin: University of Texas Press.

Jara, René, and Hernán Vidal, eds. 1986. *Testimonio y Literatura.* Minneapolis, Minnesota: Monographic Series of the Society for the Study of Contemporary Hispanic and Lusophone Revolutionary Literatures, No.3.

Jay, Alice. 1993. *Persecution by Proxy: the Civil Patrols in Guatemala.* Washington, D.C.: Robert F. Kennedy Memorial Centre for Human Rights.

Jonas, Susanne. 1991. *The Battle for Guatemala. Rebels, Death Squads, and U.S. Power.* Latin American Perspective Series, No. 5. Oxford: Westview Press.

Jones, Grant. 1989. *Maya Resistance to Spanish Rule: Time and History on a Colonial Frontier.* Albuquerque: University of New Mexico Press.

Jones, Lynne. 1990. "Committed to the Cause: Life histories of political activists (two case studies)". Paper presented to the Department of Psychiatry, University of Liverpool, 5 November.

Juarros, D. Domingo. 1981. *Compendio de la historia del reino de Guatemala*. Guatemala: Editorial Piedra Santa.

Kalish, Richard A., ed. 1972. *Death and Dying: Views from Many Cultures*. New York: Baywood Publishing Co.

Kaplan, Lucille H. 1956. "Tonal and Nagual in Coastal Oaxaca", in *Journal of American Folklore* 69:363-368.

Knapp, Steven. 1989. "Collective Memory and Actual Past", in *Representations* (Special Spring Issue: Memory and Counter Memory) 26:123-149.

Kordon, Diana R., et al., eds. 1988. *Psychological Effects of Political Repression*. Buenos Aires: Sudamericana-Planeta.

Kuper, Leo. 1981. *Genocide*. London: Penguin.

Landa, Fray Diego de. 1975. *The Maya: Diego de Landa's Account of the Affairs of the Yucatan*, ed. A.R. Pagden. Chicago: J. Philip O'Hara.

Larmer, Brook. 1989. "Religious Row Endangers Guatemala", in *Christian Science Monitor*, 10 March.

Las Casas, Bartolomé de. 1909 [*circa.* 1550]. *Apologética historia de las Indias*, Vol. I. Spain: Serrano y Sanz.

———. 1967 [*circa.* 1550]. *Apologética historia de las Indias*, 2 Vols, ed., Edmundo O'Gorman. Mexico: Universidad Nacional Autónoma de Mexico.

Laub, Dori. 1992. "Knowing and Not Knowing. Massive psychic trauma: Forms of traumatic memory". Unpublished manuscript.

Lawyers' Committee for Human Rights (LHCR). 1990. *Abandoning the Victim: The U.N. Advisory Services Programe in Guatemala*. New York: LCHR

Leach, E. 1977. *Custom, Law, and Terrorist Violence*. Edinburgh: University Press.

Le Bot, Yvon. 1983. "Guatemala: luchas sociales ante un horizonte de guerra, 1973 -1982", in *Cuadernos Políticos* 38 (October-December):23-35.

———. 1995. *La guerra en tierras Mayas: Comunidad, violencia y modernidad en Guatemala (1970-1992)*. Fondo de Cultura Económica.

Leed, E. 1979. *No Man's Land. Combat and Identity in World War I*. Cambridge: Cambridge University Press.

Lesser, Alexander. 1968. "War and the State", in Morton Fried, Marvin Harris, and Robert Murphy, eds., *War: The Anthropology of Armed Conflict and Aggression*. Pp. 92-96. New York: American Museum of Natural History: The Natural History Press.

Levett, A. 1989. "Psychological trauma and childhood", in *Psychology in Society* 12:19-32.

Levi, Primo. 1986. *Moments of Reprieve*. London: Abacus.

———. 1988. *The Drowned and the Saved*. New York: Summit.

Lévi-Strauss, Claude. 1963. *Structural Anthropology*. New York and London: Basic Books.

———. 1966. *The Savage Mind*. London: Weidenfeld and Nicolson.

Le Vine, Robert A. 1961. "Anthropology and the Study of Conflict", in *Journal of Conflict Resolution* 5(1):3-15.

Lewis, Oscar. 1951. *Life in a Mexican Village: Tepoztlán Restudied*. Urbana: University of Illinois Press.

Lifton, Robert Jay. 1967. *Death in Life: Survivors of Hiroshima*. New York: Random House.

————. 1973. *Home from the War: Vietnam Veterans, Neither Victims nor Executioners.* New York: Simon and Schuster.

————. 1983. *The Broken Connection: On Death and the Continuity of Life.* New York: Basic Books.

————. 1986. *The Nazi Doctors. Medical Killing and the Psychology of the Genocide.* New York: Basic Books.

————. 1987. *The Future of Immortality and other Essays for a Nuclear Age.* New York: Basic Books.

Lipowski, L. 1988. "Somatization: The concept and its clinical application", in *American Journal of Psychiatry* 145:1358-1368.

Lovell, W. George. 1988. "Surviving Conquest: The Maya of Guatemala in historical perspective", in *Latin American Research Review* 23(2):25-57.

Lovell, George, and William R. Sweezy. 1990. "Indian Migration and Community Formation: An analysis of congregación in colonial Guatemala", in D.J. Robinson, ed., *Migration in Colonial Latin America.* Cambridge: Cambridge University Press.

MacDonald, Sharon. 1987. "Drawing the Lines: gender, peace, and war: an introduction", in S. MacDonald et al., eds., *Images of Women in Peace and War: Cross-Cultural and Historical Perspectives.* London: MacMillan.

McClintock, M. 1985. *The American Connection: State Terror and Popular Resistance in Guatemala.* Bath: The Pitman Press.

McKendrick, B., and W. Hoffman. 1990. *People and Violence in South Africa.* Cape Town and Oxford: Oxford University Press.

Madsen, William. 1967. "Religious Syncretism", in *Handbook of Middle American Indians.* Vol 6, pp. 369-492. Austin: University of Texas Press.

Manrique, Castaneda L. 1967. "Otomi", in *Handbook of Middle American Indians.* Vol 6, pp. 602-637. Austin: University of Texas Press.

Manz, B. 1988. *Refugees of a Hidden War: The Aftermath of Counterinsurgency in Guatemala.* Albany: SUNY series in Anthropological Studies of Contemporary Issues.

Marcus, George E., and Michael M.J. Fisher. 1986. *Anthropology as Cultural Critique: An Experimental Moment in the Human Sciences.* Chicago: University of Chicago Press.

Marris, Peter. 1975. *Loss and Change.* Garden City, N.Y.: Anchor Books, Doubleday and Company.

Martin-Baro, I. 1990. "War and the Psychosocial Trauma of Salvadorian Children". Posthumous Presentation at the Annual Meeting of the American Psychological Association, Boston, Mass. From Department of Psychology and Education, Universidad Centroamericana, El Salvador.

Marwick, M.G. 1965. *Sorcery and its Social Setting. A Study of Northern Rhodesian Cewa.* Manchester University Press.

Masiello, Francine. 1987. "La Argentina durante el proceso. Las multiples resistencias de la cultura", in Balderston et al., eds., *Ficción y política: La narrativa argentina durante el proceso militar.* Pp12-13. Buenos Aires: Alianza Editorial.

Melville, Thomas, and Marjorie Melville. 1971. *Guatemala: The Politics of Land Ownership.* New York: Free Press.

Melzak, Sheila. 1992. "Secrecy, Privacy, Survival, Repressive Regimes and Growing up", in *Bulletin Anna Freud Centre* 15:205-223.

Metcalf, P. 1982. *A Borneo Journey into Death.* Philadelphia: University of Pennsylvania Press.

Milgram, Stanley. 1974. *Obedience to Authority: An Experimental View.* New York: Harper and Row.

Montejo, Victor. 1987. *Testimony: Death of a Guatemalan Village.* Willimantic, Conn.: Curbstone.

Moore, Barrington. 1954. *Terror and Progress USSR: Some Sources of Change and Stability in the Soviet Dictatorship.* Cambridge, Mass.: Harvard University Press.

Musgrave-Portilla, L. Marie. 1982. "The Nahualli or Transforming Wizard in Pre- and Post-Conquest Mesoamerica", in *Journal of Latin American Lore* 8(1): 3-62.

Nash, June. 1970. *In the Eyes of the Ancestors. Beliefs and Behaviour in a Mayan Community.* New Haven: Yale University Press.

———. 1976. "Ethnology in a Revolutionary Setting", in M. Ryniewich and J. Spradlet, eds., *Ethics and Anthropology: Dilemmas in Fieldwork.* Pp. 148-166. New York: Wiley.

Nash, Manning. 1957. "Cultural Persistence and Social Structure: The Mesoamerican calender survivals", in *Southwestern Journal of Anthropology* 13: 149-155.

———. 1967. *Machine Age Maya: Industrialization of a Guatemalan Community.* Chicago: University of Chicago Press.

Navarrete, Sergio. 1997. "Music of the Dead: The marimba in Rabinal, Guatemala". Unpublished manuscript

Neitzsche, Friedrich. 1980 [1874]. *On the Advantage and Disadvantage of History for Life.* New York: Hackett.

Nettelship, Martin A., Dale R. Givens, and Anderson Nettelship, eds. 1975. *War: Its Causes and Correlates.* The Hague: Mouton.

Neuenswander, Helen L., and Shirley D. Souder. 1977. "The Hot-Cold Wet-Dry Syndrome among the Quiché of Joyabaj", in Helen Neuenswander and Dean E. Arnold, eds., *Cognitive Studies of Southern Mesoamerica.* Dallas, Texas: SIL Museum of Anthropology, publication 3.

Nora, Pierre. 1989. "Between Memory and History: Les lieux de mémoire", in *Representations* (Special Spring Issue: Memory and Counter-Memory) 26:7-25.

Oakes, Maud. 1951. *The Two Crosses of Todos Santos. Survivals of Mayan Religious Ritual.* New York: Pantheon Books.

Oliver-Smith, Anthony. 1986. *The Martyred City: Death and Rebirth in the Andes.* Albuquerque: University of New Mexico Press.

Ortiz, Karol R. 1985. "Mental Health Consequences of Life History Method: Implications from a refugee case", in *Ethos* 13(2):27-30.

Orwell, George. 1950. *1984: A Novel.* New York: New American Library.

Otterbein, Keith, and Charlotte Swanson Otterbein. 1985. *The Evolution of War: A Cross-Cultural Study,* second edition. New Haven: HRAF Press.

Painter, James. 1987. *Guatemala: False Hope, False Freedom.* London: Catholic Institute for International Relations (CIIR) and Latin American Bureau.

Parkes, C.M. 1972. *Bereavement: Studies of Grief in Adult Life.* London: Tavistock Publications.

Parkin, D., ed. 1982. "Introduction", in *Semantic Anthropology.* London: Academic Press.

Pateman, T. 1980. *Language, Truth, and Politics.* Lewes: Jean Stroud.

Patterson, Orlando. 1982. *Slavery and Social Death: A Comparative Study.* Cambridge, Mass.: Harvard University Press.

Pearce, Jenny. 1986. *Promised Land: Peasant Rebellion in Chalatenango, El Salvador.* London: Latin American Bureau (Research and Action) Ltd.

Píel, Jean. 1989. *Sajcabaja. Muerte y resurrección de un pueblo de Guatemala 1500-1970.* Mexico: CEMCA.

Pitt-Rivers, Julian. 1970. "Spiritual Power in Central America: the naguals of Chiapas", in Mary Douglas, ed., *Witchcraft Accusations and Confessions.* Pp. 183-206. London: Tavistock.

Popkin, Margaret. 1996. *Civil Patrols and Their Legacy: Overcoming Mobilization and Polarization in the Guatemalan Countryside.* Washington, D.C.: Robert F. Kennedy Memorial Centre for Human Rights.

Popkin, Samuel L. 1979. *The Rational Peasant: The Political Economy of Rural Society in Vietnam.* Berkeley, Ca.: University of California Press.

Popular Memory Group (PMG). 1982. "Popular Memory: Theory, politics, method", in Richard Johnson et al., eds., *Making Histories: Studies in History, Writing, and Politics.* Minneapolis: University of Minnesota Press.

Poole, F.J.P. 1982. "The Ritual Forging of Identity: Aspects of person and self in Bimin-Kuskusmin male initiation", in G.H. Herdt, ed., *Rituals of Manhood.* Pp. 99-154. Berkeley, Ca.: University California Press.

"Popol Vuh". 1985. *Popol Vuh: The Definitive Edition of the Mayan Book of the Dawn of Life and the Glories of Gods and Kings.* New York: Simon and Schuster.

———. 1987. *Popul Vuh: las antiguas historias del Quiché. Version de Adrian Recinos.* Guatemala: Editorial Piedra Santa.

Raphael, B. 1983. *The Anatomy of Bereavement.* New York: Basic Books.

Redfield, Robert. 1934. "Folk Ways and City Ways", in Robert Redfield, ed., *Human Nature and the Study of Society: The Papers of Robert Redfield,* Vol. 1:172-182. Chicago: Chicago University Press.

———. 1941. *The Folk Culture of Yucatan.* Chicago: University of Chicago Press.

Redfield, Robert, and Alfonso Villa Rojas. 1934. *El chamán y el jaguar: Estudio de las drogas narcóticas entre los indianos de Colombia.* México: Siglo XXI, Editores.

———. 1962. *Chan Kom, a Maya Village.* Chicago: University of Chicago Press.

Reina, Ruben E. 1957. "Chinautla: A Guatemalan Indian community". Ph.D. dissertation, University of North Carolina.

———. 1966. *The Law of the Saints: A Pokomam Pueblo and its Community Culture.* Indianapolis: Bobbs-Merill Co.

Remesal, Antonio de. 1932. *Historia general de las Indias occidentales.* Guatemala: Sociedad de Geografía e Historia de Guatemala (Biblioteca 'Goathemala'), Tipografía Nacional.

Renner, Michael. 1989. "Enhancing Global Security", in Lester R. Brown et al., *State of the World.* Pp. 132-153. New York: W.W. Norton.

Reyes, Miguel Angel. 1986. "El índio en la lucha ideológica", in *Polémica* 20 (May-August) :5-16.

Ricadeli, Camilo. 1995. *Guatemala Weekly,* 4-10 February.

Riches, David, ed. 1986. *The Anthropology of Violence.* Oxford: Basil Blackwell.

Rigby, P. 1969. *Cattle and Kinship Among the Gogo: a Semi-pastoral Society in Central Tanzania.* London: Cornell University Press.

Rojas Lima, Flavio. 1988. *La cofradía: Reducto cultural indígena.* Guatemala: Seminario de Integración Social Guatemala.

Rollins, Judith. 1985. *Between Women: Domestics and their Employers.* Philadelphia: Temple University Press.

Rosaldo, Michelle Z. 1980. *Knowledge and Passion.* London: Cambridge University Press.

Rosaldo, Renato I. 1984. "Grief and a Headhunter's rage: On the cultural force of emotions", in Edward Bruner, ed., *Play, Text, and Story.* Proceedings of the 1983 Meeting of the American Ethnological Society. Washington D.C.: The American Ethnological Society.

———. 1989. *Culture and Truth: The Remaking of Social Analysis.* Boston: Beacon Press.

Rosenthal, Gabriele. 1989. "May 8th, 1945: The biographical meaning of a historical event", in *International Journal of Oral History* 10(3):183-193.

Rosenthal, Gabriele, ed. 1990. "Als der Krieg kam, hatte ich mit Hitler nichts mehr zu tun. Zur Gegenwärtigkeit des Dritten Reiches in Biographien", in *Erzählten Lebensgeschichten.* Opladen: Leske and Budrich.

Rubel, Arthur. 1964. "The Epidemiology of a Folk Illness: Susto in hispanic America", in *Ethnology* 3(3):268-283.

Saler, Benson. 1969. *Nagual, Brujo, and Herichero en un Pueblo Quiché.* Guatemala: Ministerio de Educación.

Sallnow, Michael J. 1987. *Pilgrims in the Andes: Regional Cults in Cusco.* Washington D.C.: Smithsonian Institute.

———. 1989. "Cooperation, Contradiction, and Terror: An Andean tragedy". Unpublished paper.

Sapir, J.D., and J.C. Croker, eds. 1977. *The Social Use of Metaphor: Essays on the Anthropology of Rhetoric.* Philadelphia: Pennsylvania Press.

Sapper, Karl. 1985. *The Verapaz in the Sixteenth and Seventeenth Centuries: A Contribution to the Historical Geography and Ethnology of Northeastern Guatemala.* Los Angeles: Institute of Archeology, University of California.

Sarlo, Beatrice. 1987. "Politica ideologia y figuracíon literaria", in René Jara and Hernán Vidal, eds., *Ficción y politica: La narrativa argentina durante el proceso militar.* P 43. Minneapolis: The Institute of Ideologies and Literature.

Scarry, Elaine. 1985. *The Body Pain: The Making and Unmaking of the World.* Oxford: Oxford University Press.

Scheper-Hughes, N. 1992. *Death Without Weeping: The Violence of Every-Day Life in Brazil.* Berkeley, Los Angeles, and London: University of California Press.

Schieffelin, Edward L. 1985. "The Cultural Analysis of Depressive Affect: an example from New Guinea", in Arthur Kleinman and Byron Good, eds., *Culture and Depression: Studies in the Anthropology and Cross Cultural Psychiatry of Affect and Disorder.* London: University of California Press.

Schmid, L. 1973. *El papel de la mano de obra migratoria en el desarrollo economica de Guatemala.* Guatemala: Instituto de Investigaciones Economicas y Sociales, Universidad de San Carlos.

Schuetze, F. 1976. "Zur Hevorlocking und Analyse von Erzaehlungen thematisch relevanter Geschichten im Pahmen scoziologischer Feldforschung", in *Arbietsgruppe Biellefelder Soziologen: Kommunikative Soziolisationsforchung.* Pp. 159-260. Muenchen: Fink.

Schultze Jena, Leonard. 1954. *La vida y las creencias de los indígenas Quiché de Guatemala.* Guatemala: Ministeria de Educacíon Pública.

Scott, James C. 1976.*The Moral Economy of the Peasant. Rebellion and Subsistence in Southeast Asia.* New Haven: Yale University Press.

———. 1985. *Weapons of the Weak: Everyday Forms of Peasant Resistance.* New Haven and London: Yale University Press.

Shengold, L. 1989. *Soul Murder. The Effects of Child Abuse and Deprivation.* New Haven: Yale University Press.

Sherman, William L. 1979. *Forced Native Labour in Sixteenth Century Central America.* Lincoln, Nebraska: University of Nebraska Press.

Shurtz, J. 1988. "The Phemonenology of Terror". Ph.D. dissertation, Union for Experimenting Colleges and Universities.

Sieder, Rachel. 1996. *Derecho consuetudinario y transicíon democratica en Guatemala.* Guatemala: Flacso.

Siegel, Morris. 1941. "Religion in Western Guatemala: A product of acculturation", in *American Anthropologist* 43:62-76.

Simon, Jean Marie. 1987. *Eternal Spring, Eternal Tyranny.* U.K.: Verso.

Skocpol, Theda. 1979. *States and Social Revolutions.* Cambridge: Cambridge University Press.

Smith, Carol. 1986. "Culture and Community: The language of class in Guatemala", in Michael Sprinker, ed., *The Year Left.* London: Verso.

———. 1988. "Destruction of the Material Bases for Indian Culture: Economic changes in Totonicapán", in R. Carmack, ed., *Harvest of Violence.* Norman: University of Oklahoma Press.

———. 1990a. "The Militarization of Civil Society in Guatemala: Economic reorganization as a continuation of war: Military impact in the western highlands of Guatemala", in *Latin American Perspectives* 17(4):8-41.

Smith, Carol, ed. 1990b. *Guatemalan Indians and the State, 1540 to 1988.* Austin: University of Texas Press.

Smith, Waldemar. 1977. *The Fiesta System and Economic Change.* New York: Columbia University Press.

Solomon, Joel A. 1995. *Institutional Violence: Civil Patrols in Guatemala.* Washington, D.C.: Robert F. Kennedy Memorial Centre for Human Rights.

Summer, Doris. 1991. "Rigoberta's Secrets", in *Latin American Perspectives* (Summer Issue 70: Voices of the Voiceless in Testimonial Literature, Part 1) 18(3): 32-50.

Stadelman, Raymond. 1940. *Maize Cultivation in Northwestern Guatemala.* Contributions to American Anthropology and History, No.33. Washington, D.C.: Carnegie Institution of Washington.

Staub, Ervin. 1989. *The Roots of Evil: The Origins of Genocide and Other Group Violence.* Cambridge: Cambridge University Press.

Sternbach, Nancy S. 1991. "Women's Testimonial Discourse", in *Latin American Perspectives* (Summer Issue 70: Voices of the Voiceless in Testimonial Literature, Part 1) 18(3):91-102.

Stewart, M., and P.E. Hodgkinson. 1988. "Missing, Presumed Dead", in *Disaster Management* 1:11-14.

Stoll, David. 1988. "Evangelicals, Guerrillas, and the Army: The Ixil Triangle under Ríos Montt", in Robert M. Carmack (ed.), *Harvest of Violence*. Norman: University of Oklahoma Press.

————. 1990. *Is Latin America Turning Protestant? The Politics of Evangelical Growth*. Berkeley: University of California Press.

————. 1993. *Between Two Armies in the Ixil Towns of Guatemala*. New York: Columbia University Press.

Storr, A. 1989. *Churchill's Black Dog and Other Phenomena of the Human Mind. Why Human Beings Become Violent*. London: Collins.

Suárez-Orozco, M.M. 1990. "Speaking of the Unspeakable: Towards a psychosocial understanding of responses to terror", in *Ethnos* 18(3):353-383.

————. 1992. "A Grammar of Terror: Psychocultural responses to state terrorism in the dirty war and post-dirty war in Argentina", in Carolyn Nordstrom and Jo Ann Morton, eds., *The Paths to Domination, Resistance, and Terror*. Pp. 219-259. Berkeley, Los Angeles and Oxford: University of California Press.

Symonds, M. 1976. "The Rape Victim: Psychological patterns of response", in *American Journal of Psychoanalysis* 36(1):27-34.

Taussig, Michael . 1984. "Culture of Terror — Space of Death: Roger Casement's Putumayo Report and the explanation of torture", in *Comparative Studies of Society and History* 26:467-497.

————. 1987. *Shamanism, Colonialism, and the Wild Man: Study in Terror and Healing*. Chicago: Chicago University Press.

————. 1990. "Terror as Usual: Walter Benjamin's theory of history as a state of siege", in *Social Text* 23:3-20. Reprinted in M. Taussig (ed.), 1992, *The Nervous System*. Pp. 11-35. London: Routledge.

Tax, Sol. 1937. "The Municipios of the Midwestern Highlands of Guatemala", in *American Anthropologist* 39(3):423-444.

————. 1941. "World View and Social Relations in Guatemala", in *American Anthropologist* 43(1):27-42.

Taylor, Charles. 1989. *Sources of Self. The Making of Modern Identity*. Cambridge: Cambridge University Press.

Tedlock, Barbara. 1982. *Time and the Highland Maya*. Albuquerque: University of New Mexico Press.

Tedlock, Dennis, trans. 1985. *Popul Vuh: The Definitive Edition of the Mayan Book of the Dawn of Life and the Glories of Gods and Kings*. New York: Simon and Schuster.

Timmerman, J. 1981. *Prisoner Without a Name, Cell Without a Number*. New York: Alfred A. Knopf.

Tranfo, Luigi. 1974. *Vida y magia en un pueblo otomí del mezquital*. México: Instituto Nacional Indigenista.

————. 1979. "Tona y Nagual", in Itala Signorini, ed., *Los Huaves de San Mateo del Mar, Oaxaca*. Pp. 177-210. Mexico: Instituto Nacional Indigenista.

Turner, Victor. 1967. *The Forest of Symbols: Aspects of Ndembu Ritual*. Ithaca,

New York: Cornell University Press.

———. 1969. *The Ritual Process: Structure and Anti-Structure*. Ithaca, New York: Cornell University Press.

Uzzell, Douglas. 1974. "Susto Revisited: Illness as strategic role", in *American Ethnologist* 1(2):369-378.

Villa Rojas, Alfonso. 1947. "Kinship and Nagualism in a Tzeltal Community, Southeastern Mexico", in *American Anthropologist* 49:578-587.

———. 1978. *Los elegidos de Dios; Etnografía de los Mayas de Quintana Roo*. Mexico: Instituto Nacional Indigenista.

Vogt, Evon Z. 1969. *Zinacantan: A Maya Community in the Highlands of Chiapas*. Cambridge: Belknap Press of the Harvard University Press.

———. 1970. "Human Souls and Animal Spirits in Zinacantan", in Jean Pouillon and Pierre Miranda, eds., *Exchanges et Communications*. Pp. 1148-1167. The Hague: Mouton.

———. 1976. *Tortillas for the Gods: A Symbolic Analysis of Zinacanteco Rituals*. Cambridge, Mass.: Harvard University Press.

Wagley, Charles. 1941. *Economics of a Guatemalan Village*. Menasha, Wis.: American Anthropological Association Memoir No. 58.

———. 1949. *The Social and Religious Life of a Guatemalan Village*. Menasha, Wis.: American Anthropological Association Memoir No. 71.

Wallace, A. 1961. *Culture and Personality*. New York: Random House.

Walter, Eugene V. 1969. *Terror and Resistance. A Study of Political Violence with Case Studies of Some Primitive African Communities*. New York: Oxford University Press.

Warren, Kay B. 1978 (second edition). *The Symbolism of Subordination: Indian Identity in a Guatemalan Town*. Austin: University of Texas Press.

———. 1993. *The Violence Within: Cultural and Political Opposition in Divided Nations*. Boulder, Col.: Westview Press.

Watanabe, John B. 1989. "Elusive Essences: Souls and social identity in two highland Maya communities", in *Ethnographic Encounters in Southern Mesoamerica: Essays in Honour of Evon Zartman Vogt, Jr*. Pp. 263-274. Albany: Institute of Mesoamerican Studies.

———. 1992. *Maya Saints and Souls in a Changing World*. Austin: University of Texas Press.

Watson, James B. 1971. "Tairora: The politics of despotism in a small society", in Ronald M. Berndt and P. Lawrence, eds., *Politics in New Guinea*. Nedlands, Western Australia: University of Western Australia Press.

Weber, Max. 1978. *Economy and Society: An Outline of Interpretive Sociology,* G. Roth and C. Willich, eds. Berkeley, Ca.: University of California Press.

Webster, David. 1975. "Warfare and the Evolution of the State", in *American Antiquity* 40:464-470.

Werbner, Richard. 1991. *Tears of the Dead: A Social Biography of an African Family*. London: Edinburgh University Press for the International African Institute.

Williams, Raymond. 1977. *Marxism and Literature*. Oxford: Oxford University Press.

Wilson, Richard. 1995. *Maya Resurgence in Guatemala. Q'eqchi' Experiences*. Norman and London: University of Oklahoma Press.

Wisdom, Charles. 1974 [1940]. *The Chorti Indians of Guatemala.* Chicago: University of Chicago Press; Midway.

Wolf, Eric R. 1967. "The Closed Corporate Community in Mesoamerica and Central Java", in Jack Potter, May Díaz, and George Foster, eds., *Peasant Society: a Reader.* Boston: Little, Brown and Row.

————. 1969. *Peasant Wars of the Twentieth Century.* New York: Harper Torchbooks.

Wolfenstein, Martha. 1957 [1911]. *Disaster: Psychological Essay.* London: Routledge Kegan Paul.

Wright, R. 1991. *Time Among the Maya. Travels in Belize, Guatemala, and Mexico.* London: The Bodley Head.

Ximénez, Fransisco. 1929. *Historia de la Provincia de San Vicente de Chiapas y Guatemala.* Guatemala: Sociedad de Geografía e Historia de Guatemala (Biblioteca 'Goathemala'), Tipografía Nacional.

Zemon Davis, N., and Randolph Starn. 1989. "Introduction to Memory and Counter-Memory", in *Representations* (Special Spring Issue: Memory and Counter-Memory) 26:1-7.

Zimbardo, Phillip G. 1969. *The Cognitive Control of Motivation: The Consequences of Choice and Dissonance.* Glencoe, Ill.: Scott, Foresman.

Zimbardo, P.G., C. Haney, W.C. Banks, and D. Jaffe. 1974. "The Psychology of Imprisonment: Privation, power, and pathology", in R. Rubin, ed., *Doing unto Others.* Engelwood Cliffs, N.J.: Prentice-Hall.

Zur, Judith N. 1994. "The Psychological Impact of Impunity", in *Anthropology Today* 10(3):12-17.

Zur, Judith N. 1996. "From PTSD to Voices in Context: From an 'experience-far' to an 'experience-near' understanding of responses to war and atrocity across cultures", in *International Journal of Social Psychiatry* 42(4):305-317.

Index

Abandonment, of families, 86; see Orphaning
Abduction, 11, 15, 16, 68, 70, 80, 130, 204, 205 as discontinuity, 224; and symbolic burial 217-218
Acción Católica. see: Catholic Action
Accords. see Peace Accords
Accusation, 143; see also Labelling
After-life, 199-201, 204, 208, 210
Agriculture, disruption of, 41
Agro-technology, impact of, 29
Aj'itz. see *Brujo*
Aj q'ij. see *Costumbrista* diviners
Aj mes. see *Costumbrista* spirit caller
Alcohol. see Drinking
All Saints' Day, 197-198,204, 290
Amnesia, historical, 159
Amnesties (1982-88), 4, 96, 122, 130; conditional, and return to village, 173; law, 2; see also Law of Reconciliation
Ancestors, 29, 102,157(n20), 195,198-201, 208, 218, 224-5(n3), 241, 260 , 295; category of, 193; see also *Castigo*
Anger and indignation, 184, 216, 272, 296; memories of 169
Anthropological abstraction, and sanitization of war, 21-22
APM, 279, 313
Arbenz, Jacobo., 25(n17)
Armed opposition. see EGP; FAR; FARM; ORPA;

URNG
Arms supplies 49(n19), 102, 124(n9)
Army. see Military
Arzú Irigoyen, A., 5, 23(n4), 292
ASC, 279, 282, 313
Assassination, 2, 11, 12, 204
Assimilation, 50(n25)
Atrocity, 19, 161, 270; as 'beginning', 70; local, and jefes,101, 110; mnemonic merger, 164; non-narratability of, 213
Autonomy, destruction of, 71, 98, 103; individual, 119, 125(n13)
AVANCSO, 3, 24(n8), 313

'Beans and Bullets Programme', 95, 97, 124(n7)
Bereaved, reduction of, 212
Beteta , Noel de Jesus, 3
Betrayal, 226(n18), 237, 238, 239, 286; fear of, 118, 253, Bin, el, 261-2, 263, 275, 277(n9)
Bombardment and bombing, 78; of Emol, 71
Bomberos Voluntarios, 78, 90(n18), 203
Boys, 139-141, 298-300, 304
Brujos and *brujería*, 88, 204, 229, 236, 237, 251, 253, 256, 260-2, 275, 276(n6); invisibility of, 73; and Jefes,120-1, 126(n35), 247, 272- 3; and spirit invasion, 110, 230, 262, 263, 283; and responsibility, 123
Burial 195, 201-203, 225(n8); symbolic, 217-218; see alsoClandestine burials

'Captive observers', 162
Cargo system, 37, 49(n20); 'revival' of, 39
Cash income, 62
Castellanización, 30, 31
Castigo, (ancestral punishment), 229, 232-4, 249(n8); and military, 241, 244, 247
Catechists, 41, 50(n23), 242; and education 31; supra-communal organization of, 81; supression of, 68, 69, 239; women as, 53
Catholic Action, 62, 102, 233, 239, 286; development of, 41; targetting of, 39, 42; and liberation theology, 41
Catholic Church, 3, 199; closure of local diocese, 15
Catholic clergy, targetting of, 69
Catholicism, charismatic, 15; conversion to, 50 (n24); Indian/*ladino* 50(n33*)*; and radicalism, 16
Catholicism, Pure: see Costumbre
Catholics, in rev. movement, 50(n29); vulnerability of 50(n32)
CDP, 313 see Patrols, renaming of
CEH, 282, 310, 313 (2, 5)
Cerezo Arévalo,Vinicio., 2
CERJ, 3, 23(n5), 100, 113, 280, 281, 313
Chajul, 5
Chaos, 161, 202
Chiché, 77
Chichicastenango, 77, 78, 80, 82, 83, 125(n20), 185; *Jefe* of, 107
Child labour, 10, 16, 58; and education, 33